ST. THOMAS AQUINAS
Theological Texts

ST. THOMAS AQUINAS

Theological Texts

SELECTED AND TRANSLATED
WITH NOTES AND AN INTRODUCTION
BY
THOMAS GILBY

THE LABYRINTH PRESS
Durham, North Carolina

Copyright 1955 by Oxford University Press

First Labyrinth Press Edition 1982
Published under license from Oxford University Press

Library of Congress Cataloging in Publication Data

Thomas, Aquinas, Saint, 1225?-1274.
    St. Thomas Aquinas, theological texts.

    Reprint: London: Oxford University Press, 1955.
    Includes index.
    1. Theology—Collected works—Middle Ages, 600-
1500. 2. Catholic Church—Collected works.
II. Gilby, Thomas, 1902-   . II. Title.
BX890.T62E6   1982   230'.2   81-14270
ISBN 0-939464-01-2   AACR2

Printed in the United States of America

TO

CATHERINE WALSTON

NIHIL OBSTAT: Fr Drostanus Maclaren, O.P.

IMPRIMI POTEST: Fr Hilarius Carpenter, O.P.
Prior Provincialis Angliae.
die 25 Novembris 1953

NIHIL OBSTAT: Patricius Morris, S.T.D., L.S.S.
Censor deputatus.
IMPRIMATUR: E. Morrogh Bernard. *Vic. Gen.*

Westmonasterii, die 28a Septembris 1954.

Contents

B 4007   a 2

Introduction

WHILE the attempt to separate St. Thomas's philosophy from his theology may be partly justified, it is an impossible task to separate his theology from his philosophy. Pure nature is a fiction, for mankind has always either possessed the supernatural or been deprived of it: grace has ever been on the stage of history. Nevertheless, the character and capacities of the rational social animal can be legitimately studied out of the complete context. The abstraction is valid, so long as it is not mistaken for the concrete reality; the notion of a scientific *type* or *kind* runs through the strictly rational disciplines of psychology, moral philosophy, and metaphysics, which includes natural theology. Christian theology, however, is less detached, for grace without human nature cannot be conceived. The gift is the entrance of God's intimate life into human beings, possessing them and shaping them to himself, but modified by the conditions of their creatureliness. It is their habitual intercourse, largely inarticulate, in the society of the three Blessed Persons, and as *theirs* responds to the nature of human intelligence, human volition, human sensation, human emotions, and even human physique.

This theme, which recurs throughout St. Thomas's theological compositions, appears in his frequent and sometimes lengthy preoccupation with the profane when he is treating the sacred; his confidence that they serve to explain one another is expressed by his stress on the reasonable notes of Christian theology. His study of God's revelation through Jesus Christ, and of the new life he brings, sets out to be science, not poetry; the spirit is explanatory, not exclamatory; the mode dialectical, not rhetorical; the purpose to investigate existing meanings, not to muster symbols charged with emotional force: and though the premises are mysteries held by faith, and not evident in themselves nor demonstrated from visible data nor postulated by practical necessity, as with the other sciences, the discourse is as severely logical as theirs.

The result should not be represented as a hybrid of faith and reason, the work of an author with a divided mind, who addresses himself to a rationalist defence of the dogmas he receives as a fideist, but as a fresh and fruitful species. But one cannot see how it is not a mixture, but a synthesis, in which nature and grace, like matter and spirit, are fused rather than juxtaposed, unless his use of *analogy* is appreciated. The reader soon perceives how many sentences and judgements, indeed whole paragraphs and arguments, swing between parallel relationships: 'as *a* to *b*, so *A* to *B*,' that is a characteristic pattern, and sometimes the comparisons are of the highest with the lowest, and conversely. Analogy is more than a trick of speech, and goes deeper than metaphor; it is taken into philosophy, and subjected to the rules of scientific thinking. Recognizing the likenesses in diversity and the kinship between all parts of reality, St. Thomas was able to mount to God, who is both transcendent and the integrator of the universe. And when this First Cause reveals himself as Father, Son, and Holy Ghost, why should the effort falter? The mind is not then invited to enter a special enclave, with its own peculiar rules. *The Word was made flesh, and dwelt among us, full of grace and truth.*

Some commentators have overstressed the rationalism of St. Thomas's theology. The system, officially recommended for the professional training of the officials of Latin Christianity, who are matter-of-fact rather than romantic and more outwardly concerned with the working of an institution than with the challenge of a mystery, tends to look like mechanics. It can be given a metallic ring; it has been rendered as though it were a legal code. A reaction is setting in, and some Catholic theologians are beginning to look elsewhere for their inspiration, to Bonaventure among the thirteenth-century Scholastics, to the Victorines of the twelfth-century, and to older, less tidy and allegedly warmer and more generous, schools of divinity. Their feeling is understandable, but their verdict would be mistaken if, consulting the manualist instead of the master, they judged him as but the greatest representative of the analytic schoolmen. In his systematic treatises, and still more in his *opuscula* and commentaries on Biblical and Neo-Platonist texts, will be discovered an appreciation of real and ranging myths and allegorical truths, accompanied by a sense of history, which together combine to form a theology which is positive as well as speculative. His power of sustained concentration on meanings is remarkable, yet he reminds himself that existents, not essences, are the objects of mind. His theology is not a study of how certain abstract ideas can be inter-related, but the account, furnished to the believing reason, of God's deeds with men.

The present collection follows the order of its companion volume, *St. Thomas Aquinas, Philosophical Texts*,[1] and adopts the plan of the *Summa Theologica*; the corresponding parts of the two anthologies can accordingly be set alongside one another. After a preliminary discussion of the nature of Christian theology, or *sacra doctrina*, the first subject is God and his works: the sections of this volume which correspond to the *Prima Pars* consider the revelation of the Blessed

[1] Oxford University Press, 1951.

Trinity and the part played by rational creatures in the drama of grace rather than in the working of the natural universe. Then come the sections dealing with man's movement to God through moral activity: this is the subject of the *Secunda Pars*, which is divided into the *Prima Secundae* and the *Secunda Secundae*; the first half of the second part treats of virtue in general, of sin, law, and grace; the second half of the second part takes the virtues in detail and the life of the spirit with God. The final sections match the *Tertia Pars*, and are about Christ, *via tendendi in Deum*, our way of going to God, and his Church, which continues the work of the Incarnation.

St. Thomas was more sparing of terms than of ideas. His repetitions are more monotonous in English than in Latin. Yet it is for the sake of accuracy, as much as of interest, that this translation is, as in the *Philosophical Texts*, a compromise between a paraphrase and a word-for-word translation, and that terms have been inflected by their sense in parallel passages. The same system of cross-reference has been employed: the figures below a text to the left sometimes dispense with a footnote, and may, it is hoped, set the reader tacking on his own course, without starting from the first page and reading through to the last.

I gratefully acknowledge the help of Murdoch Scott, Hugh Nash, Leonard Boyle, Cornelius Ernst, Timothy McDermott, Vincent Gotz, Stanislaus Parker, Henry St. John, and Catherine Walston.

The poem 'Godhead here in hiding' by G. M. Hopkins is quoted by permission of the Oxford University Press.

T. G.

BLACKFRIARS, CAMBRIDGE

1954

Biographical and Bibliographical Note

ST. THOMAS AQUINAS was born about 1225 at the Castle of Rocca Secca in the Kingdom of Naples. Entering the Order of Preachers in 1244, he studied at Paris, 1245–8, and Cologne, 1248–52. Returning to Paris in 1252 he became *Cursor Biblicus*, charged with the duty of taking the students through a rapid course of Scriptural reading. In 1254 he became *Baccalaureus Sententiarius*, publicly reading the *Sentences* of Peter Lombard, the classical theological textbook of the Middle Ages, under the direction of a *Magister*. In 1256 he himself received the licence to teach as a Master: as such his ordinary lectures were on the Scriptures; in addition he was expected to hold formal disputations. In 1259 he was called to the Papal Court as lecturer, and moved with it from Anagni to Orvieto, Rome, and Viterbo. In 1270 he was recalled to Paris to meet the threat of Latin Averroism. In 1272 he returned to Italy, teaching at Naples until 1274, when he died at the Abbey of Fossa Nova, in the States of the Church, on his way north to take part in the General Council of Vienne.

Of his writings still extant and certainly authentic, some are the direct result of his lecturing. These are the *Commentary on the Four Books of the Sentences* (1254–5), the *Commentaries on Holy Scripture*, the *Quaestiones Disputatae*, and the *Quaestiones Quodlibetales*. Nine Biblical commentaries remain, of which *Isaias* and *Romans* to *1 Corinthians vii. 10* are *expositiones* written down by St. Thomas himself, while the remainder are *lecturae* or *reportationes*, taken down by one of his students or by his secretary, Reginald of Piperno: these are *St. Matthew*, *St. Paul's Epistles*, *Lamentations*, *Jeremias*, *St. John*, *Psalms i–li*, and *Job*. The *Quaestiones Disputatae*, or *quaestiones ordinariae*, report a linked series of debates held once or twice a week throughout the academic year; the order of questions in the printed editions may not be chronological. They include the *de Veritate*, *de Potentia*, *de Malo*, *de Anima*, *de Spiritualibus Creaturis*, *de Virtutibus*, *de Caritate*, and *de Unione Verbi Incarnati*. The *Quaestiones Quodlibetales*, or Quodlibets, record occasional debates where any listener in the audience, not only the Master's own students, could put a question; the order of questions in the printed editions is certainly not chronological.

The most famous of the writings not directly rising from his actual lecturing is the *Summa Theologica* (1267–72), composed as a textbook for students: it is followed by the *Summa Contra Gentes* (1258–9), addressed to the Jewish and Muslim world. During his first years as Master he composed the commentaries on Boethius, *de Trinitate* and *de Hebdomadibus*, on the Pseudo-Dionysius, *de Divinis Nominibus*, and on the medieval extract from Proclus, the *Liber de Causis*; during his later years the commentaries on Aristotle's *Physics*, *Metaphysics*, *de Anima*, *Nicomachean Ethics*, *Politics* (to iii, *lect.* 6), *Posterior Analytics*, *Periher-meneias* (to ii, *lect.* 3), *de Caelo* (to iii, *lect.* 8), *de Generatione* (to i, *lect.* 17), *de Sensu et Sensato*, *de Memoria et Reminiscentia*, and the *Meteorologica* (to ii, *lect.* 10).

Some of the *opuscula* are pamphlets and replies to correspondents in Rome, Trent, Venice, Besançon, and Antioch; others are lengthy treatises. Among the theological *opuscula* are the *Compendium Theologiae ad fratrem Reginaldum socium suum carissimum,* the *de Articulis Fidei et Sacramentis Ecclesiae,* the *de Rationibus Fidei ad cantorem Antiochenum,* the *contra Errores Graecorum ad Urbanum IV Papam Maximum,* and the three occasioned by the controversies between the friars and the secular Masters of Paris, the *contra Impugnantes Dei cultum et religionem* (1257), the *de Perfectione vitae spiritualis* (1269), and the *contra Retrahentes homines a religionis ingressu* (1270), of which the second is of the most lasting value.

The philosophical *opuscula* include the important trilogy, the *de Ente et Essentia ad fratres socios* (1256), the *de Unitate Intellectus contra Averroistas Parisienses* (1270), and the *de Aeternitate Mundi contra murmurantes* (1270–1). Also may be mentioned the *de Principiis Naturae ad fratrem Sylvestrum,* the *de Substantiis Separatis ad fratrem Reginaldum,* the *de Regimine Subditorum ad Ducissam Brabantiae* (later called *de Regimine Judaeorum*), and the *de Regno,* or *de Regimine Principum ad Regem Cypri,* worthily completed from ii. 4 by Ptolemy of Lucca.

There remain his conferences, or *collationes,* on the *Our Father, Hail Mary, Creed,* and *Ten Commandments.* Also his sermons for Sundays and for Feastdays, some of which were preached in the Neapolitan vernacular: they are numbered in this collection according to the Venice edition of 1758. All Biblical references are to the Vulgate.

O Creator, past all telling you have appointed, from the treasures of your wisdom, the hierarchies of angels, disposing them in wondrous order above the bright heavens, and have so beautifully set out all parts of the universe. You we call the true fount of wisdom and the noble origin of all things. Be pleased to shed on the darkness of mind in which I was born the twofold beam of your light and warmth to dispel my ignorance and sin. You make eloquent the tongues of children. Then instruct my speech and touch my lips with graciousness. Make me keen to understand, quick to learn, able to remember; make me delicate to interpret and ready to speak. Guide my going in and going forward, lead home my going forth. You are true God and true man, and live for ever and ever. Amen.

Prayer, before study

Every truth without exception—and whoever may utter it—is from the Holy Ghost.

Summa Theologica, 1a–2ae. cix, 1, *ad* 1

True science is about things which really exist.

Exposition, *de Divinis Nominibus,* i, *lect.* 2

'Thomas' signifies a deep, an abyss. *The words of a man's mouth are as deep waters.*[1] He spoke with many voices—of love, *let us also go that we may die with him:*[2] of doubt, *except I see in his hands the print of the nails, and thrust my hand into his side, I will not believe:*[3] of avowal of faith, *my Lord and my God:*[4] of trust, *but, Lord, we do not know where thou art going; how are we to know the way there?*[5]

Feast Day Sermons, 78

[1] Prov. xviii. 4. [2] John xi. 16. [3] John xx. 25.
[4] John xx. 28. [5] John xiv. 5.

I

Theology[1]

1. The writer of an introduction should perform these three tasks: he should enlist the reader's favourable attention, by showing the value of the subject; he should prepare him, by proposing its plan and divisions; he should put him on his mettle by warning him of the difficulties to be encountered.

Commentary, I de Anima, lect. 1

2. The instruction of beginners, as well as of advanced students, is part of a theologian's vocation: *even as babes unto Christ I have fed you with milk, and not with meat.*[2] Accordingly, this book of mine proposes to treat Christian truths in a style adapted to novices.

[1] Between the theological virtue of faith, which assents to a supernatural mystery, and a purely rational philosophy of religion (which can, of course, discuss the natural effects of supernatural reality) lies a discipline which is both supernatural and scientific: supernatural, because its principles are held because of divine Revelation, scientific, because it scrutinizes them and infers conclusions from them acc   'ing to t'.c strict laws of evidence. This is *sacra doctrina*, Christian theology, the science of grace, which, investigating supernatural truths from within, is to be distinguished from the natural theology which it presupposes and uses. It has two branches: *positive theology* applies historical and literary criticism to establish the character and significance of the words and deeds which embody God's message; *speculative theology* contemplates and develops their meaning. By long-standing custom canonists have taught moral theology; one result has been the tendency to put it in a separate compartment from dogmatic theology. But Christian theology is a single science, and the division between 'Dogma' and 'Morals' is merely that between the theoretical part of science, which knows what is true, and its practical part, which judges what therefore is to be done.   [2] 1 Cor. iii. 1–2.

I have noticed how they are frequently held up, sometimes by heaps of useless questions, points and arguments, sometimes because the information comes out disjointedly from commentaries on texts or from disputations to meet academic occasions, sometimes because excessive repetition induces blankness and boredom.

Trusting in God's help, I shall try, therefore, to avoid these drawbacks and to expound sacred doctrine as briefly and clearly as the subject-matter allows.

To keep our inquiry within bounds, I shall first investigate what Christian theology is, and what is its field.

Next, because its main purpose is to communicate knowledge about the living God, about his life both as intimately his own and as the source and purpose of all things, especially of rational creatures, my exposition is divided into three parts. The first treats of God; the second of the movement of men to God; the third of Christ, whose humanity shows us the way of our going to God.

54, 273, 497   *Summa Theologica*, Prologue; 1a. i and ii,
Prologues

3. *Every man at the beginning doth set forth good wine, but thou hast kept the good wine until now.*[1] The tale points the moral. For a tempter begins by alluring, and shows his hand only when his victims are drunk: *it comes in sweetly, but at the last it biteth like an adder.*[2] Then again, a convert may begin well, but afterwards fall away: *are ye so foolish? Having begun in the Spirit, are ye now made perfect by the flesh?*[3]

But burdensome and bitter may be the start with Christ: *strait is the gate and narrow the way which leads*

---

[1] John ii. 10.   [2] Prov. xxiii. 31.   [3] Gal. iii. 3.

to life.[1] Then as we grow in faith and sound doctrine our movements become more lissom and easy: *when thou goest thy steps shall not be straitened, and when thou runnest thou shalt not stumble.*[2] All who will devoutly follow Christ must suffer hardship and grief to begin with: *amen, amen I say to you, that ye shall weep and lament.*[3] Afterwards comes peace and joy: *your sorrow shall be turned into joy.*[4] *The sufferings of this present time are not worthy to be compared with the glory which shall be revealed in us.*[5]

   286, 443, 526   Commentary, *St. John* ii, *lect.* 1

4. Contemplation concerns ends which serve no ulterior purpose. Play, too, is concerned with ends when you play for the fun of the thing, though with means to ends when you take exercise in order to keep fit.[6]

   352, 478   III *Contra Gentes,* 2

5. The sight of an effect rouses a natural desire to know the cause.[7] The human mind can view the whole range of things, and therefore instinctively craves to know their cause, which, ultimately, is God alone. Happiness is not attained until this natural appetite is at rest. Not any sort of understanding will do: only divine understanding will satisfy; only knowing God

---

[1] Matt. vii. 14.   [2] Prov. iv. 12.
[3] John xvi. 20.   [4] John xvi. 20.   [5] Gal. viii. 8.
[6] As being sound and worthy in itself an end is called a *bonum honestum,* as giving pleasure a *bonum delectabile*—these two objects may coincide: a means is called a *bonum utile.*
[7] Natural desire, *appetitus naturalis* or *desiderium naturale.* Sometimes used in contradistinction to conscious desire, *appetitus elicitus,* which is either emotive, *appetitus sensitivus,* or intellective, *appetitus rationalis*: this last is will, *voluntas.* The *appetitus naturalis* of the mind is its unconscious desire for complete truth. In this text, though not always when he uses a similar argument, St. Thomas takes natural desire in its widest sense.

will produce the state where restlessness is stilled. *Blessed are the pure in heart, for they shall see God.*[1] *This is life eternal, that they might know thee, the only true God.*[2] Aristotle's conclusion amounts to the same; final felicity is the pure contemplation of the noblest truth.[3]

131, 211, 662   III *Contra Gentes*, 25

I. NATURAL AND CHRISTIAN THEOLOGY

6. *For whatsoever things were written aforetime were written for our learning.*[4] The writings are bound in two volumes, of Creation and of the Holy Scriptures.

26   *Sunday Sermons*, 65

7. Of the two types of potentiality, the first is natural, and awaits actualization by a force of like nature to the subject: thus semen is developed into an animal, and the young grow adult. The second awaits actualization by a higher principle; that wood can be carved into a chest or that a blind man can be granted his sight are beyond the natural potentialities of the subjects concerned.

This difference, observed in the physical world, applies also to the human mind. Its natural potentiality is to be lit up by the ability to discern meanings,[6] an active and inborn power which is at work when we are in the act of understanding. The knowledge which comes is limited to the things we are acquainted with through our senses, and to the objects which can be imagined; it cannot comprehend our final end. We may deal with them expertly, yet a desire to know more

---

[1] Matt. v. 8.   [2] John xvii. 3.
[3] *Ethics*, x. 7, 1177ª11.   [4] Rom. xv. 4.
[5] Second Sunday of Advent.
[6] The active reason or factive intellect, *intellectus agens*, νοῦς ποιητικός; *de Anima*, iii. 5, 430ª10.

remains unsatisfied. How many things are scarcely hinted at by sense-knowledge; their existence may be suspected, but not their nature, for the world of spirits is vastly different from the world of bodies. Even in the material world there are many things which escape us; sometimes we may have an inkling of their secrets, sometimes not even that.

Hence the discontent and the desire within the mind for more perfect knowledge. Now an innate desire cannot be aimless. Yet this natural longing can be satisfied only if the mind be rendered completely in act, and so at peace, by an active principle more sublime than anything in the world about us. It is a desire to seek cause when effect is perceived. Whatever the situation, once the circumstances are apprehended, the human mind would penetrate into its very heart. A native instinct of intelligence will not rest until it reaches the first cause, seen in person, not in substitute. He is God, and therefore the final aim of rational creatures is nothing short of the vision of God, the seeing of his very self.

296, 348, 661   *Compendium Theologiae*, 104

8. Theologians occupy themselves with two kinds of divine truth, and with the corresponding refutation of hostile teachings. Merely rational inquiry can lead to the first, but the second lies beyond the unaided reason, however assiduous its activity. I say *two kinds* without implying any division in God: the doubling comes from the position of the human mind, which has to take different bearings on divine truth.[1]

81, 353   1 *Contra Gentes*, 9

9. That God exists, and other such theological truths which can be known by natural reason, are not articles

[1] The distinction is between natural theology, sometimes called theodicy, and Christian theology, or *sacra doctrina*.

of faith, but preambles to the Creed: faith presupposes reason as grace presupposes nature, or as any perfection supposes a subject capable of betterment. Nevertheless nothing bars a truth which is demonstrable in itself and open to scientific knowledge from being accepted as a matter of belief before its proof has been grasped.

364, 403   *Summa Theologica*, 1a. ii. 2, *ad* 1

10. Human philosophy examines creatures as elements of this world. Christian faith, however, does not stop short there; fire is taken, not as fire, but as representing the divine majesty and beckoning us to God: *the glory of the Lord shines through all his creation; how should his faithful servant herald his marvels enough?*[1] A philosopher and a theologian pursue different interests; one looks for inherently natural characteristics, the other for relations opening out to God. Even when they look at the same thing their point of view is different. The philosopher starts from proximate causes, the theologian from the first cause as divinely revealed; his concern is the manifestation of God's omnipotence and glory.

Theology deserves to be called the highest wisdom, for everything is viewed in the light of the first cause: *this is your wisdom and your understanding in the sight of the nations.*[2] It is the principal, and philosophy should be at its service: indeed divine wisdom uses human philosophy, just as the highest philosophy in its turn seeks for illustrations from data provided by all the other sciences.

Then also they follow different courses, for philosophy takes creatures in themselves and thence infers truths about God; creatures come in at the start, God at the end. The movement of theology is the reverse; God comes first, the creature afterwards. Hence theo-

[1] Ecclus. xlii. 17.   [2] Deut. iv. 6.

logy is nobler because liker to God, who in knowing himself looks upon creatures.

130, 365   II *Contra Gentes*, 4

11. The gifts of grace are added to us in order to enhance the gifts of nature, not to take them away. The native light of reason is not obliterated by the light of faith gratuitously shed on us. Hence Christian theology enlists the help of philosophy and the sciences. Mere reasoning can never discover the truths which faith perceives; on the other hand, it cannot discover any disagreement between its own intrinsically natural truths and those divinely revealed. Were there any contradiction, one set or the other would be fallacious, and, since both are from God, he would be the author of our deception, which is out of the question. In fact the imperfect reflects the perfect; our enterprise should be to draw out the analogies between the discoveries of reason and the commands of faith.

The principles of reason are the foundations of philosophy, the principles of faith are the foundations of Christian theology. The truths of philosophy are more restricted; they cannot be contrary to the truths of faith, but instead offer likenesses and anticipations of them. Nature is the prelude to grace. It is the abuse of science and philosophy which provokes statements against faith. These mistakes can be confuted by showing how impossible or unconvincing they are. Remember this, that as the truths of faith cannot be demonstratively proved so the denial of them sometimes cannot be demonstratively disproved, though any lack of cogency can be exposed.

Accordingly Christian theology may call on philosophy to perform three offices. First, to demonstrate the groundwork of faith, for the truths of natural religion—

for instance, that God exists, that there is one God, and so forth—can be proved by philosophy and are presupposed to religious belief and are necessary elements in the science of faith, or Christian theology. Secondly, to declare analogies common to nature and grace; thus Augustine draws illustrations of the Trinity from philosophical teachings. Thirdly, to resist attacks on faith, by showing that they are either wrongly conceived or at least unsupported and cannot be pressed.

Those who apply philosophy to the Christian Revelation should be on their guard against two faults. One is to invoke the tenets of unsound philosophy, as Origen did. The other, which would confine the truths of faith within the bounds of philosophy, as though belief could not go beyond the reach of reason, in effect turns things inside out, for philosophy should be kept within the bounds of faith: *bringing into captivity every thought to the obedience of Christ.*[1]

162, 198, 351, 410, 425, 465　Exposition, *de Trinitate*, ii. 3

12. Two things enclosed within the same order may reflect one another's likeness, but the likeness between cause and effect is not thus mutual:[2] we can say that a copy is like the original, but not conversely. We can speak of the creature resembling God in some way, but not of God resembling the creature.

74, 482　　　　　　　　*Summa Theologica*, 1a. iv. 3, *ad* 4

13. Holy Scripture applies to God the terms answering to objects found in our immediate environment. They fall into two classes. Some signify perfections which first of all are God's, and flow from him to creatures—thus, by the primary *good* and the *living* God other things are *good* and *alive*. These are the

[1] 2 Cor. x. 5.
[2] Pseudo-Dionysius, *de Divinis Nominibus*, ix. 6; *PG* III. 914.

terms considered by Dionysius in his books entitled *de Divinis Nominibus*. Others signify meanings transposed from creatures to God—thus, *lion, rock, sun* and so forth, which describe God symbolically or metaphorically. These he treats of in the book entitled *de Symbolica Theologia*.[1]

62, 129 Exposition, *de Divinis Nominibus*, Prologue

14. The first cause defies description. There is a different turn of meaning about statements which say that God is this or that and statements which attribute qualities to the things around us. The divine being is beyond our ways of making sense of things. Dionysius remarks that negative statements about God can be accurate, but that affirmative statements are clumsy and halting.[2]

62, 98, 482 Exposition, *de Causis, lect.* 8[3]

15. God is both transcendent and the cause of everything. Accordingly theologians sometimes confess that he is beyond all speech, while at other times they attribute many and various names to him.

60, 111, 143, 392 Exposition, *de Divinis Nominibus*, i, lect. 3

2. REVELATION

16. God is so good that it would be out of character for him to keep his knowledge of himself to himself and never to give himself intimately, for goodness of itself is generous.

129 Exposition, *de Divinis Nominibus*, i, *lect.* 1

[1] The first type, of absolute perfection, *perfectio simpliciter simplex*, is ascribed to God formally, *formaliter*; the second type, of relative perfection, is ascribed virtually, *virtualiter*.

[2] *de Caelesti Hierarchia*, ii. 3; *PG* v. 142.

[3] The *Liber de Causis*, a medieval extract from Proclus, Στοιχείωσις θεολογική, attributed to Aristotle before the time of St. Thomas.

17. The Word of the Eternal Father, who comprehends everything in his infinity, willed to narrow himself to our smallness, though without diminishing his majesty, in order to recall us, who are made mean by sin, to the grandeur of divine glory. Lest anybody should hold himself excused by the press of other business from waiting on his heavenly words, which students may find explicitly and copiously recorded in the books of Holy Writ, he composed a compendium of the doctrine of salvation.

The conditions of salvation, which are that our minds should not be darkened with error, that we should not pursue wrong ends and miss our true destiny, and that we should not be stained by guilt, are met through knowing what is true, purposing what is right, and maintaining what is fair.

The truth necessary for salvation is comprised in a few terse articles of faith. To describe the word we preach St. Paul quotes Isaiah, *a short word shall the Lord make upon the earth.*[1] Human purposes are straightened out in one brief prayer, in which our Lord teaches us how to pray and tells us what we should want and hope for. Human justice, which consists in obedience to law, he crowns with the single command of charity: *love is the fulfilling of the law.*[2]

St. Paul instructs us that our entire perfection is contained at present under three concise headings: *and now there remain faith, hope, charity, these three.*[3] Such is the Apostle's order, such the order of reason, for we cannot love unless we have good reason to hope, and we cannot hope unless we have knowledge.

223, 390, 488, 501   *Compendium Theologiae*, 1

[1] Rom. ix. 28; Isa. xxviii. 22.
[2] Rom. xiii. 10.
[3] 1 Cor. xiii. 13.

18. Now to come to your query as to whether we may hold that until the Resurrection the loving Virgin sorrowed seven times a day when recalling the words addressed to her by the blessed Simeon, *a sword shall pierce thy soul.*[1] I would note that the idea is unsupported by authority, and can be as easily rejected as approved. I would add this, that for myself I do not think such trivialities should be preached when such a wealth of assured truth is committed to us to communicate. However, they are not worth recanting, unless people have been bothered by them.

530   *Declaratio VI Quaestionum,* 5[2]

19. *All scripture is given by inspiration of God, and is profitable for doctrine, for reproof, for correction, for instruction in righteousness.*[3] The divinely inspired scriptures cannot be mastered by the purely rational sciences. An additional divinely inspired discipline is required. The need for such a science of divine revelation, going beyond purely rational exploration, is based on the principle that men must see at what they are aiming if they are to direct their purposes and actions. The final object of life is God, who exceeds the comprehension of reason: *the eye hath not seen, O God, besides thee, what thou hast prepared for those that wait for thee.*[4] Human salvation demands the divine disclosure of truths surpassing reason.

Even regarding truths accessible to the reason, men need to be instructed by divine revelation, otherwise few would know them, and then only after a long time, and jumbled with errors. Yet their entire salvation, which lies with God, depends on the knowledge of

[1] Luke ii. 35.
[2] To Brother Gerard, lecturer at Besançon.
[3] 2 Tim. iii. 16.   [4] Isa. lxiv. 4.

these truths, and is more expeditiously and safely pro-
moted when they are also taught by divine revelation.
    285, 380, 388   *Summa Theologica,* 1a. i. 1

20. Were there no revelation of the truths of natural
religion one embarrassment would be the restriction of
knowledge about God to very few. Three factors conspire to keep truth, which is the fruit of study, out of
reach. First, by personal temperament many people are
disinclined to follow intellectual pursuits, and especially
to press them to the utmost in order to discover God.
Secondly, the business of earning a living for themselves
and their families forbids them the leisure. Thirdly,
laziness prevents them making the preparations and
mastering the rational disciplines required.

A second embarrassment would be the years of
prolonged training needed to reach such deep truths;
even then we would hardly reach them. In youth we
are too volatile for the quiet and reflection required.
Most of us would lose ourselves in obscurity were we
left to our own devices. Yet all of us have a natural
desire to know God, and success here should not be reserved to the few and the old.

A third embarrassment would be the resulting mixture of mistakes, the consequence of our intellectual
feebleness and of thought clogged by fancies. Failing to
keep to the point, and confused by the babel of experts,
how many of us would be beset by doubts! Even well-
founded conclusions would be adulterated with strains
of fallacious and plausible argument.

By a salutary provision, then, divine clemency introduces to us the conclusions of natural theology by way
of faith, in order that all may come to divine truth
readily and without doubt or error. *Ye henceforth walk
not as other gentiles walk, in the vanity of their senses,*

having their understanding darkened.[1] *All thy children shall be taught of the Lord.*[2]

282, 353, 374, 578 1 *Contra Gentes*, 4

21. Truths above reason can be believed on authority alone; where that is lacking we have to take hints from the workings of Nature.

35, 358, 537 *Summa Theologica*, 1a–2a. ci. 1

22. We cannot have full knowledge all at once. We must start by believing; then afterwards we may be led on to master the evidence for ourselves. Some truths lie quite beyond the power of reason; these we shall never understand in this life, but must take on faith, until in heaven we come to see them with perfect vision. There are other truths which theoretically lie within the grasp of reason, but to begin with even these demonstrable truths about God must be accepted by faith.

The Rabbi Moses suggests five reasons why this should be so.[3] First, the depth and subtlety of these truths, and their remoteness from workaday experience. Second, the inherent weakness of the human mind. Third, the complication of the theological apparatus required for theological demonstrations. Fourth, temperamental inability to study. Fifth, the distraction of other work required to provide necessities of life. How serviceable, then, is the way of faith, open to all at all times, that they may draw nigh to salvation.

366, 380 *Disputations*, xiv *de Veritate*, 10

23. Our poor mental sight, which, notes Aristotle, reacts to the most evident things of nature like an owl

---

[1] Eph. iv. 17–18.   [2] Isa. liv. 13.
[3] Moses Maimonides (1135–1204), *The Guide for the Perplexed*, i. 34 (ed. M. Friedländer, London, 1928, p. 44). He is arguing that instruction should not begin with metaphysics.

blinking in the sunlight,[1] allows a truth more certain in itself to be less certain to us. Hence the doubts some people feel are not because the articles of faith are dubious, but because our minds are unsteady. Even so, a scrap of knowledge about sublime things is worth more than any amount about trivialities.

354, 377, 455   *Summa Theologica*, 1a. i. 5, *ad* 1

24. Commonplace comparisons are better than fine flights for communicating divine truths. Holy Scripture uses them, and for three reasons. First, in order the more safely to preserve the human spirit from error, for the expressions obviously cannot be applied to God just as they stand, whereas if noble figures were evoked people might easily be deceived, especially those who can imagine nothing finer than physical beauty. Secondly, gross understatement is well adapted to our present knowledge of God. We know what he is not, rather than what he is, and a modesty of expression brings home to us how far he is above us. Thirdly, crude symbolism serves to screen divine truths against those unfitted to look at them.

13, 618   *Summa Theologica*, 1a. i. 9, *ad* 3

25. We know God better through grace than through unaided reason. Natural knowledge depends on the imagination, which draws on what is provided by the outward senses, and on the power of human intelligence, which abstracts meanings from images. Both are heightened when God reveals his favours. The natural light of intelligence is strengthened by the light of grace, and sometimes images are divinely shaped which are happier suggestions of heavenly truth than those developed from the senses.

94, 179, 352   *Summa Theologica*, 1a. xii. 13.

[1] *Metaphysics*, i. 1, 993[b]10.

3. THE BIBLE

26. *This is the book of the commandments of God, and the law that is for ever. All they that keep it shall come to life.*[1]

Augustine tells us[2] that an eloquent scholar should speak to instruct, to delight, to persuade—to instruct the inexperienced, delight the bored, prevail on the reluctant. How well are these tasks performed by the words of Holy Scripture. They hold steadily to eternal truth; *for ever, O Lord, thy word standeth firm in heaven.*[3] They gladden us by the benefits they bring; *how sweet are thy words to my palate.*[4] They charge us with their power; *are not my words as fire? saith the Lord.*[5]

Our text commends Holy Scripture for three reasons: for its authority—*this is the book of the commandments of God,* for its eternal instructive truth—*the law that is for ever,* and for its attraction and promise—*all that keep it shall come to life.*

The effective authority of Holy Scripture originates from God, who *found out all the way of knowledge and gave it to Jacob his servant and to Israel his beloved.*[6] *Which, having begun to be declared by the Lord, was confirmed unto us by them that heard him.*[7] His authority is to be infallibly believed, because he is truth itself—*I am the way, the truth, and the life,*[8] possessed of the plenitude of knowledge—*O the depth of the riches of the wisdom and of the knowledge of God!,*[9] and armed with might—*the word of God is living and effectual and more piercing than any two-edged sword.*[10] Mighty it is

---

[1] Baruch, iv. 1.
[2] *de Doctrina Christiana,* iv. 4; *PL.* xxxiv. 91.
[3] Ps. cxviii. 89. [4] Ps. cxviii. 103.
[5] Jer. xxiii. 29. [6] Baruch iii. 37. [7] Heb. ii. 3.
[8] John xiv. 6. [9] Rom. xi. 33. [10] Heb. iv. 22.

because of the necessity it lays on us: *he that believeth not shall be condemned.*[1] Hence scriptural truth is proposed as a precept. Its mandates direct the mind through faith—*you believe in God, believe also in me,*[2] quicken the affections through love—*this is my commandment, that you love one another, as I have loved you,*[3] and lead us to practice what we preach—*this do, and thou shalt live.*[4] Mighty, also, because every part of Christian teaching is entirely consistent; *for whether I or they, so we preach; and so you have believed.*[5] This unity is established because all have one master—*for one is your master, and all you are brethren,*[6] one spirit—*did we not walk in the same spirit? and in the same steps?*[7] and, above all, one single loyalty—*the multitude of believers had but one heart and one soul.*[8]

Eternal and steadfast is the truth of Scripture: *heaven and earth shall pass away, but my words shall not pass away.*[9] It will last for ever, this law of an authority who is above change—*the Lord of hosts hath decreed, and who can disannul it?,*[10] who is constant—*I am the Lord of hosts and I change not,*[11] and who is true—*the lip of truth shall be steadfast for ever.*[12]

Then nothing is more useful than its teaching: *I am the Lord thy God that teach thee profitable things.*[13] Follow it and we shall come to life. First, to the life of grace, to which Holy Scripture disposes us: *the words that I have spoken to you are spirit and life.*[14] By grace our spirit lives with God: *I live, now not I; but Christ liveth in me.*[15] Then to the righteousness of good living expressed in good works, guided thereto by Holy Scripture: *thy*

---

[1] Mark xvi. 16. [2] John xiv. 1. [3] John xv. 12.
[4] Luke x. 28. [5] 1 Cor. xv. 11. [6] Matt. xxiii. 8.
[7] 2 Cor. xii. 18. [8] Acts iv. 32. [9] Luke xxi.33.
[10] Ias. xiv. 27. [11] Mal. iii. 6. [12] Prov. xii. 19.
[13] Isa xlviii. 17. [14] John vi. 64. [15] Gal. ii. 20.

justifications I will never forget, for by them thou hast given me life.[1] Finally, to the life of glory, which Holy Scripture promises and to which it conducts us: *Lord, to whom shall we go? thou hast the words of eternal life.*[2] *These things are written, that you may believe that Jesus is the Christ, the Son of God; and that believing, you may have life in his name.*[3]

571   *Inaugural Address* as Biblical Bachelor[4]

27. God, who is the author of Holy Scripture, possesses the power not only to adapt words to meanings, which we can do, but also to adapt things to meanings. What is peculiar to Holy Scripture is this, the things there signified by words may also in their turn signify other things. The first signification, whereby words signify facts, is called the historical and literal sense; the second signification, whereby the facts signified by the words also signify other facts, is called the spiritual sense. Note that the spiritual sense is based on, and presupposes, the literal sense.

619   *Summa Theologica,* 1a. i. 10

28. Truth necessary for salvation appears through the text of Holy Writ by divine design. The truth about something may be manifested either by words or by things, for words can signify things and things can signify one another. The author of the world can as well shape one thing to the figure of another as to fit a word to a thing. Accordingly, Holy Writ expresses truth in two ways, first, through the literal sense, when things are signified by words; secondly, through the spiritual sense, when things are signified by other things.

---

[1] Ps. cxviii. 93.   [2] John vi. 69.   [3] John xx. 31.
[4] *Principium fratris Thomae de Aquino quando incepit Parisiis ut Baccalaureus Biblicus, de Commendatione et Partitione Sacrae Scripturae.*

The various senses contained in Holy Writ would bring confusion were they not connected. In fact the spiritual sense is always based on the literal sense, and derives from it. Nor is the meaning clouded, though Augustine notes the advantages of not having the Bible made too easy[1]: boredom is dispelled when the attention is teased, pride cannot flatter itself when finding itself hard put to in order to catch the meaning, and disbelievers cannot jeer at what is kept away from them—*give not that which is holy to the dogs.*[2]

He also notes that nothing is occultly delivered in one text which is not plainly exposed in another. Mystical interpretations should always be supported by plain meanings. Cogent arguments cannot be developed from the spiritual sense, not from any lack of authority, but because the symbolic interpretation of history is a tricky business. One event may be figurative of so many others; if you start chopping and changing without taking care you may easily find yourself with a fallacious conclusion. For example, *lion* is the figure both of Christ and of Satan, but whatever the Bible attributes to lions cannot therefore be indiscriminately applied to either.

A meaning expressed by words, which is the literal or historical sense, is discovered by getting the hang of the sentence. You find the spiritual sense, however, by looking past the things signified by the literal sense to other realities behind them, and especially by treating things visible as figures of things invisible: that is why it is called the spiritual sense.

The purpose of the spiritual sense is twofold, first, to help right conduct; second, to help right belief. The first points a moral, and is called the moral sense, and

---

[1] *de Doctrina Christiana*, ii. 6; *PL* xxxiv. 38.
[2] Matt. vi. 6.

sometimes the tropological sense. The second is divided according to periods. The Old Testament is the figure of the New Testament, both are figures of the Heavenly Jerusalem: the Church's present state has been described as lying midway between the Synagogue and the triumphant City of God. The prefigurations of Christ and his Church in the Old Testament belong to what is called the allegorical sense; the prefigurations of the Church Triumphant in both Testaments to what is called the anagogical sense. Not every passage of the Bible is invested with all these senses; sometimes but one is present.

When rams and other creatures are used as signs of persons other than Christ they should be taken as pieces of fiction, not as historical facts; as such they enter into what we have called the literal and historical sense. The spiritual sense is restricted to the symbolism of real things and events; it is present when they have been chosen to typify Christ, shadows of his substance. Then the allegorical sense is superimposed on the historical sense. When, however, Christ is signified by pictures of fancy, this meaning remains part of their literal sense, as when Christ was symbolized by the dream-image of the stone cut out of the mountain without hands.[1]

The spiritual sense of Holy Writ is the planned symbolism of real things in their courses. He alone can give such meanings who also governs them by his Providence. We use words and images of fiction to signify what we mean; this, as we have remarked, is to employ the literal sense. God, however, can express his meaning through the unfolding of history.[2]

289, 359, 619   VII *Quodlibets*, vi. 14, *c. & ad* 1–4; 15, *c. &*
ad 1; 16, *c*

[1] Dan. ii. 34.
[2] St. Thomas does not speak of the *accommodated* sense of

29. Holy Scripture speaks of four marriages. The first in its historical and literal sense, the bodily union of a man and a woman; the second allegorical, the union of Christ with his Church; the third tropological or moral, the union of God with the soul; the fourth anagogical or eschatological, the union of God with the Church Triumphant.

570 *Sunday Sermons,* 20[1]

30. *They said unto him, Rabbi, where dwellest thou? He saith unto them, Come and see.*[2] The literal sense of the passage is that they wanted to know the house where he lived. Allegorically it means heaven, the home of God. The moral sense indicates what manner of men they should be if Christ is to dwell with them: *ye are builded together for an habitation of God.*[3]

126 Commentary, *St. John,* i, *lect.* 15

31. All the senses of Holy Scripture are built on the literal sense, from which alone, and not from allegorical passages, can arguments be drawn. The spiritual sense brings nothing needful to faith which is not elsewhere clearly conveyed by the literal sense.

568 *Summa Theologica,* 1a. i. 10, *ad* 1

32. History, etiology, and analogy fall under the literal sense. History is a plain statement of what was said or done, etiology shows its cause, and analogy harmonizes its meaning with other truths. All the

Scripture. For him the literal sense is what is meant by the words, or by images of fancy. It comprehends what is meant nowadays by the literal sense, and also the use of metaphor, parable, allegory, fable, and simile. The spiritual sense of Scripture is restricted to the symbolic meaning of real things as designed by God.

[1] First Sunday after Epiphany.
[2] John i. 38–39.
[3] Eph. ii. 22.

spiritual senses can be put under the heading of
allegory.

Summa Theologica, 1a. i. 10, *ad* 2

33. The metaphorical sense is contained in the literal
sense, for words bear imaginative suggestions as well as
their plain and proximate sense. The literal sense of a
figurative phrase is not the figure of speech itself, but
what it symbolizes; for instance, when speaking of
God's arm the Bible literally means that he wields
power, not that he has a bodily member.

62, 73   *Summa Theologica,* 1a. i. 10, *ad* 3

34. Theological argument should not fasten on figures
of speech, remarks Peter Lombard.[1] And Dionysius
says that symbolic theology is not scientific—it certainly
is not when it is not expository.[2]

571   Exposition, *de Trinitate,* ii. 3, *ad* 5

4. THE SCIENCE OF GRACE

35. The light of faith is infused, but needs to be focused
on distinct articles of doctrine: *how shall they believe
in him of whom they have not heard? and how shall they
hear without a preacher?*[3] As the understanding of first
principles of philosophy is brought out by empirical
tests so the truth of Christian teaching is supported by
miracles: *and they went forth, and preached everywhere,
the Lord working with them, and confirming the word with
the signs that followed.*[4]

To begin with, then, theology employs a narrative or
historical style in chronicling the signs confirming faith.
Yet because the principles of theology lie beyond the
grasp of the human reason, which in this present life is

---

[1] *Sentences,* i. vi.   [2] *Epistola,* x; *PG* iii. 1106.
[3] Rom. x. 14.   [4] Mark xvi. 20.

accustomed to observe and deal with things of sense, we have to treat these phenomena as symbols of the high truths on which we are bent. Consequently, theology also employs a metaphorical and parabolical style of discourse.

The purpose of theology is threefold: to refute error, to teach sound morals, and to contemplate truth. On the first count, theology is dialectical, and argues both from proved authorities and from reasonable analogies. On the second count, theology is preceptive and homiletical; in dealing with divine laws, it adopts, according to the context, the threatening or promising temper of prophetical writings or the narrative style of historical documents. On the third count, theology is also dialectical, as in patristic writings, which are the inspiration of this work of mine.

Hence Scripture is the fourfold source of theology. When we are out to discover the facts, then we must use the literal and historical sense; when we propose to edify, then the moral sense; when we want to foster contemplation, then the allegorical sense—also called the anagogical or eschatological sense when it looks ahead to heaven. When we propose to refute error, then we must keep to the literal sense, for the others deal in figures of speech, which are not the counters of formal rational argumentation.

286, 357, 469   *I Sentences*, Prologue, i. 5

36. The premisses of Christian theology are revealed truths, accepted on the word of the teacher who reveals them. Consequently its typical method is the appeal to authority. This does not impair its scientific dignity, for though to cite human authority is the poorest form of argument, the appeal to divine authority is the highest and most cogent.

Nevertheless Christian theology also avails itself of human reasoning to illustrate the truths of faith, not to prove them. Grace does not scrap nature, but improves it; reason subserves faith, and natural love runs through charity. Theology invokes great thinkers on matters where they are received authorities: thus St. Paul at Athens quoted Aratus, *in him we live, and move, and have our being; as certain of your own poets have said, For we also are his offspring.*[1] Theology treats them as sources of external evidence for its arguments. Its proper and indispensable court of appeal is to the authority of the canonical Scriptures. The writings of the Fathers of the Church are also proper sources, yet their authority is not final. Faith rests on divine revelation made through the prophets and apostles and set down in the canonical Scriptures, not on revelations, if there be any, made to other holy teachers.

11, 79, 133, 353, 537   *Summa Theologica*, 1a. i. 8, *ad* 2

37. That God can do impossibilities—this position is not heretical, though I am convinced it is untenable.

193, 291, 369   *de Aeternitate Mundi*

38. It is philosophically impossible for divine faith to profess what the reason must regard as false: not even divine omnipotence can make this otherwise.

188, 194, 585   *de Unitate Intellectus*

39. Christian theology is a science. Remember that there are two sorts of science. Some sciences are based on principles evident of themselves to the reason, for instance, arithmetic, geometry, and so forth; others on principles accepted from a higher science, for instance, optics presupposes geometry, and musical theory presupposes arithmetic. Christian theology is a science of

[1] Acts xvii. 28.

the second sort, for it works from principles known by the light of a higher knowledge, namely the vision enjoyed by God and the blessed. As music takes its principles from mathematics, so Christian theology believes principles revealed by God.

199, 368, 577   *Summa Theologica*, 1a. i. 2

40. In the order of discovery, the eternal is a conclusion at which we arrive by inference from the temporal: *for the invisible things of him from the creation of the world are clearly seen, being understood by the things that are made.*[1] But once eternal things are known then they take first place, and in the order of explanation, everything is to be examined in their light, and mundane affairs are to be disposed of according to eternal reasons.

169, 357, 465   *Summa Theologica*, 1a. lxxix. 9

41. The divine truths of faith are not closed to scientific inquiry, and its method of working from the unknown to the known can be applied. However, two sides are engaged. For our part we can discover divine truths only by working from our environment, which is composed of creatures perceived through our senses. On their side, in themselves, they are the most evident of all truths, and are so beheld by God and the blessed, though not at present by us.

Consequently there are two kinds of theology. One follows the reasonable course of inferring divine truths from meanings governing the physical world: it is thus that philosophers, claiming for fundamental philosophy, or metaphysics, the title of the divine science, have discussed theological truths. The other, while appreciating that at present when we are wayfarers we cannot see for ourselves the supreme evidence of divine

[1] Rom. i. 20.

truths, already begins through infused faith to take after and share in God's own knowledge by cleaving to his fundamental truth for its own sake.

By knowing himself, God without process of thought has simple insight into all other things. Our faith is fixed and intent on him, and catches his meaning. Thence, by using our wits and drawing conclusions, we come to know other truths as well. The prime truths held by faith play the part of premises to theological science, to which other truths are conclusions. Moreover, because it proceeds from higher principles Christian theology is nobler than natural theology.

Objections and Replies.[1]

1. It seems incongruous to call theology a science when holy writers apply the contrasting term of *wisdom* to the knowledge of divine truths.

When wisdom is set off against science it is as a complement, not a contrary. Wisdom is the mistress of the sciences, and Aristotle speaks of it as crowning them and governing them from on high by its principles.[2] All the more is this the case with a wisdom that is from and about the highest reality. To set everything in order, that is the office of the wise man. Hence theology is called wisdom because it governs the other sciences and sets them in proportion. In the mechanical arts those are called wise who direct others; they are the highest planners, while their subordinates may be compared to the scientists who deal with details. Science, also, is to wisdom what description is to definition.

2. But science presupposes that its subject can be

---

[1] This article follows the order of objections, exposition, and replies to objections, characteristic of the *Summa Theologica*: the objections are here transposed for the readers' convenience.

[2] *Metaphysics*, i. 1, 981^{a}30; *Ethics*, vi. 8, 1141^{b}25.

defined. Damascene observes that we cannot know at all what God is.[1] It follows that we can have no scientific knowledge about him.

When a cause is known through its effects, these supply the place of the cause's definition. All sciences which deal with subjects about which we are ignorant at the start have to adopt this substitute. Because there is a science which deals with God it does not follow that we are bound to know beforehand what he is. Or we might say that we can start with a notion of what he is not, for negative knowledge, as well as positive knowledge, can serve to isolate a topic for scientific examination.

3. Yet a science considers the parts and reactions of its subject. God, however, is simple, and cannot be analysed or submitted to tests.

The parts of a subject are not necessarily real components or members, but may be logical headings adopted for systematic treatment. Real changes are not induced in a thing when it is submitted to logical categories. To declare what God is not and then to draw comparisons between him and other things is relevant; by this method of negation and relation many conclusions may be proved about him from the data of faith and philosophy.

4. Nevertheless, reasoning precedes assent in any scientific inquiry, for assent is the effect of proof. When the truths of faith are discussed, however, the reverse is the case: assent precedes rationalization. Therefore it cannot be urged that the method is truly scientific.

A science is a system of principles and conclusions. Reasoning precedes assent to the conclusions, but not to the principles; it comes after and from assent to these. The articles of the faith are like principles, not con-

[1] *de Fide Orthodoxa*, i. 4; *PG* xciv. 797.

clusions, to Christian theology. Aristotle notes that
principles cannot be rigorously demonstrated, but they
can be defended by exposing the effects of denying
them, and recommended by bringing out their analogies
with the ways things work.[1]

5. Admitting that a science works from principles
which it takes for granted, then these must be either
self-evident truths or truths which can be demonstrably
taken back to self-evident truths. The articles of faith
are neither, and consequently cannot serve as scientific
premisses.

Even the human sciences suppose principles not
evident to all, but assumed from elsewhere; a physician
may take on faith the findings of physicists. Any subordinate science is backed by a higher science and
accepts certain truths as outside discussion. The articles
of faith are evident only in divine knowledge, and are
accepted as being such, though on good witness as to
their credibility.

6. Faith is the evidence of things not seen. Science,
on the contrary, deals with things which can be seen.
Therefore a science of faith seems a contradiction in
terms.

Scientific evidence derives from the evidence of
principles. Now a science does not adduce direct
evidence for its own principles, but uses these principles
to show that its own proper conclusions are evident.
Christian theology makes no attempt to demonstrate
the truths of faith in themselves, but uses them as
principles to elucidate its conclusions, and to invest
them with an equal certainty.

7. Science starts from insight, for it is from the
understanding of initial truths that we come to the
scientific knowledge of conclusions. But in matters of

[1] *Metaphysics*, iv. 4, 1006ª20.

faith there is no beginning with such intuition, which may indeed come at the end: *if you will not believe surely ye shall not understand.*[1]

Understanding certainly lies behind science, at least in the sense that science comes from understanding, but not immediately, here and now. For sometimes a subordinate science starts by believing the teachings of a superior science, though originally these teachings are clearly understood by a mind which is master of that science. Understanding, then, is the prime principle, but not the proximate principle. So it is with Christian theology: its proximate principle is human faith, but its prime principle is divine intelligence, on whose testimony we believe. The purpose of faith is to reach understanding of what is believed. In much the same way a scientific specialist may address himself to a more universal science in order to understand his own principles and prove hypotheses which to begin with were objects of his belief.

355, 374, 381   Exposition, *de Trinitate*, ii. 2

42. A hybrid results when two different kinds are mixed to produce a third, but not when one becomes the same in kind as the other. The taking of scientific arguments into Christian theology is less like mixing water with wine than like changing water into wine.

363   Exposition, *de Trinitate*, ii. 3, *ad* 5

43. A teacher should frame his words for the benefit of his hearers, not their harm. Some truths are to nobody's hurt, on the contrary all should know them; these should be plainly proposed. Others call for caution, and for two reasons: first, lest the irreligious should scoff when the privacy of faith is unveiled; secondly, lest

[1] Isa. vii 9.

simple folk should misapprehend subtleties: *I have fed you with milk, and not with meat, for hitherto ye were not able to bear it, neither yet now are ye able.*[1] Nobody should feel aggrieved: those who can may stay to study, others are not compelled.

369, 578   Exposition, *de Trinitate*, ii. 4

44. We can collect true analogies of the truths of faith which are fully evident only to those who see God. They do not amount to demonstration nor provide complete understanding. All the same, human reason is profitably employed with them, so long as the presumption of proving or comprehending is avoided, for even slight knowledge of such high matters is precious.

79, 131   I *Contra Gentes*, 8

45. Theology should resort to all the sciences, since they are its familiars, and its precursors in time though its followers in dignity.

7, 10   Exposition, *de Trinitate*, ii. 3, *ad* 7

46. Demonstrative knowledge about God leaves so much unsaid, and therefore is not final happiness.

172   III *Contra Gentes*, 39

47. Logical categories may frame the physical world, but not the first principles of reality. God's infinite simplicity rules out any attempt to classify him by genus and species; consequently he is not the subject for scientific definition.

74, 108, 367   *de Ente et Essentia*, 7

48. Realities which are inseparable in reality may yet be separated by logical analysis.

92   Exposition, *de Hebdomadibus*, 4

[1] I Cor. iii. 2.

49. We do not derogate from God's simplicity by considering him under many aspects, for they are not divisions of his essence, but consequences of our manner of understanding. There is no reason why our reason should not separately consider a variety of notes, and attribute them, each and all, to one simple being. We have to consider God from many points of view. Indeed, the simpler the being the greater and more manifest the powers we can see there: our multitudinous praises attest God's supreme simplicity.

102   II *Contra Gentes*, 14

50. God is wholly single and simple in himself. The human mind, however, which does not see him as he is, cannot know him except through many concepts. At the same time we are well aware that these different concepts answer to one and the same simple thing. The diversity is represented by the plurality of predicate and subject, the unity by the affirmation connecting them.

366   *Summa Theologica*, 1a. xiii. 12

51. In the ascending scale knowledge grows at once more closely knit and wider in its range. At the height of divine mind, all things are seen together and distinctly in one single truth, namely in God. So also sacred theology, the highest of human disciplines, is divinely held together despite the throng of objects dealt with, and without sacrificing detail or restricting attention to broad effects. Here theology is unlike metaphysics, which, discussing everything only in terms of abstract reality without regard to special variations, is therefore vague about the proper details of natural and moral objects. With theology, however, the miscellaneous objects of the other sciences are lit up by divine truth, which is one, and which runs through all theological processes, with the result that theology can be a coherent synthesis, and amount to more than a set of eclectic doctrines.

244 *I Sentences*, Prologue, i. 2. *c. & ad* 1

52. Part of philosophy is theoretical, part practical, but Christian theology is simultaneously a theoretical and a practical science, taking after God who by one act of knowledge contemplates himself and the things of which he is the artist. Nevertheless its emphasis is theoretical rather than practical; it treats of what is rather than of what we should do about it. Its principal concern is with divine truths and not with human acts, for these are considered only in so far as they promote that knowledge of God in which eternal happiness consists.

204, 421, 433 *Summa Theologica*, 1a. i. 4

53. There are two kinds of wisdom, corresponding to two kinds of judgement. One is by way of sympathy; for instance, a man who is endowed with the habit of virtue rightly judges what should be done by that virtue, for he already has a bias that way: in this sense the virtuous man is the rule and measure of human conduct.[1] The other is based on principle; for instance, a man well versed in moral science can pass sound judgements about virtues he does not possess. Theological judgement by sympathy proceeds from that wisdom which is numbered among the Gifts of the Holy Ghost: *he that is spiritual judgeth all things.*[2] And Dionysius notes that 'Hierotheus was taught by undergoing divine things, not only by learning about

[1] *Ethics*, x. 5, 1176ª15.   [2] 1 Cor. ii. 15.

them'.[1] Another kind of theological judgement is the result of scientific training: though its data are revealed, Christian theology demands this discipline.

458, 462   *Summa Theologica*, 1a. i. 6, *ad* 3

54. Hierotheus learnt divinity in the three ways, of acceptance, of keen and well-advised examination of the Scriptures, and of inspiration. He took what was taught by theologians, that is, by apostles. He wrestled with the meaning of the Holy Scriptures, and yet was gentle and delicate with their truth. He not only gathered information about divine things, but submitted himself to them; that is, he did more than study them with his mind, but fell in love with them and held them dear.

This affective condition relates to appetition rather than to cognition. Note this difference: things known are in the knower after the manner of the knower, not after their own manner of existence, whereas desire goes out to things just as they are in themselves, and the lover in a sense is changed into them. As a man of virtue rightly judges matters relating to that virtue, not from scientific theory but from a settled disposition which has become second nature to him, so to a lover of divine things is divinely given a flair for judging them aright. He is identified with them, and so knows them from 'compassion' or sympathy.

88, 381, 455, 471 Exposition, *de Divinis Nominibus*, ii, *lect.* 4

55. The Father gives his substance to the Son. Yet it cannot be said that he does not keep his substance, otherwise something of his divinity would be lost. In the case of bodily things what is given is not kept; give a horse away, and it is no longer yours. But reality may

[1] *de Divinis Nominibus*, ii. 9; *PG* iii. 647.

be both given and kept in the world of spirit, as when
you communicate knowledge.

166, 178   *Exposition, 1st Decretal*[1]

56. *Knowledge puffs up*[2]—the text applies when science
is without love.

Contra Impugnantes, 11

---

[1] To the Archdeacon of Trent, *de errore Abbatis Joachim
contra Magistrum Petrum Lombardum.*
[2] 1 Cor. viii. 1.

The Living God[1]

57. We confess the Lord *high and lifted up*,[2] who is *above all*.[3] Were he the existence of things, he would be within the universe, not above it.

15, 350, 356   1 *Contra Gentes*, 26

58. Perfect fruitfulness.

80   *Summa Theologica*, 1a. xxvii. 5, *ad* 3

59. What is real is actual, and the more actual, or fuller of reality, a thing is the more it is impelled to give of itself. Then also a thing is active because it is actual. It acts by communicating its actuality so far as it can.

[1] Twenty-five questions at the beginning of the *Summa Theologica* are devoted to the Unity of God before the mystery of the blessed Trinity is considered; despite long tracts which appear mainly of philosophical interest, the treatment is infused throughout with revealed doctrines, notably when it is argued that created minds are called to see God just as he is, in a face-to-face vision, and to share his own intimate happiness, that his goodness is expressed in a generosity exceeding the rights of a well-appointed universe, and that his personal Providence works with a mercy and equity beyond ordinary kindness and justice. The treatise culminates in the doctrine of the blessed Trinity, which is recommended, though not demonstrated, by analogies from the operations of knowing and loving, and investigated in accordance with the teachings of the Fathers and the definitions of the Councils of the Church. The mysterious goings forth within God are prolonged when the divine Persons are sent and given to the souls of men; their presence is not merely that of cause to effect but also that of object to our knowledge and love. The theme is picked up again in the treatises on the Gospel Law, Grace, Charity, and the life of the spirit with God.

[2] Isa. vi. 1.   [3] Rom. ix. 5.

The divine nature is supremely and sheerly actual, and therefore is essentially generous. God is bountiful to creatures by imparting his likeness; it is by this likeness that they are real. Above this lavishness the Catholic Faith professes another, namely the bestowal of God's very nature. When humanity is transmitted then a human being is born; when divinity itself is begotten then what issues is God.

Material forms differ from the divine nature on two counts. First, they are not complete substances; thus, human nature is not identical with a real man; there is more in the individual than a specific nature; humanity is not a man. The divine nature, however, is a complete substance; the deity is God. Secondly, the existence of created things does not spring from their inner essential principles, and consequently no created form or nature is its existence. God's proper name, however, is *I am*,[1] and that denotes his very form.

Material forms are propagated when they are embodied, that is to say, they are received in a distinct reality, namely matter, which underlies them and together with them composes physical natures. Of themselves they are not complete substances. Because neither they nor the physical natures which result from their union with matter are their existences, they take their existences from an outside principle.[2] When a material form exists in different subjects, then there are as many existences as there are things. There is one and the same specific nature in Socrates and in Plato, but not one and the same real existent nature.

[1] Exod. iii. 14.
[2] Existence, commonly used since the sixteenth-century for *esse*, that which makes a subject a real being, its ultimate substantial actuality. *Esse* indicates that a thing is: it is distinct from *essentia*, which denotes what it is.

But the imparting of divine nature, which is complete substance, requires no material to receive it or give it substance: what is begotten and what is given is no compound of form and matter. Furthermore, because the divine nature and the divine existence are identical, existence is not repeated by the subjects to which it is attributed: one and the same existence is possessed by begetter and begotten, and by giver and gift, nor are they numerically distinct individuals.

91, 141, 512 — Disputations, II *de Potentia*, I

I. THE GODHEAD

60. God is not confined in time, for he is eternal, and without beginning or end. His being is constant, ever present, never altering from past to future. Nothing can be taken away from him, nothing added. And his name is *he who is*.[1] His grandeur incomparably exceeds anything we know, for he is boundless. Sizes, however vast, can be defined by proportions and mathematical ratios. But God's magnitude is beyond the scale of creatures, and they cannot measure him. *Great is the Lord, and greatly to be praised; and his greatness is unsearchable.*[2] And again, *large beyond all bounds, high beyond all measure.*[3] He transcends mutability, and is unchangeable and unwavering: *no variableness, neither shadow of turning.*[4] His power outmatches all things, for he is omnipotent, able to do everything: *I am the Almighty God.*[5] Our definitions and conclusions are outranged, for he is incalculable, comprehended only by himself: *canst thou by searching find out God? canst thou find out the Almighty unto perfection?*[6] And again, *how sublime thy counsels, thy thoughts how high above us.*[7]

[1] Exod. iii. 13. [2] Ps. cxliv. 3.
[3] Baruch iii. 25. [4] James i. 27.
[5] Gen. xvii. 1. [6] Job xi. 7. [7] Jer. xxxii. 19.

Exceeding all speech, he is ineffable, and nobody can sufficiently sound his praises: *praise and extol him as you will, he is beyond all praising.*[1]

100, 210, 415   Exposition, *1st Decretal*

61. A created mind may see God, but cannot know all that he has done and can do: that would be to comprehend his power.

137, 523   *Summa Theologica*, 1a. xii. 8

62. No human emotions can be strictly attributed to God, with the exception of love and joy, and even these then carry no counterpart to the organic changes which take place in human affection and pleasure.

Holy Writ calls God's love to mind. *Yea, he loved the people.*[2] *Yea, I have loved thee with an everlasting love.*[3] *For the Father himself loveth you.*[4] Philosophers, too, regard love as primordial; Dionysius says that divine love is not satisfied without offspring.[5]

That God delights as well is confirmed by the authority of Holy Writ. *At thy right hand are pleasures for evermore.*[6] *I was daily his delight, playing before him always.*[7] *There is joy in heaven over one sinner that repenteth.*[8] Aristotle, too, remarks that God rejoices always with single and simple delight.[9]

Other good qualities not completely compatible with divine perfection are attributed to God metaphorically, not strictly, for they reflect some divine likeness, either in their effects or in their previous dispositions.

In their effects, because sometimes both a will ordered by wisdom and a passion out of control may

---

[1] Ecclus. xliii. 33.   [2] Deut. xxxiii. 3.
[3] Jer. xxxi. 3.   [4] John xvi. 27.
[5] Cf. *de Divinis Nominibus*, iv, *lect*. 1, 2.
[6] Ps. xvi. 11.   [7] Prov. viii. 30.
[8] Luke xi. 10.   [9] *Ethics*, vii. 14, 1154^b26.

lead to similar results. A just judge punishes, so does a man in anger. God is said to be angry when his ordered wisdom wills that somebody should be punished: *when the fire of his anger blazes out suddenly*.[1] He is said to be pitiful when his loving-kindness takes our miseries away; he is moved, as it were, by compassion: *slow to anger and plenteous in mercy*.[2] He is also said to repent, when within the eternal and immutable plan of Providence he builds up again what he had previously destroyed, or pulls down what he had previously put up: *I will destroy man whom I have created from the face of the earth; both man, and beast, and the creeping things, and the fowls of the air; for it repenteth me that I have made them*.[3] But such sayings should not be flatly interpreted, for the *Strength of Israel is not a man that he should repent*.[4]

Preceding dispositions may also reflect God's likeness, for love and joy, which exist properly in God, are the elements of all appetition—love the origin, joy the end. We may note that giving pain has its pleasure. We grieve when things happen against our will, and God is said to grieve when what we do strikes at what he loves and approves: *yea, truth faileth; and he that departeth from evil maketh himself a prey; and the Lord saw it, and it displeased him that there was no judgment: and he saw that there was no man, and wondered that there was no intercessor*.[5]

13, 200, 658, 670   1 *Contra Gentes*, 91

63. God is sheer goodness, whereas other things are credited with the sort of goodness appropriate to their natures. Justice, for example, is defined with reference to one type of activity. God's being is identical with his

[1] Ps. ii. 13.   [2] Ps. cii. 8.   [3] Gen. vi. 7.
[4] 1 Kings xv. 29.   [5] Isa. lix. 15–16.

acting; therefore for him to be good and to be just is one and the same. We do not touch this simplicity, our substance and our activity are distinct, and the goodness attributed to us because we exist is not identical with the goodness attributed to us because our dealings are fair.

Goodness is a general term, under which justice, and the other virtues, are special headings. God's is goodness at full strength, whereas not every type of goodness is discovered in other things, for the type varies from one to another. Though all are good in some way, not all possess the type of goodness called justice. Some are just, others have their different but appropriate kind of goodness. Yet all are good because they flow from the fount of goodness. God be praised through all things. Amen.

132, 143, 391   Exposition, *de Hebdomadibus*, 5

64. *Life* is an abstract term, signifying the very living of what is alive. An animal is said to be alive because of its soul; its living is the kind of existing which comes from that, its proper form. God, however, is his existence, and therefore is his living and his life.

1 *Contra Gentes*, 97

65. God so lives that he has no principle of life.

Summa Theologica, 1a. xviii. 3, *ad* 2

66. The living of a live thing is its existing; the actual understanding of the first mind is its life and existence.

Exposition, *de Causis*, 12

67. God's living is his knowing. His power of understanding, the object understood, and his act of understanding are all identical. Whatever is understood in God is, therefore, his living and his life. All things he

makes he understands. Therefore as existing in him they are his life.

85, 134, 187, 670   *Summa Theologica*, 1a. xviii. 4

68. As by one act God understands all things in his essence, so by one act he wills all things in his goodness. Therefore, as by his understanding of a cause he understands the effect in the cause, so his willing of an end is not the cause of his willing the means to that end, though he wills that means should serve that end. In short, he wills this to be for that, but he does not will this because he wills that.

187   *Summa Theologica*, 1a. xix. 5

69. God's love for things is better than ours. For our will is not the cause of goodness, but responds to goodness. Our liking does not produce the good of the thing we love: it is the other way round—the goodness, real or apparent, of the thing calls forth our love, whether that love be a love which rests content with its object as it finds it or a love which seeks to improve it. But God's love, which makes things out of nothingness, impregnates all the goodness they have.

117, 291   *Summa Theologica*, 1a. xx. 2

70. Love can be greater or less on the side either of the lover or of the beloved. With respect to the will's activity, loving is said to be more or less intense: here God does not love some more than others, for he loves all with a single and simple act, unvarying and perpetual. With respect to the object, we are said to love more—though not necessarily with greater vehemence —where there is more to love: here God loves some more than others. This conclusion is forced on us, for otherwise, since his will is the cause of goodness, some things would not be better than others.

310, 327, 407   *Summa Theologica*, 1a. xx. 3

71. God's planning and arranging immediately engages every event, though his Providence is carried out executively and the world is governed through secondary causes. He himself disposes of things great and small, first and last, without ceding any of his powers. He is not like an earthly ruler who has to delegate his responsibilities because he is unable to attend to everything at once. God knows everything simultaneously; details neither fuss him nor distract him from major issues.

183, 187, 392, 439   *Compendium Theologiae*, 131

72. God is merciful. He works above his justice, not against it. When you give two hundred pieces from your own money to a man who is owed one hundred by another, you are acting, not against justice, but from liberality and mercy. So it is when you forgive an injury, for forgiveness is like giving a present: *bestow on one another even as Christ has pardoned you.*[1] Mercy is the fulfilment of justice, not the abolition: *mercy rejoiceth against judgment.*[2]

268, 327, 435   *Summa Theologica*, 1a. xxi. 3, *ad* 2

73. Beauty and the beautiful—these are one and the same in God. Excess is of degree or of kind. The first is signified by the comparative and superlative, the second by the addition of the preposition *super*. Both are the same in God, who is most beautiful and super-beautiful —not that he can be put into any class, for every kind of beauty is his, who is the fount of all beauty.

350   Exposition, *de Divinis Nominibus*, iv, *lect.* 5

74. Hyperbole is impossible when speaking of God's perfection. Nothing can touch him. He depends on

[1] Eph. iv. 32.   [2] James ii. 13.

nothing outside. He takes from nothing. His goodness
is consummate, and lacks nothing of perfection found
anywhere.

507   Commentary, *V Metaphysics, lect.* 18

75. Whatever is desirable in any happiness whatsoever,
be it true, be it false, pre-exists wholly and supremely
in God's happiness. False happiness, precisely as
such, that is, as falling short of complete happiness, is
absent; nevertheless any likeness or promise of joy,
however thin, has its perfect original and fulfilment in
God.

131, 201, 669   *Summa Theologica,* 1a. xxvi. 4, *c. & ad* 1

76. God is most happy, and therefore supremely conscious.

661   Commentary, *III Metaphysics, lect.* 11

77. Consider how divine happiness gathers up within
itself and consummates all joys—the joys of the contemplative life, for God has the splendid and perpetual
vision of himself and others; of the active life, for he
governs the wide universe, not one man only, or one
household, or one city, one kingdom. False earthly
satisfactions are but shadows of that complete felicity,
whether they be pleasure, wealth, power, dignity, or
fame. God enjoys, without alloy, the most excellent
gladness in himself and for all things; he is rich, for he
owns everything; his power is unlimited; his dignity is
the primacy and command over all; his fame the admiration of every mind that knows him.

121, 207, 452   1 *Contra Gentes,* 102

2. THE BLESSED TRINITY

78. Jerome says that heresy comes from undue prolixity;[1] therefore we should address ourselves to discuss the Trinity with care and modesty.

587   *Summa Theologica*, 1a. xxxi. 2

79. A thing may be reasonably proved either by going to the root of the matter and producing a cogent demonstration, as when natural science argues about the uniform velocity of heavenly bodies, or by accepting it and then showing how the consequences fit the evidence, as when astronomy adopts a hypothesis to rationalize the appearances, and constructs a system of eccentrics and epicycles. This second line of reasoning is not final, for another hypothesis may be found which serves just as well.

The first method of proof is serviceable in dealing with such truths as God's unity. But the second must be adopted when we would show forth the truth of the Blessed Trinity. We start with acceptance, and then afterwards may give recommending reasons, not that they sufficiently demonstrate the mystery.

35, 41, 44, 576   *Summa Theologica*, 1a. xxxii. 1, *ad* 2

80. Goodness is generous. God is supremely good. Therefore supremely generous. But he cannot supremely give himself to creatures, for they cannot receive his entire goodness. The perfect gift of himself is not to another diverse by nature. Therefore within him there is distinctness without division.

Sheer joy is his, and this demands companionship.

Perfect love must be matched. Charity is unselfish love. But creatures cannot be loved above all; they are not attractive enough. Therefore in the divine begetting

[1] Attributed by Peter Lombard, *Sentences*, IV. xiii. 2.

is there perfect lover and perfect beloved, distinct, but of one nature.

Our profession is downright, that in God exists a plurality of persons in unity of nature; we are convinced on account of the witness of faith, not for the reasons given above.

394, 451, 543 *I Sentences*, II. i. 4

i. *Summary*

81. Truths about God open to reason have been subtly discussed by many pagan philosophers, though some have erred and others have barely reached the truth after long and laborious study. But they were unable to touch the truths delivered to us by Christianity, which through faith instructs us beyond human sense. Take this: although God is single and simple, he is nevertheless God the Father, God the Son, and God the Holy Ghost, and these are not three gods, but one God. We propose to consider this mystery as best as we can.

19 *Compendium Theologiae*, 36

82. God understands and loves himself. Moreover, his understanding and his loving are identical with his being. A thing understood is in the mind understanding; thus is God in himself. A thing as understood in the mind is, as it were, a word of mind—for what we signify by an outward word of speech is what we have understood within. Therefore, within God we set down the existence of a Word.

13, 113 *Compendium Theologiae*, 37

83. A concept, that is what ordinary usage calls the interior word contained in the mind. What is formed in the living womb by vital power is said to be physically conceived; the male gives and the female receives in such wise that the thing conceived, being of the same

kind, shares in the nature of both. What is formed in the
mind is also conceived. The thing understood gives,
as it were, and the understanding receives, and what is
apprehended in and by the mind agrees with the
quickening object, of which it is a kind of likeness, and
with the mind, because there it has intelligible reality.
Consequently what the mind knows is without strain
described as a conception of mind.

54   *Compendium Theologiae*, 38

84. But this difference should be reckoned with. What
the mind conceives seems like the offspring of the thing
understood, showing its likeness and representing its
presence. When the mind understands something other
than itself, the thing understood is like the father of the
word conceived in the mind, while the mind plays the
part of the mother, in whose womb conception takes
place. But when the mind understands itself, the word
conceived is related to mind as offspring to father.
Therefore in dealing with God's self-understanding,
the Word should be compared to God, of which it is
the Word, as son to father.

67, 499   *Compendium Theologiae*, 39

85. Observe also that with us, where substantial reality
and intellectual activity are distinct, the word conceived in our minds has only a mental reality, not
identical with the psychological state of our minds. In
God, however, to be and to understand are entirely one
and the same. The Word of God in God is God from
every point of view; the Word is one with God in
meaning and in substance, one in intelligible and in
natural being. The Word is identically the divine
nature and essence, and whatever may be predicated of
God may also be predicated of the Word.

68   *Compendium Theologiae*, 41

86. By insisting that the Son is consubstantial with the Father in the Creed we rule out two mistakes. First, of imagining that a process of physical generation is involved, where there is separation of son's substance from father's. Secondly, of imagining that a process like our thinking is involved, where the word conceived in our mind is a supervening accident, and not part of the substance of mind.

108   *Compendium Theologiae*, 42

87. The object understood is in the understanding, and likewise the object loved, when loved, is in the lover. The beloved moves the lover from within, and to this extent is inside the lover. As God understands himself so does he love himself, for good as such is always held dear. Therefore God is in himself like beloved in lover.

451   *Compendium Theologiae*, 45

88. But the beloved's presence in the lover is of a somewhat different character from the presence of the known in the knower. Understanding comes when the mind takes after its object by holding its likeness. Loving, however, comes when the lover is moved by the attraction set up by the beloved. Loving is not brought about by a likeness, as knowing is, but by a real attraction. The manner whereby God is in himself as known in knower is described by the terms *generation, father, son, word,* all of which imply a specific likeness. But the manner whereby God is in himself as beloved in lover is described by the terms *breath* or *spirit*: in this sense the Creed bids us believe in the Spirit.

53, 399   *Compendium Theologiae*, 46

89. We are drawn to goodness as by an end. What our ends are ultimately decides whether our voluntary acts are right or wrong. Consider then how the love which

loves the supreme good which is God, is so excellent
that it is called *holy*—whether that means *pure*, as
the Greeks say, for God's is sheer goodness quite un-
flecked, or *firm*, as the Latins say, for God's is immutable goodness. Fittingly, therefore, we speak of the
Spirit which is God's love of himself as the Holy Spirit.

451   *Compendium Theologiae*, 47

90. God's understanding is his very being, and so is
his loving. He loves himself by his essence and substance, not by a supervening quality. Beloved is then in
lover by very substance, not according to an accidental
mode, as in us. The Holy Ghost is like the Father and
the Son, a person subsisting in the divine substance.

118   *Compendium Theologiae*, 48

91. When the mind actually understands, understanding proceeds from the power of mind, and so does the
thing understood, which is the word. Similarly, when
the lover actually loves then the beloved is in the lover;
the being loved proceeds both from the power of loving
and from the awareness of the beloved. In other words,
the presence of the beloved in the lover comes first from
the principle of love and next from the beloved being
held in mind, that is from the word of the beloved
which is conceived. Since the Word is the Son when
God understands and loves himself, which Word is
uttered by the Father, we must infer that the Holy
Ghost, who is of the love whereby God is in himself as
the beloved in the lover, proceeds from the Father and
the Son—*ex Patre Filioque*.

120, 145, 661   *Compendium Theologiae*, 49

92. The Trinity we profess in God does not deny the
simple unity of his substance. God exists and understands and loves, but not as we do. Man by nature is a

substance and a thing, but his knowing and loving are
not his very substance—the holding of himself in mind
is not a thing, but the looking at a thing; the keeping of
himself in love is not a thing, but the outstretching of a
thing. So then we can separately consider these three
apart, namely, the self, the self knowing, the self loving.
These three are not identical, for, to repeat, man's
knowing and man's loving are not man's very being,
though both are rooted in his single substance. But
God's being and understanding and loving are identical; his existing in nature and in mind and in love are
one and the same, though each is substance. And because complete substances of an intelligent kind are
called *persons* in Latin, *hypostases* in Greek, we profess
three persons or hypostases, Father, Son, and Holy
Ghost.

49, 109, 512   *Compendium Theologiae*, 50

ii. *Divine Origins*

93. After having considered truths concerning the
unity of the divine nature, let us now turn to truths
concerning the Trinity of divine Persons. Because
the distinction between them arises from relations of
origin, the question of divine origins comes first in the
order of treatment. Then comes the treatment of the
resulting relations; finally of the divine Persons themselves.

100, 105   *Summa Theologica*, 1a. xxvii, Prologue

94. *I proceeded forth and came from God.*[1] Holy Scripture makes use of phrases which refer to a proceeding
forth within the divine reality. This has been variously
interpreted.

[1] John viii. 42.

Arius, who treated it as an issuing of effect from cause, taught that the Son proceeds from the Father as the first of his creatures, and that the Holy Ghost proceeds from the Father and the Son as the first creature of both. Consequently, neither the Son nor the Holy Ghost are true God. Against this we read of the Son, *we are in his Son, Jesus Christ, this is the true God,*[1] and of the Holy Ghost, *know you not that your members are the temple of the Holy Ghost*[2]—a temple being for God alone.

Sabellius, who treated it after the manner in which a cause is said to proceed into an effect, by moving the effect or impressing there its likeness, taught that the Father is named the Son inasmuch as he assumed flesh from the Virgin, and that the Father is also called the Holy Ghost inasmuch as he vivifies and sanctifies rational creatures. Against this is our Lord's own statement about himself, *the Son can do nothing of himself,*[3] and other statements too declaring that he is not the Father, but the Son.

A close study of their doctrines shows that they supposed *proceeding forth* to imply an outside term and object, and consequently as not being completed within the Godhead. An emanation results from activity of some sort; if that is an action going out into external material, then of course the result leaves the principle and an outside effect is produced. But if the activity is of the kind which remains inside the active substance, the result stays within it. The best example is the mind's activity; there actual understanding is performed within the mind.

Since God is above creatures, his attributes should be conceived after the fashion of intellectual substances, which are the highest, not of bodily creatures, which are

[1] John v. 20.   [2] 1 Cor. vi. 19.   [3] John v. 19.

the lowest. Emanations within God should not be imagined as if they were bodily processes, movements in space or physical actions producing external effects, as when a heater warms something up, but, following the tradition of Catholic Faith, they should be explained in terms of intellectual expression, as when a meaning is uttered yet stays within the mind.

12, 85   *Summa Theologica*, 1a. xxvii. 1

95. *Thou art my Son; this day have I begotten thee.*[1] The coming forth of the divine Word fulfils all the conditions of generation, which, properly speaking, means the origin of a living thing from an attached living principle, and an issuing in like specific nature. The Word proceeds from understanding, which is a vital activity; from an attached living principle, for the activity is immanent; according to specific likeness, for the concept is like the thing understood; and existing in the same nature, for God's being is his understanding. The proceeding forth of the Word, then, is called generation, and the Word who proceeds forth is called the Son.

129, 507   *Summa Theologica*, 1a. xxvii. 2

96. The Word issues, a complete substance within the Godhead. On this account Scripture uses terms about the begetting of life to signify the issuing of divine wisdom in person: *when there were no depths I was conceived; when there were no fountains abounding with water; before the mountains were settled, before the hills was I born.*[2]

                                    Summa Theologica, 1a. xxvii. 2, *ad* 2

97. The issuing of the Son is from understanding and then, corresponding to the conception of the known in

[1] Ps. ii. 7.   [2] Prov. viii. 24–25.

the knower, another emanation proceeds, namely of
love from the activity of will, whereby the beloved is
in the lover.

This love, as such and precisely, expresses no such
likeness as does the Word, but is rather an impulsion,
or motion towards. The result is more appropriately
named Spirit, than Begotten, or Son.

88   *Summa Theologica*, 1a. xxvii. 3, 4

98. Most Greek authorities refer to the Father as being
the cause of the Son, and to the Father and the Son as
being the cause of the Holy Ghost. This usage, which
is found in Athanasius, Basil, and Theodoret, to mention some names, can give rise to confusion, since it is
not customary among the Latins who, instead of *cause,*
speak of *principle* or *author.* They are guided by three
considerations.

First, there is no question of the Father being the
final cause, or the material cause, or the formal cause of
the Son. The originating or efficient cause remains in
question. Now in our experience cause and effect are
really different substances. And so, to avoid reckoning
the Son as of different substantial nature from the
Father, we prefer to use, instead of *cause,* such terms
as *fount, head,* and so forth, which signify both origin
and identical substance.

Secondly, *cause* and *effect* are correlative terms, and
so we do not refer to the Father as a *cause* to avoid
implying that the Son is an effect. Were we to say that
the Son had a cause, we might be taken to mean that
he was included within the universe of things created
by God.

Thirdly, we should not be freer than Holy Scripture
in attributing terms to God. There the Father is called
the principle, or beginning: *in the beginning was the*

Word.[1] Never is he called the *cause*, nor is the Son spoken of as caused. Since *cause* is a narrower term than *principle* we should not presume to employ it, especially as *principle* is a better and more general term than any to signify origin in God.[2] Since divine truths are incomprehensible and beyond definition, it is more appropriate to keep to broad terms, and avoid very pointed ones, when speaking about God. Thus his proper name is, *I am who I am*.[3]

Of course we are not alleging that the Greek Fathers, in referring to the Father as *cause*, hold that there is a difference of nature between the Father and the Son, or that the Son is a creature. Gregory of Nyssa and Basil are quite explicit on this head, yet for them *cause* is a good term to express the origin of persons; for us *principle* is a better.

    15, 580, 587   *Contra Errores Graecorum*, 1

99. Intelligent substances, the noblest of creatures, express themselves through knowledge and love. Thus they bear the image of the uncreated Trinity. Their own thoughts and their loves, however, are not persons; their understanding and affections are not their substance, but qualities about them. Only with God is understanding and loving his very self, only with him are his Word and Love persons.

    94   *Disputations*, x *de Potentia*, 1

iii. *Divine Relations*

100. Those who abide by the definitions of the Catholic Faith, and subscribe to the dogma that there are three persons in one nature, must thereby hold that in God

---

[1] John i. 1.

[2] *Cause*: a positive principle on which a reality depends. *Principle*: that from which anything starts in any way whatsoever.

[3] Exod. iii. 14.

relations are real. Number is the result of distinction, and there is distinction within God, a distinction of inward substantial reality, not just a separateness apart from creatures, who are distinct from him by their natures.

This distinction cannot be drawn between divine absolute realities; such attributes as *one*, *true*, or *good* apply to the divine nature, which is one. Were the distinction of persons conceived in those terms it would follow that they differed by nature, which is the heresy of Arius. We are left with the conclusion that the only possible distinction which can be entertained within the Godhead is between relative realities.

Yet more than a merely logical distinction is called for. While it is true that terms which signify an identical reality can be considered separately and apart (thus geometry can treat one and the same point both as a beginning and as an end), we mean more than that when we speak of three distinct divine Persons. Otherwise the Father would really be the Son, and the Son really the Father, and it would follow that the divine Persons would be merely nominally distinct, which is the heresy of Sabellius.

We infer, therefore, that relations in God are real. How this can be we must now investigate, following the teaching of sacred authorities, but not expecting to reach a full explanation.

We are first aware of real relations in situations where quantities can be compared together, or where things act on or are acted on by one another. This is bound to colour our reflections on relations in God. Yet dwelling on quantities is little help, for God is free from quantity, both numerical and continuous: the analogy here is slight—if we except the term *three* to indicate the persons. Even so, we have to go back behind the concept of number, and appreciate the divine relations which constitute the trinity of persons. Likewise the term *one* which is used to indicate the unity of the divine nature; it does not mean that God is one unit among others, for he is not in a class, and when he is related to creatures the relationship is purely logical and invests him with no additional reality.

There remain, therefore, the relations which arise from activity. Now here there can be no question of the transitive action of an active principle working on a passive principle, or the action which involves the reception of an effect in a subject. No passive principle exists in God; there is nothing like material in him, nothing by which he can be really affected by what goes on outside him. So if activity is spoken of then that kind of activity which denotes perfection and involves no change must be meant, namely, immanent activity, such as understanding and willing—sensation and emotion can be left aside, for they are bound up with organic changes, and God is wholly incorporeal.

God's perfect fatherhood is by mind and not by blood. Now four relationships can arise when our mind understands, namely, to the thing understood, to the likeness through which the object is understood, to the mind's own act of understanding, and to the concept it expresses. This last differs from the other three: from the object, which is sometimes outside the mind, whereas the concept is within the mind—also the object is like the end to which the concept is the means, for the concept is formed by the stretching out of the mind to know the real object; from the likeness, which actuates and informs the mind, and which can be taken as the principle of the actual understanding; and from the act of understanding, of which the concept is the term, for the conception, called the word of mind, is constituted by the activity of the mind conceiving a definition or judgement.

This word, by which our mind understands something other than itself, derives from that other and represents it. When, however, the mind understands itself then this word is the offspring and likeness of the mind understanding itself.

In our case this mental word is distinct from the mind; it is not the mind's substance, but a quality of mind, though part, of course, of the mind's actual understanding. But were there a mind in which substance and activity were the same, the word would be inside both the very being and the activity of that mind. Such is God's mind, and therefore his Word is co-essential with him.

Thus we can catch a glimpse of how one may originate another without any cleavage in the unity of essence. Origin always implies a real relation, either on the side of one, when what is originated is different in nature from its originator, as in the springing forth of creatures from God, or on both sides, when both originated and originator have the same nature, as in human generation where there is a real relationship between son and father. The Word of God is consubstantial with its Principle; and consequently there is a real and mutual relationship between the Word and its Begetter.

62, 111, 507   Disputations, VIII *de Potentia*, 1

101. Having affirmed that there are real relations in God, we are bound to conclude that they are the divine nature. Otherwise we are led into such heresies as saying that there are parts in God, or that the relations are accidents or modifications of his being (for every reality is either substance or accident), or that something other than God's substance is truly eternal.

To clear up the position, recall that of the nine categories of accident,[1] the very meaning of some connotes *inherence*, or existence in a subject; thus quantity and quality are attributed to a subject because they are in it. But relation is different; its very meaning denotes a reference to something else; it goes out, not in.

From observing this special mode of significance proper to relative terms, some have taught that the precise function of a relation is not 'to inhere', but 'to be about' a subject; a relation is a phase between the substance which is related and that to which it is related. Relations in created things, they continued, are not accidents, for the very being of an accident is a 'being in', its existence is an inherence. Some theologians, Gilbert de la Porrée among them, proceeded to graft this opinion on their theology of the Trinity.[2] They concluded that relations are not in the divine Persons, but, as it were, attend or accompany them; and that because the divine essence is in the persons, therefore the divine relations are not the divine essence, and that because they do not inhere, then neither are they accidents. In this fashion they interpreted Augustine's dictum, that relation is attributed to God neither as substance nor as accident.[3]

Yet it would follow from this opinion that a relation was not a true reality, but only a logical entity, for everything real is either substance or accident. Indeed, some philosophers, Averroes for example, have held that relations were purely logical categories. Gilbert de la Porrée could then be construed to teach that the divine

---

[1] The ten Aristotelean predicaments or categories: substance and the nine categories of accident—quality, relation, quantity, action, *passio* or reception of action, location, duration, posture, dress.

[2] 1076–1154. *In de Trinitate*; PL LXIV. 1292. Cf. PL LXIV. 1309.   [3] *de Trinitate*, v. 4–5; PL XLII. 913.

relations are purely logical, and, by implication, that the distinction of divine Persons is not real—which is heretical.

We should proceed as follows: there is no reason why real existence should not be inherence, although not signified as such. Indeed *action* itself denotes a 'being from', not 'a being in', the agent, nevertheless it is certainly in the agent. Similarly, *relation to*, though pointing outwardly, certainly exists inwardly—that is, of course, when it is more than a purely mental reference. In created things relation is an accident, but in God it is his substance. Therefore relations are the divine substance, though they do not explicitly state the mode of substance, for the relative terms which signify them are predicated of God in a special manner, unlike that of absolute and substantial terms.

49, 105, 507   Disputations, vIII *de Potentia*, 2

102. The essence of a relation is the contrast of one relative with another. Since real relations exist within God, so also do real contrasts. Relative opposition of itself denotes distinction. Therefore within God there is real distinction, not of his absolute being, which is his nature, supremely single and simple, but of relations within him.

47, 50   *Summa Theologica*, 1a. xxviii. 3

103. Real relations within God appear only from his cognitive and affective activities which stay inside him, not from his actions which produce an outside effect. Corresponding to the two emanations by which the Word is conceived and Love proceeds forth, two opposite relations are assigned, one on the side of the originator or principle, the other on the side of what is originated and begun. In the generation of the Word, the first relation is called *fatherhood*, the second *sonship*.

Proper terms are lacking for what comes forth by love
—an uncatalogued activity—and for the resulting relations, but the relation of the principle is called a
breathing or *spiration*, and the answering relation is
called a proceeding forth or *procession*, although both
terms denote origin rather than relation.

82, 87   *Summa Theologica*, 1a. xxviii. 4

iv. *Divine Persons*

104. Person signifies what is noblest in nature, namely
a complete substance of an intellectual kind, and therefore, with all due safeguards, the term should be applied
to God, whose nature embraces every perfection.

507   *Summa Theologica*, 1a. xxix. 3

105. To inquire into the meaning of personality in
general is one question, to inquire into the meaning of
divine personality is another. *Person* in general means
an individual substance which is intelligent, individual,
that is, single in itself and distinct from others. But
human person also implies this body of flesh and bones
and this soul: these are individuating principles for
men, but not for every kind of person.

Now distinctions in God arise from relations of
origin. A relation in God is not, as it is with us, an
accident modifying a subject, but the divine nature itself, and existing as a complete substance. As Deity is
God, so divine fatherhood is the Father. Divine personality, then, signifies a relation existing as a complete
substance. Thus a relation is denoted, which is a substance, a hypostasis subsisting in, and really identical
with, the divine nature.

Let us continue this train of thought. The term *per-*
son accordingly signifies relation directly and nature

obliquely—the relation here is a complete substance, not one of the categories of accidents. But at the same time *person* also signifies nature directly and relation obliquely when nature is synonomous with substance or hypostasis; relation enters obliquely because the distinct meaning of hypostasis when applied to God comes from relation.

The nuances of meaning in the term *person* were not appreciated before heretics began to make false statements. Previously *person* had been treated as an absolute term, and only afterwards was it accommodated to signify a relative thing. But there was no break with usage, and the sense was not strained, for relation was hinted at in the term.

100, 507, 580 *Summa Theologica*, 1a. xxix. 4

106. Absolute properties in God, such as wisdom and goodness, bring out no contrast, and therefore they are not really distinct. They are, of course, completely substantial, but do not express distinct complete substances or persons.

Summa Theologica, 1a. xxx. 1, *ad* 2

107. *Person* in God signifies a relation subsisting in the divine nature.

Summa Theologica, 1a. xxx. 1

108. Number is either abstract or concrete. Abstract or pure number, such as 2, 3, 4, exists merely in the mind and represents a merely logical arrangement; there is nothing to prevent its being applied to God, for *whole* and *part* as purely logical notions can be attributed to him. But concrete number is the numbering of real things, such as two men or two horses: if the units are creatures, then one is part of two, and two are part of three, for one is less than a couple, and a couple is less

than a trio. Such is not the case with God, where the Father is as much as the whole Trinity.

59, 86, 92   *Summa Theologica*, 1a. xxx. 1, *ad* 4

109. The numerical terms which enter into the propositions we formulate about God are not taken from number considered as a species of quantity. Numerical quantity is like other bodily properties, for instance, height and breadth, in being merely metaphorically applied to God. The numerical terms used in theological logic come from a plurality transcending the categories of the physical sciences, and this plurality is verified in the divine manifold in the manner that metaphysical unity is possessed by one single thing. When we apply *one* to God, we do not treat him as a unit, but credit him with the oneness which is identical with being, for by attributing unity to a thing we add nothing to its reality, but merely deny that it is broken up and affirm that it is undivided. Similarly, *many* as applied to God signifies things as being single and entirely themselves in what is their own.

13, 47, 100   *Summa Theologica*, 1a. xxx. 3

110. When we profess the Trinity in Unity we certainly enumerate, but we mean, not three times one, but distinct persons which can be counted.

Summa Theologica, 1a. xxxi. 1, *ad* 4

3. THE FATHER

111. As in the case of other terms which are properly applied to God, *fatherhood* and *generation* are more completely verified in him than elsewhere, as regards not their creaturely mode of signification but their inmost meaning: *I bow my knees unto the Father of our*

Lord Jesus Christ, from whom all fatherhood is named.[1]
Generation is defined by its term, the form of the object
generated: the closer this is to the form of the generating
principle so much the truer and more perfect the
generation. Like makes like—it is better to beget an
equal than to produce a thing of lower nature than oneself. With divine generation the forms of begetter and
begotten are numerically the same, whereas with us they
are specifically the same but numerically different.
Fatherhood and *generation* are superlative in God, comparative in creatures.

59, 108, 543   *Summa Theologica*, 1a. xxxiii. 2

112. A term is primarily attributed to a subject which
possesses its full meaning, not to something else which
bears some resemblance: what is borrowed comes back
to what is owned. Lion primarily means the animal, not
a lionheart or any other sort of human lion. Now fatherhood and sonship at full strength are the Father's and
the Son's who are one in nature and glory. Creatures
are not related to God with the utmost sonship, because
they and the creator are not of the same nature.

Nevertheless there are varying degrees of resemblance, and the more perfect a thing the closer it is to
divine sonship. God is called the father of non-rational
creatures because they are like his footprints; they re-
semble him because they are his traces: *hath rain a
father? or who hath begotten the drops of dew?*[2] Rational
creatures are like him because they are his images: *is not
he thy father that hath possessed thee? hath he not
created and established thee?*[3] Of some he is father by
likeness of grace, for they are called adopted sons because born of grace: *the Spirit himself beareth witness
with our spirit that we are the children of God, and if*

[1] Eph. iii. 14.   [2] Job xxxviii. 28.   [3] Deut. xxxii. 6.

children, then heirs also.[1] And of others by a greater
likeness, for they have entered into their inheritance of
glory: *we rejoice in hope of the glory of God.*[2]

Perfect fatherhood, then, is a relation of Person to
Person, and thence it is derived to include God's relationship to creatures.

13, 415, 435 *Summa Theologica*, 1a. xxxiii. 3

4. THE SON

113. The order in which we discover things governs
our language about them; frequently what is stated as
primary is in reality secondary, and etymology traces
back a meaning to an original case though it exists
beforehand elsewhere. Thus some terms attributed to
God and creatures, such as *being, good,* and so forth, are
used about creatures to start with, and are later trans-
ferred to God, though existence and goodness pre-exist
in him.

Such is our usage concerning *word.* A word of mouth,
heard by our ears, is more readily taken in than the inward word of mind. Etymologically *word* stands first for
what we say, not for what we think. Yet the word of
mind really comes first, guiding and shaping our lips;
it is the final and efficient cause of speech, the final cause
because speech is the sign of thought, adopted to express
what we are thinking about, the efficient cause because
sound is taken to signify what we please, for a word of
language is an artificial sign and, like other works of art,
is settled by the will.

Three phases may be noticed: the purpose, the
exemplar, and the finished work; these make up a threefold word. First, the inner word of our heart, the con-

---

[1] Rom. viii. 16–17.   [2] Rom. v. 2.

cept of our mind which we propose or express in speech. Secondly, the image or exemplar of the outward word we are going to chose, and this is the word of mind couched in sense. Lastly comes the utterance of the word. An artist first intends his work of art, next shapes it in his mind and fancy, and then in his material. Similarly, a speaker first conceives the meaning he intends to convey, afterwards finds a sign for it, and finally pronounces it.

A bodily word can be ascribed to God metaphorically, inasmuch as his creatures can be called his words, for they manifest his mind as effects manifest their cause. Likewise the word imagined can be attributed to God metaphorically, to stand for the divine ideas of creation. But the word of heart, which is what mind considers, and which is wholly free from matter or impediment, can be attributed to God no less strictly than the terms *knowledge* and *known*, *understanding* and *understood*.

17, 83, 137, 505   Disputations, IV *de Veritate*, I

114. The Son is not generated from nothing, but from the substance of the Father.

85   *Summa Theologica*, Ia. xli. 3

115. The Incarnate Word is like a word of speech. For as sensible sounds express what we think so Christ's body manifests the Eternal Word.

497   Disputations, IV *de Veritate*, I, *ad* 6

116. The Word bears on creatures, since by knowing himself God knows all his creatures. A concept represents all that the mind is understanding, but whereas with us there are as many words of mind as there are diverse objects of our understanding, with God, who

by one act understands both himself and everything
else, a unique Word expressed the Father and all
creation. God knows himself, but creatures he knows
and makes. So the Word is expressive of God the
Father, and both expressive and creative of the universe:
for he spake and it was done.[1]

147, 499, 562   *Summa Theologica,* 1a. xxxiv. 3

117. Dionysius says that effects are but indifferent
copies of their causes which range high above them.[2]
Such is the distance between causes and effects that
some terms which apply to effects cannot be applied to
causes. Just because delightful things give delight we
are not bound to infer that they take delight, or because
the sun gives heat that therefore it is itself heated. The
reason is that all full causes surpass the mode of the
reality communicated to their effects.[3]

When, therefore, you inquire whether things exist
more truly in themselves than in the Word, you must
draw a distinction. The phrase *more truly* can designate
either the truth of things or the truth of judgements.
Without doubt the truth of things is greater in the
Word than it is in created reality. Conversely, the predicate *man* is applied more accurately to a real subject
existing in human nature than to its existence in the
Word.

67, 91, 599   *Disputations,* iv *de Veritate,* 6

---

[1] Ps. xxxii. 9.

[2] *de Divinis Nominibus,* ii. 7; *PG* iii. 646.

[3] A principal cause, according to its full theological and philosophical meaning, is always of a higher degree of being than its
effect, and the likeness between them is analogical. When cause
and effect are of the same nature—in other words, when the likeness between them is univocal—then the cause is less a cause of the
effect's being (*causa quoad esse*) than of its coming to be (*causa
quoad fieri*).

5. THE HOLY GHOST

118. The relations arising from the proceeding forth of love are unnamed, and the Person who proceeds forth, the Holy Ghost, is wellnigh anonymous.

88, 124, 544   *Summa Theologica*, 1a. xxxvi. 1

119. We speak of spirits when we see movement springing from a hidden source.

de Rationibus Fidei, 4[1]

120. *Love* can be used either as an essential name of the divine nature or as a personal name of a divine person—then it is the proper name of the Holy Ghost, as *Word* is the proper name of the Son.

Mental processes, clearer than affective processes to us, are furnished with a more precise vocabulary for their phases. Hence we have to employ circumlocutions for the Person who rises from love. Nevertheless parallels can be found, and to the concept or word of knowledge there corresponds an impression, so to say, of the beloved on the affection of the lover.

Apart from *loving* and *holding dear*, there are few technical terms to state the relationship which results from this impression or this being in love, and from the relationship between the lover and the beloved arising from the activity of loving. The poverty of language forces us to use the common terms of endearment—as though, instead of the Word, we have to speak of *intelligence conceived* or *wisdom begotten*.

Well then, when they denote no more than a relationship of lover to beloved, the terms *loving* and *holding dear* apply to God's nature; but when they express a relationship of what proceeds forth to its principle, and conversely when, in other words, *love* means the Love

[1] To the Cantor of Antioch.

that arises and *holding dear* means a breathing forth of
affection, then *Love* is the name of a Person, and *holding dear* manifests a personal activity and is a personal
term, like uttering the Word or begetting the Son.

145   *Summa Theologica*, 1a. xxxvii. 1

121. The perfect goodness of divine happiness and
glory postulates friendship within God: nothing is
better, nothing nobler than charity, says Richard of St.
Victor.[1] There is no happiness without joy, and joy
comes from friendship above all. Nothing is sweeter, he
goes on, nothing more jocund; intelligent living experiences nothing dearer than the play of charity, and
no other enjoyment can compare with it.

Perfect glory displays a certain magnificence of intercourse, which charity provides. God's true and perfect happiness, therefore, requires a trinity of persons.
The love of oneself alone is a private love, not true
charity. Yet God cannot supremely love another, since
no creature is supremely lovable, for no creature is
supremely good. It appears then that God's charity
would not love to the utmost were he only one person.
Nor even if he were only two, for with perfect friendship the lover wills that what he loves should also be
equally loved by another. To be unable to receive love's
intercourse is a mark of great weakness; to be able to
bear it a mark of great strength. Better to receive gratefully, best to ask for more and more, says Richard.

63, 80, 286, 399   *Disputations*, IX *de Potentia*, 9

122. A gift is freely given, and expects no return. Its
reason is love. What is first given is love; that is the first
gift. The Holy Ghost comes forth as the substance of
love, and *Gift* is his proper name.

454   *Summa Theologica*, 1a. xxxviii. 2

[1] *de Trinitate*, iii. 2; *PL* cxcvi. 916.

6. THE SENDING FORTH OF DIVINE PERSONS

123. *I am not alone, but I and the Father that sent me.*[1]
Being sent, that implies two relations, to the point of
departure, and to the term of arrival. With regard to
the first, a proceeding forth appears in command, in
advice, and in origin: in command, as when a master
dispatches a servant; in advice, as when a counsellor
launches a king into war; and in origin, as when a
plant puts out a flower. With regard to the second, a
new beginning appears, for the person sent either
arrives on the scene for the first time or takes on a fresh
role.

The sending forth, or mission, of a divine Person
meets both requirements: on one side, there is a proceeding forth of origin, on the other, a new mode of
existence. Thus we say that the Son is sent by the
Father into the world, because he proceeds from the
Father and is newly born visibly into the world, although he was there already: *he was in the world, and
the world was made by him, and the world knew him not.*[2]

16, 142, 496   *Summa Theologica*, 1a, xliii. 1

124. Notice this difference among words implying
origin when applied to God. Some state only a relation
to a principle—*proceeding forth* and *going out*. Others
add a reference to an object—so we speak of *begetting*
and *breathing love*, and so also of *being sent* and *being
given*.

95   *Summa Theologica*, 1a. xliii. 2

125. The term *procession* within the Blessed Trinity
signifies a coming forth from a principle and not necessarily a going out to an object, though the coming forth

[1] John viii. 16.   [2] John. i. 10.

of the Holy Spirit, a coming forth of love, does imply a
going out to another, namely to the beloved. And because the eternal comings forth are the cause and type
of all creation, so it is that the begetting of the Son is
the exemplar of all making, and the Father's loving
of the Son is the exemplar of all granting of love to
creatures. Hence the Holy Spirit, who is the love
whereby the Father loves the Son, is also the love
whereby God loves creatures and imparts to them his
goodness.

Two comings forth of love can be considered: one is
eternal to a divine beloved, the other temporal to a
creature beloved. This second love confers something
on the creature, and from this fresh effect arises a new
relationship towards God on the creature's part.

112, 292, 387   *I Sentences*, XIV. i. 1

126. The creature can be conjoined to God in three
ways. First, by likeness only, when it reflects divine
goodness but does not reach to the divine substance:
this is the common causal presence of God in all things.
Secondly, by reaching as well to God's substance
through the activity of mind and heart, by faith cleaving
to the first truth, by charity to the first good: this is the
special presence of God in the soul by grace. Thirdly,
by reaching to God's substance by its very being, not
merely by its activity: this is God's presence in the Incarnation; there is no essential identity here, for what is
created cannot become God, but human nature is
taken into the unity of a divine Person.

401, 507   *I Sentences*, XXXVII. i. 2

127. We say that a divine Person is *sent* when he comes
to renew a creature, and *given* when possessed by a
creature. Neither situation comes about except through
sanctifying grace.

We describe God's existence in all things by one common style. His presence by essence, presence, and power, is the presence of a cause in the things which share in its goodness. But above this general presence there is another and special presence, reserved to rational beings, to whom God is said to be present as the known in the knower and the beloved in the lover. For the mind and heart can be lifted to God himself. Accordingly, he is said to dwell in souls as in his temple, and is then more than a cause in an effect. The only divine work which can show the reason how a divine Person may newly exist in creatures is sanctifying grace. In this manner a divine Person is said to proceed forth in time and be sent to us.

That only is possessed as a gift which is freely enjoyed. Nothing but sanctifying grace imparts the power of enjoying God. By the gift of grace the Holy Ghost is possessed by the soul, and dwells there. He is both sent and given.

292, 543   *Summa Theologica*, ix. xliii. 3

128. The Holy Spirit in person, not merely the Gifts of the Holy Spirit, comes forth and is given. When we receive them, our relationship is not arrested at them, but goes out to the Holy Spirit, who is now with us in a new way. Now is he said to be related to us as we are to him.

457   *I Sentences*, xiv. ii. 1 (*ii*)

129. *I, wisdom, have poured out rivers. I, like a brook out of a river of a mighty water; I, like a channel of a river, and like an aqueduct came out of paradise. I said, I will water my garden of plants, and I will water abundantly the fruits of my meadow.*[1]

[1] Ecclus. xxiv. 40.

Among the diversity of doctrines proclaimed by
various sages about where wisdom may be found, the
position of St. Paul stands out firm and strong: *Christ
the power of God and the wisdom of God, who of God is
made unto us wisdom.*[1] This does not mean that wisdom
is uniquely the Son's, for he is one by wisdom, as he is
one by nature, with the Father and the Holy Ghost, but
that wisdom is attributed to him in a special manner
because his character so well shows it forth. For this is
what the highest wisdom does: it manifests the hidden
truths of divinity; it produces the works of creation, and
furthermore restores them at need; it brings them to the
completion of achieving their own proper and perfect
purpose.

God alone knows the depths and riches of his Godhead, and divine wisdom alone can declare his secrets.
Our knowledge of him, whatsoever it may be, comes
from him, for imperfection is the shadow cast by perfection, and what is partial originates from what is complete. *Who shall know thy thoughts except thou give
wisdom?*[2] Above all the revelation of the Blessed Trinity
is found in the deeds of the Son, who is the Word of
God, uttered by the Father. *No man knoweth the Father
but the Son, and he to whom it shall please the Son to
reveal him.*[3] And again, *no man hath seen God at any
time, the only begotten Son, who is in the bosom of the
Father, he hath declared him.*[4] Therefore is wisdom
personified in the Son, of whom it is written, *I, wisdom,
have poured out rivers.* These rivers I interpret to mean
the ineffable flow of the everlasting streams, of Son from
Father, and of Holy Ghost from them both. These are
the streams which once seemed underground, or so
lost to sight in the confusion of creatures, that the

[1] 1 Cor. i. 24, 30.   [2] Wisd. ix. 27.
[3] Matt. xi. 27.   [4] John i. 18.

wisest of men could hardly come to know the mystery
of the Trinity. But now, *the depths of rivers he hath
searched, and the hidden things he hath declared*;[1] now
the Son has come, he has brought us good tidings and
opened their courses to us. *Teach ye all nations, baptizing them in the name of the Father and of the Son and of
the Holy Ghost.*[2]

Divine wisdom's next function is to create. God's
wisdom is that of an artist, whose knowledge of what he
makes is practical as well as theoretical: *thou hast made
all things in wisdom.*[3] It is Wisdom in person who
speaks: *I was with him forming all things.*[4] So we think
of the Son when calling him the image of God invisible
and the pattern to which all things are made; *the first-
born of every creature, for in him were all things created
in heaven and on earth.*[5] Since *all things were made
through him*[6] rightly do we think of the Son when it is
written, *I, like a brook out of a river of a mighty water.*
Here is suggested how all things flow from God but
without lowering him. As brooks and irrigation canals
are led from great rivers, so all the motions of creatures
derive from the eternal activity of the divine Persons. He
begot the Word, cries Augustine, and there must all
things first be if ever they are to come forth.[7] And
Aristotle declares that the original which comes first is
the cause of its copies that come after.[8] Therefore must
we look to the goings forth of the divine Persons if we
are to ascribe meaning and cause to the goings forth of
creatures. The creator floods the creature, but the level
of the main stream does not fall; the creature is distinct
from the creator, but the divine might is not drawn off.

---

[1] Job xxviii. 11.   [2] Matt. xxviii. 19.   [3] Ps. ciii. 24.
[4] Prov. viii. 30.   [5] Col. i. 15–16.   [6] John i. 3.
[7] *de Genesi ad Litteram*, i. 2; *PL* xxxiv. 248.
[8] *Metaphysics*, ii. 2, 994[a]12.

He who makes a thing is he who can repair it, and so the restoration of creation is the third function of wisdom: *by wisdom were they healed.*[1] This especially was the work of the Son, who was made man in order to change the very state of our nature and restore everything human: *through him reconciling all things unto himself, both as to the things that are on earth and the things that are in heaven.*[2] Justly then do we read these lines of the Son, *I, like a channel of a river, and like an aqueduct came out of Paradise.* This Paradise is the glory of God the Father, and from this paradise the Son descended into our vale of tears, not losing glory, but hiding it: *I came forth from the Father, and am come into the world.*[3] Here let us pause to reflect how he came, and what was the fruit. How water rushes down! how Christ was urged by love of us throughout the mystery of his life! *a violent stream, which the Spirit of the Lord driveth on!*[4] And this stream is led off into many channels to water the whole Church: *and he gave some apostles, and some prophets, and others some evangelists, and others some pastors and doctors; for the perfecting of the saints, for the work of the ministry, for the building up of the Body of Christ.*[5]

A fourth function of divine wisdom is the fostering of things to the fulfilment of their purpose. Otherwise what is left but vanity? Vanity which wisdom will not abide, for wisdom *reacheth from end to end mightily and ordereth all things sweetly.*[6] And when are we at ease but when we have arrived and rest where we desire to be? This is the doing of the Son, the true natural son of the Father, who brings us into the glory of his birthright: *for it became him for whom are all things and by whom*

---

[1] Wisd. ix. 19.   [2] Col. i. 20.
[3] John xvi. 28.   [4] Isa. lix. 19.
[5] Eph. iv. 11–12.   [6] Wisd. viii. 1.

are all things, who has brought many children into glory.[1]
Hence it is written, *I will water my garden of plants.*
Preparation is needed to get rid of whatever might
hinder this purpose, and so, in order to bring us to
eternal glory, Christ has prepared the medicine of his
sacraments for us, to cleanse our sinful souls.

First the planting, and then the harvest. The Church
is the garden: *my sister, my spouse is a garden enclosed.*[2]
Here are many plots, all different according to our call-
ings, but all planted by God, and the whole is watered
by the streams of Christ's sacraments flowing from his
side. Holy Writ exclaims at its loveliness: *how beautiful
are thy tabernacles, O Jacob, and thy tents, O Israel; as
wooded valleys, as watered gardens near the river.*[3]
Hence, also, the Church's ministers are like gardeners:
I have preached, Apollo's watered.[4]

The fruits which wisdom has abundantly watered
are the harvest. It is Christ who brings us to glory,
Christ who brings to birth the Church's faithful: *shall
not I that make others to bring forth children myself bring
forth, saith the Lord; shall I, that give generation to
others, be barren, saith the Lord thy God?*[5] The fruits are
the saints in glory: *let my beloved come into his garden
and eat the fruit of his apple trees.*[6] What abundance and
ripeness is here! *They shall be inebriated with the plants
of thy house.*[7] For indeed they are drunk, their joy surpassing all measure of reason and desire. *From the
beginning of the world they have not heard, nor perceived
with the ears; the eye hath not seen, O God, what things
thou hast prepared for them that wait for thee.*[8]

17, 568   *I Sentences*, Prologue

[1] Heb. ii. 10.   [2] Cant. iv. 12.   [3] Num. xxiv. 5.
[4] 1 Cor. iii. 6.   [5] Isa. lxvi. 9.   [6] Cant. v. 1.
[7] Ps. xxxv. 9.   [8] Isa. lxiv. 4.

III

Creation[1]

130. Creatures—vanity, because on the brink of nothingness; not vanity, because made to God's likeness.

245, 259, 356   Disputations, *de Caritate*, 1, *ad* 11

131. *I meditate on all thy works, I muse on the work of thy hands.*[2] Meditation is indispensable for well-instructed faith. Accordingly let us consider creatures in order to view and marvel at divine wisdom. A work of art represents the mind of the maker: *how manifold are thy works! in wisdom hast thou made them.*[3] God's wisdom has produced all things real; and from them we can catch a glimpse of his likeness, *poured forth on all creation.*[4] The psalmist says, *such knowledge is too wonderful for me; it is too high, I cannot attain it:* and he goes on to remind himself of God's guiding light, *even the night shall be light about me; marvellous are thy works, and that my soul knoweth right well.*[5]

In the second place, we are led to wonder at God's

---

[1] Two principles enter here and are afterwards elaborated. The first is that God is the total cause of reality; creation is the production of the whole of a thing; all reality there is from and for him. The second is that creatures are real in, though not from, themselves, and therefore good; moreover, they are real as material beings, not only as spiritual. The opening questions on morality in the *Prima Secundae* follow easily from the concluding questions in the *Prima Pars*, where man's psycho-physical unity is accepted without regrets and his place in the theological universe determined. What he can do must first be decided before he is told what he ought to do.

[2] Ps. cxlii. 5.   [3] Ps. ciii. 24.
[4] Ecclus. i. 10.   [5] Ps. cxxxviii. 6, 11, 14.

power, and so to hold him in reverence. The maker is nobler than the things he makes. We gaze at the heavens and the earth, *why then, how much greater must he be who contrived them!*[1] *For the invisible things of him from the creation of the world are clearly seen, being understood by the things which are made, even his eternal power and godhead.*[2] From wonderment we come to fear and reverence: *thy name is great in might; who would not fear thee, O King of nations!*[3]

In the third place, our hearts are warmed to love God's goodness. All perfections showered throughout the world in separate drops flow together, whole and complete, in the fount of goodness. If we are drawn to the sweetness, beauty, and goodness of creatures, how much more impetuously should we be borne away to him in whom all these little streams commingle and course. *For thou, Lord, hast made me glad through thy work; I will triumph in the works of thy hand.*[4] *They shall be abundantly satisfied with the fatness of thy house; and thou shalt make them drink of the river of thy pleasures. For with thee is the fountain of life.*[5] *So many good things seen, and he, who is sheer goodness, not known! What folly is this ignorance about God.*[6]

In the fourth place, we grow like God, who sees everything by knowing himself. Faith starts by telling us about God, and then in the light of his revelation we look at his creatures. *We all, with open face beholding as in a glass the glory of the Lord, are changed into the same image.*[7]

Studying creatures builds up beyond question the Christian Faith. *Remember the works of the Lord, recount*

---

[1] Wisd. xiii. 4.
[3] Jer. x. 6–7.
[5] Ps. xxxv. 9–10.
[7] 2 Cor. iii. 18.

[2] Rom. i. 20.
[4] Ps. xci. 4.
[6] Wisd. xiii. 1.

what you have seen; the works of the Lord are the words of the Lord.[1]

10, 77, 239, 352, 465   II *Contra Gentes*, 2

132. When you go into a house from the cold and at the entrance feel a warmth which grows as you go farther inside, you believe there is a fire in the hearth giving out heat, although you do not see it. So you see the things of this world ranged in different degrees of beauty and value, and the nigher you draw to God the handsomer and finer they appear.

129, 489   Exposition, *Apostle's Creed*

133. How false the doctrine that our opinions about creatures are no concern of faith so long as we think aright about God. For mistakes about them contribute to mistakes about God, and take our mind away from him on whom faith rests. Holy Writ threatens those who are so misled and treats them as disbelievers: *because they regard not the works of the Lord, nor the operation of his hands, he shall destroy them, and not build them up.*[2] *They have calculated and gone astray, they have not appreciated the honour of a blameless life.*[3]

41   II *Contra Gentes*, 3

134. The entire universe pre-exists in the Godhead, which is its primordial cause. Father, Son, and Holy Ghost are all in all, because in their divinity every other thing is anticipated and possessed.

129, 399   Exposition, *de Divinis Nominibus*, ii, *lect.* 1

135. For families who do not mix together to dwell under the same roof is an uncomfortable arrangement. The entire universe is one dominion and realm,

[1] Ecclus. xlii. 15.   [2] Ps. xxvii. 5.   [3] Wisd. ii. 21–22.

governed by one ruler, who is the first mover, the first truth, the first good—God, blessed for ever and ever.

182   Commentary, *XII Metaphysics, lect.* 12

I. THE UNIVERSE

136. *In the beginning God created the heaven and the earth.*[1] To create is to bring a thing into existence without any previous material at all to work on.

94, 617, 620   II *Contra Gentes,* 16

137. God's being is one, and yet he understands and produces many things, though his actual understanding is one and simple. His being and understanding is eternal and changeless; yet he can understand what is temporal and changing, and can produce fresh effects in time. Some sort of analogy may be drawn from human affairs; a task can be postponed until a future fixed date without affecting the steadfastness of the will to do it. If you urge that this happens when the passage of time brings another influence into play deferring the suitable moment, I reply that this indeed is the case within any particular system of reference constituted by God's temporal effects: he raised Lazarus to life, not immediately after he was dead, but four days afterwards; the delay was from a concern for the context and for what had gone before. But if we regard the whole universe as one system, then such considerations do not come in, for change and time were produced simultaneously with the universe; there was no preceding time or change to which this new general effect had to be accommodated. Its only measure was the mind of the maker, who understood and willed that this new effect should not be from eternity, but should begin after

[1] Gen. i. 1.

nothingness. Time is the measure of action and motion, dimension is the measure of size. If we inquire about any particular body, the earth for instance, and ask why it should be contained within its present boundaries and not spread beyond them, a reason can be found by referring to the proportions of the cosmos. But if we press the inquiry, and ask why that should not extend outside the limits of some fixed size, we cannot refer to any other magnitude. We must either hold that bodily magnitude is indefinite, as some of the ancient natural philosophers thought, or we must look for the cause of its definite size solely in the mind and will of the maker: the infinite God produced a finite universe according to the word of his wisdom. So also the eternal God could produce a new world according to the same reason and word of wisdom.

68, 95, 206   Exposition, *de Causis, lect.* 11

138. God's first effect is existence. All other effects presuppose and are based on that. He is pure existence. The existence of all other things partakes of his.

63   *Compendium Theologiae*, 68

139. Although the first cause, who is God, forms no part of the essence of created things, the existence coursing through them cannot be understood except as drawn off from divine existence. No proper effect is given its sufficient reason without invoking its proper cause.

67, 134   Disputations, III *de Potentia*, 5, *ad* 1

140. St. Peter refers to those who say, *where is his promise or his coming? for since the time that the fathers slept, all things continue as they were from the beginning.*[1] They are led into this mistake of supposing that the world has always been going on because they fail to

[1] 2 Pet. iii. 4.

consider the origin of things. Maimonides compares them to a baby, a solitary castaway on a desert island, who when he is grown up, never having seen a pregnancy or birth, is told how human beings are conceived, carried, and brought forth, and yet remains sceptical, for how can a man be in a woman's womb?[1] Similarly do they look at the present world without believing that it ever began.

148   Exposition, *Apostle's Creed*

141. Creation is ascribed to God because of his existence, which is identical with his essence and common to all three Persons, and is, therefore, an activity of the whole Trinity, not peculiar to one Person. Nevertheless, origins within the Godhead have a causal bearing on creation. God is an artist, and the universe is his work of art. An artist sets to work through an examplar in his mind and love in his will. God the Father makes creatures through his Word, who is his Son, and through his Love, who is the Holy Ghost. In this sense then, as implying the essential attributes of intelligence and will, the processions of the divine Persons account for the production of creatures.

92, 123, 500   *Summa Theologica*, 1a. xlv. 6

142. There is a twofold going forth of God, the first whereby one Person proceeds from another—and so the divine Persons are distinct; the second whereby creatures proceed—and here the multiplying and diversifying of things is the common work of the whole Trinity.

94, 125   Exposition, *de Divinis Nominibus*, ii, *lect.* 2

143. By the first essential existent and good each and every other thing exists and is good, partaking of God,

[1] *The Guide for the Perplexed*, ii. 17 (ed. Friedländer, p. 179).

and made like him, though distantly and deficiently. Everything is called good by the divine goodness, as by its first principle, which is the exemplar, efficient, and final cause of all goodness. Nevertheless, the likeness of divine goodness is intrinsic to each, and this formally is its own denoting goodness. Hence—one goodness throughout the world, yet also many goodnesses.

63, 183   *Summa Theologica*, 1a. vi. 4

144. He who acts from a debt of justice acts for the sake, not of himself alone, but also of an objective right other than himself. Because he is the first and original cause, God is not bound by any obligation when he creates. *Who hath first given to him, and recompense shall be made him? for of him, and by him, and in him, are all things.*[1] Job confesses the same truth: *who hath prevented me, that I should repay him? whatsoever is under the whole earth is mine.*[2]

268, 430   11 *Contra Gentes*, 28

145. God loves himself without deliberation, and the issuing love is the Holy Ghost. Creatures, however, do not issue forth from any necessity in the divine nature compelling the divine will. Creatures, whom he wills to be produced freely and without need, are not his ultimate end, nor does his goodness depend on them, since he gains nothing from them. A comparison may be drawn with human activity; of its nature our will is necessarily set on happiness, but not on any particular means thereto.

118, 489   Disputations, x *de Potentia*, 2, *ad* 6

146. Were natural things pure forms, without matter in their very nature, they would exist more truly as

[1] Rom. xi. 35–36.   [2] Job, xli. 11.

divine ideas than as physical objects. That is why Plato held that true man was a substance apart from the world, of which embodied men were shadows. Yet because matter enters into the very constitution of physical things, while admitting that their existence, absolutely speaking, is more perfect in the divine mind than in themselves—for in God it is uncreated and in them it is created—we should say that this sort of existence, for instance, actually to be a man or a horse, is more truly in the physical world than in the divine mind, since to be material is part of their true existence, and matter is not present in God's mind. The idea of a house is nobler in the architect's mind than in bricks and mortar, yet the latter is more truly called a house, for that is the actual, not merely the potential, building.

116 *Summa Theologica,* 1a. xviii. 4, *ad* 4

147. It is to be held with complete conviction that God brings creatures into existence of his own free will, and not as bound by natural necessity. Four arguments can be adduced.

First, we must say that a purpose runs through the universe, otherwise everything would happen by chance. All things are intentionally produced. But this all-pervading purpose works differently through natural and through voluntary processes. Knowing neither ends nor the meaning of purpose nor the relationship of means to ends, a physical reality cannot appoint its own end, nor set itself into motion towards this end, nor plan and guide its own achievement: these are the functions of a voluntary agent, able to appreciate its end and to make arrangements accordingly. Physical processes aim at ends because they are set in motion and directed by intelligence and will, like an arrow by a bowman. The work of Nature, remarks Aristotle, is the work of intelligence.[1] What is borrowed and from another always depends on what is possessed and from oneself. Therefore, the original ordainer of things to their ends must act from will; God created the world voluntarily, uncompelled by any necessity of his nature. The coming forth of the Son, begotten by nature and born before creation, is no argument against this conclusion, for the Son does not issue as part of a purpose, but as the end of all things.

Secondly, there is a narrow determinism about purely natural processes. Since like makes like, Nature always tends to repeat itself. Monotony results from oneness, variety from a multitude in shifting relationships. Nature would ever be bent on standard types but for flaws in its powers and material. No such faults are found in God's workmanship; he is almighty, and he has no need for material to work on. One being alone proceeds from him, he, who is his equal, is the Son; all other less beings issue from his will, not his nature. Many are their degrees of variety; obviously divine power is infinite, and not committed to producing one stock effect over and over again. This goes to show that God creates from choice, and not compulsion.

Thirdly, like makes like, and therefore every effect somehow pre-exists in its cause. Whatever is in another exists in the manner of the other. God is intelligence; that is why creatures pre-exist intelligibly in God: *all things were made by him, and without him was made nothing that was made; in him was life.*[2] Things are brought forth from mind only by an act of will, which is the executor of mind, and acts for the thing understood. We conclude that created things come forth from God by an act of his will.

Fourthly, Aristotle notes two kinds of operation.[3]

[1] *Physics*, ii. 4, 196ª28.   [2] John i. 3-4.
[3] *Metaphysics*, ix. 8, 1050ª30.

One is activity remaining inside its principle as perfection and act; for example, understanding, willing, and so forth. The other is action passing from the principle into an external subject, and therefore inducing perfection and actuality; for example, heating, setting in motion, and so forth. God's activity is his substance, and does not leave his substance, and consequently does not belong to this second class. It is an immanent activity, like understanding, willing, seeing—which last, however, does not here apply, for sense-activity, although not directly productive of an external effect, is stimulated from outside. God's activity, then, in producing things comes from intelligence and will, and all creatures proceed from his choice, and not because he is bound by his nature to produce them. The conclusion is not affected by what is held about the generation of the Son, for there nothing is produced outside the divine nature.

44, 116, 187, 500   Disputations, III *de Potentia*, 15

148. We take it as a fact that the world was not from eternity. Holy Writ, which cannot cheat us, testifies that its duration once began. We may still raise the doubt whether it is theoretically possible for it to have always existed.

190   *de Aeternitate Mundi*

149. That the world has not always existed is to be held by faith alone, and cannot be demonstratively proved.

140   *Summa Theologica*, 1a. xlvi. 2

150. God alone is completely immutable; for that reason true and proper eternity is his alone. Other things share in his eternity to the degree that his stillness possesses them. Some things take such stability from

God that never will they cease to be: *the earth abideth for ever.*[1] The Scriptures call them eternal because of their permanence, although they can be destroyed: *the everlasting hills,*[2] *the precious things of the lasting hills.*[3] Others more amply share in true eternity because their being is immortal, or because their activity is not intermittent, as with the angels and the blessed who enjoy the Word. In that vision, says Augustine, there is no chatter of thought.[4]

60, 661   *Summa Theologica,* 1a. x. 3

151. Origen taught that human souls and angels are of the same species. He wished to avoid the ancient heresy of explaining diversity by the dualism of good and evil. Freewill, he thought, was the cause. God made rational creatures at the beginning all equal and the same; then afterwards some progressed in the stages of life by adhering to God, while others fell away, and regressed in various degrees—some were taken into the heavens, others lapsed to the malignity of demons.

His interpretation loses sight of the whole by concentrating exclusively on the parts. A wise craftsman is not obsessed with the particular advantages of this part or that; he takes them all as subordinate to the whole. A builder does not make all the parts of a house out of the same precious material. The members of a bodily organism are not all endowed with the eye's lustre; that would make for a poor sort of animal. So also God in his wisdom has not made all equal, otherwise the universe would be imperfect and lacking the gradations of reality. It is pretty well the same question when you inquire why God makes one being better than another

[1] Eccles. i. 4.   [2] Ps. lxxv. 4.
[3] Deut. xxxiii. 15.
[4] *de Trinitate,* xv. 16; *PL* xlii. 1079.

and why a craftsman should adopt differences in what
he contrives.

324, 417, 568   Disputations, *de Anima*, 7

152. Distinction and variety in the world is intended
by the first cause. God brings things into existence in
order that his goodness may be communicated and
manifested. One solitary creature would not suffice.
Therefore he makes creatures many and diverse, that
what is wanting in one may be supplied by another.
Goodness in God is single and consistent, in creatures
scattered and uneven; he is better represented by the
whole universe than by any one thing. Things are made
distinct by the concept of wisdom, which is the Word
of God: *and God said, Let there be light; and there was
light. And God saw the light that it was good: and God
divided the light from the darkness.*[1]

63, 269, 410, 523   *Summa Theologica*, 1a. xlvii. 1

153. *Why is it that one dawn, one day, one year excels
another, when all come from the same sun? By God's knowledge are they divided.*[2] Divine wisdom is the cause why
things are distinct, also why they are unequal. It would be
an unfinished world were it all on one level of goodness.

319   *Summa Theologica*, 1a. xlvii. 2

154. Contrast and oddness come not from chance, not
from flaws in the material, not from interference with
the divine plan, not from our deserts, but from God's
own purpose, who wills to impart his perfections to
creatures, as much as each can stand.

336   II *Contra Gentes*, 45

155. Every existent, whatsoever and howsoever, is
from God, who is the perfect good. Since evil cannot be

[1] Gen. i. 3–4.   [2] Ecclus. xxxiii. 7–8.

the direct effect of good, no being as such can be evil: *every creature of God is good.*[1]

III *Contra Gentes*, 7

156. That there is one first principle for evil things, at the opposite pole to the supreme good, is a postulate without basis. For things are active only inasmuch as they are actual realities; their impact comes from what they positively are, their activity from their being actual. A thing is termed good when it is actual and complete, evil when it is lacking: body is good when living, evil when dead, for body lives by its soul, which is its act and perfection, and its evil is death, which deprives it of soul. A thing acts or is acted on inasmuch as it is good; it fails to act or to be acted on to the extent that it is bad. We criticize a bad architect for his incompetence, a bad building for its shortcomings. Evil as such, then, is not an active principle itself, nor has it an active principle: it results from a failure of activity.

236 *de Substantiis Separatis*, 15[2]

157. Since all Nature is good, no particular kind of nature can be bent on an evil object unless it be also a particular good. Nothing prevents what is for some nature a particular good appearing evil, that is repugnant, to a higher nature: it is all very well for a dog to growl, but not for a man. Since men share in animal nature they can have tendencies inimical to their rational nature. This is not the case, however, with simple intellectual natures; they are pure intelligences and directly related to universal good. Demons are intellectual without admixture of body, and therefore have no base inclinations.

231, 247 *de Substantiis Separatis*, 18

[1] 1 Tim. iv. 4.   [2] To Brother Reginald of Piperno.

158. A thing essentially evil cannot exist. The foundation of evil is always a good subject. Nor can a supreme evil exist, which can be matched against supreme good.

233   *Compendium Theologiae,* 117

159. Evil as such cannot be desired.

Disputations, 1 *de Malo,* 1

160. What is totally so is essentially so; for instance, the totally good is the essentially good. When a thing shares in goodness, a distinction lies at its centre between the reality receiving and the reality received. No reality is essentially evil; consequently an evil thing is not totally evil, but is partially good, and in proportion to this part is it real. Now can we begin to recognize what evil is: it is not a real substance, for evil things are good by their substance, but a deficiency of some good which a thing should possess, but does not.

63, 262   Exposition, *de Divinis Nominibus,* iv, *lect.* 14

161. *The Lord made heaven and earth, the sea, and all that is therein.*[1] Some heretics hold that the visible things of this world are created by an evil principle, and in support they quote St. Paul's words, *the good of this world hath blinded the eyes of unbelievers.*[2]

The position is quite untenable. For if diverse things share in one reality, we must postulate a cause of their union: diversity as such does not unite. On this account, therefore, whenever you discover one reality running through different things, you must look for the one cause from which it is received. Now existence is common to all things, however diverse they be, and all have one principle from which they possess it, be they spiritual and invisible or material and visible. When the devil is called the god of this world, it is not because he

[1] Ps. cxlv. 6.   [2] 2 Cor. iv. 4.

made it, but because we serve him with our worldliness. St. Paul uses this turn of phrase when he refers to those *whose god is their belly.*[1]

5 15, 595   *Summa Theologica,* 1a. lxv. 1

162. That God permits evil to happen in this world he governs does not derogate from his goodness. In the first place, divine Providence does not change the natures of things out of recognition, but respects them. The perfection of the universe requires that some should be indefectible, while others should suffer changes according to their nature. Were evil swept away entirely, divine Providence could not regenerate and restore the integrity of things, and this would be a greater evil than the particular ills they suffer.

Secondly, gain to one is loss to another: coming to be spells dying away. The lion must eat, so the kid is killed; the patience of the just supposes persecution from the unjust. Take away all evil, and much good would go with it. God's care is to bring good out of the evils which happen, not to abolish them.

Thirdly, goodness is set off by particular evils; bright colours are edged and emphasized by shade.

220   *Compendium Theologiae,* 142

2. ANGELS

163. Augustine says,[2] *two things hast thou made, O Lord, one near to thee*—namely angelic substance, *the other near to nothing*—namely matter.

Disputations, *de Spiritualibus Creaturis,* 1, *sed contra xiv*

164. They are intellectual natures, at the peak of creation.

II *Contra Gentes,* 42

[1] Phil. iii. 19.   [2] *Confessions,* xii. 7; *PL* xxxii. 828.

165. Substance can exist without body. All possible types of being can be discovered in the universe, which otherwise would be deficient. Possible and actual are the same in everlasting duration. Thus substances can exist complete without matter: they rank below the first substance, which is God, and above human souls united to bodies.

153, 178   II *Contra Gentes*, 91

166. Mind is richer than matter. We can think of objects which cannot exist as material things; for example, mathematics treats of terms which cannot physically exist. Let us take this as a hint, when we assess the proper natures of both, that incorporeal substances, whose reality is intellectual, are more profuse than physical substances, and that the angels outnumber physical bodies. *Thousand thousands ministered unto him, and ten thousand times ten thousand stood before him.*[1]

II *Contra Gentes*, 92

167. Angels mean messengers and ministers. Their function it is to execute the plan of divine providence, even in earthly things: *who maketh his angels spirits; his ministers a flaming fire.*[2]

181   III *Contra Gentes*, 79

168. The Canonical Scriptures tell us that the angels were created before men. Reason also suggests that they were not more recent than the physical universe, for it is unfitting that the more perfect should tag along after the less perfect. This is confirmed by scriptural authority: *when all the morning stars sang together, and all the sons of God shouted for joy.*[3]

148   *de Substantiis Separatis*, 16

[1] Dan. vii. 10.   [2] Ps. ciii. 4.   [3] Job xxxviii. 7.

169. Augustine introduces the distinction between the morning knowledge and the evening knowledge of the angels when he explains how the six days of creation represent phases of knowledge, rather than of time.[1] The temporal day starts when the land is lit by the sun; by a comparison he speaks of the spiritual day which begins from the light of mind playing on different parts of creation: here periods are reckoned not by chronology but by significance. The dawn is the opening of the day, the twilight its close; these two correspond to a thing's beginning, which is known in its originating cause, and in its finish, which is known in its actual existence. Thus the primordial knowledge of things, as conceived in the Eternal Word, is described as the morning light of mind, and the closing knowledge of things, as they exist in their own natures, as the evening light of mind.

113. 116, 523   Disputations, VIII *de Veritate*, 16

170. *The night is far spent, the day is at hand.*[2] The entire stretch of our present life may be compared to night, because of the darkness of ignorance lying heavily on it; the state of future happiness to day, for God's brightness shines on the blessed.

Commentary, *Romans*, xiii, *lect.* 3

171. Angels are called intellectual because of their immediate and complete insight into all objects within their natural field. Human souls are called rational because their knowledge is acquired by a process of reasoning. Unlike the angels, they do not apprehend at once the full evidence of an object presented to them; they are convinced by formal argument, not by intuition.

50   *Summa Theologica*, 1a. lviii. 3

[1] *de Genesi ad Litteram*, iv. 22–23; *PL* xxxiv. 316.
[2] Rom. xiii. 12.

172. We approach truth through logic, by adding a predicate to a subject. A pure spirit, however, sees immediately the truth in a subject, and by simple insight knows what we have to arrive at through affirmative or negative judgements.

47, 377 *Disputations,* XVI *de Malo,* 6, *ad* 1, ii

173. *He shall give his angels charge over thee, to keep thee in all thy ways.*[1] God is quicker to show mercy than to punish. He allows devils to tempt us—*we wrestle not against flesh and blood, but against principalities and powers, against the rulers of the darkness of this world, against spiritual wickedness in high places:*[2] all the more then are angels appointed to guard us.

God's universal providence works through secondary causes. All things are cared for, but especially rational beings, for they, born to possess divine goodness, operate from will, a principle higher than instinct or unconscious impulse. The world of pure spirits stretches between the divine nature and the world of human beings; because divine wisdom has ordained that the higher should look after the lower, angels execute the divine plan for human salvation: they are our guardians, who free us when hindered and help to bring us home.

182 *II Sentences,* XI. i. 1

3. MEN

174. God's likeness in men can be compared to that of Hercules in marble—a semblance of form, a disparity of nature.

12 IV *Contra Gentes,* 26

175. The whole body and all its members receive substantial and specific being from the soul, which exists

[1] Ps. xc. 11.   [2] Eph. vi. 12.

throughout, and is the quickening principle of the whole body directly and immediately, and of the various members as taken up into the organism.

Matter is for form, and so is suitably adapted to form. Forms of lower things are of weaker power; they have fewer functions, and scarcely require heterogeneous parts. But the soul, a higher form of richer power, is the principle of many more activities, requiring dissimilar organs for their execution. The higher the soul the greater the bodily diversity. Yet however complex the parts, they all make up the integrity of a single body.

513, 640, 665   Disputations, *de Spiritualibus Creaturis*, 4

176. The human soul is the actuality of an organism, which is its instrument—not, however, for every activity, for some activities of the soul surpass the range of body.

Disputations, *de Anima*, 2, *ad* 2

177. *The word of God is quick, and powerful, and sharper than any two-edged sword, piercing even to the dividing asunder of soul and spirit.*[1] Soul is that in us through which we have communion with animals, spirit that through which we have intercourse with spiritual substances. Nevertheless one and the same substance it is which quickens body and which, by its power called the mind, is able to understand.

354   Commentary, *Hebrews*, iv, *lect.* 2

178. *God made man unquenchable, the image of his own endless life.*[2] The immortality of the human soul is inevitable. Let us ponder on the evidence. What follows directly from something cannot be separated from it: you cannot have a man who is not an animal, nor a number which is neither odd nor even. Now existence results directly from form: for whatever is real exists as

[1] Heb. iv. 12.   [2] Wisd. ii. 25.

the kind of thing it is by its form. It is quite impossible to split existence from real form.

Things perish because they are composed of matter and form. It is by losing their form that they go out of existence. The form itself ceases to be, not directly because of itself, but indirectly because of an attached condition, namely the dissolution of the compound of which it is the specific principle. This is the case when the form in question is of the type that does not exist of itself, but is the factor giving existing meaning to the whole compound.

If, however, there be a form which exists of its own right—we shall call this a subsisting form henceforward—then it is bound to be immortal of its nature. For existence can be parted from an existent only by depriving it of its form. If the existent be a form, then this cannot be done.[1] Now the principle of human understanding is evidently a subsisting form, not merely a form whereby a compound exists, since understanding itself is not an activity wholly taking place in a bodily organ.[2] You never find a bodily organ which can receive all bodily natures, for such receptiveness argues a power that is open and wide in its range, whereas a bodily organ of any kind is committed to one determinate type of physical being. The mind, on the other hand, can welcome any physical nature. Its activity, therefore, is spiritual, and cannot be confined to a bodily organ, or be intrinsically dependent on bodily processes.

The manner of a thing's activity displays what manner of being it is. What subsists is self-acting; what does not subsist acts as part of another; for instance, the

---

[1] The argument considers the play of natural forces. Annihilation, from the cessation of God's sustaining energy, is always possible, though the evidence is against its happening.

[2] *de Anima*, iii. 4, 429^{b}2.

cause of heat is not pure heat, but a hot thing. Since intellectual activity is uplifted above the body so also is its principle not wholly dependent on the body. Mind is not composed of matter and form, for its ideas are not physical, but spiritual, as their universality declares: they are abstract, and not tied down to matter or to the material conditions of time and place.

The mind is, therefore, a subsisting form, and is consequently immortal. Aristotle agrees that the mind is divine and perpetual.[1] Nevertheless it is not a separate substance, but a part of man's nature; it is his soul, and his soul with a special part to play. To that extent is the soul immortal.

Those who deny this must demolish some of our premisses. Some say that the soul is a body, composed of matter and form, and not a subsisting form. Others that mind is the same as sense, having no operation apart from bodily organs, and so neither above the body nor existing by itself. Others go to the other extreme, and affirm that the mind is a substance separate from human individuals.

We may note two signs that they are in error. One appears from the mind's ability to embrace things mortal and make them immortal. The other appears from its inborn craving, its load of desire. No natural appetite is really purposeless. All human beings long for eternity, and reasonably too, for existence is always desirable when it is apprehended as sheer existence, not committed to here and now; then it is desired absolutely and for all time.

225, 228, 662   Disputations, *de Anima*, 14

179. Next, we ask whether the soul can understand when separated from the body. The question is clouded

[1] *de Anima*, i. 5, 410^{b}15; iii. 4, 429^{a}19.

with doubts, for sensing certainly goes with reasoning during our present life. Various solutions have been attempted—the Platonists teach that in this life the senses play an incidental role of providing the stimulus which releases the mind so that it remembers what it already knows; the Avicennists that the senses do more, for they prepare the mind to receive knowledge from elsewhere and allow a kind of world-mind to get into us. I find neither solution acceptable. I affirm that the senses bring before us the proper objects of our knowledge, and do not merely excite us into remembrance or introduce us to what we should know.

All the same, I must confess that I have landed myself more deeply in the difficulty of explaining how a disembodied mind can know anything at all. For it has no sense-images coming through and retained in bodily organs. Take these away, and how can the soul understand? How can we see a perfectly colourless landscape?

To put the question into proportion, consider that the human soul, which moves in the underworld of mind, is a meagre and lowly partaker of intellectual life. The intellectual nature of the supreme mind is so powerful that everything is understood through one intellectual concept, namely the divine essence. Minds ranged below need many concepts in order to understand. This is the rule—the higher the mind, the fewer the concepts; the stronger the intelligence, the more it can understand through fewer means. One extensive concept will provide but indistinct knowledge for an inferior mind.

The human soul, too weak-minded to master the ideas which pure spirits work with and unable to seize on singulars from a few common generalities, would have to content itself with vague and indefinite knowledge. That is why the present perfection of human knowledge postulates the union of soul with body, for knowledge is pointed and particular when the active reason, the factive intellect[1] lifts singular things from matter into mind.

All the same, the press of spiritual substances is certainly warded off by physical processes, and the sense-preoccupations involved: men asleep, or wandering in their minds, receive revelations not granted when they are in possession of their normal faculties. Consequently, when completely disembodied, the mind should more readily react to the influence of spiritual substances prompting it to understand without recourse to sense-images, which now it cannot do. Even so, the result would not compare in fullness and detail with the empirical knowledge we arrive at through the senses. Here I am not allowing for the infusion of supernatural light to enable the soul to know everything and even to see God himself. Another point to be noted is that the disembodied soul keeps its ideas from its earthly existence, and so may remember things already learnt.

523, 663   Disputations, *de Anima*, 15

180. An excellent form brings all and more than lesser forms can provide. Matter is as richly endowed by a higher form as by a lower; in addition it also becomes the proper subject of complementary perfection. Thus our body is both a physiological and a psychological object, is both organic and charged with human interests and values.

175, 665   Disputations, *de Spiritualibus Creaturis*, 3, *ad* 2

4. DIVINE GOVERNMENT

181. *Bless you the Lord, all you his hosts; you ministers of his that do his good pleasure.*[2] Were there no mediate

[1] *intellectus agens.*   [2] Ps. cii. 21.

causes, the universe would be made up only of effects, whereas it is a masterpiece of divine Providence, a plan executed through a chain of command. *Fire and hail, snow and vapour, stormy wind fulfilling his word.*[1]

131   III *Contra Gentes*, 7 7

182. All events that take place in this world, even those apparently fortuitous or casual, are comprehended in the order of divine Providence, on which fate depends. This has been foolishly denied on the assumption that the divine mind is like ours, a mistaken assumption, since our mind is abstract and cannot penetrate singular things, whereas divine understanding—and divine loving—is identical with divine being. As the power of God's being masters every turn of reality, for everything whatsoever derives from him, so also God's understanding and substantial truth embrace all knowing and everything that can be known, and his loving and his beloved all desiring and everything desirable. Inasmuch as anything at all can be known so is it held in his knowledge; inasmuch as anything at all can be loved so is it held by his will; inasmuch as anything at all *is* so does it fall under his active power, which he perfectly comprehends, since he is a fully conscious agent.

Nevertheless, if divine Providence be the direct cause of everything that happens in this world, at least of the good things, does it not then seem that everything must come about of necessity? Take God's knowledge first: that cannot fail, and therefore, if he knows an event, is it not bound to come about? Take his will next: that cannot be ineffective, and how can that which he decides fail to come about?

These difficulties crop up when the activity of God's

[1] Ps. cxlviii. 8.

mind and will is reduced to the condition of our own
mental and volitional processes. Let us take mind first,
and will afterwards.

First, with regard to knowledge, note that temporal
events stand in a different relation to a mind that is
inside the time-series and to a mind that is entirely
outside. *Before* and *after* in magnitude apply also to
motion, and consequently to time.[1] Accordingly, we
may draw a useful analogy from location in space.
Imagine many people marching in column along a road.
Each of them knows the men in front and behind him
by reference to his own position. But an observer high
above, while he sees how one precedes another, takes
in the column as a whole without having to work from
a position inside it. Human thoughts, however, are
qualified by time (whether directly or indirectly makes
no difference to our argument), for it takes time for the
mind to combine or divide parts.[2] We know events as
past, present, or future. Past events we remember, present
events we perceive actually existing somehow through
our senses, future events we know, not in themselves,
for they are not yet in existence, but in their causes—
with certitude if the causal system is governed by
determinism, with shrewd suspicion if we know how
the causes usually act, but not at all if the causes are
indeterminate. What can be is known only from what
is; potentiality is discovered only from actuality.[3]

Now God is wholly outside any system measured by
time. He dwells at the summit of eternity in a duration
entire and complete all at once. The whole stream of
things below him falls under his single and simple
regard. With one glance he sees all the events that take
place in time, and he sees them just as they are in

[1] *Physics*, viii. 11, 219ᵃ17.   [2] *de Anima*, iii. 6, 430ᵇ6.
[3] *Metaphysics*, ix. 9, 1051ᵃ30.

themselves. The causal order is appreciated, but events are not seen as past or future to him. They are eternally in his presence, and he sees them, to whatever period they may belong, as we see a man actually sitting down, not merely going to sit down.

Because we see somebody actually seated, it does not follow that the sitting down was a necessary event, not a free choice. For contingency (and necessity) is defined by reference of effect to cause. Past all doubt the man is actually sitting down, and in that sense the event is settled and beyond recall: what is is. God most certainly and unmistakably always knows everything that takes place in time: but on that account it does not follow that they are thereby necessary, and not contingent.

Secondly, with regard to the divine will, remember that it is not like ours. It transcends the system of particular things, of which it is the cause: God's will suffuses the whole of reality and all its shades of variety. Consequently necessity and indeterminancy enter into things from the divine will itself. The distinction applies to events from the nature of their proximate causes. To effects which he wills to be necessary God provides necessary causes; to effects he wills to be free he provides contingent active causes, that is, causes able to act otherwise. The nature of the proximate causes settles whether an effect should be called necessary or contingent. Yet every effect depends on the divine will as on the first cause which transcends the system.

This cannot be said of the human will, or indeed of any created cause, for all causes, except God, are confined in a system of necessity or contingency, whether they be variable or constant in their activity. The divine will cannot fail, but we cannot therefore ascribe necessity to all its effects.

275, 300, 327, 392, 441   Exposition, *Perihermenias*, i, *lect*.14

183. *Lord, thou hast wrought all our works in us.*[1] That
God works in every active thing has sometimes been
taken to mean that God alone, and no created power,
produces real effects; for instance, that fire does not
burn, but God does. This, however, is impossible.

First, because it would sap the causal structure of the
world, and even argue weakness in God, for it is from
strength that a cause gives to its effects the power of
causing. Secondly, because causal powers would be
groundlessly attributed to things if, in reality, they
did nothing. Indeed, they would be shams were you
to take away their proper activity: they exist for that.
As matter is meant for form, so form, the prime
perfection, is meant for activity, the supervening perfection.

Hence God's universal causality must be defined in
such a way that the proper activity of creatures is safeguarded. Now there are four classes of cause—material,
final, efficient, and formal. The material cause can be
left on one side; it is not the principle of activity, but
the subject receiving the effect of action. The others are
co-ordinated principles of activity. Let me illustrate
their role from the example of the production of a work
of art. First is the end, the purpose the artist has in
mind. Next is the efficient cause, the agent himself who
applies the cutting edge of his craft. Last is the form
embodied in the material, the chest or bed which is
carved. Notice that the efficient cause acts through its
own form.

God works throughout all activity after the manner
of all these three causes, final, efficient, and formal.

First, he is end, aim, purpose. All activity purposes a
good, real or apparent. Nothing is or appears good save
by sharing in some likeness to the supreme good, which

[1] Isa. xxvi. 12.

is God. It follows that he is the final cause of activity all whatsoever.

Second, he is efficient cause. In every designed system a secondary cause always causes in virtue of the first cause, which moves it to act. All things act by God's power, and he, therefore, is the efficient cause of all activity.

Third, let us take the formal cause. God applies active forces to effects, as does any artist. But he does more than that. He also makes the tools with which he works. He gives things their active forms and keeps them in being. Consequently he is the cause, not merely as providing the active form (like an engineer who makes a machine which works on the force of gravity), but also as sustaining the form and power of everything (like the sun which lights colour). Because the form is inside a thing, and because the more profound and pervasive it is the more intimate it is, and because God is the proper cause of existence which is innermost to all things, it follows that God works at the heart of all activity. *Thou hast clothed me with skin and bones, and hast framed me with bones and sinews.*[1]

137, 327, 334, 439 *Summa Theologica,* 1a. cv. 5

184. Observe a double capability in human nature, one with regard to natural power, the other with regard to the order of divine power, the bidding of which all creatures obey. The first is always fulfilled by God, who gives to each according to its due. The second is not always fulfilled, lest it should seem that he could do only what in fact he does do.

5, 380 *Summa Theologica,* 3a. i. 3, *ad* 3

185. Every cause acts by God's virtue. He grants to all things their original being and sustains them so long as

[1] Job x. 11.

they last; he gives them their active powers, and his activity runs through all theirs, so much so that all activity would stop were his activity to cease. *Without me you can do nothing.*[1] *For it is God who worketh in you both to will and to do of his good pleasure.*[2]

71, 300, 620   III *Contra Gentes*, 47

186. Impossible to better the world while keeping to the things which at present exist there. God has designed a most beautiful plan. The good of the whole is summed up in him. To improve any one thing out of recognition would ruin the proportions of the whole—overprolonging a chord spoils the melody of the strings. Nevertheless, God could make other things, or add to the things already made, and this new universe could be better.

137   *Summa Theologica*, 1a. xxv. 6, *ad* 3

187. God operates through secondary causes, but beyond shadow of doubt is quite able to manage without them. He can break the common and customary rhythm of nature by producing natural effects or fresh effects of a different kind. Light may be thrown on this conclusion from three sets of arguments which deny it.

First, the classical persuasion that physical things have no cause for their existence beyond themselves—though some of the ancients, Anaxagoras for example, allowed for mind putting things into some sort of order. It has been held that physical forms, which are the principles of natural activity, can neither be changed nor interrupted in their action by higher influences from outside, and that nothing can break the determinism which links them in a chain. This opinion can be refuted by showing that the first being is the cause of all other beings.

[1] John xv. 5.   [2] Phil. ii. 13.

Secondly, while admitting that God is the cause of all things, some have taught that his knowledge about them is so generalized (for he knows them through knowing himself as the fount of being) that it does not amount to a distinct knowledge of each. A particular effect does not follow from a common and general principle unless that be given a concrete application— I may know in the abstract that fornication is to be shunned, but when desire and opportunity meet warmly I may not hold back unless the consequences come over me. Similarly, they argued, particular effects issue from God only through a system of mediating causes, the higher of which are wide-spreading, and the lower more pointed and particular, and that he is committed to this system, and cannot tamper with it. This opinion, too, is false, for by knowing himself God knows whatever he holds, and since nothing at all exists save by reflecting him, he sees every possible flicker of likeness, and consequently knows all things in detail.

Thirdly, the doctrine that God produces from natural necessity and not from choice, and that what he does is determined by the demands of the present order of existing natures, and this he cannot infringe. This opinion also is false, because a higher cause, not acting from compulsion, rises above the level of causes determined to one effect, and is indeed their first cause and the cause of their causation.

From these three premises, that God is the complete cause of natural realities, that he has distinct knowledge of each and all, and that, uncompelled by natural necessity, he works voluntarily, it follows that he can produce particular effects apart from the ordinary run of nature. They are non-natural, either because what is produced is a fresh effect beyond natural power, for example, the life of glory, or because it is beyond natural power in the subject in which it takes place, for example, the giving of sight to the blind, or because it is beyond natural power in its mode of operation, for example, the prevention of fire from burning the three holy children in the furnace, or the stopping of the flow of Jordan that God's servants might pass over dryshod.[1]

69, 441   Disputations, vi *de Potentia*, 1

188. Nature, as well as God, works effects contrary to particular natures; Aristotle remarks that passing away and growing old and every sort of loss are unnatural.[2] No part of Nature, however, acts against the universal order of nature.

A particular system is defined with reference to a particular set of causes and effects, the universal system with reference to the first cause of the world. Particular physical causes in our environment act in virtue of the highest cosmic principles and cannot reject them; that their effects run counter to another particular system is required for the sake of the whole order of nature. We suppose that celestial causes are more universal than terrestrial causes; similarly we must suppose that God is even more universal: nothing forbids one causal system from being universal with regard to a smaller system, and particular with regard to a wider system. The highest cosmic principles can operate against a particular system without being against nature as such. Likewise God can operate against them without being against Nature; rather he is in accordance with Nature taken in its most universal sense, which includes the relationship of the whole cosmos to him. *For if thou wert cut out of the olive tree which is wild by nature, and wert grafted contrary to nature into a good olive tree, how much more*

[1] Dan. iii. 27; Jos. iv. 18.
[2] *de Coelo et Mundo*, ii. 6, 288^b15.

shall those, which be the natural branches, be grafted into their own olive tree.[1] The Gloss follows Augustine, and comments that God is the creator and sustainer of every nature, and does nothing unnatural.

290, 328   Disputations, VI *de Potentia*, 1, *ad* 1

189. Though God may interpose between one creature and another, and therefore act against some regional system, he cannot contravene the ordering of creatures to himself, in which justice mainly consists.

144   Disputations, VI *de Potentia*, 1, *ad* 3

190. Logicians and mathematicians look at formal structures, and they regard as impossible whatever is self-destructive and contradictory. Even God cannot do what they declare to be impossible. Natural scientists use *possible* and *impossible* in a different sense; for them the meaning of these terms relates to determinate physical subjects; they say, for instance, that such and such an effect cannot happen in such and such a subject. God, however, may do what is impossible to a lower cause.

147   Disputations, VI *de Potentia*, 1, *ad* 11

191. Divine art is not exhausted in the making of creatures, and therefore can be expressed otherwise than in the normal run of things. The effect may be called against nature, but not against art, for an artist can change his style, and make a thing differently from heretofore.

439   Disputations, VI *de Potentia*, 1, *ad* 12

192. Though he produces an effect apart from the action of a natural cause, God nevertheless leaves intact the order of cause to effect: fire still burns, though on

[1] Rom. xii. 24.

one occasion prevented from consuming the three holy children in the fiery furnace.

Disputations, VI de Potentia, 1, ad 20

193. Augustine speaks of a miracle as an event unusual and abrupt, above the faculty of nature, a surprise to the expectation of the wondering onlooker.[1] *Miracle* and *admiration* are related words: two conditions conspire when anything is admired, one, that the cause of the marvel is hidden; two, that it runs counter to what should have happened, as when somebody is surprised by a rising projectile apparently disobeying the pull of gravity.

Prodigies are of two kinds, relative and absolute. Prodigies are relative when their cause is hidden only to this man or that, who may find it in fact strange, though he would not if he knew the natural forces at work. A wonder to one is no wonder to another: an expert takes in his stride what to others may seem extraordinary. Prodigies are absolute when their causes are quite hidden and they run counter to all the natural factors in the situation. Of all causes the most mysterious and aloof from our sense-experience is the divine cause, which most secretly operates in everything. Only those effects which are wrought solely by divine power are called miracles in the narrow technical sense. Other effects which are produced by the occult forces of nature and also the normal effects which are produced by God alone may be called wonders or marvels, but not miracles strictly speaking.

The phrase, *above the faculty of nature*, signifies that the whole system of nature is surpassed; *abrupt*, that a miracle rises above the play of natural forces; *beyond*

[1] *In Joannis Evangelium Tractatus*, viii; *PL* xxxv. 1450; *de Trinitate*, iii. 5; *PL* xlii. 874.

expectation, that our knowledge is exceeded; *unusual,* that the normal course is not followed, and we are surprised, for we are familiar with what customarily happens.

362   Disputations, VI *de Potentia,* 2

194. Above nature, against nature, besides nature— that is a traditional division applied to God's miraculous works.

Above nature—here the effect can never be produced by natural forces, either because the reality wholly surpasses nature, for example, the Incarnation of the Word or the glory of heavenly happiness suffusing the bodies of God's elect, or because the reality, though part of nature, cannot be induced by natural forces in the subject in question; for example, nature can cause life, but cannot raise human persons from the dead.

Against nature—here God's action interrupts the trend of natural forces, as, for example, when he kept the three boys unscathed in the fiery furnace, or stopped the flow of Jordan, or caused a virgin to bring forth a child.

Besides nature—here nature can produce the effect, but not in the same way, either because the normal processes are dispensed with, as, for example, when Christ changed water into wine, but not like a vintner controlling the fermentation of grape-sugar, or because the effect is unusually prodigal, as, for example, the plague of frogs in Egypt, or because the effect happens suddenly and not gradually, as, for example, the cure of Simon's wife's mother.

361   Disputations, VI *de Potentia,* 2, *ad* 3

195. History recounts that a vestal virgin carried water from the Tiber in a perforated pitcher without spilling any,[1] a holding back of natural flow comparable to the stopping of Jordan. Therefore demons can work miracles.

I reply that it would not be at all strange if the true God worked this miracle to commend chastity. The old pagan virtues were from God. If it were not divinely done then no miracle took place: spirits, in point of fact, can locally stir or stay the flow of fluids by their natural power.

398   Disputations, vi *de Potentia*, 5, *obj. 5 and resp.*

196. Miracles lessen the merit of faith to the extent that they argue an unwillingness to believe the Scriptures, a hardness of heart that demands signs and wonders. All the same, it is better for men to turn to the Faith because of miracles than to remain altogether in their unbelief. Miracles are signs, *not to them that believe, but to them that believe not.*[2]

364   *Summa Theologica*, 3a. xliii. 2

197. The Faith of Christ believed by the saints and handed down to us has been marked by the seal of God, shown in works no creature can perform. These are the miracles by which Christ has confirmed holy apostolic doctrine. If you say, but no one has seen miracles performed, then I answer, that once upon a time everybody worshipped false gods and persecuted Christians, and then afterwards were converted, including the wise, noble, powerful, by a few poor and unlettered preachers. Either this was miraculous or not. If so, then the point is granted; if not, then I ask, what greater miracle could there have been than to convert so many without miracles?

363   Exposition, *Apostle's Creed.*

[1] Cf. Augustine, *de Civitate Dei*, x. 16; xxii. 11; *PL* xli. 295, 774.   [2] 1 Cor. xiv. 22.

5. MORALITY

198. Natural processes are presupposed to moral processes.

Disputations, de Correctione Fraterna, 1, ad 5

199. Psychology enters most opportunely into all the sciences. As regards prime philosophy, we cannot attain a knowledge of divine and highest causes except through what we acquire by our mind's power. Averroes recognized how we cannot appreciate the order of spiritual substances if we are ignorant of our mind's nature.[1] As regards ethics, we cannot discuss what we ought to do unless we know what we can do. Note that knowledge about the soul belongs to natural philosophy and physical science.[2]

52, 417   *Commentary, I de Anima, lect, 1, 2*

200. How connatural to human nature is delight. Hence it is the office of moral science, which studies human acts, to consider pleasure.

447, 660   *Commentary, X Ethics, lect. 1*

201. The essence of virtue consists in the doing rather of what is good than of what is difficult.

62, 291, 397   *Summa Theologica, 2a–2ae. cxxiii. 12, ad 2*

202. Since moral activity is concerned with particular occasions, sweeping moral judgements partly miss the point.

219, 426, 473   *Summa Theologica, 2a–2ae, Prologue*

203. Moral science is better occupied when treating of friendship than of justice.

52, 403, 434   *Commentary, VIII Ethics, lect. 1*

[1] Commentary, *Metaphysics*, xi.
[2] Psychology is regarded as more than a study of consciousness; its first subject is soul, the primary animating principle of body.

204. *I am Alpha and Omega, the beginning and the end, the first and the last.*[1] Among all the causes, the end holds the primacy. From it the others take their actual causality, for no activity is without purpose. Since a final purpose is the cause of a proximate purpose, the ultimate end is the first of all causes.

183, 415   III *Contra Centes*, 17

205. *All things are thine: and we have given thee what we received of thy hand.*[2] Whatever you have, knowledge, wisdom, beauty, all should you turn to God and use for his glory.

131, 452   Exposition, *Apostle's Creed*

206. We may state without qualification that purposes nowhere stretch out indefinitely. Remove what is primary from a co-ordinated system, and it will fall to pieces. Aristotle says that you cannot go on interminably with a series of active causes, because there would be no motion at all but for the existence of something first setting the others in motion.[3]

Two orders may be considered in the development of a plan, the order in which things are intended, and the order in which things are done. On both counts something comes first. In the development of intention, that is prime which first attracts: eliminate this, and nothing is wanted. In the development of executive action, that is prime which originates work: eliminate this, and nothing is done. The principle of intention is the last end; the principle of execution is the first means.

[1] Apoc. xxii. 13.   [2] 1 Paral. xxix. 14.
[3] Cf. Physics, viii. 5, 256^{a}28. Note first, that the causes in question are supposed to be in essential subordination, that is, dependent on one another for their causality, not in accidental subordination, that is, otherwise associated. Note second, that *motion* is not restricted to chemical or mechanical movement, but includes the rise of all activity, material and spiritual.

Consequently, bounds are to be set to all processes. Were there no last end, desire would never stir, activity never come to a stop, intention never be fixed. Were there no first means, nobody would ever get down to anything, nor would advice have any point, for everything would be shapeless. Of course, we are speaking of a planned order; purely coincidental arrangements have an indeterminateness about them, for random causes need not be limited and measurable.

140, 483, 533, 664   *Summa Theologica*, 1a–2ae. i. 4

207. There is no leisure about politics, for they are ever seeking an end outside political practice, for instance power or fame. Political life neither provides our final end nor contains the happiness we seek for ourselves or others. Such happiness ultimately is a state of mind; the purpose of temporal tranquillity, which well-ordered policies establish and maintain, is to give opportunities for contemplating truth.

4, 279, 282   Commentary, *X Ethics, lect.* 11

208. *Last end* can signify either the form or idea of goodness, or the concrete thing in which it is found. In the abstract, human beings agree in desiring goodness, for all crave to become complete and perfect. But they disagree on the second point; some choose riches, others pleasure, and so forth. Let us make a comparison: palatableness is pleasant, but some look for it most in wine, others in honey, or something of the sort. Nevertheless the most satisfying object should be that which is preferred by persons of well-cultivated tastes. Sinners turn away from the object in which goodness is truly found, but not from goodness itself, which they mistakenly seek in other things.

Again, *last end* can signify either the thing in which goodness lies or the possessing of it—corresponding

respectively in the care of a miser to his money and his
gloating over it. As regards the first, man agrees with
the rest of creation, for God, who is his own end, is last
end to everything else. But as regards the obtaining of
God, which is what we mean by happiness, man differs
from irrational creatures, for he grasps happiness by
knowing and loving God, whereas their existence, life,
and sensation are happy inasmuch as some likeness to
God is shared.

75, 352   *Summa Theologica*, 1a–2ae. i. 7, c. & *ad* 1; 8

209. We are bound to affirm that the blessed see God's
very being. Happiness is the ultimate achievement of
rational nature. A thing is finally complete when it
attains its original purpose, and without being forced.
I add that qualification, because a thing reaches God by
what it is and by what it does. First, by likeness. This is
common to every creature, and the rule is that the closer
the likeness to God the more the excellence. Second, by
activity—I leave aside the singular personal union of
man and God in Christ—by which I mean the rational
creature's activity of knowing and loving God.

Man's soul comes directly from God, and therefore
finds its happiness by returning direct to God. He must
be seen for what he is in himself; seen, that is, without
medium which acts as a likeness and representation of
the thing known, such as a sense-image in the eye or
reflection in the mirror; but not without a medium,
called the light of glory, which strengthens the mind to
have this vision.

5, 670   x *Quodlibets*, viii. 1

210. Let us ponder on how this may be possible. Since
our mind knows things only through their likenesses, it
seems that the species of one thing will not reveal the
essence of another. The further apart they are the

scantier will be the knowledge. If a bull be described in terms of an ass, the generic part of its nature will be known, namely *animal*, but less will be known if it be described in terms of *mineral*, a more remote generic heading. And nothing at all will be known if the bull be described in terms of something to which it bears no resemblance.

No genus is common to creatures and to God. Therefore the divine nature can be known through no creaturely likeness, either of sense or of spirit. If his essence is to be known, then he himself must be like form in the mind, not fused with mind so as to form one compound with it, but joined to mind as known to knower.

God himself is his own very existence, and likewise himself is his own very truth. Now, when a form is achieved, all predispositions to it are also gathered in. Since of ourselves we cannot grasp the form of ultimate truth (otherwise it would be born all ready for it), it follows that when the human mind is filled with God's truth it is elevated by a fresh additional quality, which we call the light of glory. Then is it charged by God, who alone of his nature possesses his own sheer truth.

10, 41 *Compendium Theologiae*, 105

211. When this end is attained the natural desire is stilled, for God's essence united to the mind is the principle of knowing all things and is the fount of all goodness. Nothing over remains to be desired. In this vision we reach to the most perfect manner of being like God, for we know him as he knows himself, namely by his essence. Nevertheless he alone knows himself as much as he is knowable; we can never comprehend him as he comprehends himself—not that any of his parts are hidden, for he has no parts, but that our power is not commensurate with his.

7, 655   *Compendium Theologiae*, 106

212. Divine truth measures the truth of human justice. All the same, our deeds are judged differently before men and before God. Some sins are secret and hidden from our tribunals, but to God *all things are naked and open before his eyes.*[1] Yet secret warnings precede the final judgement; they come to the sinner, wakeful or drowsy, from God through the inward remorse of conscience. *For God speaketh once, yea twice. In a dream, in a vision of the night, when deep sleep falleth upon men, in slumbering upon the bed; then he openeth the ears of men, and sealeth their instruction, that he may withdraw man from his purpose, and hide pride from man.*[2]

282, 658   Disputations, *de Correctione Fraterna*, 2, ad 3

213. When properly roused a man rightly judges that he is awake and another is asleep. But when he is asleep he cannot rightly appreciate the fact himself or the thoughts of another man who is awake. Things are as they appear to a man awake, not asleep; so also with a healthy man and a sick man when it comes to appreciating how much things weigh. Aristotle remarks that the virtuous man provides the rule and measure of what human conduct should be.[3] Hence St. Paul also says that *he that is spiritual judgeth all things;*[4] the man whose mind and affections are directed by the Spirit rightly decides matters pertaining to salvation.

414   Commentary, *1 Corinthians*, ii, lect. 3

214. The spark of reason cannot be extinguished so long as the light of mind remains; and sin can never make away with the mind.

266   *II Sentences*, xxxix. iii. 1

[1] Heb. iv. 13.   [2] Job xxxiii. 14–17.
[3] *Ethics* x. 5, 1176ᵃ15.   [4] 1 Cor. ii. 15.

215. Spiritual and inward ties are stronger than bodily and outward ones. Our duty to a human superior is material and external, for legal authority works by managing temporalities. All that will be changed at the last trump, *when Christ shall have put down all rule and all authority and power.*[1] Therefore conscience is more to be obeyed than authority imposed from outside. For conscience obliges in virtue of divine command, whether written down in a code or instilled by Natural Law. To weigh conscience in the scales against obedience to legal authority is to compare the weight of divine and of human decrees. The first obliges more than the second, and sometimes against the second.

Nevertheless, there is a difference between a sincere conscience when right and when wrong. A right conscience which runs counter to the command of a superior imposes a duty on us. For the obligation cannot be removed. Without sin you cannot divest yourself of a right conscience. Nor need there be any reservation, for by following a right conscience you not only do not incur sin but are also immune from sin, whatever superiors may say to the contrary.

When, however, an erroneous conscience conflicts with an external precept, we are bound by it only in matters morally neutral, and even so merely in a relative and imperfect sense. For it is not absolutely binding and lasting, or to be applied in every case. While it lasts it has some force, but we can, and should, correct it. We may incur no sin in following it, but only on the supposition that a superior has not commanded the contrary—we suppose, of course, that his command is not wicked. But, given an order, we are in a dilemma: if we act against our conscience we sin; if we disobey our superior we also sin. Of the two the first is the worse,

[1] 1 Cor. xv. 24.

since the dictate of conscience is more binding than the decree of outside authority.

282, 431, 652   Disputations, xvii *de Veritate*, 5

216. Virtue displays the perfection of ability.

347, 414   Disputations, *de Virtutibus in communi*, 1

217. Augustine defines virtue as a good quality of mind, whereby life is lived aright, which no one uses ill, and which God works in us apart from sin.[1]

This definition is complete, even leaving out the last clause, and applied to every human virtue. Virtue brings an active faculty to its full activity. The activity is good, the agent is good, and both are referred to by the definition.

Perfect activity, first of all, must go straight to its end—*whereby life is lived aright*; and, secondly, should be second-nature and rise from a habit fixed on good—*which no one uses ill*. It is not poised between good and evil: that is why *opinion,* which is neutral between truth and error, is not reckoned among the intellectual virtues, while *science* is, since it is bent on demonstrable truth.[2]

Three notes indicate the goodness of the subject; first, *mind,* for virtue is a properly human trait; secondly, *good,* defined by reference to the end of life; thirdly, *quality,* or mode of possession, for virtue is not an emotion, but a settled habit. All these notes are proper to evert virtue—moral, intellectual, theological, acquired, infused. The last clause, *which God works in us without us,* is reserved to infused virtue.[3]

235, 283   Disputations, *de Virtutibus in communi*, 2

[1] The definition was composed by Peter Lombard from phrases of St. Augustine. Cf. *Sentences,* ii. xxvii. 5.

[2] *Ethics,* vi. 1, 1139[b]11.

[3] By contrast with the acquired virtue described by Aristotle.

218. A principal circumstance of a virtuous act is this, that it should favour the underlying purpose of the virtue itself. What charity wants from fraternal correction is the sinner's reform; the act will scarcely be virtuous if rebuke is likely to make him worse.

408   Disputations, *de Correctione Fraterna*, 1

219. What is better absolutely may not be better in a particular case. Better to philosophize than to give money away—but not when you are faced with a person in need.

421   Disputations, XII *de Malo*, 1

IV

The Fall[1]

220. Nobody is excluded from the Kingdom of Heaven except through human fault.

IV *Contra Gentes*, 50

221. Ours is the power to disapprove of sins against God, not to forgive them.

Disputations, *de Correctione Fraterna*, 1, *ad* 14

222. To hold that sins are unforgivable is certainly wrong, even with the qualification that this indeed is not because divine power is unable to forgive, but because divine justice has so decreed that a lapse from grace is beyond repair.

Divine justice does not treat men who still have their course to run as though they had finished. Only when their life is over can human beings remain fast in evil: unalterableness and immobility mark the end of a process. All our present life is in a condition of flux.

---

[1] The problem of evil is shaped and a workmanlike theory proposed to meet it. First of all, concerning the doctrine of *original sin*, the two main lines of Latin thought which start from St. Augustine and St. Anselm are brought together by St. Thomas; concupiscence is the material element, the deprivation of *original justice* the formal element. Before his time many concepts were imprecise; *original justice* was not clearly distinguished from sanctifying grace, or even from the state of *pure nature*, nor *original sin* from personal sin; the heat of lust was often regarded as the transmitting cause of fault. Secondly, while he will not treat good and evil as two contending realities, his analysis of moral evil brings out its positive and negative parts, the action and the defect. The object of a bad human act is a misplaced good: this basis provides sins with their specific interest.

We are always travelling and never in the state of having arrived—our thorough restlessness bears this out, and every vicissitude of mind and body. That we should stick in our sins is certainly not to be expected from the way divine Providence works in the world.

Furthermore, divine benefits, least of all the best, should not threaten danger. How risky it would be for men to entertain grace if it could never return once they were to forsake it for sin. This argument is sharpened when we consider that sins which precede conversion, and which are forgiven by grace, are sometimes far worse than those which follow afterwards.

628   *Compendium Theologiae*, 145

223. Why should not human nature be raised to a higher state after sin than might otherwise have been the case? God permits evil in order to bring forth a greater good. St. Paul says, *where sin abounded, grace did more abound*,[1] and the Church sings at the blessing of the paschal candle, O *happy fault! that merited such and so great a Redeemer.*

556   *Summa Theologica*, 3a. i. 3, *ad* 3

I. RACIAL SIN

224. There are signs from which we can make out a good case for the existence of a racial sin. These are the evils which seem to bear the character of penalty resulting from some fault. Human nature is afflicted with physical ills, of which the greatest is death, and with spiritual ills, of which the chief is a mind so weak that it is carried away by emotions it cannot control, shies away from truth, and tumbles into sin.

You might say that such defects are not necessarily

[1] Rom. v. 20.

penal, but inherent consequences of human nature, which is compounded of contrary elements and divided between spirit and sense. Nevertheless, if we face the question steadily, take into account that divine Providence fits out things properly, and assume that spirit was joined to body in order that spirit might contain and master matter, we can then be reasonably persuaded that any threat to the mind's control arising from the destructive tendencies within physical nature was forestalled by a special and supernatural benefit, the *original justice* with which human nature was endowed at its first creation.

267   IV *Contra Gentes*, 52

225. The Pelagian denial that sin is transmitted at birth dispenses with much of Christ's redemptive work, which in fact was meant to cure the infection of Original Sin. *As by the offence of one judgment came upon all men to condemnation, even so by the righteousness of one the free gift came upon all men with justification of life.*[1] Pelagianism also dispenses with the need for infant baptism, which the Church's common custom holds to be Apostolic discipline. We, however, affirm without hedging that sin is inherited by all the descendants of the first parents of the human race.

The discussion will be clearer if we begin by casting any one human being in two roles. First, he is a private person; second, part of an organized social body. In both roles he performs certain acts. For those he does by his own choice and on his own he is responsible as a singular person. There are others, however, which are not his own, and yet are attributed to him; such are the corporate acts of his community, or acts done by the majority or by the governor: the State, or any systematic

[1] Rom. v. 18.

group, remarks Aristotle, is identified with the deeds of its ruler.[1]

Now this political community is reputed to be like one man, in that it contains different classes organized like the members of one single body.[2] Similarly, the entire human race is of common stock, and can be treated as one community, and indeed as a single human organism. Each member of this body, including Adam, can then be regarded either as a singular person or as a member of the whole.

Next we go on to consider how our first parents were established with a supernatural gift, namely, the grace of *original justice*, which rendered their reasons obedient to God, their sense-powers to their reason, and their bodies to their soul. The deed of gift was not granted to private persons, but to the ancestors of the human race for transmission to their posterity. The loss of the gift followed the same tenor; it went from them and from their descendants.

This deprivation is passed on just as human nature is passed on, that is to say, through partial, not total causality, for what is procreated is the body, into which God infuses the soul. As the divinely infused soul enters into a human nature through the body to which it is wedded so the soul contracts original sin, that is through the body which is propagated from Adam, not merely materially as being fleshly stuff, but also by an active impulse, as of seed which sprouts.

This congenital defect precisely as restricted to private persons carries no stigma of fault or blame, which is essentially of one's own voluntary incurring. But when men are taken as members born of one common descent-group, when they appear as one man,

---

[1] Cf. *Ethics*, ix. 8, 1168^b31; *Politics*, iii. 4, 1285^b5.

[2] Cf. 1 Cor. xii.

then sinfulness is incurred, because a voluntary factor
is at work, namely the actual sin of our first parents.

An analogy may help. When the hand is provoked to
commit murder, no sinfulness lies in the isolated member as such; it cannot help itself, for it is forced by
another power. Now take the hand as integrated in the
human organism, which is directed by will. Then hand,
by sharing in will, is imbued with sin. Murder is called
the fault of the whole man, not of the hand. So original
sin is a racial sin, not a personal sin. Nor is it incurred
by persons save in so far as they are stained by nature.
For as a man uses diverse powers to commit a crime,
will, reason, hands, and so forth, all of which are co-
ordinated into a unity by one governing principle from
which sinfulness spreads out, so because of their common origin all parts of the human race are charged with
one original sin.

 267, 295, 502, 526, 557   Disputations, IV *de Malo*, I

226. An actual sin committed through a bodily member
is the sin of that member, not as isolated from, but as
belonging to, the single human organism. Otherwise it
would not be termed a human sin. Similarly, original
sin is not the sin of this or that particular person, except
in so far as they have received human nature from our
first parents. This is the reason for terming it the sin of
nature: *we were by nature the children of wrath.*[1]

       Summa Theologica, 1a–2ae. lxxxi. 1

227. Unless he be his partner in crime, a son is not
blamed for his father's wrongdoing.

     Summa Theologica, 1a–2ae. lxxxi. 1, *ad* 1

228. Original sin fastens on the whole human race. It
is first of all found in the soul, which, although direct

   [1] Eph. ii. 3.

from God, is part of human nature. When human nature is transmitted, so also is original sin.

As physical propagation offers sufficient material cause for human nature to come into being, so the flesh is sufficient cause for the presence of original sin, though not of actual sin.

178, 246   Disputations, IV *de Malo*, 1, *ad* 2, 3

229. Resigned as we may be about the ills flesh is heir to, this urgent question still haunts us—How can the lack of original justice in the descendants of the ancestors of the human race in fact have the force of sin? For sin is culpable evil, which can be imputed only to the person responsible for it. Nobody should be blamed for what lies outside his power either to do or not to do. We did not chose to be born, either with or without original sin. Therefore, whatever else it may be, the misfortune should not be called sin.

The solution is eased by drawing out the distinction between *nature* and *person*. As in one human person there are many members, so in one human nature there are many persons: individuals, observes Porphyry, by participation in the common species are reckoned as if they were one man.[1] Take personal sin: different human acts are performed through different members, and their blameworthiness does not require that the particular members concerned should each act voluntarily of themselves, but that the whole man can be held responsible through his higher governing power. When reason and will command, the hand cannot help but strike, or the legs to walk to sin. Now to apply the analogy: the lack of original justice is a sin of nature, which derives from the inordinate will of the ancestors of the race. As affecting human nature the

[1] *Isagoge,* i.

condition is voluntary by referring back to the will of
our originators, from whom it passes by natural inheritance to all who are members of the human body.
Hence the term *original sin*, for it is congenital. Other
sins, namely actual sins, immediately affect the person
of the sinner, but original sin immediately affects our
nature, which, infected by our first parents, consequently affects the persons of its children.

Compendium Theologiae, 196

230. Augustine reads the symptom for the cause when
he maintains that lust transmits sin.

Disputations, iv *de Malo*, 6, *ad* 16

231. This man and that man share in original sin because both belong to the tribe of Adam. They are like
members of one body. The sin of one sinner is one sin.
Though executed by diverse members, it is committed
by one single organism, and comes from one will.
Original sin in this man and that man is what they both
inherit from one ancestral sin.

The human quality of the motions of hands and eyes
is communicated by the will, and it is thus that physiological and psychological processes are invested with
morality. Gestures reveal what the will is like; if it be
disordered, then it produces a corresponding outside
effect and impression. We commit a sinful act by turning to a temporal attraction without being duly directed
to our last end. In effect we turn away from eternal
blessing. There is a turning to, and a turning away; the
first, the self-indulgence and the wasteful love, represents the material element in sin; the second, the aver-
sion and the hate, represents the formal element, formal
because morality is defined with reference to our last
end. Hands share in sin when thrust to a deed which
breaks the fair order of virtue, and we can speak of the

formal element of sin being in them, because they are parts of a voluntary being. Hands and eyes are not outside instruments, like spears and swords, for if the will's influence extends to weapons, we do not think of them as receiving sin nor do we put any blame on them, though because they are wielded to accomplish a sinful design we may think of wickedness passing through them, and say that sin is with them virtually and in effect.

The sin of our first parents contained these two elements, the formal element of turning away from God, and the material element of turning to vanity. By the first they lost the gift of original justice, and by the second their sense-powers were abased instead of being lifted up. Both elements are inherited by their progeny. The sequel is that the higher parts of the soul are out of due order to God, while the lower parts rebel against reason and will and follow their own bents, and the body itself declines into dissolution.

The first human sin reaches the higher parts of the soul, and also the lower parts which should come under the control of the higher; a quality of guilt attaches to them all, for all can be culpable. But in those lower parts which lie outside the life of the reason, namely, those occupied with purely biological functions, and in the body itself considered purely biologically, the sequel comes as a penalty, not a fault—except perhaps virtually, in that physical weakness may conduce to wrong.

In any process the formal element derives from the active and initiating principle, the material element from the passive and receptive principle; the first sets in motion, the second is set in motion. In the case of original sin, the human will, which is the moving principle in human acts, is deprived of original justice, while the lower powers are prone to waste themselves— we may term this their concupiscence. Consequently, the formal element in original sin is the lack of original justice, the material element is concupiscence. We may draw an analogy with actual and personal sin: there the turning away from God is formal, and the turning to creatures is material. Likewise original sin; it estranges us from God, and commits us to this world.

255, 304, 449   Disputations, IV *de Malo*, 2

232. *Natural to man* has a double ring, natural to animal—and so we can desire anything attractive to our senses; and natural to human—and so we desire pleasure according to the measure set by reason: thus the concupiscence which is ready to scrap reasonableness for what takes our fancy is against human nature, and is the effect of original sin.

157, 448   Disputations, IV *de Malo*, 2, *ad* 1, *i*

2. PERSONAL SIN

233. Sin, the direct opposite of an act of virtue, is a disordered activity; vice, the direct opposite of virtue, is the condition of a thing out of its proper natural bearings.[1]

217   *Summa Theologica*, 1a–2ae. lxxi. 1

234. A man should not be labelled a thief or an adulterer from one act or motion of passion, but from a habit. The same applies when we set him down as just or unjust.

Disputations, VIII *de Malo*, 1, *ad* 15

235. Human virtue, which renders a man good in himself and in his deeds, is in accordance with human,

---

[1] *Peccatum*, sin, is sometimes used of any defective action, but usually means defective human activity and *culpa*, or fault, with consequent *poena*, penalty.

that is, rational nature. Vice is contrary to human nature, because against the order of reason.

316 *Summa Theologica*, 1a–2ae. lxxi. 2

236. Sinfulness abandons the art of divine wisdom and the plan of divine goodness.

Summa Theologica, 3a. i. 1, *ad* 3

237. Wanting one's own good is not vicious, unless it be to the despite of divine law.

Disputations, VIII *de Malo*, 1, *ad* 1

238. The specific interest of moral evil does not consist in the privation, that is, the absence of good which should be present, but precisely in what is abused, the abuse being incompatible with moral goodness.

161, 347 *Disputations, de Virtutibus in communi*, 2, *ad* 5

239. A good man's purposes are unified, a sinner's scattered. Virtues make us bent on pursuing the reasonable life; prudence links them together in a common plan of rightful activity. All purposes then converge. Not so with sinful intentions. For the sinner does not set himself to depart from the rules of reasonable living. He sets out to indulge himself with something that attracts him, and it is this which gives a positive tone to what he does. Variegated are the attractions for whose sake he is ready to turn away from right reason; there is no essential combination between them, one with another, indeed sometimes they are conflicting. Since they stamp specific character on sins it follows that sins are not all in alliance together. The life of sin is a fall from coherence to chaos; the life of virtue a climb from the many to the One.

254, 417, 480 *Summa Theologica*, 1a–2ae. lxxii. 1

240. Sin is a human act gone bad: a *human act* because voluntary, either elicited by the will, for instance, wishing and choosing, or commanded by the will, for instance, speaking or doing some outward deed; *bad* because lacking due measure. Measurement is by conformity to a rule; what does not fit is out of the true and therefore wrong. The rule for human acts is twofold, one proximate and of a piece with man, namely his conscience, the other ultimate, primary, and transcendent, namely the eternal law.

206, 455   *Summa Theologica*, 1a–2ae. lxxxi. 6

241. Sin is not pure hollowness, but an act showing a gap which ordered goodness should fill.

160, 231   *Summa Theologica*, 1a–2ae. lxxii. 1, *ad* 1

242. Two strains run together in the nature of sin, the voluntariness of the act, and the disorder which follows; in other words, the intention so to act in such a situation, and the turning away from God's law. Of these the first is the doer's direct and essential purpose, the second is indirect and incidental; nobody, observes Dionysius, intentionally acts for evil.[1] A kind of reality is defined by what is essential, not by what is accidental, which lies off the point of specific interest. Sins, therefore, are distinguished and denominated by objects directly engaged by voluntary activity rather than by the disorder incurred.

156   *Summa Theologica*, 1a–2ae. lxxii. 1

243. The faultiness of an act is not the motive for willing it. The attraction lies elsewhere, and through seeking this does the will incur the—unwanted—sinful disorder. In consequence of what it does will the act is sinful; and penalty is involved because the disorder is suffered in a sense unwillingly.

Disputations, 1 *de Malo*, 4, *ad* 2

[1] *de Divinis Nominibus*, iv. 31; *PG* iii. 731.

244. The division of sin into mortal and venial sins is not like the division of a genus into two species; they are not specifically different kinds of sin, determined by the objects to which they turn. The difference between mortal and venial sin is decided by the stage reached by the disordered turning away from God: it is here that sinfulness is brought to a head.

Two degrees of disorder may be marked. One turns the whole order upside down; the other leaves the principles intact, but muddles the details and subordinate pattern. The balance of health may be so utterly wrecked that life is destroyed; or it may be upset so as to cause sickness, but not death. The final purpose of life is the key to the moral order; our last end in practice may be compared to the first principles of reason in theory. When our acts are so deranged that we turn away from our last end, namely God, to whom we should be united by charity, then the sin is mortal. Short of that, the sin is venial.

Bodily death is incurable by nature, but for sickness remedies may be found. Similarly, in questions of science, a radical mistake about principles is past persuasion, while a mistake about conclusions may be put right by consulting again the principles which are still accepted. A similar difference works out in the life of the spirit: turn away from your last end, then of itself your sin is mortal and beyond repair, with everlasting penal effects. But venial sin can be repaired, and is undeserving of interminable punishment.

629   *Summa Theologica*, 1a–2ae. lxxii. 5

245. Everything good is from God. Things not good are neither to be sought nor used. All deeds which are not from sin can be done for God—not that every activity has always to be explicitly referred to him, for to be set on him by our settled disposition suffices.

In themselves creatures are no obstacles to eternal happiness. We make them so, by abusing them and by committing ourselves to them as if they were our ultimate goal.

Theologians hold that in fact no deliberate act is morally neutral: if directed to God by grace then it is meritorious; if it cannot be so directed it is sin; if it is not directed then it is vanity, which amounts to sin.

Although a man who commits a venial sin does not actually refer his act to God, nevertheless he still keeps God as his habitual end. He does not decisively set himself on turning away from God, but from over-fondness for a created good he falls short of God. He is like a man who loiters, but without leaving the way.

130, 346   *I Sentences*, 1. iii, *c. & ad* 2, 3, 4

246. *If any man build upon this foundation, gold, silver, precious stones, wood, hay, stubble, every.man's work shall be made manifest.*[1] We can take earthly things in three ways. First, we can make them our last end, and this is grave sin, for thus the foundations of our true life are not built on, but ruined. Secondly, by taking them for the glory of God, and this is to build on gold, silver, and precious stones. Thirdly, by pinning ourselves to them more than we should, yet without making them our last end, or taking them against God; this is venial sin, which is compared to wood, hay, or stubble, according to the strength of its desire.

Commentary, *1 Corinthians*, iii, *lect.* 2

247. Everything that happens has a cause. *Although affliction cometh not forth of the dust, neither trouble*

[1] 1 Cor. iii. 12–13.

springs out of the ground; yet man is born unto trouble, as the sparks fly upward.[1] Sin, which is word, deed, or desire against God's law, therefore has a cause.

This needs explanation. Sin is a disordered act. As regards the act a direct cause can be discovered. As regards the disorder we must look for the sort of cause that produces negations and privations. Here we must decide whether the defect is caused by the inaction of a cause or by the impact of a cause. In the first case the absence of causal energy is implied; here there is a negation of cause, and the result is a mere negation of effect: no cause, no effect; the sun sinks, and daylight fades. In the second case the presence of causal energy has an excluding effect, and it is the very energy of the cause which indirectly produces the resulting negation, as when fire heats, that being its principal effect, and dispels the cold.

Now the absence of causality suffices to explain simple negation. But sin, or any real evil, is the absence, not of good merely, but of good which could and should be present. In other words, since sin is not a simple negation but a privation, its disorder has an indirect cause.

What could and should be present is never absent unless some cause keeps it away. Accordingly philosophers and theologians are wont to say that evil has a deficient cause and an indirect active cause. Every indirect cause must be taken back to a direct cause. Since sin has an indirect cause as regards its disorder, and a direct active cause as regards its act, it follows that we can trace back the disorder to the cause of the act. So, therefore, the will ungoverned by right reason and divine law, and purposing some perishable good, directly causes the act of sin, and indirectly and inciden-

[1] Job v. 6–7.

tally the disorder of sin. The want of order in the act
issues from the want of direction in the will.

156, 513, 627   *Summa Theologica*, 1a–2ae. lxxv. 1

248. The cause of a sin is the will's not holding to the
rule of reason and divine law. Evil does not arise before
the will applies itself to doing something. In this sense,
then, the cause of the initial sin is not an evil, but a good,
namely the will, not joined to another good, namely the
rule of reason and divine law.

Summa Theologica, 1a–2ae. lxxv. 1, *ad* 3

249. To some extent we can share in Christ's sinless-
ness, if we walk the way trodden by him our leader, if
we seek to bend our mind to our destiny, and if we let
God rule our soul.

521   *III Sentences*, xii. ii. 1

250. Able to avoid sin, and able to persevere sinlessly to
the end, these statements are not the same. When you
say that someone can abstain from sin, the ability refers
to a negation. It is tantamount to saying that he is able
not to sin. This is possible for anyone in a state of grace,
at least with regard to grave sin. For, given grace, no
habitual disposition towards grave wrong exists in the
soul; the bias is all the other way. When a serious
temptation crops up, the tendency is to reject it, unless
you are swept by passion; even so, you are not bound
to succumb if you are not taken by surprise. Some
motions of lust cannot be prevented before the will
asserts its control, and so we cannot avoid all venial
sins. But so long as our freewill is not set on mortal sin
we can avoid it.

But if you say that someone can persevere to the end
of his life free from grave sin, the ability refers to an
affirmation. It is tantamount to saying that someone can

put himself in a state into which sin cannot enter, or that
he can make himself persevere, and, in effect, render
himself impeccable. This is not within the power of our
freewill; our effective ability does not go so far as to
execute this intention. We cannot command our final
perseverance, but must ask it from God.

305, 627   Disputations, xxiv *de Veritate*, 14

251. You cannot hold it against a man that he is so frail
that he would fall were temptation to come upon him,
though in fact the temptation does not present itself.
God does not punish people for what they would have
done, but for what they do.

157   Disputations, ii *de Malo*, 2, *ad* 4

3. SINS

252. You can be at once mean and wasteful—mean, by
getting what is not yours, wasteful by throwing things
away. There is no reason to prevent opposite sins co-
existing about different objects.

239, 480   *Summa Theologica*, 1a–2ae. lxxii. 8, *ad* 3

253. Charity is driven out, not because sin is strong,
but because the human will subjects itself to sin.

243   Disputations, *de Caritate*, 6, *ad* 6

254. Seven reasons for blindness, and seven sins. Here
is a comparison—a swollen head, and this is pride; an
overcast day, and this is envy; cross-eyed squinting, and
this is anger; dust and grit, and this is avarice; heavy
puffy lids, and this is sloth; congested veins, and this is
gluttony; spots before the eyes, and this is lechery.

Sunday Sermons, 38[1]

[1] Quinquagesima Sunday.

255. Head, *caput*, means first the physical organ, and afterwards is applied to any principle, and finally to a prince or governor. It is in the second sense that we speak of *capital sins*.

One sin can proceed from another in four ways. First, by taking away the grace which holds us from sin: *whosoever is born of God doth not commit sin, for God's seed remaineth in him.*[1] Thus an initial sin is the cause of the sins that follow after, and any type of sin may be the cause of another, by removing what would have prevented its commission. Such causality, however, is incidental, and of no interest to science and art, which are concerned with direct connexions.[2] Theology, consequently, does not speak of capital sins in this sense.

Secondly, one sin may cause another by promoting a propensity towards it. In this sense, however, the one is too much like the other to be separately catalogued. Thirdly, one sin can provide the material and opportunity for another; gormandizing prepares for lewdness, and covetousness for quarrelsomeness. But even in this sense one sin does not actively and directly cause another, but prepares its occasion.

Fourthly, one sin causes another by purposing it, as when somebody commits one sin for the sake of another, as when he defrauds because he is avaricious. Here the causal connexion is actual and formal, and it is in this narrow sense that we speak of capital sins. This also fits in with their being principal and ruling sins, for a prince uses his subjects for his own purposes as a general does an army.[3] Gregory speaks of capital sins being like officers who regiment the other sins.[4]

[1] 1 John iii. 9.
[2] *Physics*, viii. 3, 253^b6. *Metaphysics*, vi. 2, 1026^b2 (cf. also 75^a19, 1064^b30.)   [3] *Metaphysics*, xii. 10, 1075^a11.
[4] *Moralia*, xxxi. 45; *PL* LXXVI. 620.

One sin can be dependent on another in two ways:
first, because of purely personal foible; second, because
of its nature. The first connexion is merely of biographi-
cal interest, whereas the typological classification of
capital sins looks rather to stock purposes; those, therefore, are called capital sins which are centred on certain
key-points round which lesser purposes cluster.

They are arranged according to the special types of
good which attract them and which repel them. The
attractions are psychological, physical, and economic.
Pride and *vainglory* come from wanting to be held in
high honour and glory, and from preening oneself in
the imagination. *Gluttony* comes from individual high
living, *lust* from sexuality inborn to serve the race,
avarice from the gathering of wealth. The repulsions
are about good things wrongfully regarded as threatening our own proper good, and which, therefore, are
grieved about or actively combated. Spiritual values
menace our physical pleasure, hence *accidie* or boredom, a sadness about spiritual good. *Envy* is similar; it
resent another's good qualities because they lower our
own self-esteem. To flare out at them is *anger*.

414, 420   Disputations, viii *de Malo*, i

256. There are two sides to every sin, the turning to
transient satisfaction and the turning away from everlasting value. As regards the first, the principle of all
sins can be called lust—lust in its most general sense,
namely, the unbridled desire for one's own pleasure.
As regards the second, the principle is pride, pride in
its general sense, the lack of submission to God: *the
beginning of pride is man's revolt from God.*[1] Lust and
pride in this pervasive sense are not called capital sins,
because as such they are not special sins: they are the

[1] Ecclus. x. 14.

roots and sprouts of vice, as the desire for happiness is the root of all virtue.

231, 629   Disputations, VIII *de Malo*, 1, *ad* 1

257. Among the objects men naturally find desirable is their own excellence. If ruled by reason and shaped by God, then the desire is healthy and even greathearted: *we will not boast beyond our measure, but according to the measure of the rule which God hath measured to us.*[1] If it fall short of this measure, then the vice of pusillanimity is incurred; if it exceed, then the vice of pride, which is an overweening desire for one's own superiority.

237   Disputations, VIII *de Malo*, 2

258. Pride strives for perverse excellence, a very special sin when God is despised, but also present whenever our neighbour is despised.

Disputations, VIII *de Malo*, 2, *ad* 4

259. Vanity is attributed to shams which lack substance and are deceitful: *how long will you chase shadows and follow a lie?*[2] Or to things without solidity and permanence: *vanity of vanities, and all is vanity.*[3] Or to means which fail in their purpose, such as unavailing medicine: *I have laboured in vain, I have spent my strength for nought.*[4]

We may speak of vainglory in all three senses. First, when a man is puffed up and claims what is not his own: *what hast thou that thou didst not receive? now if thou didst receive it, why dost thou glory, as if thou hadst not received it?*[5] Secondly, when he boasts about some fleeting endowment: *all flesh is grass, the beauty thereof is but grass in flower.*[6] Thirdly, when the reputation he

---

[1] 2 Cor. x. 13.   [2] Ps. iv. 3.   [3] Eccles. i. 4.
[4] Isa. xlix. 4.   [5] 1 Cor. iv. 7.   [6] Isa. xl. 6.

claims serves no good purpose, for applause is profitless unless God be praised: *so let your light shine before men that they may see your good works and glorify your Father who is in heaven*.[1] Or unless others be prompted to emulate good example: *let every one of us please his neighbour for his good unto edification*.[2] Or he himself be made grateful and put on his mettle to persevere.

130   Disputations, ix *de Malo*, 1

260. Who would cry grave sin when someone brags about his singing, when in fact he was out of tune? Or when an owner swaggers because his racehorse has been successful? To disdain vainglory may be great virtue: that vainglory is great vice does not follow.

Disputations, ix *de Malo*, 2, c. & ad 8

261. Nobody can grieve about good as such, yet a man may apprehend it as a real or supposed evil; thus an envious man makes a grievance of another's worth, supposing it to threaten his own.

Disputations, x *de Malo*, 1, *ad* 6

262. Evil is less primordial than the good of which it is the deprivation. Similarly, human passions about evil objects derive from those about good objects, and are less primitive than them, indeed they derive from them. Hate and sadness pay tribute to desire and delight: so does envy to liking.

158   Disputations, x *de Malo*, 1, *ad* 5

263. Say a man voluntarily undertakes a duty of obedience, but groans at the boredom and burden. He has not fallen into *accidie*, for his sadness is about an outward temporal evil, not an inward eternal good.

Disputations, xi *de Malo*, 1, *ad* 4

[1] Matt. v. 6.   [2] Rom. xv. 2.

264. *Accidie* is a shrinking of mind, not from any spiritual good, but from that to which it should cleave as in duty bound, namely the goodness of God.

Disputations, xi *de Malo,* 3, *ad* 4

4. CONSEQUENCES OF SIN

265. *Woe unto you hypocrites! for ye are like unto whited sepulchres, which indeed appear beautiful outwardly, but are full of dead men's bones, and of all rottenness.*[1] Body is the dwelling of soul, and soul is the throne of God. The body of a sinner is a tomb, covering a soul dead by sin: *their throat an open sepulchre.*[2] Inside a corpse, though outside sometimes an effigy of the living.

Commentary, St. Matthew, xxiii

266. Since subtraction is action of a sort, let us examine some modes of action in order to assess how sin may diminish the good estate of human nature.

Complete things are the centres from which action comes; properly speaking, they are the causes of action. Yet, more loosely, we may think of modes or forms causing action. It is the whitewasher who does the wall, yet we also talk of his skill or whitening doing it. There is no less variety among causes in the wide sense of the word as among causes in the strict sense of the word.

To begin with, a cause is said to work directly or indirectly. Directly, when its nature is productive of the effect essentially; indirectly, when it removes an impediment to the production of the effect. Thus a room is directly lit by the sun, indirectly by the servant who opens the shutters. Again, a principal cause is said to produce an effect either immediately or mediately as a consequence: a generating cause produces a form immediately, and the results which follow mediately.

[1] Matt. xxiii. 27.   [2] Ps. xiii. 4.

These divisions apply both to positive effects and to
the results of deprivation, for causes which destroy or
diminish are causes as well as those which produce or
give increase. The agent who removes the shutter is
said to give light indirectly, and, more loosely, so also
does the removal of the shutter. Likewise the agent
who puts up the shutter, and the shuttering itself, can
be said to cause darkness indirectly.

As daylight from the sun is diffused into the room, so
the light of grace is infused into the soul by God. Although grace is beyond the nature of the soul, there is,
nevertheless, in every rational creature the readiness to
receive grace, and from grace the vigour to act accordingly. Sin is like an obstacle interposed between the
soul and God: *your iniquities have separated between you
and God.*[1]

Let us continue the analogy. The sun does not shine
into an interior unless the room faces that way; and a
north outlook, or anything that blocks the light, can be
called an obstacle. Similarly, the soul cannot be lit by
receiving grace unless it be turned to God. This looking
to God is hindered by sin. For by sin, which is against
God's law, the soul is turned away.

Any obstacle to a form or benefit either prevents its
reception or makes it more difficult to come by; furthermore, it holds up any good effect it might have had on
the subject. This is especially the case when the obstacle
is firmly embedded. A thing cannot move two ways at
once. Hence sin not only keeps grace out, but lessens
the soul's readiness to receive grace. The blessing is
there, but the soul is backward.

Since the aptness for grace is part of human nature's
good estate, we can now appreciate how sin diminishes
nature. And because grace perfects nature, heightening

[1] Isa. lix. 2.

mind and will and the sensitive parts which serve reason, we can appreciate also how sin, by depriving us of grace and clogging our natural abilities, also hurts nature. The results of sin are ignorance, malice, and concupiscence, and these are called the wounds of nature.

224, 296, 477, 628, 640   Disputations, II *de Malo*, 11

267. Rational and intelligent beings are especially affected by the general problem of good and evil, for whereas other creatures are occupied with the particular, their minds apprehend what is meant by goodness as such and their wills are set towards all good. One corollary is the division of the evil which afflicts them into the evil of fault and the evil of punishment.

Good is the opposite of evil, and this division of evil matches the division of good into primary good and secondary good: a thing's primary perfection is what it is by its form and condition, its secondary perfection is what it does. The first includes all our abilities, the second refers to their employment. The reverse side correspondingly displays two evils. The first is the lack of a due form or condition for acting, for instance, a gammy leg; the second is a failure in actual activity, for instance, a limp.

The division may be extended from physical activity to moral activity. The state of lacking what we need, whether with respect to soul or to body or even to external equipment, in order to act rightly is, on the Catholic view, penal. But the disorientated voluntary act bears the stigma of fault. Let us pause on this notion of penal evil.

There are three elements to be reckoned with in punishment. The first is that it is the consequence of fault: a man must take the consequences of what he has

done. The Christian tradition holds that no rational
creature can suffer damage in soul, body, or possession,
except for previous sin, either personal or corporate.
Therefore the lack of the advantages necessary, in
angels as well as men, for acting well are called punishments, or penalties. All evil affecting rational and intelligent creatures is either culpable or penal.

The second is that punishment is contrary to our inclination. For each of us wants his own good, and hates to
be deprived of it. Punishment is against our will, sometimes against its explicit act, as when we suffer a penalty
knowingly; sometimes against its interpretative intention, as when we do not know that we are handicapped
but would grieve if we did; sometimes against its instinctive drive, as when we lack a virtue we do not want
to have, although the natural move of will is towards all
virtue.

The third is that punishment consists in suffering.
For the effect is against the will; it is not spontaneous
and from within, but is imposed by an extrinsic principle.

On all these three counts fault and penalty differ.
Fault is evil in the activity, punishment is evil in the
agent. The sequence differs between physical and voluntary agents. With natural activity, a deficient action
follows from a deficient agent; the diseased or distorted
leg causes the limp. With moral activity, the reverse
holds true; punishment follows fault, and fits it according to divine Providence. Next, fault suits the will, but
punishment is repugnant. Lastly, fault consists in doing,
punishment in being done by. As Augustine says, fault
is the evil we perform, punishment the evil we undergo.[1]

2 14, 225, 526, 550, 606   Disputations, 1 de Malo, 4

---

[1] de Libero Arbitrio, i. 2; PL xxxii. 1222.

268. God's omnipotence most appears in his forbear-
ance and mercy. There his supreme power is displayed.
For he alone is able to forgive sin freely, whereas a ruler
bound by the law of a superior authority cannot pardon
as he pleases. Also, because by sparing us and having
compassion, he leads us to share his own infinite goodness—the final effect of divine power. Also, because
mercy lays the foundation for all divine works; nothing
is owing to creatures except what God gives them without title on their part.

72, 300 *Summa Theologica*, 1a. xxv. 3, *ad* 3

269. That if Adam had not sinned as many men as
women would have been born seems probable enough.

God alone knows the number of the elect; we cannot
guess whether more men than women are saved, or
whether they equal one another.

We cannot state that the same number of human
beings have been born as would have been born had
Adam not sinned. A human being would not have had
the same numerical identity had he been born from
different parents. Since many have been children of
fathers who have had many wives, and since polygamy
would not have existed in a state of innocence, we can
scarcely say that the number of human beings who
would have been born had original sin never entered
equals the number of human beings who will be saved
given the present condition of human nature.

153, 635 III *Quodlibets*, xi. 25

270. Man fell back to earth by deserting God. How
right it was for God to use the remedy of earth, and
by taking flesh to lead him back to health. *The Word
was made flesh.*[1] Flesh had blinded thee, exclaims

[1] John i. 14.

Augustine, now flesh heals thee; for Christ so came that from flesh he cures the weakness of flesh.[1]

550 *Summa Theologica*, 3a. i. 3, *ad* 1

271. *Bring forth fruits meet for repentance.*[2] Fruit after blossom, otherwise the tree is useless. Contrition is the flower, the making of amends is the fruit: *my flowers the promise of grace and glory.*[3]

Commentary, *St. Matthew*, iii

[1] *in Joannis Evangelium Tractatus*, ii; *PL* xxxv. 1395.
[2] Matt. iii. 8.
[3] Ecclus. xxiv. 23.

V

The New Creation[1]

272. *My Father is the husbandman.*[2] God tends us, nurtures our nature with loving care, weeds wickedness from our hearts, opens us up with the plough of the word, sows the seed of the precepts, and gathers the fruits of devotion.

183   Commentary, *St. John*, xv, *lect.* 1

273. *The day is at hand.*[3] This word *day* can be taken in a fourfold sense; the day of mercy, of grace, of justice, of glory. The day of mercy is the birthday of the Lord: *in that day the mountains shall drop down new wine, and the hills shall flow with milk.*[4] The day of grace is the time of grace: *behold, now is the day of salvation.*[5] The

---

[1] All law, which is a command of reason rather than an applied force of will, derives from the Eternal Law in the mind of God, the Natural Law after the manner of theoretic conclusions (which nobody has the power to alter) from the principles of understanding, the Positive Law after the manner of practical decisions of prudence (which may vary according to circumstances) from the principles of morality. Positive Law is not solely a remedy for sin —for St. Thomas, like Aristotle and unlike the patristic and early medieval authors, held that the State was a natural development and not just an artificial contrivance; all the same, its coercive power bulks large in the Old Law, beyond which we are taken by the Gospel Law of love. Three notes are emphasized: first, that Grace is a new creation, wholly from God, to which we can lay no claim of ourselves; second, that our co-operation with God spells no interaction of two partial causes, each contributing to the total effect, but the production of an act which is truly ours and yet completely subordinate to divine causality; third, that no violence is offered, for supernatural signifies 'above the level of nature', not 'against the movement of nature'.

[2] John xv. 1.   [3] Rom. xiii. 12.
[4] Joel. iii. 18.   [5] 2 Cor. vi. 5.

day of justice is the day of judgement: *the day of wrath,
that day of tribulation.*[1] The day of glory is the day of
eternity: *but it shall come one day which shall be known
to the Lord—not day, nor night; but it shall come to pass
that at evening time it shall be light.*[2]

The birthday of the Lord draws near. Let us devoutly
celebrate the day of mercy: *for the Lord is at hand.*[3] *My
salvation is near to come, and my righteousness is near to
be revealed.*[4] May we welcome the day of grace: *behold,
now is the accepted time; behold, now is the time of salvation.*[5] May we fear the day of judgement: *behold, the
judge standeth before the door.*[6] May we enter into the
day of glory: *behold, I come quickly, and my reward is
with me to give to every man according as his work shall
be.*[7]

26   *Sunday Sermons,* 2[8]

I. LAW

274. This is the definition of law by its four essential
parts: an ordinance of reason for the sake of the common
good commanded by the authority who has charge of
the community and promulgated.

430, 433   *Summa Theologica,* 1a–2ae. xc. 4

275. Law is an ordinance of practical reason. The
whole universe is governed by the divine reason. God
is the Prince of the Universe, the plan of government
he has in his mind bears the character of law, and because it is conceived in eternity and not in time is rightly
called the Eternal Law.

A law is promulgated by word and in writing.
Eternally the Eternal Law is promulgated in the divine

[1] Soph. i. 15.   [2] Zach. xiv. 7.   [3] Phil. iv. 5.
[4] Isa. lvi. 1.   [5] 2 Cor. vi. 2.   [6] James v. 9.
[7] Apoc. xxii. 12.   [8] First Sunday of Advent.

Word and in the Book of Life, temporally in those who listen and read.

183 *Summa Theologica*, 1a–2ae. xci. 1, *c. & ad* 2

276. All laws derive from the Eternal Law in so far as they are right and reasonable.

63, 71 *Summa Theologica*, 1a–2ae. xciii. 3

277. The sharing of rational creatures in the Eternal Law, which sets them towards their due acts and end, is called the Natural Law. The Psalmist says, *offer up the sacrifices of righteousness*, and then, to *the many who say, Who will show us any good?* he replies, *the light of thy countenance shines upon us, O Lord.*[1]

469 *Summa Theologica*, 1a–2ae. xci. 2

278. Particular arrangements instituted by human art which fit in with the principles of Natural Law are called human laws, given the presence of the four essential conditions of law.[2]

274, 646 *Summa Theologica*, 1a–2ae. xci. 3

---

[1] Ps. iv. 6–7.

[2] The divisions of Law may be summarized as follows. Over all law is the *Eternal Law* in the mind of God, which is variously shared in by rational creatures. Rational ordinances bound up with the nature of things, and deriving from the Eternal Law in the manner of a deductive intellectual process belong to the body of *Natural Law*. This is a system of principles and conclusions, some of which are proximate to the principles, for instance, that we should tell the truth, that we should not commit murder, while others are more remote, and not universally agreed on, for instance, that one man should have only one wife at a time, or that there should be some measure of private ownership of material goods: the Natural Law is accordingly divided into primary and secondary precepts. Rational ordinances instituted by the interposition of the will of authority belong to the *Positive Law*; they are necessary, but are, in a sense, arbitrary applications of legislative power, designed to ensure the smooth running of the political community. By the Positive Law an act is right because commanded, wrong

279. Human legislation, which is enacted for a group composed for the greater part of human beings who are not of consummate virtue, does not forbid all vices, from which the virtuous abstain, but only those grave ones which most people can avoid, those especially which damage others, and which have to be put down if civilized intercourse is to be maintained.

432, 643, 652 *Summa Theologica*, 1a–2ae. xcvi. 2

280. The commands of human law cover only those deeds which concern the public interest, not every deed of every virtue.

434 *Summa Theologica*, 1a–2ae. xcvi. 3

281. Certain deeds are said to be permitted by human law, not because they are approved, but because civil authority cannot check them.

435, 649 *Summa Theologica*, 1a–2ae. xciii. 3, *ad* 3

282. Besides the Natural Law and positive human laws, our conduct needs to be guided by a divine law, and for four reasons.

because forbidden: it is the other way round with the Natural Law; an act is commanded because good, forbidden because wrong. Positive Law, sometimes called Human Law, is divided into Canon Law, the disciplinary regulations of the Church, and Civil Law.

These are the main types of law. Then, also, four historical laws may be noted (282, 284, 286). First, the Positive Divine Law, which governed the Jewish theocracy, and still partially survives in the Christian Church. Second, the *Jus Gentium*, historically a compound of Roman Law and tribal law, which the medieval theologians and philosophers of law sometimes treat as a set of conclusions from the Natural Law and sometimes as the fundamental articles of Positive Law. Third, the *lex fomitis*, so named by Peter Lombard, the law of concupiscence, of the tinder of sin, referred to by St. Paul: this law in our members is law by analogy, and is as inferior to a judicial code as the Gospel Law is superior. This, the law of love and liberty, is also a law by analogy.

First, law should direct properly human activity to the final goal of life. Were we bound merely for an end proportionate to our natural faculties, an abstract consideration of the powers of reason would suggest no need for a higher law. In fact we are set towards the supernatural end of eternal joy, and therefore need to be guided by a divine law over and above Natural Law and codes of human law.

Secondly, all sorts of differences and disagreements arise from the uncertainty of human judgement, particularly when it comes to decisions on points of fact; these lead to diverse and conflicting laws. In order that we should not be held up by doubts as to what we should do and what to avoid, our human behaviour is regulated by a divinely given law, which, if we follow, we are assured we cannot go wrong.

Thirdly, human authority, which can legislate only about matters it is competent to judge, cannot extend to interior acts which are hidden, but is restricted to exterior acts which are manifest. Yet if virtue is to be established neither type of activity must go astray. Human law, therefore, which cannot check and is without the resources to control what goes on inside us, needs to be reinforced by divine law.

Fourthly, as Augustine notes, human law cannot catch up with all misdeeds.[1] The attempt would be too costly, for virtue is not served by official fussiness. Nor would the common good be fostered, nor the ease of social intercourse ensured. But divine law can forbid all wrong, for nought escapes its reckoning.

The psalmist touches on these four reasons: *The law of the Lord is clean*—for it permits no stain of sin, *bringing the soul back to life*—for it guides us inside and outside, *the decree of the Lord is unchallengeable*—for it

[1] *de Libero Arbitrio*, i. 5; *PL* xxxii. 1228.

appears sure and right, *making wise the simple*[1]—for it leads all to their divine and supernatural end.

20, 651   *Summa Theologica*, 1a–2ae. xci. 4

283. Law has the power to compel; indeed the ability to enforce is a condition of the ability to command. Compulsion comes from fear of penalty.[2] But when we regard the correspondence between precept and sanction, there the divine law differs from human law. A legal penalty can be imposed only in matters about which the lawgiver can judge and pass sentence. Man, the maker of human law, can form his judgement on external acts only, for *he seeth only those things which appear*.[3] The divine lawgiver alone is able to judge the inner motions of the will: *the searcher of the heart and reins is God*.[4] We conclude that virtue is covered from one point of view by both divine and human law, from another point of view by divine law alone, from another point of view by neither.

The style of virtue, according to Aristotle, contains three elements: knowledge, choice, and inclination.[5] First, a person should act knowingly: this falls under the judgement both of divine and human law, for what a man does in ignorance he does accidentally; any law must allow for that in deciding whether an action be punishable or pardonable. Secondly, that an action is willed by deliberate choice engages a double inner motion, namely towards ends and towards means. Divine law is able to judge both of these. Not so human law, for it cannot punish a man who meditates murder without committing it, though divine law can: *whoso-*

---

1 Ps. xviii, 8.
2 Cf. *Ethics*, x. 7, 1177^{a}20. St. Thomas, *lect.* 10. Aristotle is speaking about the leisureliness of perfect virtue.
3 1 Kings xvi. 7.   4 Ps. vii. 10.
5 *Ethics*, ii. 3, 1105^{a}30.

ever is angry with his brother shall be in danger of the judgement.[1] Thirdly, that an activity issues from a firm and constant bent implies the presence of a habit. That we should be rooted in virtue falls under the precept neither of human nor of divine law—I mean this, that neither law punishes a man as a transgressor who duly fulfils the precept, say, of honouring his parents, though in fact he lacks the virtue of family reverence.

217, 417, 430, 490   *Summana Theologica*, 1a–2ae. c, 9

2. OLD AND NEW LAW

284. If we are to be saved, we must know what to believe, what to hope, and what to do. Our faith is directed by the Creed, our confidence by the Lord's Prayer, our conduct by the Law.

There are four laws: the Natural Law, the law of lust, the Mosaic Law, and the Gospel Law. The first is the inborn light of reason which shows us what to pursue and what to avoid. God gave us this law and light at our creation, and although many believe they are excused by ignorance, nobody in fact is unaware that he should do to others as he himself would be done by. Over this primitive law the devil has sown another, the law of lust. We received his temptation, and now our flesh has become rebellious. Our reason tells us what to do, our concupiscence urges us to the contrary: *I see another law in my members, warring against the law of my mind, and bringing me into captivity to the law of sin which is in my members.*[2]

The Natural Law thus having been ruined, a written law became necessary to impel us to virtue and ward us from vice. Two motives here: fear and love. First of all, fear, for it is the thought of the Last Judgement and

[1] Matt. v. 22.   [2] Rom. vii. 23.

Hell that makes a man hesitate before committing sin: *the beginning of wisdom is the fear of the Lord, the fear of the Lord drives out sin.*[1] True, a man is not righteous who does not sin because of his fears. All the same, his justification is under way. In this manner did the Mosaic Law keep man from evil and promote his good: *he that despised the law of Moses died without mercy under two or three witness.*[2] Sufficient, this, to check the hand, but not the soul; and so another law was granted, the law of love, of Christ and his Gospel.

There are three differences between the laws of the Old and New Testaments. Fear makes men slaves, love sets them free: *where the spirit of the Lord is, there is liberty.*[3] Observance of the Old Law was recommended by temporal favours, *if ye be willing and obedient, ye shall eat the fat of the land,*[4] but the New Law offers spiritual blessings, *if thou wilt enter into life, keep the commandments.*[5] The Old Law was heavy, *now therefore why tempt ye God, to put a yoke upon the disciples, which neither our fathers nor we are able to bear?*[6] but the New Law is sweet, *for my yoke is easy, and my burden light.*[7] *For ye have not received the spirit of bondage again to fear, but ye have received the spirit of adoption.*[8]

  590, 654   *de Duobus Praeceptis Caritatis,* 1

285. *The law is holy, and the commandment holy, just, and good.*[9] Assuredly the Old Law was good, for as doctrine is sound when consonant with reason so law is just when consonant with right reason. Such was the Old Law, for it barred the lusts which would attack reasonable living, for example, the command, *thou shalt not covet anything that is thy neighbour's.*[10] Hence St.

---

[1] Ecclus. i. 16, 26.   [2] Heb. x. 28.
[3] 2 Cor. iii. 17.   [4] Isa. i. 19.
[5] Matt. xix. 17.   [6] Acts. xv. 10.   [7] Matt. xi. 30.
[8] Rom. viii. 15.   [9] Rom. vii. 12.   [10] Exod. xx. 17.

Paul argues, *I delight in the law of God after the inward man, with the mind I myself serve it.*[1]

But there are degrees of goodness, shading from imperfect to perfect: an imperfect means to an end needs to be supplemented, a perfect means is sufficient; a partial remedy helps to cure, a complete remedy cures.

Bear in mind that human and divine law differ in their immediate aims. Human law, the purpose of which is the tranquillity of the State, operates by policing external acts which could break the public peace. The purpose of divine law, on the other hand, is to lead us through to eternal happiness, the obstacles to which are sins, internal as well as external. The effective putting down of crime and the enforcement of sanctions suffices for human law, but not for divine law, which would adapt the whole of man to everlasting joy.

Only the grace of the Spirit can do this, the grace by which *love is shed abroad in our hearts.*[2] *The grace of God eternal life.*[3] The giving is reserved to our Lord; it was beyond the power of the Old Law: *the law was given by Moses, but grace and truth by Jesus Christ.*[4] Hence the Old Law was good, but imperfect: *for the law made nothing perfect, but the bringing in of a better hope.*[5]

17, 468, 616   *Summa Theologica*, 1a–2ae. xcviii. 1

286. The predominant note, indeed the general tenor, of the Gospel Law is the grace of the Holy Spirit given through faith in Christ: *where is then thy boasting? It is excluded. By what law? Of works? No, but by the law of faith.*[6] The grace of faith is here called a law. More expressly St. Paul says, *the law of the spirit of life, in Christ Jesus, hath delivered me from the law of sin and*

[1] Rom. vii. 22, 27.   [2] Rom. v. 5.   [3] Rom. vi. 23.
[4] John i. 17.   [5] Heb. vii. 19.   [6] Rom. iii. 27.

death.[1] Augustine remarks that while the law of works was graven on stone tablets the law of faith is written in the hearts of the faithful, and then he asks: What else are the laws of God written in our hearts but the very presence of the Holy Ghost?.[2]

Primarily, then, the Gospel is the grace of the Spirit shed in our hearts which makes us justified. Nevertheless there are also accompanying ordinances which prepare for the grace and activity of the Spirit. They concern faith and morals, and Christians have to be instructed in them. But they are secondary, for these documents of doctrine and order directing human affections do not themselves make us righteous: *the letter killeth, but the spirit quickeneth.*[3] Augustine applies this conclusion to anything written down, to any code external to our minds and hearts, even to the commandments contained in the Gospel: yes, even the Gospel words would kill but for the presence of inward healing grace.

129, 403   *Summa Theologica,* 1a–2ae. cvi. 1. 2

287. God's precepts are light to the loving, heavy to the fearful.

397   Disputations, xxiv *de Veritate,* 14, *ad* 7

288. Precepts of law deal with virtuous deeds, which may be difficult both because the external duties imposed are heavy and because of the interior effort demanded for acting promptly and cheerfully.

With regard to external observance, the Old Law was much more rigorous than the New Law, for it abounded with the obligations of observing a complicated ceremonial code. Apart from the precepts of

[1] Rom. viii. 2.
[2] *de Spiritu et Littera,* 24; *PL* xliv. 225.
[3] 2 Cor. iii. 6.

Natural Law, very few external loads were added by the teaching of Christ and the Apostles, though some have been instituted since by Church authorities. Augustine warns us to proceed with moderation in this matter, lest conversion to the Church be made a burdensome business.[1]

With regard to the spirit of obedience, the New Law is more taxing, for it inculcates a psychological attitude and forbids certain interior motions, into which the Old Law did not enter, or else affixed no penalties. The effort is extremely hard for those without virtue; Aristotle remarks that to do what a just man does may not be difficult, but if you lack justice then to do it as he does it is quite the reverse.[2] *His commandments are not heavy*[3]—not heavy, comments Augustine, to the lover, but otherwise to the non-lover.[4]

201, 586   *Summa Theologica*, 1a–2ae. cvii. 4

289. The grace of the Holy Ghost shown forth by faith working through friendship is the heart of the New Law. We reach this grace through God the Son made man, who filled his manhood with grace, from which source it flows to us: *the Word was made flesh; full of grace and truth; and of his fulness we have all received; for grace and truth came by Jesus Christ.*[5] The grace running from the Incarnate Word is admirably led along the channels of sense, and the interior grace, which charges flesh with spirit, expressed in deeds of sense.

Accordingly, external works relate to grace in two ways, first, as conducting to grace—such are the sacraments instituted by the New Law; second, as coming from grace—such are the deeds we do. Concerning them

[1] *ad Inquisitionem Januarii*. Epist. lv. 19; *PL* xxxiii. 221.
[2] *Ethics*, v. 9, 1137[a]5.   [3] 1 John v. 3.
[4] *de Natura et Gratia*, 69; *PL* xliv. 289.
[5] John i. 14, 16, 17.

we may observe a difference. Grace stands or falls by some of them; some it requires, and these are commanded, others it cannot abide, and these are forbidden. For example, the profession or denial of faith: *whosoever therefore shall confess me before men, him will I confess before my Father who is in heaven. And whosoever will deny me before men, him will I also deny before my Father who is in heaven.*[1] But some works are not indispensable for faith working through charity, and these are neither commanded nor forbidden by the New Law, but are left by Christ the Legislator to rulers in charge of subjects, who will ordain, at their discretion, what should be pursued and what avoided. This is one of the reasons why the Gospel Law is called the law of liberty.

564, 588   *Summa Theologica*, 1a–2ae. cviii. 1

3. GRACE

290. *How great is thy goodness, which thou hast laid up for them that fear thee!*[2] Christ is in the glory of the Father. That is why he is hidden from us, and why the life he gives us is a hidden life.

365, 522   Commentary, *Colossians*, iii, *lect.* 1

291. Grace is nature's perfection, and therefore impairs nothing natural.

11, 410   *Contra Impugnantes Dei*, 6

292. Man is made to the image of God, because he is created with an intelligence. Only intelligent beings are said to be made to his image; they only can be called his sons, and can be adopted through grace. Adoption goes further, for a right to the inheritance is implied. God's heritage is his own happiness, of which only intelligent creatures are capable, though they have no

[1] Matt. x. 32–33.   [2] Ps. xxx. 19.

strict title to it from the fact of their creation; such happiness is a gift, the gift of the Spirit. Sharing of possessions is not enough: there must be a sharing of the heritage. And so the adoption of creatures means their communion in divine happiness.

Christ should not be termed God's son by adoption, for he is begotten eternally by the Father, and his divine nature has the heritage by right, not by additional concession: *all things whatsoever that the Father has are mine.*[1]

123, 507 *III Sentences*, x. ii. 2. *iii*

i. *Necessity*

293. In order to know any truth at all we need divine assistance which rouses our minds into activity, but this is not necessarily supernatural, or over and above the natural enlightenment he gives us.

7, 183, 380 *Summa Theologica*, 1a–2ae. cix. 1

294. *Without me you can do nothing.*[2] When we speak of a man doing what lies in his power we also imply his being moved thereto by God.

182 *Summa Theologica*, 1a–2ae. cix. 6, *ad* 2

295. The Pelagian heresy, to begin with, denied the existence of original sin in babies, contradicting St. Paul, *by one man sin entered into the world, and death by sin; and so death passed upon all men, for that all have sinned.*[3] And also the Psalmist, who says, *behold, I was conceived in iniquity.*[4] Secondly, it held that good works starts with man himself, the finish being from God, and this despite the Apostolic teaching, *it is God who worketh in you both to will and to do according of his good pleasure.*[5]

[1] John, xvi. 15. [2] John xv. 5.
[3] Rom. v. 12.   [4] Ps. 1. 5.   [5] Phil. ii. 13.

Thirdly, it taught that the gift of grace is proportionate to merit, and this also despite the Apostolic teaching, *if by grace, then it is no more of works; otherwise grace is no more grace.*[1]

223   *de Articulis Fidei et Sacramentis Ecclesiae,* 1

296. Human nature can be considered either in its integrity before the Fall or in its present damaged condition. Under both respects divine help is necessary for man to act well. When his nature was integral, a free gift, superadded to his natural powers, was needed for him to will and work only when a supernatural end was engaged. Now, however, this is also needed for the repair of his nature, since his natural powers are unable to bring about his natural well-being.

Human nature is not completely corrupt or entirely destitute of good, and without supernatural help—though never without the divine help pervading all activity—a man can contrive particular good ends, such as building a house or planting a vineyard, but not his entire well-being. He will fail somewhere. A sick man may move about, but until he is cured by medicine his movements are not those of a healthy man. Fallen nature, therefore, needs grace, first, to be healed, and next, to act supernaturally and deserve everlasting life.

20, 267, 388   *Summa Theologica,* 1a–2ae. cix. 2

297. Since deeds of natural power are not deserving of eternal life, because they are not proportioned to it, the higher power of grace is necessary.

7   *Summa Theologica,* 1a–2ae. cix. 5

298. What is possible with God's help is not wholly impossible to us. Aristotle observes that what we can do

[1] Rom. xi. 6.

through our friends we can do in a sense through ourselves[1].

389   *Summa Theologica*, 1a–2ae. cix. 4, *ad* 2

299. *No man can come to me, except the Father, who
hath sent me, draw him.*[2] *For as many as are led by the
Spirit of God, they are the sons of God.*[3] *The charity of
Christ presseth us.*[4] To be drawn, to be acted on, to be
constrained—all these seem to argue a certain compulsion. Some have therefore thought that divine help
forces men to act well. But they are wrong.

Divine Providence manages all things according to
the proper mode of their functioning. Where human
beings are concerned, their freedom and responsibility
must be safeguarded, and therefore the employment of
force is out of the question. Notice that divine help is
the influence of the first cause on secondary causes, and
of a principal cause on instrumental causes; in both
cases the nature of the subordinate cause is respected.
God does not destroy our acts of will, indeed he causes
them, neither offering violence nor coercing unwilling
activity. *See, I have set before thee this day life and good,
and death and evil.*[5] *Man is confronted with life and
death, blessing and curse; the gift shall be the choice he
makes.*[6]

69, 182, 378   III *Contra Gentes*, 149

300. We are prepared for grace in that we are turned
to God. For this we need the help of divine grace: *turn
thou us to thee, O Lord, and we shall be turned.*[7] Moreover, a man cannot prepare himself for anything without taking thought. Here again he needs the help of

---

[1] *Ethics*, iii. 3, 1112[b]21.   [2] John vi. 44.
[3] Rom. viii. 14.   [4] 2 Cor. v. 14.   [5] Deut. xxx. 15.
[6] Ecclus. xv. 18.   [7] Lament. v. 21.

grace: *not that we are sufficient to think anything of our-selves, but our sufficiency is of God.*[1]

Let me explain, for on this topic we must beware of the error of Pelagius, who stated that man could fulfil the law and merit eternal life of his own freewill, provided he was taught what to do: *teach me to do thy will.*[2] That knowledge alone should come from God while we provide the charity required to fulfil the commands of the law seems hardly likely; on this account the Pelagians afterwards revised their teaching. They stated that man is responsible for the beginning of good works, when he consents to faith of his own freewill, but that the consummation is his from God. Since preparation begins from the very start, part of their error consisted in claiming that man could pre-pare himself for grace without the aid of grace, contrary to St. Paul: *he who hath begun a work in me will perform it until the day of Jesus Christ.*[3]

To explain further. A man needs grace, not only for good works, but also to prepare himself for grace, yet differently. For by good deeds well done he merits; these require habits of virtue,[4] and therefore habitual grace. But to prepare himself for this habit of sanctify-ing grace no other habit is called for—otherwise we should start a line of thought which went back in-definitely. What he does need is divine help, which includes, not only exterior factors, the occasions of salvation which divine Providence supplies, for in-stance, sound instruction, good example, even illness and blows, but also inward motions, divinely bending the human heart to good: *the king's heart is in the hand of God; he turneth it whithersoever he will.*[5]

The necessity for this conclusion can be confirmed

---

[1] 2 Cor. iii. 5.   [2] Ps. cxlii. 9.   [3] Phil. i. 6.
[4] *Ethics,* ii. 1. 1103ª14.   [5] Prov. xxi. 1.

from Aristotle,[1] when he argues that voluntary action turns on choice and is founded on deliberation, but that if you ask whence deliberation begins, you cannot always answer, why, from previous deliberation. You must call a stop. There must be some outside principle prompting the reason to deliberate over what is the right course. And this is God, not some heavenly body, which is inferior to intellectual natures. We may draw the following comparison—as all terrestial motion comes from outside this world in the first place, so all lower intelligences are set in motion by God. Nobody can prepare himself for grace, or do any good, without divine assistance.

That men can freely prepare themselves does not dispense with the need for divine help, any more than the fact that fire burns makes an originating thermal principle redundant. God moves all things according to their proper modes of operation, and so, by sharing in the divine motion, some things act from necessity, but others from liberty. Rational natures are poised between alternatives. God moves the human spirit to good; nevertheless it could resist. It is God's doing, then, that a man prepares himself to receive grace. If he lacks grace, then the cause of the failure lies in him, not in God: *O Israel, thou hast destroyed thyself; but in me is thine help.*[2]

70, 153, 183, 331, 385, 407   *1 Quodlibets,* iv. 7, c. & ad 1, 2

301. No conversion to God unless God turn us. To be turned to God is to be ready for grace—you must open your eyes to be ready to see: this we cannot do without the free help of God arousing us.

182   *Summa Theologica,* 1a–2ae. cix. 6

---

[1] The *Liber de Bona Fortuna,* a compilation from the *Magna Moralia* and the *Eudemian Ethics.* Cf. *Eudemian Ethics,* vii. 14, 1248ᵃ32   [2] Hos. xiii. 9.

302. Without grace a man cannot be set on his last end, nor command the necessary means thereto—faith, hope, charity, perseverance. You might then be tempted to argue that he cannot therefore be blamed if he lacks them, especially since he cannot deserve the help of grace, nor turn to God unless God turns him: how can he be at fault when the responsibility is not his?

This is an awkward conclusion, for it implies that a man without faith, hope, charity, and without perseverance in good would not be deserving of punishment, despite the express statement, *he that believeth not the Son shall not see life, but the wrath of God abideth in him.*[1] And since nobody reaches through to eternal happiness apart from grace, another consequence would be that at the end there will be some human beings who have neither reached happiness nor are being punished by God. On the contrary, all are divided at the Judgement: *then shall the King say unto them on his right hand, Come, you blessed of my Father, inherit the kingdom prepared for you from the foundation of the world. Then shall he say also unto them on his left hand, Depart from me, you cursed, into everlasting fire, prepared for the devil and his angels.*[2]

To clear up this doubt, consider that a man, though unable to acquire or deserve grace of his own freewill, can nevertheless stop himself from receiving it: *they say unto God, Depart from us; for we desire not the knowledge of thy ways.*[3] And again, *they are those that rebel against the light.*[4] To obstruct or not to obstruct the entrance of divine grace, this lies in the power of a man's own freewill; if he does so, then he is not unfairly blamed. God for his part is ready to give grace to all: *who will have all men saved, and to come into the*

[1] John iii. 36.
[2] Matt. xxv. 34, 41.
[3] Job xxi. 14.
[4] Job xxiv. 13.

knowledge of the truth.[1] Those only are deprived of grace who of themselves offer hindrances to it. The sun shines on the whole world, nobody could see but for its light; if somebody blunders into something unseeing because he keeps his eyes shut he has only himself to blame.

215, 247, 569   III *Contra Gentes*, 160

303. There are two phases in sin, the turning away from God and the turning to some attraction. Forgiveness concerns the first, and its consequences, not the second. A man may give up what attracted him, or even turn to a contrary object; his sin is not thereupon forgiven.

231, 629   Disputations, xxviii *de Veritate*, 2

304. The act of sin may pass, and yet the guilt remain.

266   *Summa Theologica*, 1a–2ae. cix. 7

305. A man fallen into sin is quite unable to rescue himself without the help of grace. His sin lay in giving up God, and he is not recovered until he holds to God again. This he can do only by charity, which comes not of his sole choice, but from *the Holy Ghost which is given to us.*[2]

407, 628   Disputations, xxiv *de Veritate*, 12, *ad* 11, ii

306. *Perseverance* may stand for a special virtue, that habit of which the act is the proposal to stick firmly to virtue; it is present in all who are in grace, though some may not in fact persevere to the end. Or it may stand for a special circumstance of virtue, namely, its actual endurance to the moment of death: this is not in our power to command.

250, 413, 629   Disputations, xxiv *de Veritate*, 13, *ad* 3

307. God's love for us is not greater in heaven than it is now.

389, 661   v *Quodlibets*, iii, 6, *ad* 2

[1] 1 Tim. ii. 4.   [2] Rom. v. 5.

ii. *Definition and Divisions*

308. God is the life of the soul—as the efficient cause, not the formal cause.

127   *Disputations, de Caritate,* 1, *ad* 1

309. Whatsoever is called good is good by the divine goodness, which is its first exemplar cause, its effective cause, and its final cause.

63, 183, 327   *Summa Theologica,* 1a. vi. 4

310. Is grace a positive effect in the soul? According to usage, grace is taken in two senses. First, to mean what is freely given, as when we say, I give you this grace or do you this favour. Secondly, to mean the acceptance and reception of such a boon, as when we say, this man enjoys the king's favour. The two are connected, for nothing is bestowed on an unwilling recipient.

Divine grace may be similarly divided. In one sense it is called grace freely bestowed, *gratia gratis data,* which in technical theology usually stands for the special gifts of prophecy, wisdom, and the like: into such grace we are not at present inquiring, for clearly it is a reality created in the soul. In the second sense, grace is called sanctifying grace, *gratia gratum faciens,* and this, which renders a man agreeable to God, is our topic. That it presupposes the activity of God accepting a man is clear; what is in question is whether it produces a real effect in the man.

Some have denied it, contending that this grace is not in the soul, but only in God. Their opinion cannot be sustained, because for God to love something is the same as for God to will it good. To all things he grants the natural benefits they have: *all things thou lovest.*[1] All

[1] Wisd. xi. 25.

things he approves: *God saw everything that he had made, and, behold, it was very good.*[1] But such endowments do not move us to say that their recipients enjoy the grace of God, for the term is restricted to those to whom God wills a supernatural good, namely, life everlasting: *the grace of God is eternal life.*[2]

By nature we are not worthy of such a blessing, since it is supernatural. Therefore, if we suppose that God shows us this favour, we suppose too that he makes us deserving beyond our natural merits. Not that anything in us influences God to bring us to eternal life, but rather the converse; because God freely moves us to eternal life he grants us that which makes us fit to receive it: *who hath made us worthy to be partakers of the lot of the saints in light.*[3]

The reason is this. As God's knowledge is the cause of all things (unlike ours which is caused by things), so God's will effects good (unlike ours which reacts to good). Hence we are said to have divine grace, not only because God moves us to eternal life, but also because he gives us the gift of being worthy, which gift is called sanctifying grace. Otherwise, if grace meant only divine acceptance, a sinner might be said to be in grace, for he may well be predestined to heaven. Sanctifying grace, therefore, can also be called grace freely given, but not every *gratia gratis data* makes us worthy of heaven.

69, 127, 300, 522   Disputations, xxvii *de Veritate*, 1[4]

311. A positive reality is put into a person who receives

[1] Gen. i. 31.   [2] Rom. vi. 23.   [3] Col. i. 12.
[4] The text introduces the distinction between sanctifying grace, *gratia gratum faciens*, and miraculous grace, *gratia gratis data*. Under the heading of sanctifying grace come actual grace, which moves the soul to conversion and acts of virtue, and habitual grace, a permanent quality in the soul. The controversies about grace and freewill concern actual grace.

grace: there is, first, the gift freely given him, and next, his response and acknowledgement.

408, 602 *Summa Theologica*, 1a–2ae. cx.1

312. God's grace does not consist solely in an act of divine will; it implies a real effect as well. *Blessed is the man unto whom the Lord imputeth not iniquity*[1]—a man who is not charged with sin is in a real and positive condition.

346, 412, 417, 564 *Summa Theologica*, 1a–2ae. cxiii. 2, *ad* 2

313. Grace in man is like a formal cause, not an efficient cause, making him gracious before God. Through grace he is justified and rendered worthy to be called pleasing to God.

286, 401 *Summa Theologica*, 1a–2ae. cxi. 1, *ad* 1

314. Grace is a glow of soul, a real quality, like beauty of body. God's favour helps us in two ways: first, by moving us to know, will, and do; at this stage his generous effect in us is not a settled quality but a transient motion: secondly, by infusing a habit into us, a supernatural settled form and disposition according to which we are moved readily by him and congenially towards everlasting life; at this stage grace is a kind of quality.

Summa Theologica, 1a–2ae. cx. 2

315. Grace is not a habit in the strict sense of the term, because it is not immediately directed towards activity, as the virtues are, but it causes a spiritual condition of being in the soul: it is a disposition to glory, which is consummate grace.[2]

347 Disputations, xxvii *de Veritate*, 2, *ad* 7

[1] Ps. xxxi. 2.
[2] In other words, habitual grace is what in later scholastic language is called an *entitative habit*, like beauty or good health, not an *operative habit*, like faith, justice, or science.

316. Grace and virtue are not identical. The powers of the soul are the immediate subjects of virtues; they are, as such, faculties of activity, ripe to be perfected by virtues which are proximate preparations to act well. Grace, however, is in the soul's substance, granting a new kind of spiritual being, rendering it like God and *a partaker of the divine nature.*[1]

4I5   Disputations, xxvii *de Veritate,* 6

317. Mind is made to the image of God when mindful of him and bearing him; mind is present to itself and to God before it is roused by ideas taken from sense.

400, 412   Disputations, x *de Veritate,* 2, *ad* 5

318. The grace which joins man to God is called sanctifying grace, *gratia gratum faciens.* The grace which makes him help another to come to God is called a special gift, *gratia gratis data,* because granted beyond natural abilities and personal merits. We do not speak of it as sanctifying grace because it is a help given, not to render the recipient righteous, but rather that he may co-operate in the sanctification of others: *the manifestation of the Spirit is given unto every man unto profit*[2]—the profit, namely, of others.

310, 462, 522   *Summa Theologica,* 1a–2ae. cxi. I

319. The recipient of these special gifts, for instance, prophecy, the working of miracles, the word of knowledge, is not thereupon himself made pleasing to God, or united to God, except by some resemblance. What joins man to God is another type of grace, sanctifying grace, which is not only freely given but also renders a man pleasing to God. It unites him to God through charity. *He who is joined in the Lord is one spirit.*[3] God dwells with him: *if any man love me, he will keep my*

[1] 2 Pet. i. 4.   [2] 1 Cor. xii. 7.   [3] 1 Cor. vi. 17.

word, and my Father will love him, and we will come to him, and will make our abode with him.[1] And he is in God: *he that dwelleth in love dwelleth in God, and God in him.*[2] Of this grace St. Paul speaks, when after enumerating special gifts he concludes, *if I have not charity I am nothing.*[3] It is common to all the saints, and Christ prayed that his followers might have it: *that all may be one, as thou, Father, in me, and I in thee; that they also may be one in us.*[4]

397   *Compendium Theologiae,* 214

320. Prophecy has no necessary connexion with charity, and for two reasons. First, prophecy is in the reason, charity in the will. Knowing precedes loving, and consequently some qualities of mind, such as faith and prophecy, do not depend on charity. Secondly, prophecy is given, not for the prophet's sake, but for the building up of the Church. In some ways a man can usefully serve the Church even when he is not good, that is, joined to God by charity. Prophecy and miracles, like ecclesiastical authority and so forth, can be present sometimes without charity.

364, 487   *Disputations,* XII *de Veritate,* 5

321. Prophecy is a transient gleam, not a steady light.

Disputations, XII *de Veritate,* 1, *ad* 12, *i*

322. *The God of all comfort, who comforteth us in all our tribulation, that we may be able to comfort them which are in any trouble.*[5] God imparts special gifts to some that they may help others; such is the providential order. Light is given to the sun, not to shine alone on itself, but also on the whole earth. Hence God wills that all our gifts, of wealth, of power, of knowledge,

---

[1] John xiv. 23.   [2] 1 John iv. 16.
[3] 1 Cor. xiii. 2.   [4] John xvii. 21.   [5] 2 Cor. i. 4.

should benefit others. We can comfort others by the example of our own happiness. You cannot know how to comfort others unless you yourself are at peace. *The Spirit of the Lord hath sent me to bind up the broken-hearted.*[1]

399, 462   Commentary, *2 Corinthians,* i, *lect.* 2

323. In prophecy we may distinguish the gift and the use. The gift surpasses human faculty, and is communicated by God, not by any created power. The use of prophecy, however, may be under human control to some extent: *the spirits of the prophets are subject to the prophets.*[2] For a person can hinder the working of prophecy, which requires certain psychological and moral predispositions.

247   Disputations, XII *de Veritate,* 4

iii. Cause and Effects

324. From all eternity some are preordained and directed to heaven; they are called the predestined ones: *having predestinated us unto the adoption of children according to the good pleasure of his will.*[3] From all eternity, too, it has been settled that others will not be given grace, and these are called the reprobate or rejected ones: *I loved Jacob, and I hated Esau.*[4] Divine choice is the reason of the distinction: *according as he has chosen us in him before the foundation of the world.*[5]

154, 335   III *Contra Gentes* 164

325. Christ's merit stands equally for all human beings as regards its sufficiency, not its efficacy, for this last comes partly from human freewill, partly from divine

[1] Isa. lxi. 1.   [2] 1 Cor. xiv. 32.
[3] Eph. i. 5.   [4] Mal. i. 2–3.   [5] Eph. i. 4.

election, by which the effects of Christ's merits are mercifully conferred on some, and by just judgement denied to others.

522   Disputations, xxix *de Veritate*, 7, *ad* 4

326. *To destine* means to aim; *to predestine* adds a reference to the future—things can be predestined which do not yet exist. On both counts predestination is a part of Providence, but on two counts it differs. First, because Providence, the universal ordering of things, applies to everything which God arranges for, whether they be rational or irrational, good or evil, whereas predestination is to an end special to rational creatures, namely everlasting life, and therefore in this world is restricted to human beings and the means to their salvation.

The other difference is this. When things are directed to an end we may distinguish between the plan and its outcome: not everything directed to an end succeeds in reaching it. Providence supplies the plan, and directs all human beings to happiness. Predestination, however, relates to the success of the plan, and applies only to those who will actually reach heaven.

God predestines because he loves. His choice is implied; he selects those who are infallibly directed to heaven from among others who are not so blessed. The choice is not dictated by any goodness to be discovered in those who are chosen; there is no antecedent merit prompting God's love. *The children being not yet born, neither having done any good or evil, that the purpose of God according to election might stand, not of works, but of him that calleth, it was said unto Rebecca, The elder shall serve the younger. As it is written, Jacob have I loved, but Esau have I hated.*[1] Predestination

---

[1] Rom. ix. 11–13.

supposes dilection and election. Two effects follow, the obtaining of the end, namely glory, and the giving of help, namely grace: these are its two effects.

300, 306   Disputations, vi *de Veritate*, 1

327. *Not by works of righteousness which we have done, but according to his mercy he saved us.*[1] God saves us by predestining us to heaven, and not because of the foreknowledge of our merits.

Predestining is an act of will; therefore we inquire into its cause by inquiring into God's motive. Now as regards the activity of divine will, that is uncaused; but as regards the things willed, they can be arranged according to causal categories. No one is silly enough to suppose that divine activity is prompted by our deserving; the question turns on this point: Can we find a reason in its course why human life should climb to heaven? In other words: Has God preordained that he will achieve the effect of predestination on account of our preceding merits?

Some have thought that the decisive factor was the merits of a previous existence. Such was Origen's position, who held that human souls are born in various stages of union with the corporeal world because of what they did long ago. But this we can pass by, for *the children being not yet born, neither having done any good or evil, that the purpose of God according to election might stand, not of works, but of him that calleth.*[2]

Others have thought that previous merits in this life provide a preliminary cause for predestination. The Pelagians held that the effort which begins a good life comes from us, its completion from God; predestination is achieved in one and not in another because he makes a start by giving himself over to preparing him-

---

[1] Tit. iii. 5.   [2] Rom. ix. 11.

self. But against this, *we are not sufficient of ourselves to think of anything as of ourselves, but our sufficiency is of God.*[1] As regards activity properly human no earlier principle can be discovered than taking thought. Therefore, the beginning of salvation is from no exertion of ours.

Others again have suggested that merits subsequent to predestination offer the clue; in this sense, that God gives grace to a person, and preordains that he will give grace, because he foresees that it will be turned to good account, as a king may present a knight with a horse well knowing that the animal will be made good use of. This, however, seems to dissect one single living activity into what is from grace and what is from free-will. Clearly the role of grace is an effect of, and gathered up under, predestination, and therefore cannot be its cause. Could we isolate anything on our part which caused predestination, it would be antecedent or concomitant to predestination. But in truth you cannot split what is from freewill from what is from predestination, just as you cannot split the activity of a secondary cause from that of its first cause. Divine Providence produces its effects through secondary causes; therefore the result of freewill is also the result of predestination.

We are well advised to look twice at the effect of predestination, first, at its particular detail, next at the total situation. Taking it phase by phase, there is nothing to stop one effect of predestination from being the reason and cause of another; a later phase may be the purpose or final cause of an earlier, and that phase may be the meritorious cause of a later—a meritorious cause is a type of dispositive cause which prepares the material, and can be placed under the heading of the material

[1] 2 Cor. iii. 5.

cause.[1] Thus we may say that God preordains that he will give grace that glory may be merited, and that he will give glory from merits. But if we judge the whole sweep of predestination, then we must conclude that in ourselves alone there are no grounds at all for the whole general effect. Anything human that serves salvation is entirely comprehended in the effect of predestination, including man's preparation for grace: *turn thou us unto thee, O Lord, and we shall be turned.*[2] God's goodness provides the reason, his goodness which is both the final purpose and the active beginning of predestination.

68, 70, 182, 441   *Summa Theologica,* 1a. xxiii. 5

328. Because we are subject to mutation and time, in which there is a *before* and *after,* we know events successively—we remember the past, see the present, and foretell the future. But God, who is immune from all change, *I am the Lord and I change not,*[3] is beyond the passage of time, nor is there found in him past or future, for everything is present before him. From eternity he foresees that such a one is about to die at such a time, but this is to speak after our fashion; we should rather say that God sees him dying, as I see Peter sitting down when he does sit down—notice, my vision imposes no necessity on his sitting down.

182, 328   *Letter,* to Bernard, Abbot of Monte Cassino

329. *I work a work in your days, a work which you will not believe, if any man shall tell it you.*[4] Such is God's

---

[1] Recall the four causes: the *final cause,* which answers the question, why?; the *efficient cause,* which answers the question, who?; the *formal cause,* which answers the question, what?; the *material cause,* which answers the question, out of what?

[2] Lam. v. 21.   [3] Mal. iii. 6.

[4] Acts xiii. 41; Hab. i. 5.

love and favour that he does more for us than we can
conceive.

Exposition, *Apostles' Creed*

330. Habitual grace, a gift settled on us by God, calls
for some preparation, for a form cannot exist except
in properly disposed material. Actual grace, which is
God's help moving the soul to good, requires no previous preparation on our part, as though we could make
ourselves ready for divine help. Whatever our preparedness, all comes from God's help moving us to
good. The very movement of freewill itself towards
good which fits us to receive grace is an act of freewill
itself moved by God.

Sometimes a person's preparation for grace is simultaneous with the infusion of grace: his activity is then
meritorious, not of grace, which is already possessed,
but of glory, which he has yet to acquire. Sometimes
the preparation is partial, and so continues some time
before the gift of habitual grace is received: even so, it is
from divine motion, and is not enough for merit, since
the person is not yet justified, and there is no merit
apart from grace.

He cannot prepare himself for grace unless God
anticipates and premoves him to good; it makes no
difference whether the preparation be achieved suddenly or gradually: *it is easy for God to enrich the beggar
in a moment.*[1] Sometimes a person is moved by God
to some particular value, and not to the complete and
eventual good of life; this is anterior to grace. But
sometimes he is completely responsive and receives
grace all at once. *Every one that hath heard of the Father
and hath learned cometh to me.*[2] So it befell Paul

[1] Ecclus. xi. 23.
[2] John vi. 45.

unexpectedly on the road of sin; his heart was touched, he learned, he came.

299, 300, 346 *Summa Theologica*, 1a–2ae. cxii. 2, *c. & ad* 1, 2

331. *Behold, as the clay is in the potter's hand, so are you in my hand.*[1] Nobody receives grace of himself howsoever he prepares himself, even though he does all that lies in his power. Being prepared for grace can be taken in two ways: one, as the effect of human freewill alone, and thus no necessity is postulated that grace must be received, for grace surpasses all human effort; second, as the effect of God's motion, and then a necessity enters, a necessity, not of coercion, but of infallibility, for God's purpose cannot fail. For if it be God's will to touch the heart then grace will infallibly follow.

183   *Summa Theologica*, 1a–2ae. cxii. 3

332. *So then it is not of him that willeth, nor of him that runneth, but of God that showeth mercy.*[2] A man's good intentions and deeds are anticipated by divine help. Success is attributed to the first and overriding cause, rather than to the proximate agents, victory to the general rather than to the rank-and-file. Not that a man's freewill is ruled out, as some have misconstrued, for he is master both of his interior and of his exterior activity, but that he is subject to God.

69   III *Contra Gentes*, 150

333. The more generous and beyond our deserving the deed the more it manifests the gracious goodness of God.

72   III *Sentences*, iv. i. 1

334. One difference between cause and effect is this: cause of cause is also cause of effect, but cause of effect

[1] Jer. xviii. 6.   [2] Rom. ix. 16.

is not necessarily cause of cause. The difference appears in a causal series where the first cause produces its effect through a secondary cause, which consequently somehow causes the effect of the first cause, of which, however, it is not the cause. Now there are two periods in predestination, the eternal ordination, and its temporal effect, which is twofold, grace and glory. Human activity is the meriting cause of glory, but no purely human act merits grace, though natural goodness may dispose to its reception. It does not follow that the cause of our predestination is our activity, either before or after grace.

To discover the cause of predestination, recall that predestining is directing to a goal; it is an act of mind moved by will. Accordingly, to find the reason for predestination we should look for the will's motive. Here we should draw a distinction, and note, first, how the will acts as it needs must from its nature, and secondly, how all the same it can reserve its action. Let me explain. Its bounden activity is set by its last end, from which nothing can divert it; no man can wish not to be happy. The necessity is absolute, and carries with it the hypothetical necessity of willing those things without which this end cannot be gained. But everything else, not being indispensable for this end, though sometimes regarded as helpful to it, is willed, not from the press of the will's nature, but from the will's own free inclination. All the same, on the supposition that the will does make this choice, it becomes committed to all those objects without which its purpose cannot be executed, as when a king of his bounty knights one of his men, and is then obliged to provide him with a horse, for you cannot have a knight without a mount; the horse is due and necessary on the supposition of the preceding royal favour.

Now divine goodness itself is the end and purpose of

the divine will, and it depends on no other good. God
possesses it, and he needs no other good. Therefore, and
in the first place, his will is not set on doing anything
as from obligation, but purely from generosity. However, on the supposition that he wills to create things, it
follows, with some show of right, that they should be
endowed with whatever is needful for their integrity;
if men are to be produced, then they should be made
reasonable. Effects not essential to the things which
God choses to make, however, issue from his sheer
liberality, without our being entitled to them. Both
grace and glory are such perfections, for human nature
can exist without them and they belong to another
world; if God decides to grant them, then they are
pure presents. The motive of such liberality is his over-
flowing love; his own infinite goodness, therefore, is the
cause of predestination.

So may we settle a controversy. Some say that everything comes from God's caprice; others that he has no
choice. Both sides are in the wrong, for the former
treats everything as arbitrary and dissipates the necessary connexions among divine effects, while the latter
treats everything as emanating from God by a kind of
natural necessity. A middle way is to be taken: God's
simple will and pleasure lie at the origin of things, but
they are then given what is their due, always, however,
on the supposition that they have no fundamental claim
in justice. God owes it to himself that they should be
provided with what is meet and proper. Thus his will
is fulfilled. But he is nobody's debtor.

185   Disputations, vi *de Veritate*, 2

335. The causality of reprobation is unlike that of predestination. For predestination is the cause both of
what is awaited in the future, namely glory, and of what

is received in the present, namely grace. Whereas reprobation is not the cause of present fault, but of future
result, namely, of being abandoned by God. Fault is
born of the freewill of the person who deserts grace, and
who, consequently, is rejected.

658   *Summa Theologica*, 1a. xxiii. 4, *ad* 2

336. Why does God choose some and reject others? His
will is the sole reason. Why does he draw this man and
not that? Augustine warns us not to try to judge between them if we do not wish to err.[1] God is not unfair
if he renders unequally to men not unequal. It would
be against justice were the effect of predestination a
debt and not a gift. But without prejudice to justice
you can give presents just as you please, here more, here
less, so long as no one is deprived of what is owing to
him. *Take what is thine, and go thy way. Is it not lawful
for me to do what I will with my own?*[2]

147, 152, 383   *Summa Theologica*, 1a. xxiii. 5, *ad* 3

337. *God our Saviour will have all men to be saved, and
to come to the knowledge of the truth.*[3] The event, however, is otherwise. Therefore, it may be argued, God's
will is not always fulfilled.

I answer that the text can be interpreted in three
ways. First, by accommodating the phrase *all men* to
mean that God wills those to be saved who are saved;
not that no man exists whom he wills not to be saved,
but that no man is saved whom he does not wish to be
saved. Secondly, by taking it to stand for all kinds of
each, not for each of all kinds, meaning that God wills
all conditions of mankind to be saved, men and women,
Jews and Gentiles, great and small, but not all men of

---

[1] *in Joannis Evangelium Tractatus*, xxvi. 6; *PL* xxxv. 1607.
[2] Matt. xx. 14–15.   [3] 1 Tim. ii. 4.

B 4007   N

every condition. Thirdly, the text can refer to his wish, or antecedent will, not to his effective, or consequent will. This distinction arises on the side of the things willed, not on the side of the divine will itself, in which there is no before and after.

To understand the position, reflect that everything inasmuch as it is real and good is willed by God. But something considered at first sight and in the abstract may be good or evil, which then on second thoughts and when placed in its context changes its character. It is good for man to live, bad for him to be killed; but that is in the abstract: taken in the concrete, he may be a murderer and a menace to the community; in which case, it is good for him to be killed, bad for him to live. We can say that a good judge starts off by wanting all men to live, and ends by sentencing a man to be hanged.

Similarly, God antecedently wills all men to be saved, but consequently wills some to be damned, according to the requirements of his justice. Now that which is antecedently willed is not willed outright, but only in a manner of speaking. Things are only downrightly willed when all their surrounding circumstances are taken into account: this is called consequent will. We can say that the just judge chooses the death-sentence in the main, that is what he simply wills, though part of his intention is to let a man go free: this is better called a wish, not a decisive will. Whatsoever God simply wills, that he does; whatsoever he wishes, that may not come about.

183, 380   *Summa Theologica*, 1a. xix. 6 *obj.* 1 *& resp.*

338. Grace has five effects in us: first, our soul is healed; second, we will good; third, we work effectively for it; fourth, we persevere; fifth, we break through to glory.

408   *Summa Theologica*, 1a–2ae. cxi. 3

339. Fundamental health of mind and the first cure from sin come through faith, when we see God's distant brightness through a glass darkly. The next is when we are cured of all fault, penalty, and misery, and are brought to see him face to face. *For we see now through a glass in a dark manner; but then face to face.*[1]

374   Disputations, x *de Veritate*, 11, *ad* 9

340. *To live is Christ, to die is gain.*[2] St. Paul is speaking strictly, for anybody reckons it gain when his life is bettered, as when from sickness he recovers his health. *Your life is hid with Christ in God.*[3] This is not yet full life: *whilst we are at home in the body, we are absent from the Lord.*[4] When we die, our life will be improved, for then we shall be present to Christ.

290, 400   Commentary, *Philippians*, i, *lect.* 3

341. The sinner is justified by God moving him to righteousness: *it is God that justifieth the ungodly.*[5] Now God moves all things according to the mode of each, and men according to the proper condition of human nature, to which freewill is essential. In those who can exercise their freewill the motion from God to righteousness is not without a motion of freewill; he infuses justifying grace in such wise that he moves at the same time the freewill to accept the gift.

331   *Summa Theologica*, 1a–2ae. cxiii. 3

342. No one who has the use of freewill can be justified without its exercise in the very instant of his justification. In those, however, who are not responsible agents, such as babies and children, this is not required.

607   Disputations, xxviii *de Veritate*, 3

---

[1] 1 Cor. xiii. 12.   [2] Phil. i. 21.
[3] Col. iii. 3.   [4] 2 Cor. v. 6.   [5] Rom. iv. 5.

343. Effectual causal activity covers effects as to their mode of coming into existence and remaining in existence as well as the mere fact of their production. The divine will, the most effectual of all causes, gets its effect in every way. God wills that some things should come about as necessary effects, and others as contingent effects, in order to compose the harmony and integration of the universe. The principles of determinism and of indeterminacy are both at work, for he furnishes necessary and unfailing causes for some effects, and contingent and variable causes for others. The contingency of these last is defined by their nexus with their proximate causes, not with their first cause. They are contingent because God wills them so to happen by equipping their contingent causes.

183, 417   *Summa Theologica*, 1a. xix. 8

344. Reward is what you receive, merit what you do. The first is in the mind, the second in the will through charity.

327, 461, 465   *Disputations*, xiv *de Veritate*, 5, *ad* 5

345. Eternal life consists in enjoying God. The motion of the human spirit to this end is the proper act of charity, which sets in order all acts of the other virtues, since all are summoned by charity. The meriting of eternal life relates primarily to charity, secondarily to the other virtues.

399, 486, 554   *Summa Theologica*, 1a–2ae. cxiv. 4

346. Any deliberate act without exception done from a state of grace is meritorious.

294, 314   *II Sentences*, xl. i. 5

VI

The Theological Virtues[1]

347. Habits[2] vary in kind according to the formal differences of the objects with which they deal. The object of any theological virtue is God himself, the final end of everything, here taken precisely as existing outside the field unaided reason can work. The objects of the other two classes of virtues, namely the intellectual virtues and the moral virtues, are inside this field. The theological virtues, therefore, differ from them in kind.

216, 283, 315, 355, 371, 407, 416
Summa Theologica, 1a–2ae. lxii. 2

348. Although the theological virtues co-exist with the intellectual and moral virtues in the same human subject, their object is different, being our ultimate end

---

[1] Sanctifying grace quickens the human substance and thence spreads into the psychological abilities, or faculties of activity. The heightened qualities of these powers of action are called virtues. The highest are the three theological virtues, which not only go to God but also touch him. Faith is the mind's assent to his truth above all, hope the will's trust in his powerful and promised mercy, charity our love of God for his own sake. Charity, however, is more than a sublime and disinterested affection; it is an act of friendship which, taking as well as giving, is founded on intercourse with God's intimate life and communicates in the knowledge and love of the blessed Persons of the Trinity.

[2] A habit (*habitus*, ἕξις), a psychological quality which gives a psychological ability, or faculty, a bent to a type of action. Virtues are good habits, and are defined by the kind of moral good they achieve. Fair dealing with others is not precisely identical with controlled emotion within oneself; justice, therefore, and temperance are correspondingly distinct.

itself, not, as with the other types of virtue, a penulti-
mate end leading to it.

292, 457   Disputations, XIV *de Veritate*, 3, *ad* 9

349. They are the virtues which make us well adjusted
to our last end, which is God himself: hence they are
called theological, for they not only go out to God
but also reach him. To be well adjusted to an end we
must know and desire it; the desire demands that we are
in love with this end and are confident we can attain
it. The theological virtues are therefore three—*faith*,
which makes us know God; *hope*, which makes us look
forward to joining him; *charity*, which makes us his
friends.

284, 571, 642   Disputations, *de Virtutibus in communi*, 12

350. *Praise him and extol him as you will, he is beyond
all praising.*[1] A theological virtue strikes no mean
between extremes. For the virtuous mean of which the
moralists write is taken by reference to some standard
or measure, and is observed neither by excess nor defect.
A theological virtue can be measured either by what the
virtue itself demands or by what our capacity allows.
Regarding the first, God himself is the rule and mode
of virtue: our faith is measured by divine truth, our
hope by the greatness of his power and faithful affection, our charity by his goodness. His truth, power,
and goodness outstretch any measure of reason. We
can certainly never believe, trust, or love God more
than, or even as much as, we should. Extravagance is
impossible. Here is no virtuous moderation, no reasonable mean; the more extreme our activity, the better
we are.

74, 439, 452   *Summa Theologica*, 1a–2ae. lxiv. 4

[1] Ecclus. xliii. 33.

351. The real meaning of existents rules and measures truth in the human mind. The accuracy, or otherwise, of our perception depends on adjustment to an object just as it is, no more, no less; so the intellectual virtues strike a mean regarding their proper objects. Theological virtues, however, are engaged with the first measure of all reality, and this is a measure which cannot be measured. About their activity, consequently, there is no balance between extremes, no question of having their objects 'just so', they are not poised between *more* and *less*; indeed, to touch the ultimate at all is enough for them. All the same, some sort of centre can be found in their material context. For example, Christian faith goes midway between confusing the divine Persons with Sabellius and dividing the divine nature with Arius. Then again, although we cannot rely too extravagantly on divine help, Christian hope nevertheless must pick a path among the means to salvation.

11, 177, 374   Disputations, *de Spe*, 1, *ad* 7

352. Our interior activities can be about ends, which are desired for their own sakes, or about means to ends, such as exterior activities, whereby we offer our bodily service to God. There is no economizing with ends; the more we press towards them so much the better. Means, however, are measured by ends; a doctor, though seeking to give health as much as he can, will not be unstinting with his medicine. No limit can be drawn to faith, hope, and charity: the more a man believes, trusts, and loves, the better he is. Let discretion, however, mark their exterior expression, which should be tempered by loving kindness.

73, 483   Commentary, *Romans*, xii, *lect.* 1

I. FAITH

353. *Now thanks be unto God, who always causeth us to triumph in Christ, and maketh manifest the savour of his knowledge.*[1] Between knowledge through science and knowledge through faith there is this difference: science shines only on the mind, showing that God is the cause of everything, that he is one and wise, and so forth. Faith enlightens the mind and also warms the affections, telling us not merely that God is first cause, but also that he is saviour, redeemer, loving, made flesh for us. Hence the phrase, *maketh manifest the savour of his knowledge*; its fragrance is diffused far and wide. *Behold, the smell of my son is as the smell of a field which the Lord hath blessed.*[2]

10, 17, 19, 413   Commentary, *2 Corinthians*, ii, *lect.* 3

354. By faith the Christian soul enters, as it were, into marriage with God: *I will espouse thee to me in faith.*[3] Human virtue will disappoint us, even the noblest, unless we recognize eternal and immortal good. Before Christ's coming no philosopher by his entire sustained effort could have known as much about God and the truths necessary for salvation as can a humble old woman now that Christ has come. Were we able of ourselves to understand all things, visible and invisible, it might be foolish to believe what we do not see. But in fact our knowledge is so meagre that no scientist can ever completely expose the nature of a midge—we read of one researcher who spent thirty years in solitude in order to learn all about bees.

22, 179, 458   Exposition, *Apostles' Creed*

[1] 2 Cor. ii. 14.   [2] Gen. xxvii. 27.
[3] Hos. ii. 20.

i. *Object*

355. A thing engaged by a habit of knowledge can be taken at two levels: first, there is the underlying subject or *material-object*; second, the special aspect or *formal-object* which is studied. For example, geometry draws conclusions about things in the world about us; these, which are its material objects, on being treated in the medium of its theorems, then light up with the formal demonstrated truth of geometry. So also with faith. Nothing less than First Truth is its formal object; the motive for every assent it makes is divine revelation. The medium in which it works is divine truth, and yet it takes as its material many other things, although these enter only when they bear some relation to God, being effects of the Divinity which help men in their pilgrimage towards enjoying God. Even so First Truth remains the main object of faith, just as *health* dominates every medical interest.

8, 347, 577   *Summa Theologica*, 2a–2ae. i. 1

356. Let us try to describe how First Truth is the object of faith. No habit is a virtue unless its activity is reliably good, otherwise a virtue would not be the steady perfection of an ability. An intellectual act is good by engaging what truly is; no habit of mind is a virtue unless its activity is infallibly set on expressing truth. For this reason the habits of insight into principles and of inferring scientific conclusions are virtues, but opinion is not a virtue.[1] Now faith cannot be ranged with the intellectual virtues because its object is evident, for in fact it is unseen. If faith is a virtue then this can only be because it holds fast to testimony which cannot deceive or be deceived. As creaturely reality is

[1] *Ethics*, vi. 3, 1139^{b}10.

vanity and loss unless embraced in uncreated reality,
so creaturely truth is deceptive unless supported by
uncreated truth. Men, and angels too, promise no
infallible witness unless God's authority speaks through
them.

The virtue of faith causes the mind to assent to
a truth which, transcending human understanding,
is held in divine knowledge. The believer, observes
Dionysius, is freed from variable and inconstant error
by God, who possesses simple and constant truth.[1]
Immediately and principally this truth is of uncreated
reality, and thence descends to creatures. Men accept
God's knowledge by faith and are joined thereby to
him. Faith's principal object is God himself; other
things are subsidiary and dependent.

40, 204, 217, 417   Disputations, xiv *de Veritate*, 8

357. Among the many articles of faith some are about
the divinity, others about the manhood assumed by the
Son of God, others about the effects of God, yet the
whole basis of faith is God's own first truth, on which
rest all the other truths that faith takes in. *You believe in
God, believe also in me*,[2] says our Lord, so giving us to
understand that he is believed because he is God.

34, 525   Exposition, *First Decretal*

358. The authority of faith derives from the revelation
of the Father through the Son and the Holy Ghost, not
from angels or miracles, though in certain cases truths
of faith have been disclosed through angels, for instance, to Zachary and Mary, also to Joseph, and many
miracles have been wrought to support them.

193, 197   *Contra Errores Graecorum*, 30

---

[1] *de Divinis Nominibus*, vii. 14; *PG.* iii. 871.
[2] John xiv. 1.

359. Though they may be about the same fact, for example, Christ's Passion, faith and prophecy do not deal precisely with the same meaning there. Faith bears on the underlying eternal truth, namely that God suffered for us, and this is its formal interest, embodied in the historical event, which is its material context. With prophecy, however, it is the other way round, the fulfilment comes first, the religious truth afterwards.

27, 319   III Sentences, XXIV. 1. *iii, sol.* 1, *ad* 3

360. Miracles demonstrate the veracity of the announcer, not directly the truth of what he preaches.

193   III Sentences, XXIV. i. 4, *ad* 3

361. An author who writes about a far country he has never seen is not believed as though he had actually travelled there. Before Christ's coming, the patriarchs and prophets talked to us about the Kingdom of God, but we do not believe them as we do Christ, who was with God, who indeed is one with God.

86, 123, 496   Exposition, *Apostles' Creed*

362. *The Samaritans said to the woman, We now believe, not for thy saying, for we ourselves have heard him, and know that this is indeed the Saviour of the world.*[1] Natural reason, the testimonies of the Law and Prophets, the preaching of the Apostles and others—these three lead us to faith in Christ. But once a person has been led to believe, then can he confess that these are not the reasons why he believes; instead his motive is divine truth itself.

196   Commentary, *St. John,* iv, *lect.* 5

363. The first motive for belief may come either from created things, as when we are led by prodigies to believe truths about God or other things, or from uncreated truth itself, as when we believe what God

[1] John iv. 42.

tells us through his ministers. The first sort of faith exists in demons, for by their natural intelligence as well as by the miracles they see—and much more penetratingly appreciate than we do—they are forced to believe truths beyond their natural powers. Their assent, however, arises not from the infused virtue of faith, but from their natural ingenuity.

194   *III Sentences*, xxiii. iii. 3. *ii, sol.* 1

364. A truth of faith is assented to because the will so commands, not because the inner evidence is immediately seen or inferred. The will's own motives are of two kinds. First, when its impulse to moral good is at work; then belief is praiseworthy. Second, when the object of belief, though not evident in itself, is recognized to be credible and to demand belief: for instance, if a moral teacher foretold a future event, and backed up his exhortations by raising somebody from the dead, the listener would be convinced that he was hearing the word of the Lord, who cannot deceive, though the future event itself is not yet verified. Such corroborative proof leaves the character of faith intact.

Faith as a good moral act exists and is praised among Christ's faithful. Notwithstanding their lack of the virtue of faith, the devils assent from merely intellectual conviction: *the devils also believe and tremble.*[1] They see manifest signs; they well apprehend that the Church's doctrine is from God, though they do not see into its mystery. They believe that God is three in one, but without sight of this mystery. Their conviction, as it were forced from them by the evidences, is not a gift of grace; the very perspicacity of their natural intelligences drives them to assent.

370, 374, 377   *Summa Theologica*, 2a–2ae. v. 2, c. & *ad* 1, 2

[1] James, ii. 19.

365. The senses cannot penetrate into intellectual truth; neither they nor the natural reason can search into the things that are of the Spirit of God; the Spirit of God knows them, but no creature of himself. Nevertheless the mind of the spiritual man is enlightened by the Spirit of God, and his will is kindled; he himself can no more be judged by a sensual man than a man awake by one asleep.

458, 462   Commentary, *1 Corinthians*, ii, *lect.* 3

366. Known is within knower after the mode of the knower. The proper mode of the human mind is to know truth by passing affirmative or negative judgements: things in themselves simple are expressed in a composite manner. Conversely, the divine mind conceives in simplicity things that are composite. Consequently, the object of faith can be doubly considered, in itself and in the human mind. Though in reality the thing believed by faith is simple, in the believer it takes on the complex form of a proposition.

172, 463, 579   *Summa Theologica*, 2a–2ae. i. 2

367. The Creed does not say *that God is almighty*, but, *I believe in God almighty:* the turn of phrase indicates that the believer's mind goes out to the thing believed, without delaying on a proposition about it. As in science so in faith—we formulate propositions in order to reach things.

47, 351, 577   *Summa Theologica*, 2a–2ae. i. 2, *ad* 2

368. *When he shall appear, we shall be like him; for we shall see him as he is.*[1] The heavenly vision will be of First Truth itself, not of any substitute for it; the act will be a simple sight, not a judgement expressed in a proposition.

172, 670   *Summa Theologica*, 2a–2ae. i. 2, *ad* 3

[1] 1 John, iii. 2.

369. Propositions pertain to faith directly and indirectly. Directly, when they deal with key-points of revelation—that God is three and one, that the Son of God was made flesh, and so forth—here false statements introduce heresy, particularly when they are clung to. Indirectly, when they deal with points from which conclusions contrary to faith can be inferred—for instance, if by denying that Samuel was the son of Elkanah you implied that Scripture was at fault: such false opinions may be entertained without danger of incurring heresy before the implication has been drawn, particularly if you are not stubborn about them. But when their consequences become manifest, and, above all, when the Church has issued a ruling on the subject, then heresy is incurred if the errors are persisted in. That is why people are heretics now who would not have been reputed such before their conclusions had been pressed.

37, 458, 583   *Summa Theologica*, 1a. xxxii. 4

370. The infused light of the habit of faith discovers the meaning of the articles of the Creed just as the mind's natural power of abstraction discovers the first evidences of reason.

41, 462   *III Sentences*, xxiii. ii. 1, *ad* 4

371. A habit is more directly concerned with its specific interest than with the surrounding context. Change the first, and the appropriate type of habit too is altered. The specific interest of faith is First Truth, manifested through the teaching of the Church, just as the specific interest of a science is the kind of truth it demonstrates. Imagine a student who has learnt by heart some geometrical conclusions, and repeats them; his assent to them is from opinion, not from scientific knowledge; he possesses the science of geometry only when they are established in his mind by geometric means. A person who holds to the truths of faith without assenting to them through the authority of Catholic doctrine is in a similar case; he lacks the virtue of faith. Accept the authority, and you accept all it teaches: otherwise you follow your private judgement rather than the Church's teaching. So then, if a person pertinaciously disbelieves one article, he is without faith in the other articles of the Creed—I speak of the infused virtue of faith, not of one's own private belief, which is one's own opinion.

347, 458, 583   Disputations, *de Caritate*, 13, *ad 6*

372. The mystery of the Incarnation was announced in two stages. First, the main idea; next, the historical circumstances. The high truth was revealed to angels at the beginning of their beatitude: *the mystery of godliness appeared unto angels.*[1] And for the reason that their occupations are affected by this ruling: *are they not all ministering spirits, sent to minister for men who shall receive the inheritance of salvation?*[2] The historical surroundings, however, of the mystery were not disclosed to all at the beginning.

387, 497, 501   *Summa Theologica*, 1a. lvii. 5

373. *One Lord, one faith, one baptism.*[3] Hold firmly that our faith is identical with that of the ancients. Deny this, and you dissolve the unity of the Church.

Some urge: Cannot we believe different dogmas and yet hold to the same underlying reality? Faith, they say, assents to a thing, not to a proposition about it. Thus, to take one instance, Christ's resurrection is essential to faith, but whether it be put in the past, or the present, or the future is accidental.

[1] 1 Tim. iii. 16.   [2] Heb. i. 14.   [3] Eph. iv. 5.

Yet they are in error, for the assent of faith operates only through a judgement of reason: there is the crisis between human truth or falsehood. When I profess, *I believe in the Resurrection*, you rightly take me to be committed to an assertion about a past historical event; an element of time comes into all our affirmations and negations.[1]

At this point we can pause to note how the object of faith can be considered as it exists in itself and as it exists in us. The real thing is outside the soul, and this, which is the object of belief and makes the virtue of faith what it is, is one and the same for all. But when our minds lay hold of this object, it becomes qualified by our acceptance, and is multiplied into different propositions. Despite this diversification, however, faith is not divided into fragments.

23, 571, 580   *Disputations*, xiv *de Veritate*, 12

ii. *Act*

374. *Faith is the substance of things hoped for, the evidence of things not seen.*[2] Some writers are of the opinion that St. Paul was not proposing to describe what faith is, but what faith does. But may he not provide what amounts in effect to a final definition? True, proper scholastic form is lacking, but all the essential requisites are touched on. After all, philosophers themselves are not always explicit about every logical technicality they use; they suggest that a formal display of definition and demonstration can be provided if called for. So the above definition of faith is complete, exclusive, and not to be improved upon, though it may be paraphrased to advantage.

One characteristic of faith is that the believer's mind

[1] *de Anima*, iii. 6, 430[b]6.   [2] Heb. xi. 1.

is made up for him by his will, which is moved by its own object, namely the good which draws him to his final goal. Consequently he is engaged by a double object, the good and the true, namely the will's own object and motive, and the object to which the mind assents under the will's influence. The ultimate good attracting and moving the will is both natural and supernatural. As natural it lies within the scope of our natural powers; it is the felicity matching human nature about which philosophers discourse—the contemplative happiness of active wisdom, the practical happiness of active prudence spreading out into the activities of the other moral virtues. As supernatural, it exceeds unaided human nature and cannot be reached by our inherited powers; we cannot think it or wish it of ourselves. We are set on this happiness solely by divine liberality: *for since the beginning of the world men have not heard, nor perceived by the ear, neither hath the eye seen, O God, besides thee, what he hath prepared for him that waiteth for him.*[1]

The end is in the beginning: no one is directed to an end unless he be already proportioned to it. Otherwise he would not desire it, for like likes like. The motion of human nature towards happiness starts from the first principles of reason, which are like the seeds of wisdom, and the first principles of the Natural Law, which are like the seeds of the moral virtues. The parallel applies to the world of grace: it is consonant with the way things work that the happiness of eternal life should already be planted in him who has received the promise. Eternal life consists in the full knowledge of God: *this is eternal life, that they may know thee, the only true God.*[2] This supernatural knowledge is now entered into

[1] Isa. lxiv. 4. Cf. 1 Cor. ii. 9.
[2] John xvii. 3.

by faith, which believes, through infused light, truths exceeding our natural wits.

When we discuss a systematic and heterogeneous whole we are accustomed to refer to the first part or the beginning as the substance: thus, the foundation of a house, or the keel of a ship. Hence faith is called the *substance*, and *of things hoped for*, for this touches on the reference of faith to the good which moves the will to influence the mind decisively. The will proposes an object unseen, and therefore not of the sort to elicit a purely intellectual assent, and determines the mind to assent to it.

When an object is evident, and appears clearly to the mind, then it makes up our mind for us. The mind, however, can also be settled by an unseen object, and be quite convinced, because of the influence of the will. Hence the phrase, *the evidence*—another text has *the conviction*—*of things not seen*, indicates the nature of the mind's assent by faith.

To sum up, St. Paul gives us the material of faith— *the things which appear not*; the act of faith—*the evidence*, or *conviction*; and the purpose of faith—*the substance of things hoped for*. The act implies the habit and the subject, namely the mind. No more is required, and his definition can then be set out in more formal fashion: faith is a habit of mind, which begins eternal life in us, and induces a reasonable assent to things unseen.

This formula separates faith from other functions of mind and will. *Things unseen*—hence it differs from the understanding of principles and the scientific knowledge of conclusions; *evidence*—hence it differs from opinion or doubt, and also from non-cognitive habits; *substance of things hoped for*—hence it differs from belief in the vague sense of the term, including any strong persuasion based on human authority, and also from prudence and other cognitive habits which neither directly deal with ultimates nor immediately set us in proper relation to the things we finally hope for.

11, 209, 217, 459   Disputations, xiv *de Veritate*, 2

375. The will's activity, though perhaps extrinsic to the activity of pure reason, is intrinsic to the activity of faith—just as reason, though outside emotion, is inside temperance.

447, 655   Disputations, xiv *de Veritate*, 3, *ad* 10

376. Will plays the principal role in the knowledge of faith; the mind assents from the impulsion of will, not from any infallible attraction exercised by the very evidence of truth.

290   iii *Contra Gentes*, 40

377. To believe is to assent with cogitation[1]— Augustine's phrase is a good enough definition, and, as I will now explain, enables us to discriminate between faith and all other intellectual operations.

According to Aristotle,[2] our mind has two main operations. The first conceives a simple meaning, such as what we signify by the term *man* or *animal*; neither these simple apprehensions nor their utterance involve truth or falsehood. The second is the act of judgement, affirmative or negative as the case may be; here, and in the sentence which expresses it, the mind adopts a position which is true or false. Now faith resides in a judgement, not in a simple apprehension: we believe or disbelieve true or false statements.

The human mind can be compared to primary matter, which is indeterminate of itself and potential

---

[1] *de Praedestinatione Sanctorum*, 2; *PL* xliv. 963.
[2] *de Anima*, iii. 6, 431ᵃ30.

to all physical forms. Left to itself the mind is able to receive all intelligible objects, and is no more set on a positive statement than on a negative statement about any topic. This indifference disappears when it is moved by a factor other than itself to one or other of alternatives. This movement can come either from its own proper object, namely an evident truth, or from the will, which commands the specifically human activity of our faculties.

Faced by a yea or nay, the receptive mind can be affected in various ways. Sometimes it is swayed neither to one side nor to the other, either because evidence is lacking for both, as in problems about which we have no clue, or because the conflicting evidence appears counterbalancing: this is the state of *doubt*, wavering between alternatives. Sometimes the mind tends more to one side than to the other, yet without being entirely committed; though partially resolved in favour of one, it is not finally decided: this is *opinion*, which accepts one side, yet with the fear that the opposite may be true. Sometimes the mind is quite made up in favour of one side; this may come either from the evidence of the object or from the influence of the will. The evidence of the object may be immediate, as when the truth of a proposition infallibly and at once appears from its very terms (here we have the act of *understanding principles*), or mediate, when the terms of the proposition, having been appreciated, are taken back to evident principles (here we have the *scientific knowledge of conclusions*).

Yet it may happen that the mind cannot take a stand on the internal evidence, either immediately seen, as with principles, or mediately demonstrated, as with conclusions, but comes to a decision under the influence of the will, which resolutely and decisively chooses to

adopt one side, because this is the right and advantageous course to take. The motive is sufficient to
sway the will, though not the mind. Such is *faith*. One
person takes the word of another for the sake of
decency and common sense. Likewise with religious
faith, which is moved by revelation because of the
promise of the reward of eternal life, though the mind
remains blind to the inner evidence of what is proposed.
We can be unwilling about other acts, but believing
can only be willing: Augustine notes that we may go
into the church, approach the altar, take the sacrament
without internal intention about what our body is
doing, but we can make an act of faith only if we
want to.[1]

I have already remarked that neither assent nor
dissent is conveyed by the simple apprehension of
meanings. No judgement is passed, no position either
adopted or rejected. The understanding of principles
conveys an assent, but without deliberation; conviction
comes without pondering the pros and cons. Scientific
knowledge is marked by deliberation and conviction,
but the first causes the second, and the second then
cancels out the first; the scientific process brings principles to bear, and the conclusion is resolved in them.
Once the scientific conviction has been excogitated the
discussion is over. Consequently, cogitation and assent
are not evenly matched.

In the case of faith, however, cogitation and assent
are simultaneous. The assent is effected by the will, not
by taking thought. The mind does not arrive at an
object through its own proper motion, namely by
coming to see the truth; and so it remains restless, and
picks at and turns over what is believed. Its assent is completely unwavering, but nevertheless the mind itself is

[1] *in Joannis Evangelium Tractatus.* xxvi. 6; *PL* xxxv. 1607.

not satisfied, for it has been settled from outside, not from its own object. Hence the believer is said to be captive: *bringing into captivity every thought to the obedience of Christ.*[1] Consequently thoughts may rise up in the believer which are contrary to what he believes: this does not happen in the case of the understanding of principles or the demonstrated knowledge of conclusions.

To sum up: the phrase of the definition, *to assent,* separates faith from simple apprehension, doubt, and opinion, while the phrase, *with cogitation,* separates it from understanding, and the two co-existing separate it from scientific knowledge.

41, 459   Disputations, xiv *de Veritate,* 1.

378. The author of faith is he who produces the believer's assent to the truth declared. Mere hearing is not a sufficient cause. The assent is caused by the will, not by any necessity of reason. And therefore a preacher or herald cannot produce faith. God is the cause of faith, for he alone can alter our wills.

301, 574   Disputations, xxvii *de Veritate,* 3, *ad* 12

379. Faith does not quench desire, but inflames it.

iii *Contra Gentes,* 40

iii. *Necessity*

380. *Without faith it is impossible to please God.*[2] The perfect functioning of a subordinate element in a system requires the combination of two conditions, its own proper motion and the motion of a higher nature, and the concurrence of the two—water's own movement is governed by gravity, its tidal movement by the moon.

Only things of rational nature are immediately

[1] 2 Cor. x. 5.   [2] Heb. xi. 6.

related to God. Lesser things are occupied with particular events, not with universal Being; they partake of divine goodness either because they exist, thus inanimate things, or because they live, thus plants, or because they know incidents, thus animals. Rational beings, on the other hand, are directly related to the universal principle of reality because the universal import of truth and goodness comes to them. The perfection, therefore, of rational natures cannot be estimated from their own native resources, for what they expect from supernatural sharing of divine goodness must also be reckoned with. It is with such considerations in mind that we come to the conclusion that man's ultimate happiness consists in a supernatural vision of God.

Nobody can arrive at this end except by learning the way from God. *Every man that hath heard, and hath learned from the Father, cometh to me.*[1] The discipline has to be undertaken gradually, not suddenly; that is the characteristic process for educating human nature. At the beginning lies belief; as Aristotle remarks, a learner must take things on trust.[2] A disciple must accept what his master teaches him, and so belief in God is a necessary preliminary to the perfect vision of happiness.

19, 40, 293, 503, 569 *Summa Theologica*, 2a–2ae. ii. 3

381. An act, such as faith, which deals with objects outside the range of our natural powers postulates an active settled quality which is given to us, not acquired. The habit of faith helps our minds in two ways: it makes us easy and assured about what should be believed, and discerning about what should be rejected.

53, 414 *III Sentences*, XXIII. iii. 2

---

[1] John vi. 45.
[2] *de Sophisticis Elenchis*, 2, 165[b]3.

382. Nicodemus had not yet arrived at faith when he acknowledged that our Lord was his master and a great man who had wrought marvels. Our Lord, wishing to help Nicodemus to higher knowledge, and suggesting that it was not strange that he himself should be reputed no more than a man, for the secrets of divinity can be reached only through a spiritual rebirth, said, *Amen, amen, I say to thee, unless a man be born again of water and the Holy Ghost, he cannot enter into the kingdom of heaven.*[1] As much as to say, it is not surprising you do not see the kingdom of God, for nobody sees it unless he has received the Holy Ghost, in whom he is born again, a son of God.

299   Commentary, *St. John*, iii, *lect.* 1

383. Divine care supplies everybody with the means necessary for salvation, so long as he on his part does not put up obstacles. If a person, who has been brought up in the backwoods or among beasts, follows his conscience and seeks good and avoids evil, then most assuredly is it to be held that God's internal inspiration will reveal to him the truths necessary for salvation or God will send him a preacher, as when Peter and Cornelius were brought together.[2]

298, 336   Disputations, XIV *de Veritate*, 11, *ad* 1, *i*

384. As sweeping statements the following are false: *he who actually thinks about the articles of faith is bound to believe them*, and, *he who actually thinks about the divine goodness is bound to love it.* A man does not sin when he thinks about the truths of faith without devotion, for topics can be considered merely theoretically and debated in cold blood.

Declaratio CVIII Dubiorum, 88, 89[3]

[1] John iii. 5.   [2] Acts x. 5.
[3] To the Dominican Master General, John of Vercelli, on

385. When reason dawns and deliberation begins, what then first occurs to a person is to take thought about himself. If then he sets himself to his rightful end the grace of forgiveness from original sin descends on him.

222, 607, 629   *Summa Theologica,* 1a–2ae. lxxxix. 6

386. *The Holy Ghost was not yet given, because that Jesus was not yet glorified.*[1] Some heretics have presumptuously seized on this text for saying that God did not dwell by grace among men before the Incarnation. What is true is that the Spirit was not then given with the fullness received by the Apostles after the Resurrection, and that the richness of grace comes to the Church from the Incarnation: *the law was given to Moses, but grace and truth came by Jesus Christ.*[2]

551, 569   *Contra Errores Graecorum,* 16

387. Are the invisible comings of the Divine Persons to men now more full and frequent than they were before the Incarnation? God is always the same, and without shadow of change, though according to historical fitness his wisdom pre-ordains this or that to be done at one period and not at another. It is on the human side that the situation changes. And here we can say that Christ's coming has broken down the old barrier of damnation. The entire human race is now more open to receive grace than before, both because satisfaction has been made and the devil defeated and because Christ's teaching has more clearly revealed divine truth to us.

doubts arising from the *Commentary on the Sentences* by Peter of Tarentaise, a colleague of St. Thomas, afterwards Pope Innocent V.

[1] John vii. 39.   [2] John i. 17.

To speak generally, we have now received more of
God's fullness, although in Old Testament times some
persons received more than we possess, and were better
men. Even so, it was of Christ they received, being
saved by faith in the Mediator. And this, too, is to
speak of their personal grace. For as regards the state
of human nature, it was then still under the sentence
for the sin of our first parents, and still barred against
going to glory. But now the Gospel has been preached,
and all is set for every imperfection of our humanity to
be cleared away.

123, 372, 607   *I Sentences*, xv. v. 2, c. & ad 2

388. *I know that my Redeemer liveth.*[1] The revelation
of Christ was made to many pagans. The Sybils her-
alded some of Christ's mysteries, as Augustine notes.[2]
Roman History records that in the reign of Constantine Augustus and Irene his mother, a tomb was
discovered in which a body was lying with a golden
plate on the breast inscribed, *Christ will be born of a
Virgin, and I believe in him; O Sun, you will see me
again in the time of Constantine and Irene.*[3] If any were
saved to whom revelation was not given, it was not
without faith in the Mediator; the faith, if not explicit, was implicit, for they believed that God would
liberate men and reveal his truths at his own time and
pleasure: *who teachest us more than the beasts of the
earth.*[4]

195, 296, 302   *Summa Theologica*, 2a–2ae. ii. 7, *ad* 3

[1] Job xix. 25.
[2] *Contra Faustum*, xiii. 15; *PL* XLII. 290.
[3] Theophanes, *Chronographia*; *PG* CVIII. 918.
[4] Job xxv. 11.

2. HOPE

389. As such to disbelieve God or to hate him are worse than not to trust him, but as regards their effect on us sins against hope are more dangerous than sins against faith or charity, for when hope dies we lose heart and flounder in wickedness: *if thou faint in the day of peril, little will thy strength avail.*[1]

Summa Theologica, 2a–2ae. xx. 3

390. Hope implies seeking and pursuing, in other words, the appetition of desire, not of delight and joy. It differs from simple desire, first, because desire wants any good that may be offered, and therefore is prompted by that part of us which likes pleasure and shrinks from pain, whereas hope is for a difficult good, and is prompted by that part of us which is prepared to tackle opposition. Secondly, desire may simply want something without reckoning whether it be possible or not, whereas hope is excited by a good which can be secured —indeed it wears an air of confidence.

Thus by four notes of its object is hope distinguished —from fear, because its object is *good*; from joy, because *future*; from desire, because *difficult*; and from despair, because *possible*. An object is possible either because you can obtain it through your own efforts or because you can rely on the help of friends, in which case two elements enter, the good hoped for, and the person who will back you up. No man is able of himself to grasp the supreme good of eternal life; he needs divine help. Hence there is here a twofold object, the eternal life we hope for, and the divine help we hope by.

You cannot hope too much in God; you cannot go amiss by confiding in his help. Hope goes wrong and is

[1] Prov. xxiv. 10.

mistaken when you rely on your own strength, as
when you presume on salvation though remaining
committed to sin.

16, 350, 439   *Disputations, de Spe,* 1, *ad* 1

391. *Be ye therefore followers of God, as dear children;
and walk in love:*[1] this text strikes the authentic note of
living in divine familiarity. God's love cultivates no
private preserve, but goes out universally to all. *All
things that live thou lovest,*[2] and men especially: *yea, he
loved people.*[3] Cyprian declares that this is why our
religion is public and corporate; we pray not for one
alone but for all, for together we form one community.[4]
We must needs pray for ourselves, but love of the
fellowship bids us pray for others. Therefore, we say
Our Father, not *My Father.*

Although our hope rests on divine help, be mindful
how we should lean on one another in order to gain the
more readily what we seek: *in God we trust, who doth
deliver us out of so great dangers, you helping withal in
prayer for us.*[5] And again, *pray for one another, that you
may be saved.*[6] Ambrose notes how petty individuals
wax mighty when they are unanimous and stand
together.[7] The prayers of many cannot fail to be fulfilled. Let us then be emboldened by the promise: *if
two of you shall agree on earth concerning anything they
shall ask, it shall be done for them by my Father who is in
heaven.*[8] Therefore we do not privately petition, but in
common say *Our Father.*

Remember also that we hope in God through
Christ. *Being justified therefore by faith, let us have peace*

---

[1] Eph. v. 1.   [2] Wisd. xi. 27.   [3] Deut. xxxiii. 3.
[4] *de Oratione Dominica,* viii; *PL* iv. 524.
[5] 2 Cor. i. 10–11.   [6] James v. 16.
[7] *Commentaria in Epistolam ad Romanos,* xv. 30; *PL* xvii. 177.
[8] Matt. xvii. 19.

with God through our Lord Jesus Christ: by whom we have access through faith into this grace wherein we stand, and glory in the hope of the glory of the children of God.[1] Through him who alone is God's only begotten and natural son we become God's adopted children: *God sent his son, that we might receive the adoption of sons.*[2] Let not the burden of our prayer diminish his prerogative: Augustine says that we should not claim as ours what belongs to Christ alone; God is the Father of Christ singularly, of the rest of us in common; Christ he begets, men he creates.[3] Therefore we pray, *Our Father.*

72, 77, 129, 551   *Compendium Theologiae*, 251

392. A common cause why hope dies is the failure of the friend on whose help we have relied. That he would like to help is not enough; he must also command the ability. By calling on God as *Our Father* we acknowledge his readiness to help, but lest any doubt linger as to his power to help we add, *Who art in heaven.* In heaven—not as though content to stay there, but as comprehending the universe in one sweep of power: *none but I span the vault of heaven.*[4] He rides above the skies: *thou hast set thy glory above the heavens.*[5] To confess our confidence is to stress his might. Thereby one obstacle to prayer is removed, namely the persuasion that human affairs are settled by the influence of the planets: *be not dismayed by the signs of heaven, as the heathens are.*[6] This strikes at the root of prayer, for if we are bound by fate, how can we, whatever we do, gain blessing and be kept from woe? By appealing to our Father who is in heaven we address ourselves to the mover and master of the high heavens which cannot thwart him.

[1] Rom. v. 1–2.   [2] Gal. iv. 5.
[3] *Sermones dubii*, lxxxiv. 1; *PL* xxxix. 1908.
[4] Ecclus. xxiv. 8.   [5] Ps. viii. 1.   [6] Jer. x. 2.

For prayer to be effective our petitions should be for benefits worthily to be expected from God. *Ye ask, and receive not, because ye ask amiss,*[1] namely for things which smack of earthly, not heavenly wisdom. Chrysostom observes that when we say *who art in heaven,* we do not locate God there, rather our desire forsakes this earth and sets itself on the heavenly places.[2]

Another obstacle to confident prayer is set up when human life is reckoned remote from Providence, as in the ungodly advice of Job's comforter: *thick clouds are a cover to him, that he seeth not, and he walketh in the circuit of heaven.*[3] And again, *hast thou seen what the elders do in the dark, every man in the chambers of his imagery. For they say, The Lord seeth us not, the Lord hath forsaken the earth.*[4] This is the opinion St. Paul attacked in front of the Athenians: *he is not far from every one of us, for in him we live, and move, and have our being.*[5] God sustains our existence, governs our life, and directs our actions: *from the start thy fatherly Providence bringest all things home.*[6]

Even the least and smallest animals are not outside his Providence: *are not two sparrows sold for a farthing? One of them shall not fall on the ground without your Father. The very hairs of your head are numbered.*[7] In comparison with them, how much more are men cherished by Providence: *doth God take care for oxen?*[8] Indeed he does, but not so much as for men, whom he chastises and rewards and pre-ordains to eternity. Let us banish our diffidence, for our Lord heartens us: *fear ye not therefore, ye are of more value than many sparrows.*[9]

[1] James iv. 3.
[2] *In Matthaeum hom.* xix. 4; *PG* LVII. 278.
[3] Job xii. 14.　　　　　　　　[4] Ezek. viii. 12.
[5] Acts xvii. 27–28.
[6] Wisd. xiv. 3.　　　　　　　　[7] Matt. x. 29–30.
[8] 1 Cor. ix. 9.　　　　　　　　[9] Matt. x. 31.

So the Psalmist sings: *the children of men put their trust under the shadow of thy wings.*[1]

He reserves his most special care for those who seek to approach him by faith and love: *draw nigh to God, and he will draw nigh to you.*[2] And again: *the Lord is nigh unto all them that call upon him in truth.*[3] Draws nigh?—more than that, he dwells in them: *thou O Lord art in the midst of us.*[4] Thus is hope increased when we say, *Who art in heaven;* in heaven, that is, expounds Augustine,[5] in the saints. The spiritual distance between the just and sinners is greater than the physical distance between heaven and earth. Symbolically we face the east when we pray and turn to where the heavens light up, for through Christ every saint is granted the dignity of being a heaven in himself: *I have put my words in thy mouth, and I have covered thee in the shadow of mine hand, that I may plant the heavens, and lay the foundations of the earth, and say unto Sion, Thou art my people.*[6]

112, 182, 439   *Compendium Theologiae,* 252

393. Three servants looked forward to the return of their master. One said, 'He will come quickly; I will wait up for him.' The second said, 'He will be late; therefore will I keep awake.' The third said, 'I know not when he will come; therefore will I remain watchful.' Which of these spoke best? The first was at fault, and, if his master delays, will be in danger of falling asleep. The second may also have made a mistake, but he runs no such risk. The third spoke well; he leaves the time open, but remains alert.

[1] Ps. xxxv. 8.   [2] James iv. 8.
[3] Ps. cxliv. 18.   [4] Jer. xiv. 9.
[5] *de Sermone Domini in Monte,* ii. 5; PL xxxiv. 1276.
[6] Isa. li. 16.

It is not good to fix the day and hour of the Lord's coming.

658   Commentary, *St. Matthew*, xxiv. 50

3. CHARITY

394. The beloved may be absent or present, but love stays on.

Summa Theologica, 1a–2ae. xxviii. 1, *ad* 1

395. Love is the effective cause of real union, moving the lover to desire and seek the actual presence of the beloved. But in itself love is but an affective union, a joining of affection. Augustine says that love is a living force, uniting two together, or seeking to unite them.[1]

121, 455, 660   *Summa Theologica*, 1a–2ae. xxviii, 1

396. By knowledge is the beloved said to be in the lover, because embraced in mind: *I hold you in my heart*.[2] Lover is said to be in beloved, because, not content with superficial acquaintance, he strives for an intimate experience and to enter into the very soul of the beloved. Thus Holy Writ speaks of God's Love, who is the Holy Ghost: *he searcheth all things, yea the deep things of God.*[3]

87, 454, 660   *Summa Theologica*, 1a–2ae. xxviii, 2

i. *Friendship*

397. *I will not now call you servants, for the servant knoweth not what the master doeth. But I have called you friends.*[4] This friendship, what is it but charity?

According to Aristotle,[5] not all love amounts to

---

[1] *de Trinitate*, viii. 10; *PL* xlii, 960.
[2] Phil. i. 7.   [3] 1 Cor. ii. 10.
[4] John xv. 15.   [5] *Ethics*, viii. 2, 1155[b]29.

friendship, but only that which goes with active well-wishing. Then others are loved for their own sake; their good is willed; they are sought for themselves, not merely wanted because they are good for us—as when we like wine and horses and so forth, not from friendship, but from desire, for true friendship with a wine or a horse makes little sense.

Nevertheless disinterested affection does not go so far as friendship. For friendship furthermore requires a mutual loving between two persons; friend is friend to friend. There is a basis for such joint devotion, and it is fellowship.

Now men have intercourse with God inasmuch as he shares his own happiness with them. St. Paul speaks of this communion and fellowship which is the basis of friendship: *God is faithful, by whom you are called unto the fellowship of his Son, Jesus Christ our Lord.*[1]

80, 120, 526, 637   *Summa Theologica*, 2a–2ae. xxiii. 1

398. *He who is joined to the Lord is one spirit.*[2] Unity of substance is not signified, but union of friendship, which exists between lover and beloved. Charity is rather the principle than the go-between of this union, for its act of friendship goes out to God directly, without delaying on its own dispositions.

80, 412   *Disputations, de Caritate*, 1, *ad* 3

399. For friends to converse together is the proper condition of friendship. Men's conversation with God is through contemplation. The Holy Ghost makes us God's lovers; therefore also his beholders: *we all with open face beholding as in a glass the glory of the Lord, are changed into the same image from glory to glory, even as by the Spirit of the Lord.*[3]

[1] 1 Cor. i. 9.   [2] 1 Cor. vi. 17.   [3] 2 Cor. iii. 18.

B 4007   P

Next, friends delight in each other's presence, enjoying each other's actions and talk, and finding comfort there in their anxieties. Does trouble come? Then straightaway we seek our friend. We are made friends with God, he dwelling in us and we in him; and so the Holy Ghost, he who is called the Paraclete, the Comforter,[1] consoles us in the set-backs and losses we suffer from this world.

Lastly, friends agree together. Accordingly, instructed by his precepts and moved by the Holy Ghost to fulfil them, we consent to God's will. We are treated like free persons, not like slaves. A freeman is himself responsible for what he does; his will is his own, unlike a slave's, which is another's. The Holy Ghost so moves us that our acts are voluntary, for we are in love, and it is from love we act, not from servile fear. *For ye have not received the spirit of bondage again to fear, but ye have received the Spirit of adoption.*[2]

218, 478, 503, 616, 669   IV *Contra Gentes*, 22

400. God is in things, first, because he is their cause, secondly, because he is the object of their activity, as the known in the knower and as the desired in the lover, and this, the familiar presence of which Gregory speaks,[3] which is proper to human souls, is God's special presence by grace to rational creatures who know him and love him, actually or habitually.

317   *Summa Theologica*, 1a. viii. 3

401. God is in men who are sanctified by grace, and his presence there is of a special kind, not common to other creatures. Not that it sets up any real difference in him, for he is not differently affected by different

---

[1] John xiv. 26.   [2] Rom. viii. 15.
[3] *Glossa ordinaria*, on Cant. v. 17. Cf. *Moralium Liber*, ii. 12; *PL* LXXV. 565.

things. The difference lies on our side. People in grace
have what others lack. Now this is either the Divine
Being or a special divine effect. Not the first, for it is
out of the question for men to be assumed by the Spirit
into a personal union comparable with that of Christ,
the Son of God. It is an effect then, yet not that type of
effect called an activity, otherwise it would be absent
when we were asleep. It is a habit, a settled quality
infused into the soul, whereby the Holy Ghost is said
to dwell in human beings.

123, 310, 452, 485   *I Sentences*, XVII. i. 1

402. The love of our neighbour is included in the love
of God.

131, 143, 409, 486   Commentary, *Galatians*, v, *lect.* 3

ii. *Human Quality*

403. *Master, which is the great commandment of the
law? Jesus said unto him, Thou halt love thy God.*[1]
God's commandments are about virtues. Beyond all
doubt charity is a virtue. Since virtue makes a person
good and render a good account of himself, the virtues
appropriate to him adapt him to his proper good. What
is proper depends on what you mean by man. Man as
such is a rational animal; it follows that his good should
be a reasonable good. Take him as an artist; then what
is good will be found in his work of art. Take him as
a citizen, then in the well-being of the commonwealth.
But always virtue works for good, indeed for good well
performed, that is, voluntarily, readily, pleasurably,
and firmly—these are the characteristics of virtuous
activity, and they cannot be present unless you love
what you are aiming at.

[1] Matt. xxii. 36–37.

Man as man has a certain affinity with the object of human virtue; this is that kind of good called reasonable living. His will has an innate bent towards it. Put him in a less primitive scene, and then he needs virtues additional to these natural aptitudes in order to achieve success. An artist has to be trained to love works of art, a citizen educated to love political probity.

When a man is admitted to citizenship he should have the virtues ensuring that he loves and serves the State. Likewise, when by divine grace a man is set on sharing eternal bliss, which consists in the joyful vision of God, he becomes a citizen and a companion in the blessed society of the Heavenly Jerusalem: *you are fellow-citizens with the saints, and of the household of God.*[1] Definite virtues are required of a man thus enrolled. They are the infused virtues freely given to him, and their activity is prompted by the love of the common good of that perfect society, namely, the divine good which is the heart of happiness.

Loving the community may mean either wanting it or serving it. The first is not necessarily a mark of good citizenship, for a tyrant may seek the public good, but for himself, not for the State; what he seeks in political life is his own aggrandizement. It is the second, a genuine love of the commonwealth, which makes a good citizen; a patriotism which recks little of private interest and risks mortal danger—this is holding one's country dear. Similarly, the desire to possess for oneself the joys of heaven does not necessarily set a person well on the way to them: even the wicked want to be happy. But to love the communion of the saints for its own sake, working to sustain and extend this fellowship, commits us and identifies us with it, and such is charity. Charity loves God for himself, and our neighbour as

[1] Eph. ii. 19.

ourself—for he also is called to the same happiness.
Charity defies the barriers which grave sin would set
up to keep us out. Charity, therefore, is a virtue, indeed
the most potent of virtues.

356, 381   Disputations, *de Caritate*, 2

404. Virtue builds up the good life. But what is good?
Above all it must be measured by the final purpose and
end of human life, and by nothing less.

Ends are twofold, and so, therefore, are human
values. One is ultimate, the others proximate and
particular. Our ultimate and principal good is the
enjoying of God: *it is good for me to cleave to God.*[1]
Secondary ends are themselves twofold: some are true
goods, which mount to the principal good and ultimate
end; others are shams, and entice us away.

Virtue with no reservations about it clearly sets us
on the supreme good of life. Hence Aristotle defines
virtue as the disposition of the perfect to the best.[2] Such
virtue cannot flourish without charity. But if defined
by reference to immediate and particular ends, then
virtue can exist without charity. Any propensity towards
what is good merely in appearance is no true virtue,
but a false show of virtue—thus the prudence of misers
gloating over their gains; their justice disdaining the
property of others only lest they have to pay damages;
their temperance checking luxury because it is expen-
sive; their courage prepared to go through fire and
water to escape poverty.

11, 417, 428   *Summa Theologica*, 2a–2ae. xxiii. 7

405. Charity is the form, mover, mother, and root of
all the virtues.

Disputations, *de Caritate*, 3

[1] Ps. lxxii. 28.   [2] *Physics*, vii. 3, 246^{b}23.

406. Charity is love; not all love is charity.

245   *Summa Theologica*, 1a–2ae. lxii. 2, *ad* 3

407. Peter Lombard held that charity was not a
created reality, but the Holy Ghost dwelling in the
soul[1]—he did not mean that the Holy Ghost was
identified with our movement of love, but that charity,
unlike the other virtues, such as faith and hope, was not
elicited from a habit which was really ours. He was
trying to enhance charity.

Ponder well, and this opinion tends rather to dis-
credit charity. It would mean that active charity rises
from the Holy Ghost so moving the mind that we are
merely passive, and not responsible for our loving or
otherwise. This militates against the character of a
voluntary act. Charity would not then be a voluntary
act. There is a snag here, for our loving is very much
our own.

Nor is the situation eased by the additional qualification that the Holy Ghost moves the will as a principal
cause moves an instrumental cause. An instrument, of
course, is a principle, but not of the kind which decides
its own activity or inactivity. The implication would be
that the voluntary character of charity was made away
with, and merit banished.

No, the Holy Ghost moves the will to love, but in
such a way that we are principal causes.

Active powers perfectly develop their activities only
when these become connatural through qualities which
are part-principles. God, who moves all things to their
due ends, implants in them dispositions to follow the
purposes he assigns to them: *wisdom disposes all things
gracefully*.[2] Certainly charity surpasses the nature of
human will-power, but all the same supernatural

---

[1] *Sentences*, i. xvii. 1.   [2] Wisd. viii. 1.

friendship would compare unfavourably with the physical and psychological dynamism of natural functions and virtues unless a form were granted conducing to its activity. Nor would its exercise be easy and delightful, whereas no virtue compares with charity in eagerness to act and happiness in acting.

For these reasons, then, the activity of charity presupposes the existence within us of a settled disposition over and above kindliness and good-nature, an active quality inclining us to love promptly and pleasurably.

300, 310   *Summa Theologica*, 2a–2ae. xxiii. 2

408. Charity brings to life again those who are spiritually dead. It is the formal cause, not the efficient cause, of this revival; its effective power is limited. You may compare it to the soul of Lazarus, which did not make him rise again, but was a living man because his soul was reunited with his body.

308, 417, 627   *Disputations, de Caritate*, 1, *ad* 24

iii. *Characteristics*

409. *Love thy neighbour as thyself*[1]—*as thyself*, that states the mode for this commandment, composed of the five notes of truth, order, decisiveness, constancy, and fairness.

We should love others truly, for their own sakes rather than our own. There are three types of friendship, one for utility, another for pleasure, a third for virtue. The first will lapse when no further advantage is to be gained, and with the second it is our own pleasure we are after. *Thy boon companions will desert thee when trouble is afoot.*[2] But the third genuinely loves another for his own sake.

[1] Lev. xix. 18; Matt. v. 43.   [2] Ecclus. vi. 10.

We should love others ordinately, and not treat them as though they were God. *He that loveth father and mother more than me is not worthy of me; and he that loveth son or daughter more than me is not worthy of me.*[1]

We should love others effectively, bringing them blessings and protecting them from evil. *Let us not love in word, neither in tongue, but in deed and in truth.*[2] To the same effect St. Paul speaks of *love without dissimulation.*[3]

We should love perseveringly: *a friend loveth at all times, and a brother is born for adversity.*[4] Patience and modesty are among the qualities that strengthen friendship: on the contrary *a wrathful man stirreth up strife*[5] and *by pride cometh contention.*[6]

Lastly our friendship should be pure and holy, not abused by sin. For God says, *abide in me;*[7] he it is *who gives birth to all noble loving.*[8]

486   *de Duobus Praeceptis Caritatis*, 5

410. Some spiritual writers have been persuaded that we should love all our neighbours equally, even our enemies. They were speaking of inward affection, not of outward effect, for where the giving of benefits is concerned the order of love puts the persons who are close to us before those who are distant.

Their position, however, is quite unreasonable, for the affection of charity, following the predilection of grace, is no less unequally distributed than is natural love. Both spring from divine wisdom. Natural attractions vary according to the properties of the things engaged, and the attraction exercised by grace, which comes out through the affection of charity, is modulated by our environment; our attachment is deepest and

[1] Matt. x. 37.   [2] 1 John iii. 18.   [3] Rom. xii. 9.
[4] Prov. xvii. 17.   [5] Prov. xv. 18.   [6] Prov. xiii. 10.
[7] John xv. 4.   [8] Ecclus. xxiv. 24.

most intense to those we respond to most easily. Let us analyse this.

Every activity is proportionate to its object and to its subject. The object determines what kind of activity is put forth, the subject determines its intensity. The object of that friendship called charity is God; the subject is the man who loves. Such differences as are found under the first heading are measured by reference to God: here the governing principle is this, the nearer a person is to God the greater the good we will him. For though charity wills the same kind of good to all, namely eternal happiness, this has different degrees which vary according to their nearness to divine happiness. After all, charity should be fair and observe God's justice, according to which the nobler the soul the more intimately it shares in his joy. Mind you, we are speaking precisely of charity—there are other types of devotion which seek the good of the beloved object. The intensity of charity is measured with reference to the subject, the lover, and here the governing principle is this, the nearer the dearer; we seek the good of those we are in love with more intensely than the greater good we theoretically wish for those who are better.

70, 151, 397   *Summa Theologica*, 2a–2ae. xxvi. 6 and 7

411. For three reasons ought we to be given to hospitality. First, we gain grace, as did the Samaritan woman who talked with Christ. Second, we may frequently receive saints and angels: *be not forgetful to entertain strangers, for thereby some have entertained angels unawares.*[1] Third, we ourselves shall be welcomed into eternal and heavenly dwellings: *I was a stranger and ye took me in.*[2]

400   *Sunday Sermons*, 19[3]

[1] Heb. xiii. 1.   [2] Matt. xxv. 33.
[3] On Epistle, First Sunday after Epiphany.

412. Because we cannot know for certain that we are in charity it does not follow that we cannot love from charity. That we love from charity, that is what is asked of us, not that we know we do: *I know nothing by myself, but he that judgeth me is the Lord.*[1]

206, 350   Disputations, *de Caritate*, 7, *ad* 16

413. Christ dwells in our head through the faith of our mind;[2] we can be certain he does when we know that we believe what the Catholic Church holds and teaches. He dwells in our heart through faith quickened by charity;[3] we cannot be certain about this, or that we have charity, unless a special grace or revelation be granted us. All the same we can form a confident conjecture if we find ourselves so prepared and ready that no temporal object will be allowed to make us act against Christ. *Beloved, if our heart condemn us not, then have we confidence toward God.*[4]

353, 356, 487   Commentary, *2 Corinthians*, xiii, *lect.* 2

[1] 1 Cor. iv. 4.

[2] *Fides informis*: the theological virtue of faith which can be considered apart from charity, and may exist without it, as in a believer who is in grave sin, but not of infidelity.

[3] *Fides formata*.

[4] 1 John iii. 21.

VII

The Cardinal Virtues[1]

414. Commenting on the words, *Blessed be ye poor*,[2] Ambrose says that four cardinal virtues are recognized, namely, prudence, justice, fortitude, and temperance.[3] Cardinal comes from *cardo*, a hinge on which a gate turns: *as the door turneth upon his hinges, so does the slothful man turn upon his bed*.[4] The cardinal virtues support the portals that open into a properly human way of life. The life of the senses we share with animals, the life of the mind we share, though imperfectly, with angels; the life of practical reasonableness is our appointed level. The life of a voluptuary is that of a beast, the life of a contemplative is more than human. The active life, exercised through moral virtue, that is proper to man; the cardinal virtues are those on which the other reasonable virtues are based and revolve.

A virtuous act has four characteristics. First, it is a measured kind of operation, appropriate to the circum-

---

[1] The theological virtues are not superimposed on the natural virtues described in Aristotle's *Ethics*, as though the Christian had to live at two different levels. The natural virtues, sometimes called the acquired virtues, are charged with grace, and given a new mode and object: these are the infused moral virtues. About forty of them are studied in the *Secunda Secundae*, clustered round the four cardinal virtues of prudence, justice, fortitude, and temperance. Three themes may be noted: the directing role of prudence which, through the act of conscience, applies the rule of intelligence to the contingent events of life; second, the supreme role of equity, or non-legalistic justice, in fair dealing; third, that fortitude and temperance are qualities of emotion, for the mind enters into passion to enhance, not weaken, it.   [2] Luke vi. 20.

[3] *Expositio Evangelii secundam Lucam*, v. 49; *PL* xv. 1649.

[4] Prov. xxvi. 14.

stances of its situation. Secondly, it evinces a certain steadiness in acting that way; there is a reliability about the person who does it. Thirdly, it is well adapted to achieve an end which is not merely his own self-betterment. Fourthly, it is done deliberately. Aristotle refers to these elements when he says that fair and temperate types of activity are not enough for virtue, but that he who does them should also be in a certain state, that he should act knowingly, with deliberate preference in the light of purpose, and from a stable and constant disposition.[1] The traits of knowledge, rightness, moderation, and firmness, though present in all virtuous activity, are respectively more prominent in four specific fields.

The practical knowledge requisite for virtue goes through three phases, namely, taking counsel, forming a judgement, and making a choice. The first two have their counterparts in the inquiry instituted and the conclusion arrived at by the theoretical reason, but there is none for the third, when the practical reason comes to the decision of going on or not. The first phase is perfected by the virtue called *eubulia*, or good counsel, the second by *synesis*, or good judgement, which is called *gnome* when applied to exceptional cases;[2] both prepare for the act of prudence commanding what should be done. Prudence, then, plays the principal part in the knowledge directing moral activity, and so is set up as a cardinal virtue.

A human act is assessed by its consonance with real purposes in the world outside us; praise and blame can be apportioned even when it is done in solitude, but more especially when it relates to others. Then activity is correct with respect, not to one person alone, but also to the other people with whom he dwells in the social community. We can observe not a few who seem to

[1] *Ethics*, ii. 3, 1105ᵃ29.   [2] *Ethics*, vi. 10, 1142ᵃ28.

practice moral virtue by regulating their own private conduct but who seem incapable of doing so in their dealings with their neighbours. Justice, then, is set up as a principal virtue, for it squarely meets the claims of others: what is just is what is fairly adjusted.

Moderation and restraint are especially good and praiseworthy where the emotions are strongest and most need control. Our most powerful impulse is to seek the most vehement pleasures, and here is set up the cardinal virtue of temperance, which checks lust for the delights of touch. Firmness is conspicuously good and praiseworthy where the emotions are most fearful and most require to be made intrepid, and here is set up the cardinal virtue of fortitude or bravery, which steadies us in the face of great perils and danger of death.

Of these four, prudence is in the reason, justice in the will, temperance in the sense-appetites which seek pleasure, fortitude in the sense-appetites which meet emergencies. The sense-appetites, the seats of our emotional life, can be entered by reason and will, and therefore can be regarded as abilities for acting voluntarily and in a human manner. Hence the fourfold division of the cardinal virtues matches the essential elements of virtue, the situations with which virtues deal, and the faculties in which they reside.

217, 283, 447, 626 Disputations, *de Virtutibus Cardinalibus*, 1

415. Macrobius records that 'Plotinus, who was like Plato, a prince among philosophers, discovered four virtues in each of the four classes, namely of what are called the political virtues, the purgative virtues, the virtues of the already purified soul, and the exemplar virtues'.[1]

Augustine notes that virtues grow in the soul by

---

[1] *Commentarius ex Cicerone in Somnium Scipionis*, i. 8.

climbing to their cause, which is God: strive after him, and we shall live well.[1] All virtues pre-exist in God, as do the full values of everything; these are exemplar virtues, the prototype of the moral virtues. Prudence is his providence, justice his observance of eternal law, fortitude his immutability, temperance his agreement of love with mind.

Then because men should be borne away to divine things—for this we may quote Aristotle[2] and follow up with Holy Writ, for example, *be ye perfect as your heavenly Father is perfect*[3]—we should also postulate certain virtues which come midway between the exemplar virtues, which are God's, and the political virtues, which belong to man as a reasonable social animal. These intermediate virtues can be taken at two stages; at the first they are in process of coming to the second, when they have reached their goal.

At the first stage, when men are striving to capture the divine likeness, virtues are described as purgative. Then prudence despises worldly goods in order to pursue divine contemplation, and bends every thought to divine things alone; then temperance renounces, so far as nature allows, what the body wants; then fortitude is not frightened at the effort of leaving physical reassurance behind in order to live in the supernatural; then justice whole-heartedly consents to the steps these standards demand.

At the second stage, when men have caught the divine likeness, virtues are ascribed to the purified soul. Then prudence gazes only at divine truths; then temperance feels no earthly lust; then fortitude no fear; then justice seals an eternal compact, and men are com-

---

[1] *de Moribus Ecclesiae*, 6; *PL* XXXII. 1314.
[2] *Ethics*, v. 5, 1140ª24.
[3] Matt. v. 48.

panions with the divine mind. Such are the virtues of
the blessed, and of some holy persons in this life.

63, 486, 534   *Summa Theologica*, 1a–2ae. lxi. 5

416. Divine wisdom teaches *temperance and justice,
prudence and fortitude*.[1] Effects match their origins and
causes; accordingly all the virtues, intellectual and
moral, which are acquired by our own exertions, are
developed from certain natural pre-existing principles.
In the life of grace the divinely imparted theological
virtues play the part of these principles. It is right, then,
that other habits divinely infused in us should supple-
ment and match these theological virtues—habits which
are to the theological virtues what the acquired moral
virtues are to the natural principles of virtue.

These infused moral virtues are different in kind
from the natural virtues. The difference appears from
both their formal objects and their immediate purposes.

The formal object of a virtue is a certain measured
good—for instance, with temperance, which is concerned with good through and in the pleasures of touch,
the reasonable measure, its formal element, comes from
the reason, the material elements from the emotions.
Clearly the measure imposed by right reason alone and
by divine rule do not exactly coincide. For instance,
where food is concerned, the reasonable standard is
that the body should be kept healthy and the mind
clear, whereas the divine standard goes further in commanding self-denial and abstinence from food and
drink: *I chastise my body and bring it into subjection*.[2]
Acquired temperance and infused temperance are
therefore different in kind; the same distinction holds
good for the other moral virtues as well.

Furthermore, habits are specifically distinct when

[1] Wisd. viii. 7.   [2] 1 Cor. ix. 27.

their immediate purposes are different in kind: the nature of a horse is different from the nature of a man, the health of a horse different from that of a man. Aristotle argues that civic virtues differ according to the type of regime in power.[1] From this point of view also the acquired moral virtues, by which we behave properly in the human community, are different from the infused moral virtues, by which we comport ourselves as *fellow citizens with the saints and familiars of God.*[2]

310, 380, 568   *Summa Theologica*, 1a–2ae. lxiii. 3, 4

417. Virtues may be treated as either complete or inchoate. Complete virtues are all interconnected, but inchoate virtues are not necessarily. Let us make the position clearer.

Consider that virtue perfects both the doer and the deed. Complete virtue makes a person good all round, whereas imperfect virtue makes him and his deed good only in one respect. Good without reserve is applied to our lives and conduct when we are well-adjusted personalities and keep the rules of life. Some of these rules are part of the code of reasonable decency, and are implied in the demands of civilized human nature. But behind them is the first and transcendental measure of activity, and this is God. We are made capable of living in a reasonable fashion by the virtue of prudence,[3] and in a divine fashion by the virtue of charity: *he that dwelleth in love dwelleth in God, and God in him.*[4]

Three stages of virtue can therefore be marked. In the first stage virtue is incomplete, for it is without prudence, and not suffused with reason. Moral predispositions to certain deeds of virtue are proper to this stage; they may be congenital: *from my infancy mercy*

[1] *Politics*, iii. 2, 1275^b.   [2] Eph. ii. 19.
[3] *Ethics*, vi. 5, 1140^b20.   [4] 1 John iv. 16.

grew up with me, and it came out with me from my mother's womb.[1] They are not equally distributed; some persons have a bent to this virtue, others to that. Nor are they fully fledged virtues, for nobody misuses properly developed virtue, whereas these dispositions may be undiscerning, and lead us to act ill or harmfully —a blind horse crashes all the harder the stronger its galloping. Gregory says that the other virtues are not virtues at all unless they carry a strain of prudence.[2]

At the second stage a reasonable standard is attained, yet without reaching to God through charity. A good life is established according to the standards of humanism; virtue is perfect enough by the test of reason, but falls as far short of perfect virtue, which is measured by the primary rule and last end, as moral predispositions do from genuine reasonable virtue.

The third stage is attained when all virtues are good without qualification, and they are charged with charity. Then is a person good simply speaking, that is, in right relation to his ultimate end.

Consider also that prudence can no more exist without the moral virtues than they can exist without prudence. Prudence is the application of right reason to moral practice; application here, as elsewhere, calls for critical appreciation of the principles at work: you cannot draw right geometrical conclusions except from right premises and principles. The principles of practice are ends, and thence we infer the reasons which decide how we should act. When moral ends are under debate, right judgement rises from the habit of virtue; as a man is, so does the end seem to him—if he is virtuous then he likes true worth, if vicious then what smacks of his weakness; it is the same with a healthy or sick sense of taste.[3]

[1] Job xxxi. 18.   [2] *Moralium Liber*, xxii. 1; *PL* LXXVI. 212.
[3] *Ethics*, i. 1, 1094ª16.

Therefore, given prudence, all the other moral virtues are present, and, given charity, all the other virtues are present.

Charity is infused by God: *the love of God is shed abroad in our hearts by the Holy Ghost, who is given to us.*[1] When God makes us want something he also provides us with the abilities to secure it. In this case these are the appropriate springs of activity towards himself: *he ordereth all things sweetly.*[2] Fittingly then is charity accompanied by other habitual settled qualities which are ready to produce acts in accordance with the claims of love. Such are all the virtues. Charity's object is our ultimate end, and this enfolds all virtuous activity. Any art or virtue dealing with an end governs the whole approach to it and all the means; military art controls cavalry training, cavalry training the farrier department. How fairly then does divine wisdom and goodness infuse all the virtues with charity: *charity is long suffering, is kind; charity envieth not, vaunteth not itself, is not puffed up, doth not behave unseemly, seeketh not her own, is not easily provoked, thinketh no evil, rejoiceth not in iniquity, but rejoiceth in the truth, beareth all things, believeth all things, hopeth all things, endureth all things, and never faileth.*[3]

310, 401, 407, 455   Disputations, *de Virtutibus Cardinalibus*, 2

418. Qualities can be classified either according to their formal principles or according to their subjects; on both counts four cardinal virtues can be catalogued.

The formal principle of moral virtue is reasonable good. This can be considered at two stages, the measured judgement of reason itself—here is the principal virtue of *prudence*—and the medium in which it works and on which it is imposed: this is either what we do

[1] Rom. v. 5.   [2] Wisd. viii. 1.   [3] 1 Cor. xiii. 4–8.

—here is *justice*—or what we feel—as regards our fears, here *fortitude*, as regards our lusts, here *temperance*.

The same fourfold division appears from the faculties concerned with morality. The reason itself—*prudence*; the will—*justice*; the emotions about dangers—*fortitude*; the emotions about pleasures—*temperance*.

347 *Summa Theologica*, 1a–2ae. lxi. 2

419. Three sorts of part are relevant when analysing a cardinal virtue: an *integral part*, thus foundations, walls, and roof make up a house; a *subjective part*, thus *bos* and *leo* are species of animal; and a *potential part*, thus the nutritive and sensitive powers are parts of the soul. The integral parts of a cardinal virtue are the components of its full activity; the subjective parts are its species or kinds; the potential parts are those other virtues which are closely associated with one of the four principal virtues, without, however, possessing its full character.

Take first the integral parts of the cardinal virtues. Eight characteristics can be collected from Aristotle,[1] Cicero,[2] and Macrobius,[3] namely, memory, grasp of meaning, docility, shrewdness, wit, ability to plan, circumspection, and caution: all can be regarded as elements of the virtue of prudence. Augustine speaks of justice rendering what is due and shunning what is unfair:[4] these can be regarded as composing justice. Aristotle speaks of fortitude as attacking and defending; both attitudes enter into *fortitude*.[5] Similarly, delicacy and a sense of honour are components of temperance.[6]

---

[1] *Ethics*, vi. 9, 1142^{b}2.
[2] *de Inventione Oratoria*, ii. 53.
[3] *in Somnium Scipionis*, i. 8.
[4] *de Correptione et Gratia*, 1; *PL* xliv. 917.
[5] *Ethics*, ii. 7, 1107^{a}33; iii. 6, 1115^{a}6.
[6] Cf. *Ethics*, ii. 7, 1108^{a}32; iv. 9, 1128^{a}32.

Next take the subjective parts of the cardinal virtues. First of all, with respect to prudence. Its species are *personal* (or *monastic*) *prudence*, whereby a man governs himself; *domestic* (or *economic*) *prudence*, whereby he governs a family or household; and *political prudence*, sovereign prudence in the ruler of the State, and ordinary political prudence in the citizens. Secondly, with respect to justice. Its species are *general justice*, also called *legal justice*, which directs the acts of the moral virtues to the common good, and *particular justice*, which renders what is due to private persons. This particular justice, or justice towards individuals, is divided from another point of view into *commutative justice*, which regulates the transactions of individual persons among themselves, and *distributive justice*, which fairly allots to them their proper share of community honours and burdens. Thirdly, with respect to fortitude; this is a highly specialized virtue, and is not divided into specific types. Fourthly, as regards temperance, this is a generic virtue diversified according to its various kinds of object. In the pleasures of feeding, we have *abstinence* concerning food, and *sobriety* concerning drink; in the pleasures of sex, *chastity* concerning intercourse, and *purity* concerning the circumstances of making love.

Finally, the potential parts of the cardinal virtues. The principal act of prudence is the practical executive command of right reason; the following virtues come into its orbit, *eubulia*, or *good counsel*, *synesis*, or *sound judgement* when the ordinary rules of conduct are concerned, and *gnome*, a flair for dealing with exceptional cases. Now as regards justice. Its classical type renders what is due between equals, but other virtues come under the general heading of justice. Some render what is owing to another, but not as to an equal; others deal with a situation where both parties are equal, yet the due or debt, though demanded by decency, cannot be enforced by law, and so is not an affair of strict justice. In the first class of these potential parts of justice comes *religion*, which offers our service and worship to God, then *piety* or *patriotism*, which renders our duty to parents and country, then *observance*, which shows reverence to superiors, and *obedience* to their commands. In the second class comes *gratitude* for past favours, and *vindication* when injury has been done; also *truthfulness*, without which social decency is impossible, *liberality* in spending money, and *friendliness*, or social good manners. The potential parts of fortitude, on the attacking side, are *confidence*, carried out with *magnificence*, which reckons not the cost, and *magnanimity*, which does not shrink from glory: on the defensive side, *patience*, which keeps an unconquered spirit, and can be protracted into *perseverance*. The potential parts of temperance are *continence*, which rides lustfulness yet without having completely broken it in, *clemency*, which tempers punishment, *meekness*, which tempers anger, *modesty* in our deportment, and this includes *disciplined study*, *playfulness*, and *good taste* in clothes.

435   *Summa Theologica*, 2a–2ae. xlviii. 1; lviii. 5, 6; lxi. 1, 2; lxxix. 1; lxxx. 1; ciii, Prologue; cxxviii. 1; cxliii. 1; cxliv. 1; clv. 1; clvii. 1; clxi, Prologue; clxvi. 2; clxviii. 2; clxix. 1

420. The four cardinal virtues can be considered as signifying either the main characteristics of every virtue or special types of virtue.

Some authors treat the cardinal virtues as general characteristics of every virtue—all directing knowledge is prudence, all balanced fairness is justice, all firmness of soul in misfortune is fortitude, all moderation about earthly values is temperance. Augustine takes this line,[1]

[1] *de Moribus Ecclesiae*, 24; *PL* xxxii. 1330.

and so does Gregory when he says[1] that prudence is not
genuine unless just, courageous, and temperate; nor
temperance perfect unless strong, just, and prudent;
nor courage complete unless prudent, temperate, and
just; nor justice true unless prudent, strong, and temperate. The moral virtues are then divided into four,
not because they are specifically different habits dealing
with diverse types of object, but because they strike
different notes.

Other authors follow Aristotle[2] and treat them as
special virtues each occupied with its own proper type
of situation. Even so, Gregory's observation is still to
the point, for in fact one virtue flows into another, and
the four virtues are named from opportunities which
make the four general modes of virtue conspicuously
commendable. Fortitude is temperate, and temperance
brave, for he who can contain his lusts can well control
himself in face of danger; and he who can face death
unflinchingly can well withstand allurements. The
principal function of temperance enters into fortitude,
and conversely; indeed this overlapping is found with
all the other virtues.

316, 416   Disputations, *de Virtutibus Cardinalibus*, 1, *ad* 1

I. PRUDENCE

421. Prudence is concerned with moral issues. Final
happiness does not lie in the activity of the moral
virtues. Moreover, happiness is man's noblest act, and
this is occupied with enjoying the sublime, not with
contriving particular arrangements. Furthermore, happiness is ultimate, while prudence, like all working

----

[1] *Moralium Liber*, xxii. 1; *PL* LXXVI. 22.
[2] *Ethics*, ii. 7, 1107[a]29.

knowledge, deals with means to ends. For these reasons, then, prudence does not reach to the heart of happiness.

198   III *Contra Gentes*, 35

422. The office of prudence is to dispose means to ends in due order. The premisses of its process of reasoning are the ends themselves; they give meaning to our conduct, as clearly as the artist's intention does to his works of art. If a person is to be prudent he must first be adjusted to the ends of life. He cannot come to right conclusions unless his principles are sound. Therefore prudence presupposes that his intelligence has a habit of insight and that his affections are rightly mustered by the moral virtues.

213   Disputations, v *de Veritate*, 1

423. Prudence is praised, not only for arriving at the right diagnosis, but also for applying effective treatment.

52   *Summa Theologica*, 2a–2ae. xlvii. 1, *ad* 3

424. The moral virtues are independent of some of the intellectual virtues; they can manage without wisdom, scientific habits of knowledge, and art; not, however, without insight and prudence. All the intellectual virtues, except prudence, can exist apart from the moral virtues.

36, 417   *Summa Theologica*, 1a–2ae. lviii. 4, 5

425. The difference between habits of knowledge comes from the range of their principles: thus wisdom looks at things from a higher point of view than the sciences do. This holds true also of practical habits of judgement. Infringements of the order of a lower system can sometimes be accommodated in the order of a higher system: monsters are against the rules of eugenics, and a biologist may be at a loss for an explanation, nevertheless a theologian can sometimes fit them in the plan of divine Providence. It may happen that a

course has to be adopted which breaks the usual rules of conduct: the case has then to be judged in the light of higher principles than suffice for ordinary working prudence. Then the decision has to be taken by a higher virtue, namely that part of prudence called *gnome*: the word implies a certain sharpness.

202, 458, 473   *Summa Theologica*, 2a–2ae. li. 4

426. If moral science is hesitant and imprecise in the abstract, much more is this so when we come down to apply it in detail to concrete instances, which are covered neither by art nor by precedents. For the factors at work in human deeds are indefinitely variable. Accordingly, decisions must be left to each person's prudence. Let him take into account all the particular circumstances, and then his is the responsibility for considering and purposing what should be done at that time: he is like the doctor in charge of a case, the captain in command of a ship. Although no particular situation entirely conforms to a pattern, nor is any one exactly like another, we may rely on help being given us to direct our lives.

203   Commentary, *II Ethics*, lect. 2

427. The virtue of prudence is able to govern our deeds, prudence which does not merely consider generalities—for these do not set us going—but also the singular and particular things which are the objects of action. Prudence is practical; that is to say, it is a principle of acting. Because they are more experienced, some people who lack a scientific theory can be more successful with practical issues than those who possess it: thus a doctor who knows what is in fact the right food is more effective than one who is merely a theoretical dietician.

52, 473   Commentary, *VI Ethics*, lect. 6

428. Some vices are obviously defects of prudence, such as inconsiderate haste, shilly-shallying, negligence —imprudence in short. Others, however, wear a false guise of prudence—worldly prudence, *the wisdom of the flesh is an enemy of God;*[1] slyness, guile, and fraud, *but we renounce the hidden things of dishonesty, not walking in craftiness;*[2] *we be no more children tossed to and fro and carried about by every wind of doctrine by the wickedness of men, by cunning craftiness by which they lie in wait to deceive.*[3]

11, 255   *Summa Theologica*, 2a–2ae. liii, Prologue, 2. lv.
                    1, 3, 4

2. JUSTICE

429. Simply speaking, a moral virtue is the nobler for the amount of reasonable goodness suffusing it. Accordingly justice, as such, excels among the other moral virtues, and is called the brightest, outshining morning and evening star.[4]

Summa Theologica, 1a–2ae. lxvi. 4

430. Justice can be discussed in three senses. First, as a special virtue, one of the four cardinal virtues, directing men's business among themselves, for example, contracts: this justice is the direct opposite, not of all sin indiscriminately, but of unfair dealings and sharp practice, of theft, robbery, and so forth. In another sense justice stands for legal or general justice, which, though it may be considered apart, really coincides with all virtue, for, according to Aristotle,[5] it orders all our transactions to the common good. The common good is the purpose of legislation, hence the epithet *legal*, because such justice observes the law. Every virtue after a fashion comes under legal justice; but not every act of virtue is

[1] Rom. viii. 7.   [2] 2 Cor. iv. 2.   [3] Eph. iv. 14.
[4] *Ethics*, v. 2, $1129^{b}29$.   [5] *Ethics*, v. 1, $1129^{b}30$.

an act of legal justice, but that only which is ordained to the well-being of the commonwealth: consequently, not every act of sin is opposed to legal justice. Thirdly, justice can stand for a certain state, proper to men who bear themselves well to God, to their neighbour, and to themselves in that their lower powers are subordinate to reason. Aristotle calls this metaphorical justice, since strict justice is always between different persons. Every sin hits at this justice, which is also called righteousness, for every sin upsets the proper order of human acts.

239, 274, 435   Disputations, xviii *de Veritate*, 1

i. *Equity*

431. Human law cannot repeal any part of divine law or Natural Law. In the natural order of things, instituted by divine Providence, material goods are provided for the satisfaction of human needs, and therefore the division and appropriation of property, which comes from human law, should not prevent natural needs being provided for. Whatever a man possesses in superabundance is owing, of natural right, to the poor for their sustenance. Such is the teaching of Ambrose echoed in Gratian's *Decretum*,[1] 'The bread which you withhold belongs to the hungry; the clothing you pack away belongs to the naked; the money you hoard should relieve the penniless.' How many needy persons there are, and since all cannot be assisted from one fund, it is left to individual initiative to provide for them from wealth possessed. If, however, the necessity is so urgent and evident that instant relief should be afforded, if, for instance, a person is about to collapse and no other way appears of satisfying his want, then he may take, either

---

[1] I. xlvii. 8. Ambrose, on Luke xii. 18 (*PL* xvii. 613–14). Cf. Basil, on Luke xii. 16 (*PG* xxxi. 1752).

openly or secretly, what he needs from the possessions of another, nor is this, strictly speaking, theft or robbery.

215, 286, 654   *Summa Theologica*, 2a–2ae. lxvi. 7

432. When the legislative authority intends the genuine common good, conformably to divine justice, then the observance of law will make good men. But if it intends what is merely opportunist, or pleasing to its own sense of importance, or repugnant to divine justice, then observance will make men good only in a manner of speaking, namely, in relation to the regime. Such good is found even in thoroughly bad men; thus we speak of a good thief, meaning an expert.

279, 652, 657   *Summa Theologica*, 1a–2ae. xcii. 2

433. All law is directed to the common well-being. From this it draws its force and meaning, and to the extent that it falls short of this it does not oblige in conscience. Hence legal authorities say, that neither the sense of justice nor the benignity of equity permit that what has been usefully established for human interests should become harsh and damaging through too rigid an interpretation.[1]

The observance of some regulation, though useful to the community in the majority of cases, may happen on some occasions to be extremely damaging. Unable to foresee all particular contingencies, the legislative authority frames laws to meet the usual run of things. The intention is that the common benefit should be served. Should it happen that observance would harm the general well-being, then such a law is not to be observed.

Note, all the same, that if there is no crisis calling for an emergency decision and instant action against the letter of the code, then it is not open for anybody to

[1] *Digest*, I. III. 25: Modestinus.

interpret what is, or is not, in the best interests of the community. Such verdicts are reserved to the ruling authority, which alone possesses the power of dispensation. All the same, when the danger is so imminent that no time can be allowed to submit the matter to the authorities, necessity carries its own dispensation, for necessity knows no law.

188, 649   *Summa Theologica*, 1a–2ae. xcvi. 6

434. Laws are enacted about human acts which in themselves are always singular and contingent instances, and therefore can vary indefinitely. Flat regulations to meet every case cannot be laid down. Legislators reckon on what happens in the majority of cases, and frame their laws accordingly. It may happen that insistence on the normal rule will be against the fair balance of justice and the common good intended by the law. For example, a law may command that deposits should be returned; in some cases, however, this may be harmful, as when a weapon is restored to the owner when he is in a raging fury, or when something is returned to the damage of the commonwealth. In such and similar cases to follow the law just as it stands will be wrong; to forsake the letter for the true purpose of justice and procure the common benefit will be right. The virtue of *epieikeia*, which we call equity, meets these situations.

If it be objected that equity cannot be a virtue, for it is opposed to strict justice, I answer that it does not depart from right itself, but from a right as formulated in a code. Nor is it opposed to the severe and exact discharge of judicial duty, which is virtuous only when the law is accurately brought to bear in the proper circumstances, not by harsh insistence on its letter outside them. This is vicious. Accordingly the *Codex* affirms that there is no doubt that the law is infringed when the letter is stressed to the exclusion of the legislator's purpose.[1]

If again you object that while a law may be freely instituted, but once instituted must be punctiliously kept, I answer that equity does not criticize a law as though saying it was not well enacted, but merely judges that its terms do not fit this particular case; what is judged is not the law, but some particular situation which has cropped up.

Lastly, if you object that the interpretation of law is reserved to the legislator and cannot be legally performed by others, I answer that the occasions for rulings are doubtful points; there admittedly it is unlawful to depart from the letter of the law without authoritative arbitration. But we are discussing emergencies, when the need is for rapid action, not interpretation.

72, 279, 286, 426 *Summa Theologica*, 2a–2ae. cxx. 1, c. & ad 1, 2, 3

435. Three kinds of parts may be attributed to a virtue. First, the *integral parts*; these are the components making up its activity. Second, the *potential parts*, or associated virtues. Third, the *subjective parts*, which are its kinds or species, the virtue being taken as a genus: such specific parts are more specialized and narrower in scope than the generic virtue. Now the inclusion of a specific type under a general heading may be either univocal or analogical: *univocal*, when the generic nature is predicated of the species with exactly the same force and meaning, as when animal is predicated of a horse or an ox: *analogical*, when the general nature is possessed by one type primarily and by others secondarily and derivatively, as when *being* is predicated of substance and accident.

[1] *Codex Justinianus*, I. xiv. 5.

Classify justice as a general heading, then equity becomes a special section; it is one of the types of justice, and accordingly may be grouped as a *subjective part* or species of justice. Nevertheless the full character and nature of justice is displayed by equity more freshly and excellently than by legalistic justice. For equity provides, as it were, a higher ruling for our conduct; it should govern the way we act according to the laws of our community. Yet equity and legal justice should work together. Indeed, if legal justice means that the application of law is tempered by the terms of the law or, and this is more important, by the intention of the legislator, then equity comes into it, and is the dominant part. If, however, legal justice means no more than the legalism which applies the letter of the law, then equity is not contained in it, but, instead, should be treated as a function of justice in the widest sense: equity then exceeds and overrides legalistic justice, and may be pitted against it.

144, 415, 419, 430   *Summa Theologica*, 2a–2ae. cxx. 2, c. &
ad 1

ii. *State Demands*

436. Some writers have held that, if a tyrant's excesses grow intolerable, then strong men must do away with him and free the people even at the risk of their own lives:[1] it is their virtuous office. They cite the example of Ehud, who thrust a dagger into Eglon, King of Moab, who had ground down the people of Israel:[2] afterwards he became judge of the people. Their opinion, however, does not agree with apostolic teaching: *be subject to your masters with all fear, not only to*

[1] Cf. John of Salisbury, *Policraticus*, iii. 15; *PL* cxcix. 512.
[2] Judges iii. 15.

the good and gentle, but also to the froward.[1] The strength to suffer patiently for conscience's sake comes from grace; when Roman Emperors tyranically persecuted the followers of the Cross, many persons of high and low degree were converted, and suffered cheerfully and without resistance—on this account we praise the Theban Legion. Better to say that Ehud slew an enemy aggressor, not the oppressive ruler of his people.

We read in the Old Testament that those who slew King Joas of Juda, though he had fallen away from God's true worship, were themselves put to death; with the proviso of the Mosaic legislation that their children were exempted from punishment.[2] How harmful to the community and civil authority if private presumption could plot the death of rulers even when they were tyrannical: more often than not, it would be bad citizens, not good ones, who would embark on these dangerous courses. Indeed, they find a good ruler as burdensome as a tyrant; Solomon remarks, *a wise king scattereth the wicked.*[3] Were the presumption to be admitted, the community would stand to lose more from the removal of a good king than from that of a tyrant.

It seems, therefore, that a tyrant's barbarism should be proceeded against by public authority, not by private presumption. In the first place, the right of instituting a ruler may belong to the people; and then, without injustice, they can rid themselves of a ruler, or curb his power, when he abuses his prerogatives. There is no question of disloyalty, even if previously they had subjected themselves to him for life; it is what he deserves if he has not observed his engagements with them and faithfully conducted himself in his office of ruling. In the second place, a higher authority may have appointed

---

[1] 1 Pet. ii. 18.   [2] 4 Kings xiv. 5–6.

[3] Prov. xx. 26.

the ruler; and then subjects can look there for a remedy
against wicked tyranny.

But when no chance remains of human aid against
tyranny, recourse must be had to God, the king of all
and *in due season the helper of the oppressed.*[1] His is the
power to soften harshness: *the heart of the king is in the
hand of the Lord; whithersoever he will he shall turn it.*[2]
He moved King Ahasuerus to pity when he meditated a
pogrom;[3] he converted King Nabuchodonosor so that
he confessed divine might: *now indeed, I Nabuchodonosor,
do praise and magnify and glorify the King of Heaven
because all his works are true and his ways judgments,
and them that walk in pride he is able to abase.*[4] As for
those tyrants who are counted unworthy of conversion,
he can cut them down in their prime or humble them:
*God hath overturned the thrones of proud princes and hath
set up the meek in their stead.*[5] Seeing the affliction of his
people in Egypt and hearing their cries, he engulfed
oppressive Pharaoh and his army in the sea. He deposed
proud Nabuchodonosor, and banished him like a beast
from human company. Nor is his power now any less
or his arm shortened. Through Isaiah he promised
peace to his people after they had been subjugated,
scattered, and enslaved. Through Ezekiel he said: *I will
deliver my flock from their mouth.*[6] To deserve such benefits from God men must abstain from sinning, for the
rule of the impious is permitted as punishment for sin:
I will make a king in my wrath.[7] And again, *He maketh
a man who is a hypocrite to rule because of the sins of the
people.*[8] Wash guilt away, and we shall be free of
tyrannical affliction.

649   *de Regimine Principum,* i. 7

[1] Ps. ix. 10.   [2] Prov. xxi. 1.   [3] Esther iii.
[4] Dan. iv. 34.   [5] Ecclus. x. 17.   [6] Ezek. xxxiv. 10.
[7] Hos. xiii. 11.   [8] Job. xxxiv. 30.

437. For a war to be just three conditions are necessary—public authority, just cause, right motive.

First, the command of sovereign authority. To declare war is not the business of a private person; he can defend his rights by recourse to a higher tribunal, but has no right to mobilize the people. The care of the commonwealth is entrusted to the prince; his the responsibility for the defence of the province, city, or realm committed to him. As he rightly defends the State against internal disturbers of the peace by punishing criminals with the civil arm—*he beareth not the sword in vain, for he is God's minister, an avenger to execute wrath upon him that doth evil*[1]—so has he the duty of defending the State with warlike weapons against external enemies. Therefore are rulers commanded, *rescue the poor, and deliver the needy out of the hand of the sinner.*[2] Augustine declares that the decision and authority of declaring war lies with rulers if the moral order is to be peacefully composed.[3]

Secondly, just cause. Those who are attacked should deserve to be attacked. Augustine observes that those wars are generally counted as just which avenge some wrong, when a nation or State has failed to make amends or restore what has been injuriously annexed.[4]

Thirdly, right intention. Those who go to war should fight to achieve some good or avoid some evil. Thus it is noted that for the true followers of God there is peace even in war,[5] for they are belligerent, not from greed or cruelty, but from love of peace, to restrain wickedness and assist righteousness. A war declared by legitimate authority and for a just cause may be vitiated

---

[1] Rom. xiii. 4.   [2] Ps. lxxxi. 4.

[3] *Contra Faustum*, xxii. 75; *PL* xlii. 448.

[4] *Quaestiones in Heptateuchum, super Josue* vii. 10; *PL* xxxiv. 781.   [5] Gratian, *Decretum*, II. xxiii. i. 6.

by evil intentions. Augustine points out that the desire
to hurt, the cruelty of feud, an unappeased and un-
appeasable spirit, arrogance in victory, lust for power,
and similar faults, all these are justly blamed in war.[1]

657   *Summa Theologica*, 2a–2ae. xl. 1

iii. *Religion*

438. God has no need for our worship. It is we who
need to show our gratitude for what we have received.

484, 642   *III Sentences*, ix, i. 3, sol. iii

439. The plan of divine Providence disposes all things
that they may reach their ends each in a style befit-
ting their natures; so also are men appointed to obtain
the things they hope for from God; which come to them
in accordance with the tenor of human life as it is lived
at present. Our condition is such that we have to address
our pleas to those who can help us, and especially when
they are our superiors. With these thoughts in mind we
broach the subject of praying to God to get our hearts'
desires.

Petition is different when addressed to men and
when addressed to God. With human intercession we
seek to inform another person of our wants, and then
to sway his will on our behalf, but neither of these considerations apply when we pour out our prayers to God.
Our intention is not to divulge our needs and hopes,
for God knows all things: *Lord, all my desire is before
thee.*[2] Our Lord told us, *your heavenly Father knoweth
that ye have need of all these things.*[3] Nor can the divine
will be persuaded to alter a decision: *God is not a man,
that he should lie; neither the son of man, that he should
repent.*[4] For our sake is prayer necessary, that we should

[1] *Contra Faustum*, xxii. 74; *PL* XLII. 447.
[2] Ps. xxxvii. 9.   [3] Matt. vi. 32.   [4] Num. xxiii. 19.

consider our own needs and bend our desire fervently and devoutly to receive what God wishes us to have so that we may become worthy to receive his blessings.

Another point of difference may be mentioned. Pleas to men require some previous acquaintanceship with them, but prayer to God brings us into his presence. Our minds are lifted up into loving intercourse when we worship him in spirit and in truth. We are of his household; we have access to him and trustfully may plead again: *I have called upon thee, thou wilt hear me, for he heard me.*[1] He begins by receiving us into his intimacy, and we are encouraged to continue our confidence. That is why perseverance and frequent petitions are welcomed by God, and are not over-importunate as they may be when addressed to human power: *men ought always to pray and not to faint.*[2] God invites us: *ask, and it shall be given you; seek, and ye shall find; knock, and it shall be opened to you.*[3]

17, 182, 390   *Compendium Theologiae,* 248

440. To will change is not the same as to change will.
68   *Summa Theologica,* 1a. xix. 7

441. In order to satisfy your request that I should write on the lawfulness of coming to decisions from reading the stars, I have been at pains to give you the patristic position.

You should know, to begin with, that the powers of heavenly bodies influence lower bodily processes. Augustine recognizes no absurdity in allowing for the part they play in bodily changes.[4] Consequently, there is nothing wrong in consulting the stars in order to foretell bodily effects, for instance, the weather, health and

---

[1] Ps. xvi. 6.   [2] Luke xviii. 1.   [3] Matt. vii. 7.
[4] *de Civitate Dei,* v. 6; *PL* XLI. 146.

sickness, the harvest and so forth, all of which depend on bodily and physical causes. To observe the heavens is general practice: farmers sow and reap at times determined by solar movement, sailors navigate by the moon, doctors choose critical periods settled by the heavens. There is no impropriety, then, in taking more occult phases of the stars into account when dealing with physical processes.

This, however, should be held unwaveringly—man's will is not determined by the stars. Otherwise his freedom would go by the board, and with it any merit for his good deeds, and censure on his evil ones. Every Christian is bound to hold that acts which issue from a man's own will, namely all his human acts properly so called, are not subject to determinism: *be not dismayed at the signs of heaven, as the heathens are dismayed at them.*[1] In order to lead people into error, the devil occupies himself in the business of those who calculate human events by the stars. Augustine declares that when astrologers hit off a true prediction we should acknowledge that they speak from an occult inspiration to which human minds are unconsciously susceptible, and that inasmuch as such statements deceive us they are the work of unclean seducing spirits, to whom a knowledge of temporal affairs is allowed.[2] He also grants that such observations can be based on a pact with demons,[3] which is wholly forbidden to Christians: *I would not that you should have fellowship with devils.*[4] Therefore to decide by the stars those issues which depend on man's freewill is certainly gravely wrong.

326   *Letter* to Reginald of Piperno

[1] Jer. x. 2.
[2] *de Genesi ad litteram*, ii. 17, *PL* xxxiv. 278.
[3] *de Doctrina Christiana*, ii. 24; *PL* xxxiv. 53.
[4] 1 Cor. x. 20.

442. In four ways sin may come into the casting of lots. First, if by tossing for the decision we seek a sign of divine judgement as a substitute for exercising our own wits. Then it verges on the sin of tempting God. Only when we are completely at a loss may we look for a special sign: *we know not what to do, but our eyes are upon thee.*[1] Secondly, if by casting lots we act without due reverence and devotion. Bede says that when people have no alternative than to copy the example of the Apostles, then let them gather together in a brotherly meeting and offer prayers to God.[2] Thirdly, when divine oracles are degraded. For though we may rule out any consort with demons when we take a text from the Bible by chance, it is, as Augustine says,[3] a displeasing custom to turn divine oracles to secular business and the vanities of this life. Fourthly, if we use the casting of lots as a substitute for divine inspiration, for instance, when it comes to the promotion of men to ecclesiastical dignities. That should be done through the concord of election wrought by the Holy Ghost. To cast lots to settle such matters is unlawful, for it insults the Spirit who instructs our senses to decide rightly: *He that is spiritual judges all things.*[4]

334 *de Sortibus,* 5[5]

3. FORTITUDE

443. The term *fortitude* can be read in two senses. First, as implying a certain firmness of mind; in this sense it is a general virtue, for as Aristotle notes, virtue requires firm and steadfast activity.[6] Secondly, as imply-

[1] 2 Chron. xx. 12.
[2] *super Acta Apostolorum Expositio,* i. 26; *PL* xcii. 945.
[3] *Epist. ad Inquisitiones Januarii,* li. 20; *PL* xxxiii. 222.
[4] 1 Cor. ii. 15.   [5] Letter to James of Tongres.
[6] *Ethics,* ii. 4, 1105^{a}32.

ing firmness in enduring and attacking under specially difficult circumstances of grave danger, when we must not run away, but, as Cicero says, take calculated risks and make arduous efforts.[1] Then it is a special virtue with its own determinate subject-matter.

414, 416, 458   *Summa Theologica*, 2a–2ae. cxxiii.2

444. Courage is more an affair of repressing fears than of moderating rashness. The first is the more difficult, for danger, which is the special concern of rashness and fear, of itself brings a repressive influence to bear on rashness, and so of itself tends to augment fear. To attack is that part of courage which moderates rashness, but to hold fast is the result of repressing fear. The principal act of courage is to endure and withstand dangers doggedly rather than to attack them.

Summa Theologica, 2a–2ae. cxxiii. 6

445. Aristotle observes how wild beasts attack either from pain, as when they are wounded, or from fear of it, as when they go for men because they are angered, whom they would leave alone if they were unmolested.[2] They are not virtuously brave, for they face danger from pain or rage, not from choice, as do those who act with foresight. True courage is from deliberate choice, not emotion. A hungry donkey who continues to graze though walloped is not virtuously brave, nor a man who acts boldly from hot blood.

217   Commentary, *III Ethics, lect.* 17

446. Many adversities confront those who would devoutly follow Christ. But they are not heavy, for the suffering is lightened with love. When somebody is in love he does not feel overburdened with the sufferings

[1] *de Inventione Oratoria*, ii. 54.
[2] *Ethics*, iii. 8, 1116^{b}34.

he endures for the sake of his beloved. He makes light
of them. And so the New Law is not a burden.

3, 476, 609   Commentary, *St. Matthew*, xi. 30

4. TEMPERANCE

447. Customary speech sometimes restricts common
terms to their most prominent examples, as when *Urbs*
is reserved for Rome. *Temperance* can be taken in
two ways, either according to its common meaning
or according to metonomy. According to its common
meaning it is a general virtue, not a special virtue, for
then it signifies a tempering or moderating of human
activities and emotions by the reason which is present
in all virtue. Though even so temperance and fortitude
differ, for temperance holds us back when we are un-
reasonably attracted, whereas fortitude holds us steady
or spurs us on when we are inclined to shirk. According
to its principal sense, however, when temperance reins
our appetites for the most alluring pleasures, then it is a
special virtue, with its own determinate subject-matter.

200, 375, 414   *Summa Theologica*, 2a–2ae. cxli. 2

448. As fortitude controls rashness and fear in the face
of the major pains which threaten to unbalance human
nature, so temperance controls desire for the major
pleasures. And because pleasure follows from connatural activity, so therefore are pleasures the more
vehement when they attend our most natural activities.
These are those which serve the individual through
food and drink and the species through intercourse of
male and female, and it is with them that temperance is
properly engaged. They come from the sense of touch;
hence we conclude that temperance, in its most precise
sense, is concerned with tactile pleasures.

200, 629   *Summa Theologica*, 2a–2ae. cxli. 4

449. The term *chastity* has both a proper and a metaphorical sense. Technically, it is a special virtue, that part of temperance occupied with the special matter of desire for sexual pleasure. This is centred on bodily intercourse, which is the special subject-matter of chastity properly so called, as also of the contrasting vice of lechery. But the terms may be extended to apply also to our spiritual intercourse with things, for here also is delight given. By a figure of speech, accordingly, spiritual chastity is engaged when our spirit enjoys God, with whom it should be joined, and refrains from enjoying things God does not mean us to mingle with: *I have espoused you one husband, that I may present you a chaste virgin to Christ.*[1] So also may we speak of spiritual fornication, when our spirit delights in embracing things against God's fair order: *thou hast played the harlot with many lovers.*[2] Chastity in this sense is a characteristic of every virtue, each of which holds us back from contracting illicit unions. Yet charity is at the centre of every virtue, and so also are the other theological virtues, which unite us immediately with God.

    131, 231, 461   *Summa Theologica*, 2a–2ae. cli. 2

450. Abstinence as such has no essential bearing on salvation: *the kingdom of God is not meat and drink.*[3] *Wisdom is justified by her children*[4]—Augustine explains that the apostles understood that the kingdom does not consist in eating and drinking, but in resignation to either lot.[5] They were neither elated by abundance, nor depressed by want.

    492, 547   *Summa Theologica*, 3a. xl. 2, *ad* 1

---

[1] 2 Cor. xi. 2.   [2] Jer. iii. 1.
[3] Rom. xiv. 17.   [4] Matt. xi. 19.
[5] *Quaestionum Evangeliorum Lib. super* Luc. vii, 7; *PL* xxxv. 1338.

VIII

Holiness[1]

451. Dionysius uses the phrase 'unmerging friendship' —how true it is that mutual help and delight are without prejudice to distinctness.

88, 395   Exposition, *de Divinis Nominibus*, iv, *lect.* 6

452. Nothing should be lacking in our friendship with God. Every act should go to him, actually or habitually. This is a precept laid on all. *Whether therefore ye eat, or drink, or whatsoever ye do, do all for the glory of God.*[2] A person loves God with his whole heart when he leads his life in God's service; all his deeds are virtually ordained to God, those excepted which lead him away. With his whole mind he commits himself to revealed truths: *bringing into captivity every thought to the*

---

[1] Though perhaps rare *de facto*, Christian perfection is not considered as extraordinary *de jure*, for all are called to it by the grace implanted in them at Baptism. St. Thomas was of the tradition which drew a clear line between the supernatural and the preternatural, between holiness and the miraculous, between the grace of union with God and *gratia gratis data*, a special divine gift of which the purpose is to benefit others, by so attracting their attention or awakening their gratitude that their salvation is helped. Holiness grows through the activity of the Gifts of the Holy Ghost, qualities complementary to the virtues; they are touched by genius, and their activity is not from deliberation, but from a divine instinct and sympathy. Holiness mounts to contemplation, but it consists in loving God with our whole heart, and our neighbour as ourself—the two precepts of the New Law. The canonical life of perfection, which is not for all, and not necessarily for the best, consists in being dedicated to certain means, the evangelical counsels, in order that these commands of love may be fulfilled.

[2] 1 Cor. x. 31.

obedience of Christ.[1] All his loves are brought into the love of God: *for whether we be beside ourselves, it is to God; or whether we be sober, it is for you; for the love of Christ constraineth us.*[2] Every power is engaged when every deed and word is based on love: *let all your things be done with charity.*[3] Such is the perfect mode of charity, to which all are bound by necessity of precept.

75, 396, 400   *de Perfectione Vitae Spiritualis,* 5

453. Not to go on along the way to God is to go back.

89   Commentary, *Ephesians,* iv, *lect.* 5

I. THE GIFTS OF THE HOLY GHOST

454. *And there shall come forth a rod out of Jesse, and a branch shall grow out of his roots; and the spirit of the Lord shall rest upon him, the spirit of wisdom and understanding, the spirit of counsel and might, the spirit of knowledge and piety, the spirit of the fear of the Lord.*[4] Virtues and Gifts are not in themselves contrasting terms, since the former are defined as good habits while the latter are defined by reference to their cause: there is no reason why a gift from another should not also be a quality of acting well, as we have seen in the case of the moral virtues infused in us by God. We must look elsewhere for their point of difference.

Some writers have held that in fact they are not different. But then no small difficulty remains why some virtues should be called Gifts, but not others, and why some Gifts, for instance, the fear of the Lord, are not reckoned among the virtues. Wherefore other writers have held that they are different, yet they have not succeeded in reaching to the root of difference, or in assigning the specific and exclusive characteristics.

[1] 2 Cor. x. 5.   [2] 2 Cor. v. 13–14.
[3] 1 Cor. xvi. 14.   [4] Isa. xi. 1.

Remarking that four of seven Gifts of the Holy Ghost, namely Wisdom, Knowledge, Understanding, and Counsel, pertain to the reason, while the remaining three, namely Fortitude, Piety, and the Fear of the Lord, pertain to the appetitive powers, some writers have explained that as a faculty of reason our freewill is endowed with the Gifts, whereas as a faculty of will it is endowed with the virtues—for but two of the virtues, namely faith and prudence, reside in the reason, while the remainder reside in the affective parts of the soul. This would be a strict division only on the supposition that all the Gifts were cognitive and all the virtues affective or appetitive.

Other authors, enlarging on Gregory's remark, that the sevenfold Gift of the Spirit shapes prudence, justice, fortitude, and temperance in the obedient mind and arms it against all temptation,[1] have emphasized this difference, that whereas the virtues strengthen us to act well, the Gifts arm us against temptation. But this does not touch the essential difference, for the virtues are well capable of resisting the temptations contrary to them—charity is a conspicuous case: *many waters cannot quench love.*[2]

Other authors again, observing that Holy Scripture prophetically sets forth the Gifts as qualities possessed by Christ, have inferred that the virtues are directed to good living, whereas the Gifts are directed to make us conformed to Christ, especially in his Passion, where they were gloriously manifested. Even this, however, does not bring out the main difference; our Lord bade us be like him through the virtues of humility, meekness, and charity: *learn of me, for I am meek and humble of heart;*[3]

[1] *Moralium Liber*, ii. 49; *PL* LXXV. 792.
[2] Cant. viii. 7.
[3] Matt. xi. 29.

love one another, as I have loved you.[1] These are virtues which shone out through his Passion.

Holy Scripture provides the clue; there the Gifts are referred to as spirits, not as gifts, which suggests that they come to us by divine inspiration, which signifies motion from outside. Let us fit this in with Aristotle's teaching about the two dynamic principles, one which is within us, namely our reason, the other which is outside us, namely God.[2] Whatever is set in motion should be adapted to its mover; and the disposition whereby it can be readily moved is one of its perfections. The higher and nobler the mover, the more necessary a better disposition; for instance, the higher the doctrine proposed, the more attentive and highly equipped should be the learners.

Now the virtues perfect our inborn tendency to be set going by our reason in our inner and outward life. But we need higher dispositions in order to be stirred by the Divinity which transcends us. These dispositions are called Gifts, not only because they are infused by God, but also because by them we are prepared to be promptly responsive to divine inspiration: *the Lord God hath opened my ear, and I was not rebellious, neither turned away back.*[3] Aristotle notices how persons touched by a divine instinct have no need to take counsel by human reasoning, for they are excited by a nobler principle. In this manner the Gifts rouse men to acts higher than the capabilities of virtue.

23, 205   *Summa Theologica*, 1a–2ae. lxviii. 1

455. It is where our own reasonable instincts are inadequate that the Gifts of the Holy Ghost are required.

God carries human reason through to its natural per-

---

[1] John xv. 12.
[2] *Eudemian Ethics*, vii. 14, 1137ᵃ5.   [3] Isa. i. 5.

fection by its native light, and to its supernatural perfection by the theological virtues. Although the supernatural is more sublime than the natural, it is less securely established in us—natural perfection is our own full endowment, whereas grace is, as it were, not quite grasped, for we imperfectly know God and love him. God works in every nature and purpose; all the same, we can think of ourselves as acting by our own powers and abilities. Yet when it comes to acting through full virtues, we need the assistance of another, for in this matter we are not completely self-possessed and self-contained. We are like the moon, or like a half-fledged student: the sun shines by its own light, the moon by a reflected light; a qualified doctor can operate without supervision, but not a medical student.

Well then, within the field of reason and as regards the natural purposes of human life, we can be regarded as competent to act from our own reasoned judgement. Any help here from divine inspiration will be from superabundance of divine goodness: philosophers note that not all equipped with acquired moral virtues are endowed with heroic or divine virtues. But with respect to our ultimate and supernatural end, on which our reason is set, though without being fully charged with the theological virtues, the motion of the reason is not enough unless borne onward by the motion and instinct of the Holy Ghost. *For as many as are led by the Spirit of God, they are the sons of God. The Spirit itself beareth witness with our spirit, that we are the children of God.*[1] Nobody can come into the inheritance of the blessed unless led by the Holy Ghost: *let thy gracious spirit lead me on into the good country.*[2]

54, 128, 415   *Summa Theologica*, 1a–2ae. lxviii. 2

[1] Rom. viii. 14, 16.
[2] Ps. cxlii. 10.

456. The Gifts excel the virtues, not in what they do, but in how they do it.

660   *Summa Theologica*, 1a–2ae. lxviii. 2, *ad* 1

457. The theological virtues join the human mind to God; the intellectual virtues are good qualities rendering the reason ready to know the truth; the moral virtues are perfections bringing the appetites under the control of right reason; the Gifts of the Holy Ghost are dispositions whereby every power of the soul can be played on by God.

Hence the Gifts are to the theological virtues (which unite men to the Spirit which moves them) what the moral virtues are to the intellectual virtues (which perfect the reason, which governs morality). As the intellectual virtues precede and rule the moral virtues, so the theological virtues should be set above the Gifts which they govern. Wherefore, Gregory observes that nobody obtains the sevenfold gift unless his entire activity be quickened by faith, hope, and charity.[1]

122, 347   *Summa Theologica*, 1a–2ae. lxviii. 8

458. The Gifts of Piety, Fortitude, and the Fear of the Lord are qualities of our appetitive powers. The differences between the Gifts of Understanding, Wisdom, Science, and Counsel, all of which are qualities of our cognitive powers, are not obvious. It has been suggested that Understanding, which is speculative or theoretical, differs from Science and Counsel because these two are practical, and that it differs from Wisdom, which also is theoretical, because it denotes insight or penetration into the truths that come before it, rather than a judgement about them. Earlier in the *Summa Theologica* I enumerated the Gifts along these lines.[2]

[1] *Moralium Liber*, i. 27; *PL* lxxv. 544.
[2] 1a–2ae. lxviii. 4.

Careful examination, however, shows that Understanding is not limited to questions of theoretical truth, but enters into practical issues, which should be ruled by eternal reasons: *a good understanding have they that do his commandments.*[1] Similarly, Science is at once speculative and practical. Consequently we have to prospect elsewhere for the ground of difference.

All four are concerned with supernatural knowledge, which is based on faith. Now *faith comes from hearing*;[2] truths are proposed for belief as things heard of, not seen; in that condition do we assent to them. Faith is engaged first of all and mainly with First Truth, secondarily with created truths, and last of all with the direction of our human deeds: *faith, which worketh by love.*[3]

When things are proposed for belief, on our side is required, first, some insight into their meaning, which is the function of Understanding, and second, discernment and right judgement about their implications. We should know what should be accepted, and what rejected. With respect to divine things, this is the function of Wisdom; with respect to creatures, of Science; with respect to individual courses of action, of Counsel.

52, 356, 369, 443   *Summa Theologica*, 2a–2ae. viii. 3, 6.

459. Faith merely assents to what is proposed, but the Gift of Understanding brings some insight into the truth, and this, where our ultimate end is concerned, supposes sanctifying grace.

377   *Summa Theologica*, 2a–2ae. viii. 5, *ad* 3

460. About what is not necessary for salvation people with sanctifying grace may be dull, but about what is

[1] Ps. cx. 10.   [2] Rom. x. 17.
[3] Gal. v. 6.

necessary they are sufficiently instructed by the Holy Spirit: *his unction teacheth you all things.*[1]

370   *Summa Theologica,* 2a–2ae. viii. 4, *ad* 1

461. Augustine says that the sixth operation of the Spirit, which is Understanding, characterizes the clean of heart, for, their eyes being pure, they see what other eyes have not seen.[2] The sixth beatitude, *Blessed are the pure of heart for they shall see God,*[3] contains two clauses, as do the other beatitudes; one refers to merit, namely cleanness of heart, the other to reward, namely seeing God. Both in a sense correspond to the Gift of Understanding.

There are two stages of purity, one preparatory, the other final. Preliminary to the sight of God is a cleansing of the affections from inordinate desires, performed by the virtues and the Gifts in the appetitive parts of man. Then there is a final development of purity, when the mind is purified from errors and phantasies, and receives divine truths without anthropomorphism or heretical distortion. This cleansing comes from the Gift of Understanding.

Similarly, there are two stages in our seeing of God, one is imperfect, which, though not gazing on God in himself, well perceives what he is not: we know him the better in this life the more we appreciate how far he is beyond our comprehension. The other is perfect vision which sees his essence. Both visions correspond to the Gift of Understanding; the first to its beginnings on earth, the second to its consummation in heaven.

5, 449   *Summa Theologica,* 2a–2ae. viii. 7

462. Of the two kinds of instructed knowledge about the truths of faith, one knows what we should believe,

[1] 1 John ii. 27.
[2] *de Sermone Domini in monte,* i. 4; *PL* xxxiv. 1235.
[3] Matt. v. 8.

discerning what is of faith from what is not—this comes from the Gift of Science which accompanies sanctifying grace; the other is a more special gift, a *gratia gratis data* not given to everybody, which knows how to expound the Faith, to bring it to others, and to refute hostile critics.

53, 318, 322 *Summa Theologica*, 2a–2ae. ix. 1, *ad* 2

463. Although its real object is divine and eternal, faith nevertheless is a temporal event in the soul of the believer. The business of the Gift of Science is rather to control our knowledge of the historical surroundings to belief, whereas the business of the Gift of Wisdom, which closely matches charity, is to perceive divine and eternal things through real union with them.

39 *Summa Theologica*, 2a–2ae. ix. 2, *ad* 1

464. Pure truth, that is the first and main concern of the Gift of Science, which also, secondarily, takes in what we do and think about it, for our life should be governed by the knowledge of divine truth and its consequences.

11, 52 *Summa Theologica*, 2a–2ae. ix. 3

465. Augustine says that Science befits those who mourn, the people who have been taught by hard experience of their defeat by the evils they sought as goods.[1] The office of Science is to pass right judgements on creatures, which can be the occasions for our turning away from God: *they have entangled men's souls, and laid a trap for the foolish.*[2] Creaturely goods do not stir us to spiritual joy unless they be taken in relation to Divine Good, from which rises spiritual peace and consequent joy—the fruits of the Spirit corresponding to

[1] *de Sermone Domini in monte*, i. 4; *PL* xxxiv. 1234.
[2] Wisd. xiv. 11.

the Gift of Wisdom. Sorrow for past mistakes, this answers to the Gift of Science; then comes consolation, when creatures are accepted as God would have us do. Accordingly, in the third beatitude, *Blessed are they that mourn, for they shall be comforted,*[1] mourning is by way of merit, comfort by way of reward—a comfort that already begins now but will be complete only in heaven.

131   *Summa Theologica,* 2a–2ae. ix. 4, c. & ad 1

466. Fear is of various kinds. Worldly fear, the fear that caused Peter to deny Christ, is not a gift of God, as Augustine notes.[2] What is from God is the *fear of him who is able to destroy both soul and body in hell.*[3] Servile fear also, the fear of punishment, though from the Holy Ghost, should not be numbered among the Gifts, for, as Augustine also notes, it can accompany the will to sin,[4] whereas a Gift can be present only with charity.

The fear which is the Gift of the Holy Ghost is filial fear, or chaste fear, which shrinks from offending our Father and from being separated from him. The Gifts are settled dispositions in the soul's powers which render them easily moved by the Spirit without setting up resistance. Such a quality is filial fear, which reverences God and shrinks from being parted from him. It holds the first place among the Gifts in the ascending order, *the fear of the Lord is the beginning of wisdom,*[5] and the last place in the descending order.[6]

10, 286   *Summa Theologica,* 2a–2ae. xix. 9

467. Filial fear grows with love, for the more we are in love the more we hate to displease or to be separated

---

[1] Matt. ii. 4.
[2] *de Gratia et Libero Arbitrio,* 18, *PL* xliv. 904.
[3] Matt. x. 28.
[4] *de Natura et Gratia,* 57; *PL* xliv. 280.   [5] Ps. cx. 10.
[6] *de Sermone Domini in monte,* i. 4; *PL* xxxiv. 1234.

from the person we love. The servility of servile fear is entirely displaced by charity, but the fear of punishment remains in substance, though its activity is lessened. The more we love God the less we fear punishment, first, because then we care less about any threat to our own advantage, and secondly, because then our firmer friendship makes us the more confident of its happy ending.

Summa Theologica, 2a–2ae. x. 10

468. *Blessed are the poor in spirit, for theirs is the kingdom of heaven.*[1] When a person subjects himself to God, he ceases to vaunt himself or to attach overmuch importance to other things apart from God: *some trust in chariots, and some in horses, but we will remember the name of the Lord.*[2] Perfectly fearing God, he does not exaggerate his own importance. He lays little store by honours or external riches. His is a poverty of spirit, which comes from the instinct of the Holy Ghost, a poverty explained by Augustine[3] as an emptying of pride, and by Ambrose[4] and Jerome[5] as a giving up of external goods.

492   *Summa Theologica*, 2a–2ae. xix. 12

469. Aristotle says that the wise man's office is to consider the highest cause of things, and by this norm to judge them with the utmost certainty and direct all his actions.[6] The highest cause can mean either the First Cause absolutely or the first cause in a particular class or series. A person who tests and disposes of subordinate things through his knowledge of the first cause in a

---

[1] Matt. v. 3.   [2] Ps. xix. 8.
[3] *de Sermone Domini in monte*, i. 1; *PL* xxxiv. 1231.
[4] *in Lucae Evangelium*, vi. 20; *PL* xv. 1735.
[5] *in Mattaei Evangelium*, v. 3; *PL* xxvi. 34.
[6] *Metaphysics*, i. 2, 928[a]9.

particular province is said to be wise in that respect;
thus we speak of a wise physician or architect: *as a wise
masterbuilder I have laid the foundation.*[1] But when he
knows the First Cause simply speaking, which is God,
then he is wise without qualification, for all his judgements and arrangements are measured by the Eternal
Law. *He that is spiritual judgeth all things,* and he does
so by the Holy Ghost; *the Spirit searcheth all things,
yea the deep things of God.*[2]

    10, 277, 425   *Summa Theologica,* 2a–2ae. xlv. 1

470. Wisdom which is the Gift of the Holy Ghost,
descending from above,[3] differs from the wisdom which is
an intellectual virtue and is acquired by human study.
Because it appreciates divine things it also differs from
faith, which simply assents to their truth.

    53   *Summa Theologica,* 2a–2ae. xlv. 1, *ad* 2

471. Wisdom implies a rightness of judgement. Now
this can come about in two ways, either by close and
reasoned application or by a flair. Questions of chastity,
for instance, can be accurately decided by a scientific
moralist, but also, through another approach, by a
person who possesses the habit of chastity. A sound
verdict may be reached about divine things both
through the intellectual virtue of wisdom and through
the soul's being in sympathy with them. This last
is the effect of the Holy Ghost; thus Dionysius says
that Hierotheus is perfect in matters of divinity, not
only by learning about them, but also by experiencing
them.[4] This sympathy and connaturality comes from
charity, which unites us to God: *he who is joined to the*

---

[1] 1 Cor. iii. 10.   [2] 1 Cor. ii. 10, 15.
[3] James iii. 14.
[4] Cf. *de Divinis Nominibus,* ii, *lect.* 4.

Lord is one spirit. [1] Will is the agent of charity, though wisdom itself is an act of mind.

54   *Summa Theologica,* 2a–2ae. xlv. 2

472. *Blessed are the peacemakers, for they shall be called the children of God.* [2] Peacemaking, which brings peace to oneself and others, is the merit of Wisdom. It is the result of setting values in their proper order, for peace, says Augustine, is the tranquillity of order. [3] To set things in order is wisdom's office; its role is eirenical. The children of God—here the reward of Wisdom is touched on. For we are called God's children by taking on the likeness of his natural and only-begotten Son: *predestinate to be conformed to the image of his Son,* [4] who is begotten Wisdom.

129, 551   *Summa Theologica,* 2a–2ae. xlv. 6

473. The virtues of prudence and good counsel, whether acquired or infused, direct men when investigating matters open to the reason, and make them shrewd for themselves and good advisers to others. The human reason, however, cannot comprehend every singular and contingent case which can arise: *our human thoughts are hesitating, our conjectures hazardous.* [5] Our calculations need to be directed by God, who comprehends everything, through the Gift of Counsel, by which a person is guided by God's advice—just as when we find ourselves at a loss in human business we seek the advice of people more experienced than ourselves.

202, 421   *Summa Theologica,* 2a–2ae. lii. 1, *ad* 1

474. Counsel befits the merciful ones; the only remedy for great evils, says Augustine, the only way of plucking

---

[1] 1 Cor. vi. 17.   [2] Matt. iv. 9.
[3] *de Civitate Dei,* xix. 13; *PL* xli. 460.
[4] Rom. viii. 29.   [5] Wisd. ix. 14.

them out is to forgive and to give.[1] Good advice is about
what is useful: *godliness is profitable unto all things*.[2] In a
special manner mercy answers to good counsel, which
directs it, though it does not elicit it, and the beatitude
corresponding to the Gift of Counsel is, *Blessed are the
merciful, for they shall obtain mercy*.[3]

72　　　　　　　　　　　*Summa Theologica*, 2a–2ae. lii. 4

475. *You have received the Spirit of adoption, whereby
we cry, Abba, Father*.[4] We reverence and serve our
parents through the virtue of piety, and therefore it is
fitting that the worship and service we offer to God our
Father through the instinct of the Holy Spirit should be
a Gift. All related to us by blood are served through
the virtue of piety; likewise the Gift also not only wor-
ships God but also reverences his children. The saints
are honoured, misery is relieved, the Holy Scriptures
are not contradicted, whether they be understood or
not. At present the saints are compassionate towards us,
though they will not need to be after the Last Judgement. Regarding its principal act, namely, of filial
reverence for God, the Gift of Piety remains in heaven.

661　　　　　　　　　　*Summa Theologica*, 2a–2ae. cxxi. 1

476. The Holy Ghost moves us past the virtue of
fortitude despite all dangers to the successful accom-
plishment of what we have begun. This is beyond
human power, for sometimes we are not strong enough
to win through and to override all evils and perils,
which press us down to death. The Holy Ghost leads
us to eternal life, which is the final achievement of all
we do, the escaping from all ills and dangers. To this end

---

[1] *de Sermone Domini in monte*, i. 4; *PL* xxxiv. 1234.
[2] 1 Tim. iv. 8.　　　　　　　　　　[3] Matt. iv. 7.
[4] Rom. viii. 15.

the Holy Ghost infuses in us the Gift of Fortitude, a
confidence of mind banishing all fear.

443 *Summa Theologica*, 2a–2ae. cxl. 1

477. Four lessons may be learnt from our Lord's descent
into hell, lessons of hope, of fear, of care, of love.

First, firm hope in God. The deeper we are sunk in
misery the more we should trust and have confidence.
Nothing could be more grievous than being in hell, and
if Christ freed men there, how strongly should we, who
are his friends, rely on him to rescue us whatever our
straits. Wisdom *forsook not the just when he was sold, but
delivered him from sinners; she went down with him into
the pit; and in bands she left him till she brought him the
sceptre of the kingdom.*[1] God specially cherishes those
who follow him. If we serve him, how secure we should
feel: *he that feareth the Lord shall tremble at nothing and
shall not be afraid: the Lord is his hope.*[2]

Secondly, we should conceive fear and expel presumption. For though Christ suffered for sinners, and
descended into hell, he did not free all, but those only
who were free from grave personal sin. The others he
left. All who die in their sins may abandon hope of
forgiveness when they go down into the shades: *these
shall go into everlasting punishment, but the just into life
everlasting.*[3]

Thirdly, let us take heed. Christ went down into the
depths for our salvation. Let our thoughts often go there
too, and dwell on retribution, imitating the holy King
Hezekiah: *I said, in the midst of my days I shall go to the
gates of hell.*[4] A mind which goes down to hell often in
life will not easily go down there in death. Men avoid
wrongdoing by reminding themselves of the penalties:

[1] Wisd. x. 13–14.   [2] Ecclus. xxxiv. 16.
[3] Matt. xxv. 46.   [4] Isa. xxxviii. 10.

reflect on damnation and we are warned against sin, for how long, keen, and manifold are the pains of hell: *in all thy works, remember thy last end, and thou shalt never sin.*[1]

Fourthly, appears an example of love. Christ descended into hell to liberate his own. We also should come to the assistance of our friends who are in purgatory. How mean a person not to relieve a dear one held in prison; how harder-hearted when the prison is purgatory, for there is no comparison between the pains of this world and the next. *Have pity on me, have pity on me, at least you my friends, because the hand of the Lord hath touched me.*[2] And so *it is a holy and wholesome thought to pray for the dead, that they may be loosed from sin.*[3] Three deeds, according to tradition, principally bring them relief: masses, prayers, and alms; a fourth is added, namely fasting, which is well understandable, for even in this world friend can satisfy for friend.

266, 527, 550   Exposition, *Apostles' Creed*

2. THE CONTEMPLATIVE LIFE

478. The contemplative life is better than the active life, if we leave special circumstances out of account, and for the half-dozen reasons given by Aristotle.[4]

First, contemplation is the activity of the best in man, namely his mind, occupied with its proper object, namely pure truth, whereas action is about external business. The contemplative life is signified by Rachel and her direct gaze, the active life, according to Gregory, by Leah who was blear eyed.[5]

Secondly, the contemplative life can be more con-

---

[1] Ecclus. vii. 40.   [2] Job. xix. 21.   [3] 2 Macc. xii. 46.
[4] *Ethics*, x. 7, 8, 1177^{a}12, 1178^{a}9.
[5] *Moralium Liber*, vi. 63; *PL* lxxv. 764.

tinual than the active, though not always at its highest pitch. Mary, the type of the contemplative, is described as sitting at the Lord's feet.[1]

Thirdly, the contemplative life affords greater delight. Augustine notes how Martha was fretting while Mary was enjoying herself.[2]

Fourthly, the contemplative life is more self-sufficient and needs lesser apparatus: *Martha, Martha, thou art careful and troubled about many things.*[3]

Fifthly, the contemplative life is sought after for its own sake, the active life for the sake of something else: *one thing have I desired of the Lord, that will I seek after, that I may dwell in the house of the Lord all the days of my life, to behold the beauty of the Lord.*[4]

Sixthly, the contemplative life is a kind of holiday: *be still, and see that I am the Lord.*[5]

Seventhly, the contemplative life is lived with divine things, the active life with human. Augustine says that *in the beginning was the Word*—attend to what Mary listened to, counsels Augustine; *and the Word was made flesh*—attend to what Martha served.[6]

Eighthly, the contemplative life pursues man's proper course, namely the way of mind, whereas the active life is occupied with the interests we share with animals.

We may add a ninth reason from the words of our Lord: *Mary hath chosen the better part, which shall not be taken away from her.*[7] Not that the one is bad, remarks Augustine, but that the other is better. Why better? Listen. It shall not be taken away. A time will

---

[1] Luke x. 39.
[2] *Sermones ad Populum*, ciii. 4; *PL* xxxviii. 614.
[3] Luke x. 41.
[4] Ps. xxvi. 4.
[5] Ps. xlv. 11.
[6] *Sermones ad Populum*, civ. 2; *PL* xxxviii. 617.
[7] Luke x. 42.

come when the burden of our necessities will be lifted,
but the sweetness of truth remains eternal.[1]

4, 399   *Summa Theologica*, 2a–2ae. clxxxii. 1

479. The contemplative life, to speak without qualification, is more perfect than the active life occupied
with the bustle of business. Yet that way of active life
which leads a person by teaching and preaching to
deliver to others the fruits of his contemplation is better
than a way which stops at contemplation, for it expresses
a greater abundance of truth. Such was the life chosen
by Christ.

547   *Summa Theologica*, 3a. xl. 1, *ad* 2

480. Perfection is reached when you are single-hearted;
the more united and compact you are, the liker you are
to God: *one thing have I desired of the Lord*.[2] This unity
breaks up when you seek riches and the things of this
world; your desires are scattered, your heart is tugged
this way and that.

239, 255   Exposition, *I Timothy*, vi, *lect.* 2

481. The signs made use of in our thoughts about God
are not such that our minds can rest on them.

14   Exposition, *de Divinis Nominibus*, i, *lect.* 2

482. To realize that God is far beyond anything we
think, that is the mind's achievement.

74   Exposition, *de Divinis Nominibus*, i, *lect.* 3

483. Creatures are set in motion towards some definite
goal, not for some boundless object stretching out indefinitely. But since God is infinitely beyond us, we
may well ask, how can we set ourselves to think about
him?

[1] *Sermones ad Populum*, ciii. 4; *PL* xxxviii. 614.
[2] Ps. xxvi. 4.

I answer that no one moves towards God as ever to be his equal; nor yet is he our goal precisely as being infinitely beyond us. Yet we are meant to become more and more like him, and according to our condition should ever be set on knowing him. Hence Hilary says that he who reverently pursues the Infinite, even though he may never attain it, will yet advance by pressing on.[1]

206   Exposition *de Trinitate*, ii. 1, *ad* 7

484. God is worshipped in silence—not that we can think or say nothing about him, but that we should appreciate how far he surpasses our comprehension: *glorify the Lord as much as you can; for he will yet far exceed, and his magnificence is wonderful: blessing the Lord, exalt him as much as you can, for he is above all praise.*[2]

60   Exposition, *de Trinitate*, ii. 1, *ad* 6

3. THE LIFE OF PERFECTION

485. *Above all these things put on charity, which is the bond of perfection.*[3] For charity binds, as it were, all the other virtues into close unity. Each and everything is said to be perfect in so far as it attains its proper end; and this is its ultimate perfection. Charity unites us to God, the ultimate end of the human mind: *he that dwelleth in love dwelleth in God, and God in him.*[4] Therefore we must look for the perfection of the Christian life in charity.

394   *Summa Theologica*, 2a–2ae. clxxxiv. 1

486. Divine law, which commands nothing impossible, commands us to be perfect: *be ye therefore perfect,*

---

[1] *de Trinitate*, ii. 10; *PL* x. 59.   [2] Ecclus. xliii. 32.
[3] Col. iii. 14.   [4] 1 John iv. 16.

even as your heavenly Father is perfect.[1] Therefore it seems that a person can be perfect even in this present life.

We have said that the perfection of the Christian life consists in charity. Now perfection implies a certain fullness, for, as Aristotle notes, that is perfect to which nothing is lacking.[2] At this point, it will be useful to distinguish between three degrees of perfection.

The first is absolute; all capacity is filled, on the side both of the lover and of the beloved. Charity is then perfect when God is loved as much as he can be loved. Such perfection no creature can reach. God alone can love like that, and in no other is there complete and essential good.

A lower degree of perfection is that which fills the capacity of the lover, who goes out to God with his full power by actual and constant affection. Such perfection is not possible to men who are wayfarers, but must wait for heaven.

The lowest degree of perfection requires that everything inimical to God's friendship is excluded. Augustine remarks that cupidity is poison to charity, while the absence of cupidity is charity's perfection.[3] Such perfection is possible here below, and in two ways.

First, when human affection excludes everything contrary to charity, in other words, mortal sin. Charity cannot exist without this perfection, which is commanded as necessary for salvation. Next, when human affection excludes everything which hinders our being wholly in love with God. Charity can exist without such perfection, as it does in those who are beginners and in those who are making progress in the life of perfection.

[1] Matt. vi. 48.   [2] *Physics*, iii. 6, 207ᵃ8.
[3] *de Diversis Quaestionibus LXXXIII*, 36; PL XL. 25.

This conclusion about loving God bears also on loving our neighbour. Our present state of life does not permit us to be actually always loving God, nor always actually loving each and all of our fellows. It is enough that our charity should reach out to all in general and to each as a habit of mind, a state of preparedness for the occasion when active love for particular persons will be called for. The distinction we have applied to our loving of God applies also to our loving of our neighbour: there is a certain completeness without which charity cannot exist, and that is that there be nothing in our affections contrary to love of the fellowship. But another and consummate completeness is not strictly necessary, I mean that charity can lack it and yet observe the three following points of perfection.

First, concerning love's extent, when strangers, and even enemies, are loved, and we do not restrict ourselves to friends and acquaintances: this, observes Augustine, is part of the perfection of God's children.[1] Secondly, concerning love's recklessness, when for love of his neighbour a person is prepared to undergo, not only loss of property, but also bodily affliction and even death: *greater love hath no man than this, that a man lay down his life for his friends.*[2] Thirdly, concerning love's effect, when a person gives of himself, not only of his belongings: *I will very gladly spend and be spent for you.*[3]

17, 409, 537   *Summa Theologica,* 2a–2ae. clxxxiv. 2, *c. &*
ad 3

487. A man is unreservedly called perfect in the spiritual life because of what is most important there; in a manner of speaking he is called perfect because of some accompaniment. Above all the spiritual life consists in charity; without charity it is so much waste.

[1] *Enchiridion.* 73; *PL* XL. 266.
[2] John xv. 13.   [3] 2 Cor. xii. 15.

Though I have the gift of prophecy, and understand all mysteries, and all knowledge; and though I have all faith, so that I could remove mountains, and have not charity, I am nothing.[1] And John the Divine says, *we know that we have passed from death unto life because we love the brethren. He that loveth not his brother abideth in death.*[2]

To speak therefore without qualification, that man is perfect spiritually who has perfect love. To speak relatively, however, perfection can be judged by certain accompanying qualities. Thus, the Apostle enumerates *the bowels of mercy, kindness, humbleness of mind, meekness, long suffering;*[3] and then links them all together in charity: *but above all these things put on charity, which is the bond of perfection.*[4]

412, 417   *de Perfectione Vitae Spiritualis*, 1

488. *Thou shalt love the Lord thy God with thy whole heart.*[5] *Thou shalt love thy neighbour as thyself.*[6] These are the two commandments of which our Lord spoke: *on these two commandments hang all the law and the prophets.*[7] The perfection of the Christian life, therefore, consists in keeping these precepts.

To explain more fully. A requirement may be either direct and essential or indirect and secondary. Christian perfection directly and essentially lies in charity, primarily in the love of God, secondarily in the love of our neighbour. On these two heads are precepts given—not that loving God can be measured by a regulation, as if what was over and above were a matter of counsel; indeed the very terms of the command are without stint, for we are bidden to love God with our whole heart: as Aristotle notes, the whole and the perfect are the same.[8]

---

[1] 1 Cor. xiii. 2.   [2] 1 John iii. 14.
[3] Col. iii. 12.   [4] Ibid. 14.   [5] Deut. vi. 5.
[6] Lev. xix. 18.   [7] Matt. xxii. 40.
[8] *Physics*, iii. 6, 207ᵃ13.

The same abandon appears in the command to love our
neighbour as ourselves, for how greatly we love ourselves! So no measure is demanded in our loving, the
reason being that *the end of the commandment is charity*.[1]
For measure is imposed on means to ends, not on the
end itself. The doctor does not measure health, but the
medicine he uses, or the diet he recommends.[2] Obviously
then, perfection consists essentially in the precepts, and
though nobody in this life may achieve it, we may well
ask, with Augustine, why this perfection should not be
commanded.[3]

Perfection lies in the counsels derivatively and instrumentally. The counsels are like the precepts in being
ordained to charity, but with this difference. For whereas the precepts are designed to exclude whatever is
contrary to and incompatible with charity, the counsels
rule out things not in themselves contrary to charity, for
instance, getting married, secular business, and so forth.
Augustine says that there are some things which God
commands, of which one is, *thou shalt not commit
adultery*, and there are some things which he does not
demand, but warns us about by spiritual counsel, of
which one is, *it is good for man not to touch a woman;* that
these are properly observed when they are done for
love of God and our neighbour.[4] Hence the Abbot
Moses says, that fastings, vigils, meditations on the
Scriptures, nakedness, mortification in every faculty—
these are not perfection, but the instruments of perfection; to that end are we disciplined by working through
them, not by staying with them.[5]

416, 638, 644   *Summa Theologica*, 2a–2ae. clxxxiv. 3

[1] 1 Tim. i. 5.   [2] *Politics*, i. 9, 1257^{b}30.
[3] *de Perfectione Justitiae*, 8; *PL* xliv, 301.
[4] *Enchiridion*, 121; *PL* xl. 288.
[5] Cassian, *Collationes Patrum*, i. 7; *PL* xlix. 490.

489. To reckon that divine blessings are grudged is poetic licence; so also to think that God from jealousy would not have us accept them. The opinion is completely baseless. Any touch of envy, or sadness about another's good fortune because it lessens one's own self-esteem is quite out of keeping with divinity. Sadness can never touch God; he is subject to no evil, nor is his good diminished by anyone else's. It is from his goodness, as from an unfailing fountain, that all goods flow to us.

131   Commentary, *I Metaphysics, lect.* 3

490. *Man looketh on the outward appearance, but the Lord looketh on the heart.*[1] Divine judgement assesses a man's state by his interior disposition, but the Church assesses him by what he does outwardly. Consequently, a person is in a canonical state of perfection because he has bound himself perpetually and with some solemnity to observing some means to perfection, not because he acts from perfect love. It can happen that one may so oblige himself and yet not keep his engagement, while another may fulfil that to which he is not bound, like the two sons in the parable, of whom one said he would not go to work in his father's vineyard, but afterwards repented and went, while the other said, *I go, sir, and went not.*[2] Nothing stops those from being perfect who are not in the religious state of perfection, and others from being in the state of perfection and yet not being perfect.

279, 650   *Summa Theologica,* 2a–2ae. clxxxiv. 4

491. *Religion,* in its original sense, meant binding yourself to God's due service through faith. Everybody undertakes this on entering the Christian religion by

[1] 1 Kings xvi. 7.   [2] Matt. xxi. 28–31.

baptism when Satan and all his pomps are renounced. But religion also has a narrower meaning, namely, of binding yourself to certain deeds of charity, deeds which in some special manner serve God and renounce the world: it is in this sense that we speak of the religious life, or the life of religion.

Charity offers due service to God through the activities alike of the contemplative life and the active life. The functions of the active life are diversified according to the different services of charity we offer our neighbour. Some religious orders are instituted to spend their time with God in contemplation, others to serve God in his members, such as the orders dedicated to nursing the sick or ransoming captives. There is no work of charity to which a religious order cannot be committed, even if it has not yet been founded.

438, 644   *Contra Impugnantes*, 1

492. *If thou wilt be perfect, go and sell all thou hast and give to the poor.*[1] Not that a man thereupon becomes perfect straightaway, but that he makes a beginning.

Commentary, *St. Matthew*, xix. 21

493. There were reasons why Christ should have led a life of poverty in this world. First, because this was in keeping with the duty of preaching: *for this purpose am I come.*[2] If preachers are to give all their time to the gospel they must be quite free from the cares of worldly business, which is not possible for the wealthy. Wherefore in sending his apostles and disciples our Lord commanded them, *do not possess gold or silver.*[3] And they said, *it is not reasonable that we should leave the word of God and serve tables.*[4] Secondly, just as he took upon

[1] Matt. xix. 21.   [2] Mark i. 38.
[3] Matt. x. 9.   [4] Acts. vi. 2.

himself bodily death in order to bestow spiritual life on us, so did he bear bodily poverty in order to enrich us spiritually: *you know the grace of our Lord Jesus Christ, that he became poor for our sakes, that through his poverty we might become rich.*[1]

450, 547, 653   *Summa Theologica*, 3a. xl. 3

494. People truly penitent, however depraved they may have been, can embark at once on the life of the evangelical counsels.

627   *Contra Retrahentes*, 5

495. Charity forms a union of affection, for friend holds friend an alter ego. Nevertheless, the beloved may be far away and therefore charity and hope can go along together.

394   Disputations, *de Spe*, 1, *ad* 11

[1] 2 Cor. viii. 9.

IX

The Incarnation[1]

496. *Drop down, ye heavens, from above, and let the clouds rain down righteousness; let the earth open, and bud forth a saviour.*[2] The heavens, plural—as though to indicate the three Blessed Persons: the Father sending, the Son taking flesh, the Spirit causing the conception. The skies raining down—picture the angel of the Annunciation coming from God: *who maketh the clouds his chariot; who walketh upon the wings of the wind; who maketh his angels spirits.*[3] The earth opening: *our land shall yield her increase.*[4] The blessed Virgin opened herself to the privilege of grace, her mind to receive, her womb to conceive: *fear not, Mary, for thou hast found favour with God.*[5]

538   Exposition, *Isaiah*, xlv

---

[1] An Aristotelean and convinced of the reality of material things, St. Thomas was not tempted to treat the Incarnation as a shadow-play; it is the real embodiment of the Word in human history, an event which is physically effective as well as morally instructive. Christ is true God, with all the attributes of divinity; he is true man, with human mind, will, emotions. So noble is the union of God with human nature that some theologians have argued that it would have taken place even if man had not sinned. St. Thomas is cautious; God's free choices can be discovered only from divine Revelation, and there all the indications are that Christ came to restore. The Atonement he made is explained in terms of sacrifice, satisfaction, merit, redemption, example, and effective influence: there are but few echoes of the doctrine of the Dark Ages that Christ recaptured us or bought us back from the devil.

[2] Isa. xlv. 8.   [3] Ps. ciii. 3.
[4] Ps. lxxxiv. 13.   [5] Luke i. 30.

497. The blessed evangelist John descends from high keen truths to the Word made gentle flesh. When the Word was in the Father's bosom he was known only by the Father, but when he became a spoken and embodied word of mouth then was he made manifest to us: *he was seen upon earth, and conversed with men.*[1] A word uttered is heard by ear, but is not read until set down in letters. The Word of God could be both seen and felt, being written in our flesh.

17   Exposition, *Apostles' Creed*

498. Because our Saviour Jesus Christ, as the angel testified, *saves his people from their sins*[2] and demonstrates in himself the truth which is the way to deathless happiness, it is right that we should meditate on him and the blessings he brings us after considering questions of moral theology. First, let us consider our Saviour himself; secondly, his sacraments; thirdly, the goal of immortality we reach through his rising from the dead.

Summa Theologica, 3a. Prologue

499. Is the mind filled, you ask, by knowing Christ? Most certainly yes, I reply, for in him are all the treasures of wisdom. God knows all things and his knowledge is compared to a treasure: *wisdom is an infinite treasure to men.*[3] A treasury is where riches are amassed, and in divine wisdom all riches are heaped together. All reality is treasured in the Word, notwithstanding the divine generosity which scatters goodness abroad, for God pours wisdom *out upon his works, and upon all flesh, according to his gift.*[4]

St. Paul adds that the treasures are hidden.[5] Things are hidden either because our observation is poor or because they are covered: we fail to see a light either

---

[1] Bar. iii. 38.   [2] Matt. i. 21.
[3] Wisd. vii. 14.   [4] Ecclus. i. 10.   [5] Col. ii. 3.

because we are blind or it is shuttered. The treasures of understanding and wisdom in the Word of God are unseen either because our eyes are clouded and not clear, or because divine truths are eclipsed by creatures and things of flesh. All the same, creatures are like God, and through the flesh we may catch a glimpse of him: *for the invisible things of him from the creation of the world are made manifest, being understood by the things which are made.*[1] Moreover, reflect on the text, *the Word was made flesh.*[2]

A man with a dark lantern has no need to search for a light; all he has to do is to open the shutter. A man with a book which tells him what he should know has only to open the book. We have no need to look outside Christ: *I judged not myself to know anything but Christ Jesus.*[3] *We know that when he shall appear,* that is, when God shall be revealed, *we shall be like to him.*[4]

84, 116, 372   Commentary, *Colossians,* ii. 3

I. THE NEED

500. A means is judged necessary either because the end cannot be secured without it, thus food is necessary for life, or because the end is better and more conveniently reached through it, thus a horse is necessary for a journey. The first kind of necessity does not enter into the Incarnation, for God's almighty power could have restored human nature in many other ways. The necessity was of the second kind, for, as Augustine declares, other ways were not closed to God, who equally commands everything, but no means was more suitable for healing our woe.[5] Let us, then, consider this

[1] Rom. i. 20.   [2] John i. 14.
[3] 1 Cor. ii. 2.   [4] 1 John iii. 2.
[5] *de Trinitate,* xiii. 10; *PL* XLII. 1024.

beneficial course, with respect, first, to our advancement in good, second, to our withdrawal from evil.

Under the first heading let us take faith. We have better guarantee when we believe that God himself is speaking to us. Augustine says that it was that we might set forth more trustfully to the truth that the Son of God, having become man, founded and built faith.[1] Next, take hope, so highly lifted up, for, as Augustine asks, what better could have raised our hope than this proof of God's deep love for us, what more cogent than the Son of God deigning to become our partner in human nature?[2] Then take charity, thereby strongly enkindled, for, as Augustine also asks, what mightier cause is there for the Lord's coming than to show us his love? He adds, that if we have been slow to love in the past let us now hasten to love in return.[3] Fourthly, take right conduct, where an example is set us. Augustine points out that men can be seen but should not be followed, God should be followed but cannot be seen, and therefore God became man that he might both be seen and followed.[4] Finally, with regard to our full sharing in the divinity, which is our true end and bliss bestowed on us through Christ's manhood, Augustine says that he became man that man might become God.[5]

Under the second heading, let us first meditate on how man is taught by the Incarnation not to rank the devil above himself or to be cowed by the author of evil. Augustine reflects that when a human nature can be so joined to God that there is but one person there, let no

---

[1] de Civitate Dei, xi. 2; PL xli. 318.
[2] de Trinitate, xiii. 10; PL xlii. 1024.
[3] de Catechizandis Rudibus, 4; PL xl. 314.
[4] Sermones ad Populum, ccclxxi. 2; PL xxxix. 1660.
[5] Sermones Supposititii, cxxviii; PL xxxix. 1997.

proud spirits vaunt themselves above men because they
are unearthly and without flesh.[1] Secondly, we are
taught how great is human dignity lest we sully it with
sin. Augustine says that God has now shown us the
high place human nature holds in creation, for he
entered into it by genuinely becoming man.[2] And Pope
Leo cries, Know your worth, O Christian; you are
made a partner of the divine nature: refuse, then, to
return to your former worthlessness by degenerate intercourse.[3] Thirdly, in order to do away with our presumption, the grace of God, says Augustine, is commended
in Jesus Christ, through no preceding merits of our
own.[4] Fourthly, man's pride, says Augustine in the
same place, his greatest hindrance to clinging to God, is
rebuked and cured by humility so great. Fifthly, in
order to free us from the bondage of sin: this, says
Augustine, should be done in such a way that the devil
is overthrown by the justice of a man, and by Christ
making satisfaction for us.[5] A mere man could not make
satisfaction for the whole human race, and this is no
office of God's. How right, then, that our Saviour
should be both God and man. Pope Leo says that
weakness is assumed by strength, lowliness by majesty,
mortality by immortality, in order that one and the same
mediator between God and men might die in the one
and rise in the other.[6] Unless he were God, he could
not have brought the remedy; unless he were man, he
could not have set the example.

147, 353, 389, 394, 552   *Summa Theologica*, 3a. i. 2

[1] *de Trinitate*, xiii. 17; *PL* XLII. 1031.
[2] *de Vera Religione*, 16; *PL* XXXIV. 134.
[3] *Sermones*, xxi. 3; *PL* LIV. 192.
[4] *de Trinitate*, xiii. 17; *PL* XLII. 1031.
[5] *de Trinitate*, xiii. 13; *PL* XLII. 1027.
[6] *Sermones*, xxi. 2; *PL* LIV. 192.

501. *The Son of Man is come to seek and to save that which was lost.*[1] Therefore, Augustine concludes, if man had not sinned the Son of Man would not have come.[2] St. Paul says, *Christ Jesus came into this world to save sinners:*[3] the Gloss on this text says that there was no cause for Christ to come into this world except to save sinners; abolish disease and injury, and there is no call for medicine.

Theologians think differently on this point. Some hold that even if man had not fallen the Son of God would have become incarnate. Others hold the contrary. Personally I think their opinion is to be preferred.

Follow this rule of interpretation: deeds done by the divine will above our deserving can come to our knowledge only when they are revealed in Holy Scripture which declares God's intentions to us. There the cause of the Incarnation is always put down to man's sin. Accordingly, it is safer to teach that the Incarnation was ordained by God as a remedy for sin, and that if no sin had come in the Incarnation would not have taken place. Nevertheless, God's power should not be circumscribed: he might have become incarnate even if sin had never entered.

16, 372   *Summa Theologica*, 3a. i. 3

502. Christ came to take away sin—was this original sin chiefly and mainly? Simply speaking, he came to take away all sin. Now his grace exceeds Adam's wrong: *if through the offence of one many be dead, much more the grace of God, and the gift by grace, which is by one man, Jesus Christ, hath abounded unto many.*[4] The greater the sin the greater its importance in Christ's project.

---

[1] Luke xix. 10.
[2] *Sermones ad Populum*, clxxiv. 2; *PL* xxxviii. 940.
[3] 1 Tim. i. 15.   [4] Rom. v. 15.

The sin which men contract at birth, although less grave and guilty than their actual sins, is more widespreading: *for that all have sinned.*[1] To that extent, therefore, it may be said that Christ came principally to take away original sin: *behold the Lamb of God who taketh away the sin of the world.*[2] The sin of the world, that is, says the Gloss, original sin, which is common to the whole world.

224, 557 *Declaratio XLII Quaestionum,* 28[3]

503. *God so loved the world, that he gave his only begotten Son, that whosoever believeth in him should not perish, but have everlasting life.*[4] The cause of every good that comes to us is God and his love. To love is to wish a person well, and since God's will is the cause of things, blessings are showered on us because he loves us. It is his love which causes every perfection, of nature and of grace: *I have loved thee with an everlasting love; therefore with loving kindness have I drawn thee.*[5]

His giving of grace issues from great friendship, yes, the very greatest, as appears on four counts. First, because of the person of the lover—*God so loved the world.* Second, because of the condition of the beloved, that is, human beings, earthly and sinful: *God commendeth his love towards us, for when we were enemies, we were reconciled to God by the death of his Son.*[6] Third, because of the magnificence of the gift, for, as Gregory observes, love is proved by deeds.[7] God gives us the costliest gift, his own Son, of same substance with himself, natural, not adopted, his only Son, not one among many, who holds all his love. So does he commend his

---

[1] Rom. v. 12. [2] John i. 29.
[3] To the Dominican Master General.
[4] John iii. 16. [5] Jer. xxxi. 3. [6] Rom. v. 8–10.
[7] XL *Homil. in Evang.* ii. 30; *PL* LXXVI. 1220.

love for us. Fourth, because of the richness of the fruit, everlasting life, giving which he gives himself, for everlasting life is enjoying God.

59, 397   Exposition, *St. John*, iii, *lect.* 3

504. If by coming close to Christ men were thereupon taken past suffering and death they would be as if swept away, and their merit of faith would be less.

374   iv *Contra Gentes*, 55

2. THE HYPOSTATIC UNION

505. *In the beginning was the Word,* and then the Gospel adds, *and the Word was made flesh.*[1] The Word who was with God assumed flesh, not a man already existing and then deified by the grace of adoption. *I came from heaven, not to do mine own will, but the will of him that sent me.*[2]

Compendium Theologiae, 202

506. Had it been an individual man who became God the Bible would not have spoken of the Son's being sent by the Father, or of his going from the Father to come into the world, but only of his going to the Father. In point of fact, both are declared: *but now I go my way to him that sent me;* and, *I came forth from the Father and am come into the world; again, I leave the world, and go to the Father.*[3]

iv *Contra Gentes,* 27

i. *One Person*

507. Was the union of the Word with man a union of natures? It seems that it was for—

1. The Athanasian Creed professes that as one man is rational soul and flesh so one Christ is God and man.

[1] John i. 1.   [2] John vi. 38.   [3] John xvi. 5, 28.

But rational soul and flesh compose one human nature. Therefore God and man are united in Christ's single nature.

2. Damascene declares that to maintain that nature and hypostasis are identical is heretical error.[1] But is it so false? For in a simple thing, in God above all, the nature and the complete substantial subject are the same. Surely if there is but one person there must be also but one nature. Are the heretics then so much at fault?

3. Damascene adds that the two natures, human and divine, were united unchangeably and unalterably, which implies a natural union, and therefore a union of natures.

4. A real distinction can be drawn between the complete substance, or *suppositum*, and the specific nature in those things where the *suppositum* includes reality over and above the specific nature, whether this be the reality of the supervening accidents merely or whether it be part of the individual substance.[2] If the union of human nature with the Word be not a union of natures then it must lie elsewhere than in the specific nature of the Word; it will follow that the complete substance, or *suppositum*, of the Word differs from the divine nature, which is impossible.

5. A union is posterior to the uniting. The unity of the Word's person is eternal, and therefore cannot be posterior to the union which was wrought in fullness of time. It follows that the union we are considering did not take place in the person of the Word.

6. When we speak of a union we imply an addition.

---

[1] *de Fide Orthodoxa*, iii. 3; *PG* xciv. 992.

[2] *Metaphysics*, vii. 6, 1031ᵃ15, e.g. the notion of Peter includes individuating notes, accidental and substantial, which are additional to the notion of *humanity*.

What is complete and simple cannot be united to something else. Consequently the person of the Word, who is true God and supremely simple, cannot suffer addition and enter into union.

7. Realities of different genera cannot be brought together: thus *length* and *colour* do not make up a single unity. But human nature and divine nature are vastly more different than realities of different genera. Therefore they cannot be joined in one person.

8. The difference between *person* and *nature* in the Word is purely logical. We define the person of the Word by a relationship of origin, namely, by a relationship of sonship towards the Father, which has no reference to human nature. As regards human nature, both *nature* and *person* in the Word have the same bearing. It follows that if the union is made in person, then also in nature.

9. The Incarnation stirs us to love the incarnate God. But we should not love one divine Person more than the others: their goodness is the same, and so also should be the devotion they call forth. Therefore, the Incarnation was wrought in the nature common to all three.

10. According to Aristotle, the life of living things is their existence.[1] In Christ, however, there are two lives, the divine life, and the human life. There are, consequently, two existences, and therefore two persons, for existence is proper to the complete substance, the rational *suppositum* or person. Therefore the union is not achieved within one single person.

11. The form of the whole is to the complete substance what the form of a part is to its matter. The form of a part can exist only in its proper matter. Therefore the form of the whole, namely its nature, cannot exist

[1] *de Anima*, ii. v, 411^{b}29.

except in its proper complete substance, which is a human person. The same reasoning applies also to the divine nature in a divine Person. If two natures are present in this union, then two persons are also present.

12. Whatever is truly predicated of a subject can be substituted for the subject in propositions about the subject. But the divine nature is truly predicated of the Word, indeed the two terms are synonymous. If we speak of the union as being within one divine Person, then we ought also to say that it is within one divine nature.

13. Whatever is really united to another is united either accidentally or essentially.[1] But human nature is not united to the Word accidentally—for then it would keep its own complete individuality and there would be two complete persons, for any substance that is merely attached to another retains its own singularity, like the cloak you put on, or the horse you ride. Therefore human nature enters essentially into the Word, as though belonging to its very essence or nature. In other words, the union is of nature.

14. Whatever is comprehended under another cannot extend outside: what is in one place is not outside that place. But the complete substance of any nature is comprehended under that nature, for which reason it is called a *res naturae*, a thing of a certain nature. In this fashion is the individual comprehended in the species and the species in the genus. Since the Word is a complete substance of divine nature it cannot go outside that nature, and certainly not so as to become a complete substance of another nature. The only hypothesis is that the two natures in the Word become one.

---

[1] That is, the two realities *either* remain distinct, though forming a pattern, which is an accident, or mode of a thing or things— this may come about naturally, or artificially, or casually—*or* they combine to form one thing or substance.

15. *Nature* is compared to *thing* as what is more formal, simple, and constitutive to what is less. But human nature cannot be so related to the person of the Word. It follows that the person of the Word cannot be a person of human nature.

16. Activity is attributed to the person, or complete substance, for it comes from the singular substance.[1] But there are two activities in Christ, as Damascene proves.[2] Consequently in him there are two persons, and the union is not in person.

17. Person is described as a nature with its own peculiar cast. If the union is made in person, it follows also that it is made in nature.

Against these arguments we acknowledge, with Fulgentius,[3] that two natures truly persist in Christ's one person, and that there are two natures in the one person of the Son.

To make the question clear we must consider, first, what *nature* is, secondly, what *person* is, and thirdly, how the union of the Incarnate Word is of person, not of nature.

The term *nature* was first used about the *nativity*, or the being born, of living things, plants and animals, and later applied to their inborn qualities. Because native principles are intrinsic (and not imposed from without, as in the case of the violent and artificial) the term later came to signify the inward principle of motion; in this sense *nature* is the principle of instinctive impulses which well up essentially from within the subject and not from outside.[4] And because such natural movement, as we especially see in generative activity, reaches to a

---

[1] *Metaphysics*, i. 1, 980^b13.
[2] *de Fide Orthodoxa*, iii. 15; *PG* xciv. 1045.
[3] *de Fide ad Petrum*, ii; *PL* lxv. 678.
[4] *Physics*, ii. 1, 192^b12.

thing of a specific kind, the term a *nature* comes last of all to stand for the determinate *kind*, *type*, or *essence*, signified by the definition. Thus, Boethius speaks of a nature as the informing specific difference in a thing.[1] In this sense do we speak of nature in the present question.

To appreciate what the term *person* implies, reflect that if there be a thing in which there is only a specific essence, that specific essence will be individually complete in itself; the complete substance and the nature will be really identical, and merely logically distinct. By *nature* I here mean the specific essence, and by *person* the complete substance.[2] But if there be any reality in a thing distinct from the specific essence (which is signified by the definition), whether that be accident or individual matter, then the complete substance will not wholly coincide with the specific nature, but will possess some additional reality. Such is the case with anything composed of matter and form, and also with a person, which Boethius defines as an individual substance of rational nature.[3]

So then, what prevents a reality from being united in person, and not in nature? For an individual substance of a rational nature possesses some reality not proper to his specific nature; this belongs to his person, not his nature. Here we have a hint how human nature can be conceived to be united to the person, and not the nature, of the Word of God, and how manhood can be attributed, not to the divine nature, but to the person of the Word who assumes it.

[1] *de Duabus Naturis*, 1; *PL* LXIV. 1342.

[2] Scholastic writing sometimes uses *substance* and *essence* or *nature* as equivalent terms—commonly in the adverbial form, *substantially* and *essentially*. This translation keeps to the rule of restricting *substance* to denote the complete existing thing, while *essence* or *nature* denotes the abstract meaning there.

[3] *de Duabus Naturis*, 3; *PL* LXIV. 1344.

Doubt and dissension crop up when we start explaining the manner of this conjunction. For, in the usual run of things, when one reality is joined to another, both either fuse essentially or remain separate things arranged together, that is accidentally united.[1] Nestorius, therefore, and Theodore of Mopsuestia before him, were persuaded that human nature was conjoined to the Word accidentally, namely through the indwelling of grace; he meant that the Word was in the man Christ like a divinity in a temple. Here we should notice that when any substance is accidentally conjoined to another it keeps its own exclusive singularity, like the garment a man puts on, or the house which shelters him. Consequently, on this reading, the man Christ would have kept his own distinctive singularity, which is his personality. The Nestorian conclusion was that the human personality of Christ was distinct from the divine personality; the Son of Man is one thing, the Son of God another; and the Blessed Virgin was acknowledged as the Mother of Christ, not as the Mother of God.

This doctrine disagrees with the Holy Scriptures, which speak differently of Christ and of men in whom the Word of God dwells by grace; of such prophets it is said that the Word of God comes, but of Christ that *the Word was made flesh*,[2] that is, a man: the meaning is that the Word of God becomes personally a man. St. Paul speaks of this union as an emptying of the Son of God,[3] not a phrase one would chose to signify indwelling by grace, otherwise it could be applied to the Father and the Holy Ghost who come to us: *if any man love me, my Father will love him, and we will come to him, and make*

---

[1] That is, the union consists of a relation of two complete substances; relation is an accident, and the union is therefore called *accidental*.

[2] John i. 1.   [3] Phil. ii. 5.

our abode with him; and, *the Spirit dwelleth with you, and shall be in you.*[1] For these and other reasons this error was condemned at the Council of Ephesus.[2]

Some, however, while sustaining the doctrine that human nature was assumed by the Word yet remained separate, and wanting also to avoid having to profess a duality of persons, held that the Word assumed soul and body before they were united and before human personality had been constituted. The main difficulty about this interpretation is that Christ would not have been a true man, for human nature is composed of this union of body and soul. In fact their error was condemned by the Council of Tours presided over by Pope Alexander III.[3]

Others swung to the opposite extreme. They held that human nature entered essentially into the Word, and that one nature was formed from the divine and human natures. Apollinaris of Laodicea put out three dogmatic points: Pope Leo touches on them in his letter to the clergy and people of Constantinople.[4] The first was that the Word took the place of soul, and so came to the flesh: one nature was formed from the Word and the flesh, as with us one nature is formed from soul and body. Here Apollinaris followed Nestorius. But because the Holy Scriptures refer to Christ's soul—*I have the power to lay it down, and I have the power to take it up again,*[5] he modified his teaching, and declared, secondly, that in Christ there was an animal or sensitive soul, but not a rational soul: the Word substituted for a human mind in the man Christ. This conclusion, which cannot

[1] John xiv. 23. 17.
[2] 3rd Œcumenical Council, 431; Denzinger, 117.
[3] 1163. The condemnation appears later in a letter to William of Sens. *PL* cc. 685. Cf. Hefele-Leclerc, v. ii, p. 974.
[4] *Epist.* lix. 5; *PL* liv. 871.   [5] John x. 18.

be justified, is refuted by Augustine:[1] it would mean
that the Word assumed an animal nature, but not a
human nature. His third point, that the flesh of Christ
was not taken from a woman but was wrought from the
Word who is thereby altered and changed, is quite impossible, for the Word, who is true God, is supremely
immutable. Apollinaris was accordingly condemned at
the Council of Constantinople.[2] Eutyches, who followed his third tenet, had been condemned, at the
Council of Chalcedon.[3]

If the union were not in person, but only by an indwelling, as Nestorius taught, then the Incarnation
would have brought nothing fresh. On the other hand,
for the union to be of natures, as Apollinaris and
Eutyches taught, is out of the question: species are like
numbers; add or subtract, and you change them.[4] A
properly constituted nature cannot be incremented by
another nature, and if another was added then the
resulting nature would not be the same as before. The
divine nature is quite complete, and cannot possibly be
added to; for that matter, human nature is complete
enough to disallow the entrance of another nature. In
any case, the result would be a compound, neither divine
nor human, and Christ would be neither man nor God,
which is inadmissible.

We are led then to the conclusion that human nature
is united to the Word neither essentially nor accidentally, but substantially, hypostatically, and personally:
substance here means the hypostasis, or complete thing.
Among created beings, no example is nearer than that
given by the Athanasian Creed, namely, of the union of

[1] *Lib.* LXXXIII *Quaest.* 80; *PL* XL. 93.
[2] 5th Œcumenical Council (Constantinople II), 553.
[3] 4th Œcumenical Council, 451.
[4] *Metaphysics*, viii. 3. 1043^{b}36.

rational soul with body. The analogy is not with the soul as the form of body, for the Word's relation to human nature cannot be like that of form to matter, but with the soul as using the body as its instrument. In this case the instrument is inborn and conjoined, not adventitious and extraneous: wherefore Damascene calls human nature the organ of the Word.[1] A closer example is mentioned by Augustine: imagine a cosmic soul, as in fact some do, which takes material disposed to receive all forms, and makes of it one person with itself.[2]

Nevertheless, all such examples fall short: thus, to mention one point, principal cause and instrumental cause working together form an accidental whole. Indeed, the Incarnation is a unique union, surpassing every communion known to us. As God is his existence and goodness, so is he essentially his unity. And as his virtue is not limited to the styles of existence and goodness discoverable among creatures, but is capable of expressing itself in manners hitherto undreamt of, so by his infinite power can he make a union in which human nature is taken into the person of the Word. Augustine says about this mystery that, if explanation be sought, let us acknowledge that it is a marvel, and, if precedent, then that there was nothing like it before; what God can do let us own we cannot probe, for in such cases the whole reason of the fact lies in the might of the maker.[3]

We may now turn to the replies to the objections.

1. The analogy lies in the making of one man, not one nature, from the union of body and soul.

2. Although nature and person are not really dif-

---

[1] *de Fide Orthodoxa*, iii. 15; *PG* xciv. 1049.

[2] The reference, *contra Felicianum*, is to Virgil of Tapse, *de Unitate Trinitatis*, 15; *PL* lxii. 344.

[3] *ad Volusianum*, 2; *PL* xxxiii. 519.

ferent in God, they are different according to our way of thinking. Just because the thing which subsists in divine nature is identical with the thing which subsists in human nature, we cannot infer that one single nature or essence is present. What we say is that the union is in person, which means that there is one complete existent, not in nature, in other words that there is not one kind of existent.

3. The two natures are truly united in Christ, but in person, not in nature; this is what is meant by saying that they are inconvertibly and unalterably united.

4. The heretics who affirm that the union is in nature, not in person, draw no distinction, either real or logical, between nature and person: hence their misreading of the situation.

5. We say that something is united because of a union; we say similarly that it is one because of its unity. We attribute union to a divine Person because it is united to human nature in time, not because it is one in itself from eternity. In the order of our thoughts we may think of the union preceding the person, considered not in its own unity, but as united to human nature.

6. When we speak of the hypostatic union we do not imply that the divine Person is composed of two realities united together: this would militate against his supreme simplicity. What we mean is that one simple divine Person subsists in two natures, divine and human.

7. When two objects come under different genera they cannot be united in one specific essence or nature. There is no reason, however, why they should not be united in the same complete substance. Length and colour do not together make one nature, but they can co-exist in the same subject.

8. The person of the Son of God can be considered

from two aspects. First, according to the common meaning of personality, which signifies complete substantiality, and it is in this sense, as already explained, that God and man are one in Christ. Secondly, according to the peculiar and Trinitarian meaning of personality, namely the Son's relationship to the Father. But this meaning is not denoted by the hypostatic union of two natures.

9. The Incarnation adds no extra goodness to any divine Person, and makes him no more lovable in himself. The person of the Word Incarnate is no more to be loved than the person of the Word Eternal in himself, and other reasons for loving which appear are comprehended in the universal goodness of the Word of God. Hence the objection is inconclusive.

10. Existence may be attributed both to the complete substance or person and to the nature in which it subsists, for a person exists as a kind of thing. The existence of the Incarnate Word is one and single with respect to the person, not the natures.

11. The relationship of nature to complete substance differs from that of form to matter. Matter is not shaped into existence save through form, and conversely, form requires determinate matter for it to be actual. But a complete substance is not constituted by a specific nature alone, for it contains other reality as well. Consequently nothing prevents one nature from being possessed by a complete substance of another nature.

12. The divine nature is predicated of a divine Person on account of the identity of the realities signified, not according to the strict propriety of logic. Therefore one term cannot be used interchangeably for the other in propositions. Thus when speaking of God, we can say a person begets, but not the divine nature begets.

13. Human nature is united to the Word neither accidentally nor essentially (as though entering into the divine nature) but substantially, that is, hypostatically, as belonging to the hypostasis or person of the Word.

14. The person of the Word is comprehended in the nature of the Word and cannot extend beyond. But the nature of the Word, because infinite, comprehends every finite nature. Therefore when the person of the Word assumes human nature, he does not stretch outside, but takes what is below the divine nature; *who, being in the form of God, thought it not robbery to be equal with God, but humbled himself.*[1] The greatness of God was not cast off, but the slightness of human nature was put on.

15. As the nature of the Word is infinite so also is the person of the Word infinite. Nature and person, accordingly, there are equal. Human nature meets the divine Person because the Word is made flesh. It does not follow that human nature, which constitutes a man's being human, is more simple and formal than the human being who is the Word made flesh.

16. Activity issues from a complete substance according to its nature or form; therefore activities are multiplied by diversity of nature as well as by diversity of complete substance. Seeing and hearing are diverse activities in one single man because they come through diverse faculties. So from Christ, although he was one person or hypostasis, issue two kinds of activity because of his two natures.

17. When person is defined as a peculiar nature, nature then means substance, and substance signifies hypostasis, not essence.

94, 104, 113, 517   Disputations, *de Unione Verbi Incarnati,* 1
[1] Phil. ii. 6, 7.

508. The divine nature is really and entirely identical with each of the three persons, all of whom can therefore be called one: *I and the Father are one.*[1] But human nature is not wholly identical in reality with any person, or complete substance, in human nature. Consequently, human nature and a human person are not equivalent terms. So then, just because there are two natures in Christ, you cannot conclude that there are two Christs.

81   Disputations, *de Unione Verbi Incarnati,* 2, *ad* 7

509. The following proposition is untrue, *a man is humanity,* for the subject and the predicate have not wholly the same sense. Humanity signifies that whereby a thing is a man, and includes only those specific notes required for being that kind of thing. A man, however, signifies a thing which has humanity, and contains many notes outside the specific characteristics.

Disputations, *de Unione Verbi Incarnati,* 3, *ad* 14

510. Although born from the Father in one way, and from his mother in another, we do not say that Christ was two sons.

94   Disputations, *de Unione Verbi Incarnati,* 3, *ad* 11

ii. *Two Natures*

511. God the Son is equal with God the Father. He was subject to death, not in his divine nature, which is the living fountainhead of all things, but in our nature which he assumed into the unity of his person.

de Rationibus Fidei, 5

512. In proclaiming the undivided Christ some heretics went to the length of saying that God and man were not just one single person, but one nature as well. The

[1] John x. 30.

error started from Arius. From those texts of Holy Scripture which refer to Christ—meaning his human nature—being less than the Father, he concluded that Christ's animating principle was solely the Word of God. This took the place of soul in his body. And when he said, *my Father is greater than I,*[1] and when we read that he prayed or grew sad, these words, deeds, and sufferings were attributed by the Arians to the nature of the Son of God. The conclusion was pushed, and the union of God with man explained as being in nature as well as in person, since body and soul constitute the unity of human nature.

The underlying mistake concerned the mystery of the Trinity, and is corrected by professing that Father and Son are equal. Concerning the Incarnation, the doctrine that the Word was the substitute for a human soul can be disproved in several ways.

Soul is united to body as substantial form of body. God cannot be the substantial form of anything. If perhaps you urge that Arius would have granted this where the supreme God, the Father, was in question, then it should be pointed out that the same is also true of angels, which by nature cannot be united to bodies as forms, since essentially they are completely spiritual. Much less, then, can the Son of God, through whom, as Arius professed, the angels were made, enter into such union.

Moreover, we deny what Arius falsely declared, that the Son of God is a creature. All spiritual creatures reach their happiness through him, and now such is their joy that sorrow cannot touch them. Much less, therefore, can God the Son grieve in his nature, or fear. Yet we read, *he began to fear and be heavy,*[2] and he told

[1] John xiv. 28.
[2] Mark xiv. 33.

his sorrow, *my soul is sorrowful unto death.*[1] Sadness is
not just a bodily reaction; it is experienced by a conscious substance. Together with the Word and the
flesh, there was a substantial reality in Christ which
could feel sadness, and this we call the soul.

Again, if Christ assumed what was ours in order to
cleanse us from sin, and since it is more necessary for
our souls to be cleansed than our bodies—for the soul
is the source and subject of sin—he took soul, the predominant part of us, with body, not body without soul.

94, 175   *Compendium Theologiae*, 204

513. Apollinaris began by agreeing with Arius in
holding that there was no other soul in Christ save the
Word of God. Since, however, he did not subscribe to
the doctrine of Arius that the Son of God was a creature,
and since he recognized that many traits of Christ are
proper neither to the Creator nor to the human body
alone, he was compelled, though still thinking that
the Word took the place of reason and intelligence,
to postulate a soul, non-rational and non-intellectual,
which sensitively quickened the body and was the seat
of emotion.

This doctrine strikes alike at the genuineness of
human nature and at the purpose of the Incarnation.
It means that the form of Christ's human body was not
a rational soul, whereas nothing queer or unnatural
should be imagined about the Incarnation. Moreover,
the restoration of human nature is principally an affair
of its intellectual part. That is where sin begins, and
that, therefore, should be taken over by God. Furthermore, we read that Christ marvelled. Now admiring is
an act of the rational soul, and is quite impossible to
God. Christ's sadness leads us to infer the presence of

[1] Mark xiv. 34.

a sensitive soul, his wonder the presence of an intelligent soul.

175, 507 *Compendium Theologiae*, 205

514. Eutyches went some of the way with Arius and Apollinaris. True, he did not deny a human soul or mind to Christ, nor any integral part of human nature. All the same he postulated one nature for both God and man after the Incarnation.

That his opinion was mistaken appears on several counts. The divine nature, complete and beyond all change, cannot enter into the make-up of another nature. One kind of thing unites with another either by being absorbed, like food into living tissue, or by consuming it, as fire destroys wood, or by the transmutation of both into a third thing, as when elements make a compound. The immutability of the divine nature forbids its entering into any of these three processes.

Again, when we view the scale of reality, we notice that the addition to a subject of a greater perfection changes its type: thus an animate thing is different in kind from an inanimate thing, a sensitive thing from an animate thing, an intelligent sensitive thing from a merely sensitive animate thing. Had the one nature Eutyches credited to Christ possessed essentially divine characteristics in addition to the human it would have been specifically different from human nature. He would not have been a man true to human type, whereas the Gospel declares he was born according to the flesh: *the book of the generation of Jesus Christ, the son of David, the son of Abraham.*[1]

150 *Compendium Theologiae*, 206

515. Photinus lessened the mystery of the Incarnation by denying Christ's divine nature; the Manichees did

[1] Matt. i. 1.

the same by denying his human nature. Fancying all
bodily nature to be caused by the power of evil, and
thinking how unfitting it would have been for the Son
of God to assume a creature of the devil, they therefore
laid it down that Christ had flesh only in appearance,
not in reality, and that the Gospel narratives about
his humanity are pieces of imagination, not accounts
of physical fact.

They contradict the express statements of Holy
Writ, that Christ was born of a virgin, that he was
circumcised, was hungry, ate food, and performed
the functions appropriate to human nature. Were the
Manichees right, then the Gospel narrative would be
wrong. Christ said of himself: *to this end was I born,
and for this cause came I into the world, that I should
bear witness to the truth.*[1] He would instead have
attested a falsehood, especially as he foretold sufferings
that would have been unreal had he lacked true flesh,
for he foretold that he would be betrayed into men's
hands, and that they would spit on him, scourge him,
crucify him. To say that he was merely acting a part
would be to load him with a lie.

To shake a true conviction is the work of a deceiver.
Christ set himself to remove from men's minds any
idea that he was a phantom. When he appeared to his
disciples and they thought they saw a spirit or ghost he
said, *handle me, and see, for a spirit hath not flesh and
bones, as you see me to have.*[2] Before that, when they
were troubled as he came walking to them on the waves
and fancied they saw an apparition, *have a good heart,*
he said, *it is I, fear ye not.*[3]

156   *Compendium Theologiae,* 207

[1] John xviii. 37.
[2] Luke xxiv. 39.
[3] Mark vi. 51.

516. Though he acknowledged that Christ possessed a truly human body, Valentinus nevertheless taught that Christ's flesh was not taken from the Virgin, but that a body was transmitted from heaven through her, without taking anything from her. It was as though water ran along a conduit. But this gainsays Bible truth: *Jesus Christ our Lord was made of the seed of David according to the flesh.*[1] And again, *God sent forth his Son, made of a woman.*[2] And again, *Jacob begat Joseph the husband of Mary, of whom was born Jesus, who is called Christ.*[3] And Mary is called *his mother.*[4] These statements would not be true had he possessed a heavenly kind of body, not born of the Virgin. When St. Paul says, *the first man is of the earth, earthy; the second man is the Lord from heaven,*[5] he means that Christ's divinity, not his bodily substance, descended from heaven. Why should a heavenly body enter the Virgin's womb if nothing was to be taken from her? The history would have been fiction, the process a mock-birth. All deceit is alien to Christ. We should confess quite bluntly, that Christ came forth from the Virgin's womb having been formed from her body.

537, 540   *Compendium Theologiae,* 208

517. The Catholic Faith professes that Christ's body is of the same kind as ours, and with this body goes a true rational soul, and simultaneously the perfect Deity, all three substantial and together in one person, not in one nature.

Some writers have gone astray when expounding this truth. Observing that whatever comes to an already substantially complete subject is then joined to it in accidental union—thus a man and the clothes he wears

---

[1] Rom. i. 3.   [2] Gal. iv. 4.   [3] Matt. i. 16.
[4] Matt. i. 18.   [5] 1 Cor. xv. 47.

are not combined in substantial union, for they do not make up one substance—they concluded that Christ's humanity was connected to the Divinity in the person of the Son like a vesture put on; they adduced St. Paul's words in support, *in habit found as a man*.[1] Again, observing that an individual of rational nature, in other words, a person, results from the union of soul and body, they concluded that from the direct union of Christ's soul with his body a human personality could not fail to result. Consequently there were two persons in Christ, the person assuming and the person assumed, as there would be in a man clothed were his garments a person.

To avoid such a conclusion others postulated that Christ's soul was never directly united to his body, but that the person of the Son separately assumed soul and body. Striving to avoid one difficulty they landed themselves in a greater. One unavoidable consequence of this doctrine would be that Christ was not a genuine man, for human nature is a composite of soul and body. Another consequence: he would be without true flesh and true bodily members, for eye is not truly human apart from soul, nor is hand, nor flesh and bone: they would be human only in a manner of speaking, as in a picture or statue. Another consequence: Christ would not really have died, for death is the deprivation of life, and cannot happen either to the Divinity or to a body which had never been alive. Another consequence: Christ would not have felt, for body does not feel unless quickened by soul.

175, 664   *Compendium Theologiae*, 209

[1] Phil. ii. 7.

3. THE SON OF MAN

518. By his divine nature Christ is simple, by his human nature he is complex.

Disputations, de Unione Verbi Incarnati, 2, *ad* 18

519. Not from necessity was Christ a debtor to death, but from love of God and man.

500, 552   *II Sentences*, xx. i. 5

520. Contrary and conflicting characteristics can be found in the same subject in different parts. By his body, man decays; by his soul, he is deathless. So also paradoxes meet through divine and human nature in Christ's single person.

178   *Disputations, de Unione Verbi Incarnati*, 3, *ad* 13

i. *Grace and Wisdom*

521. Christ's humanity was like an instrument of his divinity. Because an instrument's condition and quality should match its purpose and be worthy of the person using it, we should accordingly consider the quality of the human nature assumed by the Word of God. The purpose was the restoration of the human race; therefore Christ's human nature should be such as to ensure his being the author of this salvation.

Human salvation lies in the enjoyment of God, who gives bliss to men. How right then that Christ's manhood should have delighted in God, for the originator of a process should also be its master. We are happy in God through mind and will, the mind perfectly knowing him by the light of wisdom, the will perfectly cleaving to him by grace and love: so is man justified, *being justified freely by his grace.*[1] Rightly was the Word

[1] Rom. iii. 24.

Incarnate perfect in grace and true wisdom: *the Word was made flesh, and dwelt among us, and we beheld his glory, the glory as of the only begotten of the Father, full of grace and truth.*[1]

595   *Compendium Theologiae*, 213

522. Let us consider his fullness of grace. The term *grace* suggests two ideas, not far removed from one another: first, of being in favour; second, of being given a present. For we give gratis to those who are after our own heart and to our own liking. We may like them either reservedly or unreservedly; reservedly, when we would give them what is ours, but without entering into intimacy; unreservedly, when we would draw them close to us according to the kind and degree of our liking. Consequently, anybody who has grace has received a gift, but not everybody who has received a gift is held dear. Hence two sorts of grace can be distinguished, one is only a free gift, the other is also a grant of friendship.

Of course by the very force of the idea, grace is never a matter of right. There are two kinds of right, namely, what is due to what we are and what is due to what we do. The first is involved in the demands of our nature: thus it is due that man should have reason and hands and feet; the second is what we deserve by our acts, for example, the reward for labour. All the gifts freely given to men by God surpass the claims of nature and are not acquired by merit—though supernatural rewards are not without the name and style of grace, for grace is the principle of merit, *the gift of God is eternal life*,[2] and they are given more abundantly than we deserve.

Now some of these gifts, while exceeding the powers

[1] John i. 14.   [2] Rom. vi. 23.

of human nature and granted without our deserving,
do not of themselves make us pleasing to God; for
example, the gift of prophecy, the working of miracles,
special gifts of knowledge and teaching, and so forth.
They do not join us to God, though they reflect some
divine likeness to God, and have some share in divine
goodness, as do all things. But there are also other
gifts, freely given, which render us dear to God and
united to him.

Union with God can be by affection or by substance.
The first is through charity. St. Paul says that without
charity all the other gifts *profit us nothing*.[1] Such grace
is common to all the saints. The second union is more
than an identification by love and divine indwelling,
but is the real unity of one single person or hypostasis.
Jesus Christ alone has this unity; he is both God and
man. This is the singular grace who is joined to God
as one single person; a gift freely given, exceeding
natural power, rewarding no merits, and making Christ
most dear to God: *this is my beloved Son, in whom I am
well pleased*.[2]

Between these graces lies a difference. The first is
an habitual state of soul infused by God; the soul cleaves
to God by an act of love, a perfect act coming from a
habit. But the substantial existence of two natures conjoined in one person is not a habit. The nearer a created
reality comes to God the nearer it shares in his goodness
and the more lavish the gifts which fill it: the closer
the flame the greater the warmth and light. Nothing
nearer to God than a human nature hypostatically
united to him could exist or be thought of.

As a result Christ's soul is fuller of grace than any
other soul. This habitual grace, however, did not lead
up to the hypostatic union, but flowed from it. This is

[1] 1 Cor. xiii. 1–3.   [2] Matt. iii. 17.

suggested by the Evangelist's turn of speech: *we beheld his glory, the glory as of the only begotten of the Father, full of grace and truth.*[1] The man Christ is the only begotten of the Father because he is the Word made flesh, and because he is the Word made flesh was he made full of grace and truth.

The plenitude of nobility is more conspicuous when it gives to others; the brightness of light is judged by the area it illuminates. From Christ's fullness grace is outpoured on us. The Son of God was made man that men might be made gods and become the children of God: *when the fullness of the time was come, God sent forth his Son, made of a woman, made under the law, to redeem them that were under the law, that we might receive the adoption of sons.*[2]

Because of this overflow of grace and truth Christ is called the Head of the Church. Motion and sensation spread from the head to other members within the same organism: *God hath put all things under his feet, and gave him to be the head over all things to the Church, which is his body, the fullness of him that filleth all in all.*[3] He can be called the head, not only of men, but also of angels, because of his dignity and efficacy, not because he is himself of angelic nature: *God raised him from the dead, and set him at his own right hand in the heavenly places, far above all principality, and power, and might, and dominion, and every name that is named, not only in this world, but also in that which is to come.*[4]

To summarize: theological tradition ascribes to Christ a threefold grace. First, the grace of hypostatic union, whereby a human nature is united in person to the Son of God. Second, sanctifying grace, the fullness of which distinguishes Christ above all others. Third,

[1] John i. 14.
[2] Gal. iv. 4–5.
[3] Eph. i. 22–23.
[4] Eph. i. 20–21.

his grace as head of the Church. All three are duly set out by the Evangelist: first, *the Word was made flesh*; second, *and we beheld his glory, full of grace and truth*; third, *and of his fullness we have all received.*[1]

310, 554, 568, 659   *Compendium Theologiae*, 214

523. Next let us consider his fullness of wisdom. At once we reflect that, since in Christ there are two natures, the divine and the human, whatever is credited to either must be doubled. Consequently we profess two wisdoms in Christ, the uncreated wisdom of God and the created wisdom of man. As the Word of God he is the conceived and begotten wisdom of the Father: *Christ the power of God, and the wisdom of God.*[2] As a man, two kinds of knowledge can be distinguished, one is godlike, the other springs from human effort.

He beheld God's essence and all things in God: that we are bound to say. For the master-principle of a movement should be high above the process of movement. The vision of God, in which our eternal salvation is achieved, was rightly anticipated in the author of our salvation. We are the subjects of the process; he is the origin. From the beginning of his life he saw God; unlike the blessed he did not arrive at the vision of God.

No one was so near to God. Rightly then was his beatific knowledge greater than any other person's. For there are degrees of vision; God, the cause of all things, is beheld more clearly by some than by others. A cause is seen the more fully the more effects we perceive in it, for the power of a cause is known only by its effects, which, as it were, measure its range. Some gaze on more effects and see their divine meaning better than do others who also see God: theologians work with this

[1] John i. 14, 16.   [2] 1 Cor. i. 24.

clue when they arrange the hierarchies of angels, where the higher ranks instruct the lower. Christ's human soul is set above all other created intelligent substances. With perfect insight he beheld all God's works, past, present, and future. He enlightens the highest angels. In him *are hid all the treasures of wisdom and knowledge.*[1] *All things are naked and opened unto the eyes of him with whom we have to do.*[2]

Not that his soul attained to comprehension of the Divinity. For comprehending means knowing an object as much as it can be known. God's infinite being is infinite truth, and no created mind, even though knowing the infinite, can know it infinitely, or by seeing God can comprehend him. Christ's soul is created, as all about his human nature was created, otherwise no other nature would exist in Christ apart from the divine nature which alone is uncreated. He is the person of the Word, uncreated and single in two natures: it is for this reason that we do not say that Christ was a creature simply speaking, for his proper name indicates his personality. But we can speak of his body or soul as created. His uncreated wisdom, not his human mind, comprehends God: *no man knoweth the Son but the Father; neither knoweth any man the Father, save the Son.*[3] His soul, therefore, does not know all God's possible actions, nor all his reasons for acting. All the same, even as man, he is set by God as governor over all creation. Fittingly then he sees in God everything that God does, and in this sense can be called omniscient.

Besides this beatific knowledge in which things are known in the vision of God, there is another mode of knowledge. This starts from creatures themselves. Angels know things in the Word by their morning knowledge; they know things as natural objects in

[1] Col. ii. 3.   [2] Heb. iv. 13.   [3] Matt. xi. 27.

themselves by their evening knowledge. Now this second mode of knowing differs in men and in angels, for men acquire knowledge from their senses, discerning meanings in phenomena through the process of abstraction, whereas angels have an infused knowledge, and carry from their creation the impression of the meaning and likeness of things. Then to both men and angels is given supernatural communication with divine mysteries, and to foster this knowledge angels are enlightened by angels, and men are instructed by prophetic revelation. Since no created nobility should be denied to Christ's soul, which of all souls is the most excellent, it is fitting that, in addition to the beatific vision, three other types of knowledge should also be possessed.

The first is the empirical knowledge which other men also enjoy, for it is proper to human nature that truth should be discovered through the senses. The second is divinely infused, and informs the mind about all truths which human knowledge reaches or can reach, for it is right that the human nature assumed by the Word of God, which restores human nature, should itself lack no human perfection. The third concerns the mystery of grace. Since Christ was not only the restorer of human nature but also the propagator of grace, he also most fully knew those truths exceeding reason which can be perceived by the Gift of Wisdom and the spirit of prophecy.

To sum up: Christ's soul was raised to the highest level of knowledge possible to any created mind, first, as regards seeing God's essence and all things in God, secondly, by knowing the mysteries of grace, and thirdly, all objects of human knowledge. Here no advance was possible. Obviously in course of time Christ's bodily senses grew more experienced about

their environment, and therefore his empirical knowledge could increase. *The boy grew in wisdom and
stature.*[1] The text can be differently interpreted, to
mean, not that he grew wiser, but that his wisdom grew
more manifest and instructive to others. It was a providential dispensation to show that he was like other
men, for had he displayed adult wisdom in his boyhood,
the mystery of the Incarnation might well have appeared
a piece of play-acting.

   5, 179, 528   *Compendium Theologiae*, 216

ii. *Human Weakness*

524. Our Lord's words display the humble and human
together with the sublime and divine. On one side—
my Father is greater than I,[2] and, *my soul is sorrowful
even unto death;*[3] but on the other—*I and the Father
are one,*[4] and, *all things that the Father hath are mine.*[5]

His deeds as well manifest his two natures; the
human, in that he feared, grieved, hungered, and died;
the divine, in that by his own power he cured the sick,
raised the dead to life, commanded the elements, cast
out devils, forgave sins, rose again when he willed, and
ascended into heaven.

   507, 533   iv *Contra Gentes*, 27

525. The Son of God assumed the infirmities of
human nature in order to build up our belief in the
Incarnation. For since we experience human nature not
otherwise than by undergoing these trials, had he not
gathered them in, he might have seemed, not a real
man of flesh and blood, but a ghostly semblance, as the
Manichees held. He *emptied himself, taking upon himself the form of a servant, being made in the likeness of*

---

[1] Luke ii. 52.   [2] John xiv. 28.   [3] Matt. xxvi. 38.
[4] John x. 30.   [5] John xvi. 15.

men, and being found in fashion as a man.[1] Thus it was that Thomas, at the sight of his wounds, was recalled to his faith.[2]

372   *Summa Theologica,* 3a. xiv. 1

526. Human salvation, for which the Son of God assumed human nature, was anticipated by his surpassing grace and wisdom. The reverse side is not inconsistent, that he bore blows also and nobly conquered for us our liberty. That men who perish from injustice should be rescued by justice is all of a piece. Fairness demands that a man who owes a debt because of his wrongdoing should be set free on paying the penalty. What our friends do and endure on our behalf are in a sense our own deeds and sufferings, for friendship is a mutual power uniting two persons and making them somehow one: for this reason a man may be justly discharged because his friend has made restitution.

With the sin of our first parents perdition fell on all of us. One man alone cannot pay sufficient ransom for all; any satisfaction he offered could never amount to strict compensation for the wrong everybody shares in. Nor would it be sufficient even if an angel, moved by love of mankind, tried to make amends, for his endowments are too limited to counterbalance unlimited sins.

God alone is of such infinite dignity that atonement can be complete in the flesh he assumes. His human nature, therefore, existed in such a condition that expiation could be made for the sins of everybody. But not all penalties which men incur are of the kind that renders satisfaction. Sin has two phases, the turning to transient advantage, and the consequent turning away from God. Punishment corresponds to both, for, first, a man is hurt by the shortcomings of the things he has

[1] Phil. ii. 7.   [2] John xx. 26.

chosen to give him pleasure, and, secondly, he has lost grace and the other gifts of God's friendship. How right it is that he should be reclaimed through his very vexation and sadness over the fleeting pleasures to which he has committed himself. As for the penalties which separate him from God, these tell against recovery, for what satisfaction can be offered when the heart is graceless, the mind ignorant, the desires deranged? All these are the penal effects of sin. It is from the other phase of sin that satisfaction can spring, namely, from the sinner's own experience of inward grief and outward loss.

That Christ should assume those consequences of sin which keep men away from God cannot be entertained. How could they have enabled him to make restitution? Indeed he had to be full of grace and wisdom. But the other failings in which man has landed himself, death and distress of mind and body, these Christ chose to share, that by laying down his life for men he might redeem them.

Notice, however, that these common sufferings fall differently on him and on us. We incur them willy-nilly, for we are born of tainted stock. But Christ, who was born immaculate, chose to accept them. Our weaknesses are inherited, his are adopted. He could have embraced human nature without them, as he did without stigma of blame. It stands to reason that he who is free from wrong should be free also from punishment. Hence he was clearly under no necessity, either congenital or legal, of bearing these weaknesses. Instead, he freely shouldered them.

Our bodily disabilities are punishments for sin. We were exempt from them before our lapse. Christ put them on, and accordingly is said to have worn the likeness of sin: *God sent his own Son in the likeness of sinful*

flesh, and for sin, condemned in the flesh[1]—here St. Paul
calls suffering sin. Also, *in that he dies, he dies unto sin
once*.[2] And, what is more of a marvel, Christ was *made
a curse for us*;[3] by taking on himself the weight of pain
he broke up the burden of our crimes and their
penalties.

Notice, furthermore, that our bodily afflictions are of
two kinds: some are common to all, for instance, hunger,
thirst, fatigue, pain, death; others are special to individuals, for instance, blindness, leprosy, fever, bodily
injury. There is this difference between them: the
former are inherited by our descent from our first
parents, the latter are induced by individual factors.
No reason existed in Christ why he should have been
subject to any afflictions, either from his soul, united
to the Word of God and full of grace and wisdom, or
from his body, well knit, healthy, and formed from
the overshadowing of the Holy Spirit. By his own
dispensation he laid himself open to the weaknesses
deriving from our common origin, and he did this in
order to earn our salvation. But since he came to restore
human nature, he took those only which are everybody's heritage, not those peculiar to individual cases.
Damascene says that he assumed our ineradicable
defects.[4] Had he submitted himself to ignorance and
gracelessness, or even to leprosy or blindness, he might
have been dishonoured or lowered in men's estimation,
for which his sharing in our common lot gives no
occasion.

156, 267, 399, 550   *Compendium Theologiae, 226*

527. *For consider him that endured such contradiction of
sinners against himself, lest ye be wearied and faint in*

[1] Rom. viii. 3.   [2] Rom. vi. 10.   [3] Gal. iii. 13.
[4] *de Fide Orthodoxa*, iii. 20; *PG* xciv. 1081.

your minds.[1] Christ's lover is bidden to consider, that is, ponder well: *in all thy ways acknowledge him, and he shall direct thy paths.*[2] The reason is that any tribulation finds its remedy in the Cross. Obedience to God was there: *he humbled himself and became obedient unto death, even the death of the cross.*[3] There love and care for his mother, there charity towards his neighbour, praying even for enemies: *Father, forgive them for they know not what they do.*[4] There patience in adversity: *thus I was as a man that heareth not, and in whose mouth are no reproofs.*[5] There perseverance to the end: *Father, into thy hands I commend my spirit.*[6] Every variation on virtue there was played: the cross, cries Augustine, was not only a victim's scaffold, but also a master's chair.[7]

500   Commentary, *Hebrews*, xii. *lect.* 1

528. Some human weakness Christ took, not from compulsion but from choice, to provide for our well-being. Power and ability is for activity, that is its purpose; therefore being able to suffer, without actual suffering, does not suffice for satisfaction or merit. Nobody is called good or bad from how they can act, but from how they do act; praise and blame are awarded for performance, not promise. For this reason Christ assumed not only our vulnerability in order to save us, but also, to make good our sins, chose actual suffering.

For us he underwent the suffering owing to us from original sin, sufferings which culminate in death: *the wages of sin is death.*[8] He willed to suffer death for our sins so that he might pay the price and free us from the charge of death, although he himself was without

---

[1] Heb. xii. 3.   [2] Prov. iii. 6.
[3] Phil. ii. 8.   [4] Luke xxiii. 34.
[5] Ps. xxxviii. 14.   [6] Luke xxiii. 46.
[7] *Tract cxix in Evangel. Joann., PL* xxxv. 1950.
[8] Rom. vi. 23.

crime. He also willed that his own death should not only make redress for us, but also be a sacrament of salvation, in that by the likeness of his death we may die to carnal life and be carried over into spiritual life: *Christ hath suffered once for our sins, the just for the unjust, that he might bring us to God, being put to death in the flesh, but quickened in the spirit.*[1]

Death also he willed in order that by dying he might leave us a perfect example of virtue. Of charity, *for greater love hath no man than this, that he lay down his life for his friends.*[2] Of fortitude, which cannot be stronger than when holding fast to righteousness despite mortal fear: *consider him that endured such contradiction against himself, lest ye be wearied and faint in your minds.*[3] Of patience, for he did not allow himself to be overwhelmed by sadness, but calmly sustained death, as was spoken of him in prophecy, *he was oppressed, and he was afflicted, yet he opened not his mouth.*[4] Of obedience, for the greater the task the more famous the obedience: *he became obedient unto death, even the death of the cross.*[5]

477, 551, 665   *Compendium Theologiae*, 227

iii. *Single Existence and Twofold Will*

529. Let us now consider where unity should be attributed, and where plurality, to one person with two natures. Plurality marks the attributes proper to the different natures. Thus, to begin with, since the term *nature* comes from nativity or birth, and there are two natures in Christ, we profess two generations or births, one eternal, whereby he receives divine nature from the Father, the other temporal, whereby he receives human nature from his mother. Moreover, the natural

[1] 1 Pet. iii. 18.   [2] John xv. 13.
[3] Heb. xii. 3.   [4] Isa. liii. 7.   [5] Phil. ii. 8.

attributes of divinity and humanity are twofold in
Christ, and therefore we profess two minds and two
wills, the divine and the human, also a twofold knowledge and a twofold charity, uncreated and created.

But unity marks the attributes of a complete substance or hypostasis. Inasmuch as the existence of one
complete substance is regarded as unique, then it seems
that we should say there is one existence in Christ.
Obviously each and all of its parts have their own
proper kind of existence when they are considered in
isolation, but when they are integrated in the whole
then all exist with its single existence. If we consider
Christ as a substance complete and whole in two
natures, then his is a single existence as his is one complete substantial reality.

Since what really acts is the complete substance, or
thing, not this faculty or that, it has seemed to some
theologians that Christ therefore has a single activity:
But they neglect the typology of behaviour. Different
kinds of activity issue from one individual when there
are diverse proximate abilities or faculties of activity:
a man's sensing and understanding are different because
they come from different faculties or abilities. Activities
correspond to the kind of thing that elicits them; nature
is the principle of operation. Because Christ is one complete substance, it does not follow that he has one single
activity: he has two types or kinds of activity because of
his two natures. On the other hand, all three Persons
in the blessed Trinity have one nature and one essential
activity is common to all.

Nevertheless, Christ's human activity takes on a
divine character. When many come together in one
complete substance then the others instrumentally serve
the principal: for example, all other human powers are
instruments of the human mind. The humanity of

Christ is therefore described as the organ of the Divinity. An instrumental cause acts in virtue of the principal cause; in this way its action contains the power, not only of the instrument, but also of the principal: for example, as when a work of art is carved through the action of a tool. Christ's human activity had a virtue of divinity above human power. He touched a leper, that was the act of a man; the leper was cured, that was from divine touch. In this manner all his human deeds and sufferings were health-giving and salutary.

507, 596   *Compendium Theologiae*, 212

530. *Father, if thou be willing, remove this chalice from me: nevertheless, not my will, but thine, be done.*[1] Those were the words of Christ's prayer in the Garden. Ambrose reminds us that *mine* is the will he calls his own, *mine* the sorrow he took;[2] and he explains, that his own will refers to the man, his Father's to the Godhead; the human will is temporal, the divine will eternal.[3]

Some have taught there was only one will in Christ, but not all were persuaded by the same arguments. Apollinaris maintained there was no rational soul in Christ, but that the Word took the place of soul and even of mind: and since, as Aristotle says, the will is in the reason,[4] it would follow that in Christ there was no human will, but one single will. Eutyches likewise, and all who held there was but one composite nature in Christ, were compelled to allow but one will. Nestorius, too, came to the same conclusion, though from the different premises that the union was one of will and affection. Later, Macarius, Patriarch of Antioch, Cyrus of Alexandria, and Sergius of Constantinople, and some

[1] Luke xxii. 42.
[2] *de Fide ad Gratianum*, ii. 7; *PL* xvi. 594.
[3] *Expositio Evangelii secundum Lucam*, xxii. 42; *PL* xv. 1911.
[4] *de Anima*, iii. 10, 433[b]5.

of their followers, taught that there was but one will
in Christ, although they held there were two natures
united in one hypostasis: this was because they believed
that Christ's human nature was not active with its own
motion, but only because it was moved by the Godhead, as appears from the synodical letter of Pope
Agatho.[1]

Hence the decision of the Sixth General Council,
held at Constantinople, that we must confess, in accordance with what the prophets of old and Christ himself
taught us, handed down in the creeds, two natural wills
in Christ and two natural operations.[2] The definition
was opportune. For it is certain that the Son of God
assumed a perfect human nature. Now the will is like
the mind, a natural power which is part of the perfection of human nature; hence we must say that the Son
of God assumed a human will together with human
nature. By the assumption of a human nature the Son
of God suffered no diminution of his divine nature, to
which a will also is attributed. Therefore, we are bound
to profess two wills in Christ, one human, the other
divine.

524   *Summa Theologica*, 3a. xviii. 1

531. How was he obedient? Not by his divine will,
which sets the rule, but by his human will, measured in
all matters by his Father's.

439   Commentary, *Philippians*, ii, lect. 2.

532. The Son of God took human nature together
with all that pertains to it. Human nature contains
animal nature, as a species contains a genus. Therefore,
together with human nature he took whatever pertains
to the perfection of animal nature, including the sensi-

[1] *Epist.* iii; *PL* lxxxvii. 1221.
[2] 3rd Council of Constantinople, 680–1; Denzinger, 290–1.

tive appetite, which is the seat of the emotions. These are designed to serve reason; they are said to be rational by sharing in reason,[1] and are therefore volitional by sharing in will.

443, 447　　　　　　　　　　*Summa Theologica*, 3a. xviii. 2

533. The term *will* stands both for a faculty and for an activity. As an activity it includes willing and choosing—willing an end, choosing the means that conduce to it. To its final purpose the will is borne simply and unreservedly, as towards what is good without qualification. But regarding the means to the end it must make a reckoning, inasmuch as their goodness is relative to something else. Accordingly we can distinguish the reaction of the will to an end desirable for its own sake —to health, for instance—which is called *thelesis* by Damascene and *voluntas ut natura* or instinctive will by the scholastic masters, from the reaction of the will about a thing which is desirable for the sake of something else—medicine, for instance—which is called *boulesis* by Damascene and *voluntas ut ratio* or deliberate will by the scholastic masters.[2]

This differentiation of function does not go so deep as to set up different faculties or powers of activity, for both functions are concerned with the same formal object, namely, what is good. Hence, in speaking of Christ's human will, if we mean the faculty of will (that is, the rational faculty or essential will, not the derivative will which is found in the emotions), then there is but one will in Christ, but if we mean the activity of will, then there is both the non-deliberate and the deliberate willing.

208　　　　　　　　　　　*Summa Theologica*, 3a. xviii. 3

[1] *Ethics*, i. 13, 1102^{b}30.
[2] *de Fide Orthodoxa*, ii. 22; *PG* xciv. 944.

534. *Not what I will, but what thou wilt*[1]—these words of our Lord show that he willed an object his Father did not will; this will, according to Augustine, could be only from his human heart, since he transfigured our weakness, not into his divine love, but into his human love.[2]

We have already noted in Christ's human nature a twofold power of will, the sensitive appetite or derivative will, and the rational appetite, which acts both non-deliberately and deliberately. When he embarked on his Passion he allowed his flesh to do and suffer whatever was natural to it. In like manner he allowed the powers of his soul to follow their bent. Clearly it is the nature of the sensitive appetite to shrink from bodily pain and hurt. So also the non-deliberate will shrinks from what is hostile to nature and what by itself is evil, such as death and the like. For example, the emotions and instinctive will of an ordinary man shrink from cauterization, which may yet be chosen all the same for the sake of health. It was God's will that Christ should undergo pain, suffering, and death, not for themselves, but for the sake of human salvation. Hence his sensitive appetite and non-deliberate will could want what God did not will, though deliberately he willed always what God willed: *nevertheless, not what I will, but as thou wilt.* By his reasoned will he willed to fulfil God's will; by another will he showed that he wished otherwise.

415   *Summa Theologica,* 3a. xviii. 5

535. Though Christ's sensitive and instinctive will wished what God did not will, he was not torn by contradictions. For he did not reject the reason which

---

[1] Matt. xxvi. 39.
[2] *Contra Maximinum,* ii. 20; *PL* XLII. 789.

moved his divine will and his deliberate human will to choose the Passion. His unconditional will was for human salvation, but to connect this end with the fact of suffering was no part of its office, nor could the motions of his sense-appetites go so far as to appreciate such a purpose. Moreover, his divine will and his deliberate will were neither frustrated nor delayed by his emotions and natural instincts. Conversely, neither were they shunned nor slowed up by his divine will and his deliberate human will.

His mental agony was not such that his will suffered a conflict of reasons, as with us when we are caught with a divided mind. This comes from our weakness and inability to discern what is simply for the best. Such was not the case with Christ, whose reason was quite decided that the best course for him was to suffer if we were to be saved. The conflict lay in his sensitive appetites, which as Damascene notes[1] dreaded the coming ordeal.

Summa Theologica, 3a. xviii. 6, c. & ad 3

536. Christ knew that his Passion was willed by God, and yet he shrank from it. So also did the blessed Virgin, and sorrow came upon her at the thought: *thy soul a sword shall pierce.*[2] Yet both deliberately accepted it—and so, too, must all the saints—though it be against their instincts.

18, 497   *I Sentences*, xlviii. i. 4, *ad* 3

537. If, therefore, all God's words are likenesses of the Word who is the Son of God, we should freely listen to them to begin with, and then believe them: *that Christ may dwell in your hearts by faith.*[3] Next, we should

---

[1] *de Fide Orthodoxa*, iii. 14, 18, 23; *PG* xciv. 1037, 1073, 1087.

[2] Luke ii. 35.   [3] Eph. iii. 17.

meditate continuously on what we have believed and on the Word abiding in us. Also, we should give the Word to others, testifying to the truth, advising and cheering them. Finally, we should put the truth into practice: *be ye doers of the word and not hearers only, deceiving yourselves.*[1]

All these Mary observed when the Son of God was born from her. First, she heard: *the Holy Ghost shall come upon thee.*[2] Secondly, she consented by faith: *behold the handmaid of the Lord.*[3] Thirdly, she held the Word and carried him in her womb. Fourthly, she brought him forth. Fifthly, she fed and nursed him.

474, 516   Exposition, *Apostles' Creed*

538. *The desert shall blossom like the rose; it shall blossom abundantly, and rejoice even with joy and singing.*[4] The blessed Virgin conceived without loss, carried with comfort, and gave birth in joy.

517   Exposition, *Hail Mary*

539. The angel said, *Hail, full of grace.*[5] St. Jerome expounds: Indeed full of grace, for to others it is given in portions, but on Mary its fullness is showered.[6] The closer a thing is to its originating cause the greater the share in its effects. Christ is the principle of grace, authoritatively in his Godhead, instrumentally in his manhood: *grace and truth came by Jesus Christ.*[7] But, of all persons, the blessed Virgin Mary was closest to his manhood, which he received from her, and therefore fair it was that she should receive a greater measure of grace, above others.

496, 510, 638   *Summa Theologica,* 3a. xxvii. 5

[1] James i. 22.   [2] Luke i. 35.   [3] Luke i. 38.
[4] Isa. xxxv. 1–2.   [5] Luke i. 28.
[6] *Epistola IX, ad Paulam et Eustochium*; PL xxx. 131.
[7] John i. 17.

540. It was right and proper that the angel of the Annunciation should have appeared by physical presence to the eyesight of the Mother of God, not merely to her imagination or mind. A phrase occurs in one of Augustine's sermons: 'to me came the archangel Gabriel with glowing countenance, gleaming robe, wondrous step.'[1] It was in keeping, first, with what was announced, second, with her dignity, third, with human certainty. For it was right that an invisible creature should assume visible form to declare the incarnation of the invisible God; all the more the Old Testament theophanies and appearances led up to the real appearance of God's Son in the flesh. Next, the Mother of God was to receive the Son in her bodily womb, not only in her mind, and therefore how suitable it was that her bodily senses should have been refreshed by the angelic vision. Finally, we apprehend with greater certainty what is before our very eyes than what appears solely in the imagination. Wherefore Chrysostom says that the angel came to the Virgin when she was awake and stood visibly before her.[2]

516, 595   *Summa Theologica*, 3a. xxx. 3

541. Eve sought the fruit, but did not find there what she wished for. In her fruit the blessed Virgin found all that Eve had wanted.

635   Exposition, *Hail Mary*

542. The second man is said to be from heaven, not because of his bodily matter, which was earthly and taken from Adam, but because of his divinity and the power of the Holy Ghost which formed his body.

Summa Theologica, 3a. xxxi. 1

---

[1] *Sermones Supposititii*, cxcv; *PL.* xxxix. 2108.
[2] *Homil.* iv; *PG* lvii. 452.

543. The whole Trinity effected the conception of Christ's body. Nevertheless, it is attributed to the Holy Ghost, who is the Love of the Father and the Son, for God's exceeding great love was the motive of the Son's taking to himself flesh from the Virgin's womb.

123, 129 *Summa Theologica*, 3a. xxxii. 1

544. *The Holy Ghost shall come upon thee,*[1] therefore shalt thou conceive without sadness and waste; *and the power of the highest shall overshadow thee*, and therefore shalt thou carry without heaviness; *and the holy one which shall be born of thee shall be called the Son of God*, and therefore shalt thou bring forth without labour. Mary bears the price of our redemption. The water which gushed out of the rock to refresh the people of Israel is her symbol.[2] Hers is the integrity of maidenhood, the fruitfulness of wedlock, the purity of chastity. Let us all bless her often, and sing her praises: *for, behold, from henceforth all generations shall call me blessed.*[3]

120 *Sunday Sermons*, 47[4]

4. THE LIFE OF CHRIST

545. Christ was circumcised in order that he might free others from the yoke of the Law by bearing its burden. *God sent forth his Son, made under the Law, to redeem them that were under the Law.*[5]

666 *Summa Theologica*, 3a. xxxvi. 1

546. One difference between Christ and other men is this: they do not chose when to be born, but he, the Lord and Maker of history, chose his time, his birthplace, and his mother.

Summa Theologica, 3a. xxxv. 8

[1] Luke i. 35.   [2] Numb. xx. 8.   [3] Luke i. 48.
[4] 4th Sunday of Lent.   [5] Gal. iv. 4.

547. Christ's manner of life was shaped to the purpose of his incarnation. He came into the world, first that he might proclaim the truth: *for this was I born, and for this came I into the world, that I should give testimony to the truth.*[1] It would have been inappropriate for him to have hidden himself away and led a solitary life; instead he appeared openly and preached in public. He said to those who wished to stay him: *To other cities also I must preach the kingdom of God, for therefore am I sent.*[2]

Secondly, he came in order to free men from sin: *Christ Jesus came into this world to save sinners.*[3] Chrysostom observes that although Christ might have drawn men to hear his preaching without moving from one centre yet he chose to give us the example of venturing out and seeking those who perish, like the shepherd who searches for lost sheep, and the doctor who visits the sick.[4]

Thirdly, he came that we might have *access to God.*[5] It was fitting that he should give men confidence to approach him by associating familiarly with them: *it came to pass as he was sitting in the house, behold many publicans and sinners came, and sat down with Jesus and his disciples.*[6] Jerome comments that they had seen the publican converted from a sinful to a better life, why then should they despair of their own salvation?[7]

His deeds are for our instruction. In order to teach preachers that they ought not to be always in the public gaze, our Lord withdrew himself sometimes from the crowd. We are told of three reasons for his doing this.

[1] John xviii. 37.   [2] Luke iv. 42, 43.
[3] 1 Tim. i. 15.
[4] Chrysostom, so quoted by *Catena Aurea*, Luke iv. 42.
[5] Rom. v. 2.   [6] Matt. ix. 10.
[7] *in Matt.* ix. 10; *PL* xxvi. 58.

First, for bodily repose: *come apart into a desert place,*
he said to his disciples, *and rest a little; for there was
much coming and going; and they had not so much as time
to eat.*[1] Secondly, for the sake of prayer: *it came to pass
in those days, that he went out into a mountain to pray;
and he passed the whole night in the prayer to God.*[2]
Thirdly, in order to teach us to avoid the favour of
men: *Jesus, seeing the multitudes, went up into a mountain.*[3]

    488, 493   *Summa Theologica,* 3a. xl. 1, c. & ad 3

548. For Christ to be a hermit would not have advanced the purpose of the Incarnation; therefore he
mingled with men: *the Son of Man came eating and
drinking.*[4] Good manners demand that we should
conform to the fashions of those with whom we asso-
ciate: *I became all things to all men.*[5] For this cause he
avoided eccentricity in food and drink.

    479   *Summa Theologica,* 3a. xl. 2

549. It was fitting that Christ should have been buried.
First, to establish the fact of his death. Nobody is laid
in the grave unless they are assuredly dead, and we read
that Pilate made certain by careful inquiry that Christ
was dead before giving leave for the burial.[6] Secondly,
that by Christ's rising from the tomb hope of rising
through him may be given to us for whom it yawns: *all
that are in their graves shall hear the voice of the Son
of God, and they that hear shall live.*[7] Thirdly, for an
example for them who are dying spiritually to their
sins, who *are hidden away from the disturbance of men.*[8]
You are dead, says the Apostle, *and your life is hidden
with Christ in God.*[9] The baptized, who die to sin

---

[1] Mark vi. 31.   [2] Luke vi. 12.   [3] Matt. v. 1.
[4] Matt. xi. 19.   [5] 1 Cor. ix, 22.   [6] Mark xv. 44–45.
[7] John v. 25, 28.   [8] Ps. xxx. 21.   [9] Col. iii. 3.

through Christ's death, are, as it were, buried with Christ by immersion: *we are buried together with Christ by baptism into death.*[1]

605　　　　　　　　　　　*Summa Theologica,* 3a. li. 1

550. It was fitting that Christ should have descended into hell. First, because he came to bear our burden that he might free us from punishment: *surely he hath borne our griefs, and carried our sorrows.*[2] Because of sin our lot was hell. And as Christ dies to deliver us from death, so he went down to hell that we might not have to stay there: *O death, I will be thy death; O hell, I will be thy bite.*[3] Secondly, that the devil might be conquered and his captives rescued: *thou also by the blood of the testament hast sent forth thy prisoners out of the pit.*[4] So it is written, *Despoiling the principalities and powers, he exposed them, triumphing over them in it.*[5] Thirdly, that he might show forth his power by visiting and enlightening hell as well as by living and dying on earth: *lift up your gates, O ye princes!*[6] And the Gloss interprets, Ye princes of hell, now is your power taken away which hitherto held men fast in hell. *At the name of Jesus every knee should bow, of things in heaven, and things in earth, and things under the earth.*[7]

231, 266, 477　　　　　　*Summa Theologica,* 3a. lii. 1

5. THE ATONEMENT

551. *He loved us, and washed us from our sins in his own blood.*[8] In three ways is Christ's Passion the true and proper cause of the forgiveness of sins. First, by prompting us to charity, through which we gain pardon: *many sins are forgiven her, because she loved*

[1] Rom. vi. 4.　　[2] Isa. liii. 4.　　[3] Hos. xiii. 14.
[4] Zach. ix. 11.　　[5] Col. ii. 15.　　[6] Ps. xxiii. 7.
[7] Phil. ii. 10.　　　　　　　　　　[8] Apoc. i. 5.

much.[1] Second, through redemption, for since he is our head, then by the Passion endured from obedience and love he delivered us, who are his members, by paying the cost of sin: thus a man by the good wrought by his hands may redeem himself for the wrong into which his feet have walked. A natural body is a single organism composed of diverse members; likewise the whole Church, Christ's mystical body, is reputed to be one single person, of which the head is Christ. Thirdly, by efficient causality, for the flesh in which he suffered his Passion was an instrument of the Godhead, and by divine virtue his sufferings and death actively drive sin out.

391, 568, 595   *Summa Theologica*, 3a. xlix. 1

552. There was no better method of healing our miseries, Augustine decides, than by Christ suffering on our behalf.[2] A course of action is the more advantageous the better it serves the purpose in view. By suffering in order to save us Christ conferred benefits on us over and above the mere escaping from sin. First, because now we realize how much God loves us, and now we can be roused to love him in return; this friendship is the heart of spiritual health. *God commends his love towards us, in that, while we were yet sinners, Christ died for us.*[3] Secondly, he left us the example of the virtues necessary for salvation, of obedience, humility, constancy, justice, and the others, all of which were displayed in his Passion: *Christ suffered for us, leaving us an example, that you should follow in his steps.*[4] Thirdly, through his Passion Christ also deserved justifying grace for us, and the glory of happiness.

[1] Luke vii. 47.
[2] *de Trinitate*, xiii. 10; *PL* xlii. 1024.
[3] Rom. v. 8.   [4] 1 Pet. ii. 21.

Fourthly, because now we are provided with a stronger motive for keeping ourselves immune from sin: *for you are bought with a great price; therefore glorify God in your body and in your spirit, which are God's.*[1] Fifthly, human dignity is enhanced, for as man was tricked and defeated by the devil so man also conquered the devil, and as man deserved death so did man vanquish death: *thanks be to God, who gives us the victory through our Lord Jesus Christ.*[2] How much better then that we should be liberated through Christ's Passion than solely through God's good pleasure.

500   *Summa Theologica*, 3a. xlvi. 3

553. The proper office of a mediator is to join opposed parties, for extremes meet in a middle. To achieve our union with God is Christ's work: *God was in Christ reconciling the world unto himself.*[3] He alone is the perfect mediator between God and men, forasmuch as the human race was brought into agreement with God through his death: *there is one mediator between God and men, the man Jesus Christ,* says St. Paul, and then adds, *who gave himself a ransom for all.*[4]

There is no reason why creatures should not be called mediators after a fashion, in that they co-operate in our reconciliation, disposing and ministering to men's union with God.

The Spirit itself maketh intercession for us,[5] by causing us to plead, but, being in all things equal with God, the Holy Ghost should not be called a go-between or mediator: *now a mediator is not a mediator of one.*[6] This is for Christ alone, who is equal to the Father by his divinity, less by his humanity.

386, 472, 625   *Summa Theologica*, 3a. xxvi. 1, c. & ad 3

---

[1] 1 Cor. vi. 20.   [2] 1 Cor. xv. 57.   [3] 2 Cor. v. 19.
[4] 1 Tim. ii. 5–6.   [5] Rom. viii. 26.   [6] Gal. iii. 20.

554. On the text, *Therefore God hath highly exalted him*,[1] Augustine comments that in the Passion of Christ merit lay in the abasement of sublimity, reward in the ennobling of lowliness.[2] Now he is glorified not in himself alone, but also in his faithful: *I am glorified in them*.[3] It seems, then, that he merited glory for his faithful.

He was given grace not as a singular person alone, but also as Head of the Church, that life might flow from him to his members. Therefore the effect of what he does on himself and his members is like the effect of an ordinary person on himself alone. A person who from grace suffers in the cause of justice merits salvation for himself: *blessed are they who are persecuted for righteousness' sake, for theirs is the kingdom of heaven*.[4] Therefore, Christ deserved heaven for his members as well as for himself.

To the objection that nobody gains merit from what is done to them from outside, I answer that physically Christ's Passion was inflicted by violence, but psychologically and morally it was accepted from within.

His whole life, from its earliest stages, entitles us to heaven. The point of the Passion is to break down the obstacles on our side which prevent us profiting from his merits. Its saving effect on us is additional to that of his other deeds, not as expressing greater charity on his part, but as exciting us to greater love.

344, 521   *Summa Theologica*, 3a. xlviii. 1, c. & ad 1, 2, 3

555. Strict satisfaction is rendered when the person offended is given what he loves as much as, or more than, he hated the offence. By suffering from charity,

[1] Phil. ii. 9.
[2] *in Joannis Evangelium Tractatus*, civ; *PL*. xxxv. 1903.
[3] John xvii. 10.   [4] Matt. v. 10.

Christ offered to God more than what was demanded as recompense for the sin of the entire human race. First, from the greatness of his charity. Secondly, from the preciousness of the life he laid down, the life of a man who was God. Thirdly, by the extent and depth of what was accepted. Christ's Passion was more than sufficient, it was superabundant. *He is the propitiation for our sins; and not for our's only, but also for the sins of the whole world.*[1]

Head and members make up, as it were, one mystical body. Therefore the amends made by Christ are made also by all his members. For when two persons live in friendship, one may make satisfaction for the other. It is true that one cannot act as a substitute for the other's contrition and confession. Satisfaction, however, is an external deed, for which we adopt auxiliaries, among which are reckoned our friends.

522, 526   *Summa Theologica*, 3a. xlviii. 2, *c. & ad* 1

556. Although by his death Christ sufficiently merited salvation for the whole human race, each of us must there seek his own cure. Christ's death is like the universal cause of deliverance, as the sin of our first parents was like the universal cause of perdition. Nevertheless even a universal cause must be applied to be effective. The effects of original sin come to us through bodily birth; the effects of Christ's death through the spiritual rebirth whereby we are incorporated in Christ.

477, 595   iv *Contra Gentes*, 55

557. Original sin is a sin of nature. It came to Adam through his actual fault, in other words, his personal

[1] 1 John ii. 2.

sin. Here person corrupted nature. Through this corruption the sin of our first parents descends on their
progeny. Here nature corrupts person. Grace, however,
comes to us from Christ, not through human nature, but
solely through his personal action. Consequently, there
is no need to extend the parallel between Christ's grace
and Adam's actual and original sin. Christ's personal
sanctifying grace and his grace as Head of the Church
are essentially the same; they differ merely as different
topics for study.

225, 502, 526   *Summa Theologica*, 3a. viii. 5, *c. & ad* 1

558. By dying he destroyed our death,[1] and by the
pains he underwent he freed us from pain. That was
why he chose to suffer a painful death. His mother's
labour was no part of his work to make satisfaction for
our sins, and therefore it would have been unseemly for
his mother to have suffered in bearing him.

267, 526   *Summa Theologica*, 3a. xxxv. 6, *ad* 2

559. *Now in the place where he was crucified there was
a garden.*[2] Christ was captured in a garden, he suffered
his agony in a garden, and he was buried in a garden.
These facts are symbols. The virtue of his Passion frees
us from the sin Adam committed in the garden of Eden,
and consecrates the Church which is a garden enclosed.[3]

Commentary, *St. John*, xix, *lect.* 6

560. *He delivered himself up for us, an offering and a
sacrifice to God, for a sweetsmelling savour.*[4] A sacrifice,
strictly speaking, is something wrought for the honour
properly due to God in order to appease him. Augustine
describes a true sacrifice as a good work done that we
may cling to God in holy fellowship and be brought to

[1] Easter Preface of the Mass.   [2] John xix. 41.
[3] Cant. iv. 12.   [4] Eph. v. 2.

where we can be truly blessed.[1] He adds that Christ
offered himself up for us in the Passion. What was most
acceptable to God was his voluntary enduring of his
Passion, because it sprang from the highest charity.
Clearly Christ's Passion was a true sacrifice.

Later Augustine goes on to say[2] that the primitive
sacrifices of the ancient Fathers were many and various
types of this true sacrifice, one being prefigured by
many, as when a single meaning is expressed through
many words, in order that it may be put forward
without tedious repetition. He applies also to the one
true Mediator who reconciles us with God through his
sacrifice of peace the four qualities which may be noted
in any sacrifice, namely, to whom, by whom, what, and
for whom it is offered. Christ stays one with him to
whom he offered his sacrifice, is one with them for
whom he offered it, and is himself the offerer and the
oblation.[3]

616, 625   *Summa Theologica*, 3a. xlviii. 3

561. *You were not redeemed with corruptible things, as
silver and gold, from your vain conversation received by
tradition from your fathers; but with the precious blood
of Christ, as of a lamb without blemish and without spot.*[4]
And again, *Christ hath redeemed us from the curse of the
law, being made a curse for us*[5] he is called a curse
because he died for us on a gibbet.

Man was held captive in that he was enslaved to sin:
whosoever committeth sin is the servant of sin,[6] and again,
*by whom a man is overcome, of the same also is he the
slave.*[7] Since the devil overcame man by inducing him

---

[1] *de Civitate Dei*, x. 6; *PL* xli. 283.
[2] *de Civitate Dei*, x. 20; *PL* xli. 298.
[3] *de Trinitate*, iv. 14; *PL* xlii. 901.
[4] 1 Pet. i. 18.   [5] Gal. iii. 13.
[6] John viii. 34.   [7] 2 Pet. ii. 19.

to sin man was in bondage to the devil. Then, also, man was held captive as to a debt of punishment, to the payment of which he was bound by divine justice: this, too, is a kind of bondage, for it is the mark of slavery to have done to you what you do not will.

Now because Christ's Passion was the sufficient and superabundant satisfaction for human guilt and the consequent debt of punishment, his Passion was a kind of price, which paid the cost of freeing us from both obligations. The satisfaction a man makes to free himself or another is called a ransom: *redeem thou thy sins with alms.*[1] Christ rendered satisfaction, not by giving money or anything of the sort, but by spending for us what was of the highest value. He gave himself, and therefore his Passion is called our redemption.

224   *Summa Theologica*, 3a. xlviii. 4

562. *I have made you and I will bear you. I will carry and will save.*[2] Christ suffered in his members from the beginning of the world. He suffered on the cross in his own person: *who in his own self bore our sins in his body on the tree.*[3]

116   Commentary, *Hebrews*, xii, *lect.* 1

563. *The word of the cross to them that are saved is the power of God.*[4] Of the two kinds of efficient cause, the principal and the instrumental, the principal cause of our salvation is God. Christ's manhood is also an efficient cause, because it was the instrument of the Godhead: all he did and suffered worked for human salvation as the instrument of divine power.

289   *Summa Theologica*, 3a. xlviii. 6

---

[1] Dan. iv. 24.   [2] Isa. xlvi. 4.
[3] 1 Pet. ii. 24.   [4] 1 Cor. i. 18.

564. Christ as God possesses authoritative power to give grace and the Holy Spirit. As man he has instrumental power, for his humanity was the instrument of his divinity. By divine power his actions brought us to salvation; he causes grace in us, both by meriting it and by effectively producing it.

310 *Summa Theologica,* 3a. viii. 1, *ad* 1

565. The human body has a natural relation to the soul, which is its proper form and mainspring. By this form it comes alive and receives the proper characteristics of a human body; to this active force it serves as an instrument. We say, therefore, that the manhood of Christ, because united to the Word of God, the body being united through the soul, has causal power. His entire manhood, both soul and body, affects men's souls and bodies. Their souls primarily, their bodies secondarily, first, *because the members of the body are presented as instruments of justice*[1] in souls that live through Christ, and next, because the life of glory suffuses the body: *he that raised up Jesus from the dead shall quicken also your mortal bodies, because of his Spirit that dwelleth in you.*[2]

175, 659, 662 *Summa Theologica,* 3a. viii. 2

566. Christ's Passion is the cause of our salvation in various ways—the efficient cause when related to his Godhead; the meritorious cause when related to his human will; the satisfying cause in that it liberates us from the debt of punishment; the redemptive cause in that it frees us from the bondage of sin; the sacrificial cause in that it reconciles us with God.

343, 526 *Summa Theologica,* 3a. xlviii. 6, *ad* 3

[1] Rom. vi. 13.   [2] Phil. iii. 21.

567. A double death we can suffer, and a double life can live. One the death of the body, by separation from soul; the other the death of the soul, by separation from God. Christ killed both by the bodily death he suffered —spiritual death had no place in him. Then one is the life natural to body quickened by soul, the other the life of grace and righteousness from God, which comes through faith, when God dwells in us: *the just shall live by faith.*[1] Correspondingly there is a double resurrection, one of the body, when soul rejoins body, the other spiritual, of soul reunited to God. Christ's bodily resurrection produces both in us—though he himself never rose again spiritually, for he had never been separated from God.

Although God alone is the author of our life, Christ's body is his instrument. Now in virtue of the principal cause an instrument truly acts. Both our resurrections derive from Christ's body as from a cause. All his actions bring salvation to us, for they come from his humanity conjoined to his divinity. His bodily resurrection works our spiritual resurrection: *he was raised again for our justification.*[2] It also works our bodily resurrection: *if Christ be preached that he rose from the dead, how say some among you that there is no resurrection from the dead ?*[3]

Admirably then does St. Paul link as effects to cause the forgiveness of sins to Christ's death and sanctification to his resurrection. Sin when forgiven is cast away—the dying Christ threw down his mortal life made to the likeness of sin. Justification is the beginning of a new life—the risen Christ throws open the way into life. His death produces the forgiveness of our sins: it is the instrumental efficient cause, the sacramental

[1] Hab. ii. 4.　　　　　　　　[2] Rom. iii. 25.
[3] I Cor. xv. 12.

exemplar cause, and the meritorious moral cause. His resurrection produces ours: it is the instrumental efficient cause and the sacramental exemplar cause, but not the meritorious cause, for when Christ had risen from the dead his struggle was over, the time for merit had passed, and he had entered into his reward.

344, 662   *Compendium Theologiae,* 239

X

The Church[1]

568. The entire Church is called a single mystical body, by analogy with a human physical body which performs different functions through different members, as described by St. Paul.[2] Christ is called the Head of the Church—*God hath made him head over all the Church*[3]—by analogy with the human head. The comparison should not be laboured, for a resemblance is stated, not an exact correspondence or identity.

We may pause on these three points: order, perfection, and power. Order, because the head is the top; hence beginnings or principles are customarily called headings or heads: for example, *at every head of the way, thou hast set up a sign of thy prostitution.*[4] Perfection, because all the senses are there centred; of counsellors it is written, *the honourable, he is the head.*[5] Power, because the force, control, and human quality of other bodily members come from the head; hence the ruler is called the head of the people: *when thou wast a little one in thine own eyes, wast thou not made the head of the tribes of Israel?*[6]

---

[1] St. Thomas was a strong churchman, but less clericalist than many of his contemporaries: his writings do not favour what is now called religious totalitarianism. The Church is described as a mystical body only by metaphor. He had a well-defined sense of the limits of ecclesiastical authority, and stood apart from the Canonist Movement of his times which would have made the Pope, to whose spiritual prerogatives he was devoted, the supreme lord in temporalities. The Church's sacraments, which accept and bless man's physical nature, are not repositories, but instruments of grace; their operation is not magical and they require due dispositions on the part of the minister or recipient.

[2] Rom. xii and 1 Cor. xii. [3] Eph. i. 22.
[4] Ezek. xvi. 25. [5] Isa. ix. 15. [6] Kings xv. 17.

These three are applied figuratively to Christ. The first, because he is close to God, and his grace comes first, though not in time, and is over and before the grace received by all others, which derives from his: *whom God foreknew, he also predestined to the image of his Son; that he might be the first-born of many brethren.*[1] The second, because of his plentitude of grace: *we saw him, full of grace and truth.*[2] The third, because his is the energy which pours grace into every member of the Church: *of his fullness we have all received.*[3]

28, 34, 129, 522, 555 *Summa Theologica*, 3a. viii. 1, c. & ad 2

569. *He is the saviour of all men, especially of the faithful.*[4] It is as the Head of all mankind that Christ saves and atones: *he is the propitiation for our sins, and not for ours only, but also for those of the whole world.*[5]

One difference between an organic body and the Church's mystical body is this: the members of an organism are all knit together at one given period of time, whereas the members of the mystical body are dispersed throughout the ages, for the Church's body is made up of people of every century, from the beginning to the end of the world. They are not all contemporaries even in the world of grace, for at any given period there are some who then are lacking grace, and yet afterwards will receive it, while others already possess grace. We can reckon, therefore, with actual and potential members of the Church. Some are potential and will never be actual, others will be actual, either by faith, or by wayfarer's charity as well,[6] or by the enjoyment of our heavenly home.

[1] Rom. viii. 29. [2] John i. 14. [3] John i. 16.
[4] 1 Tim. iv. 10. [5] John ii. 2.
[6] A *viator*, a person travelling to God; contrasted with a *comprehensor*, one of the blessed who has arrived in heaven.

Looking at the whole course of history, then we say that Christ is the Head of all mankind, but not of all men in the same way. First and principally, of those who are united to him in glory; secondly, of those who are actually united to him by charity; thirdly, of those actually united to him by faith; fourthly, of those not yet united actually but who are predestined to heaven; fifthly, of those who could be united but will not be— these are human beings living in the world who are not predestined, and who will, on their passing away, wholly cease to be members of Christ, even potentially.

299, 383, 387, 551   *Summa Theologica*, 3a. viii. 3

570. *Christ loved the Church and delivered himself up for it, that he might present to himself a glorious Church, not having spot, or wrinkle, or any such thing.*[1] A glorious Church, that is the culmination achieved through Christ's Passion. This is our heavenly country, not discovered during our pilgrimage here below, where *if we say we have no sin, we deceive ourselves.*[2]

653   *Summa Theologica*, 3a. viii. 3, *ad* 2

571. *There was a wedding feast, and the mother of Jesus was there.*[3] Mystically the wedding feast means the Church: *this is a great sacrament, but I speak concerning Christ and the Church.*[4] That marriage began in the Virgin's womb, where the Father espoused the Son to human nature in unity of person: *he hath set a tabernacle in the sun.*[5] It was solemnized when the Church was joined to him by faith: *I will betroth thee unto me in faithfulness.*[6] It will be consummated when the bride, that is, the Church, shall be brought into the bridal chamber of heavenly glory.

29   Commentary, *St. John*, ii, *lect.* 1

[1] Eph. v. 25, 27.   [2] 1 John i. 8.   [3] John ii. 1.
[4] Eph. v. 32.   [5] Ps. xviii. 6.   [6] Hos. ii. 20.

572. As in one single human being there is one soul and one body but many members, so the Catholic Church has one body but many members. The soul animating this body is the Holy Ghost. Hence the Creed, after bidding us believe in the Holy Ghost, adds, *the Holy Catholic Church.*

Church means congregation. Holy Church is the congregation of believers of which each Christian is a member: *draw near to me, ye unlearned; and gather yourselves together into the house of discipline.*[1]

The Church has four marks, being one, holy, catholic or universal, and strong or lasting. Heretics lack the first, for because they have invented a variety of sects and are split into factions they do not belong to the Church, which is one: *one is my dove; my perfect one is but one.*[2] This unity has a threefold cause; it comes from agreement of faith, of hope, of charity. Of faith, for all Christians who belong to the body of the Church believe the same truths: *now I beseech you, brethren, by the name of our Lord Jesus Christ, that you all speak the same thing, and that there be no schisms among you.*[3] And again, *one Lord, one faith, one baptism.*[4] Unity of hope, for all are comforted by the same confidence of coming to life eternal: *one body and one spirit; as you are called in one hope of your redemption.*[5] Unity of charity, for all are bound together in the love of God and of one another: *the love which thou hast given me, I have given them; that they may be one, even as we are one.*[6] The genuineness of this love is shown when the members of the Church care for one another and are compassionate together: *doing the truth in charity, we may in all things grow up in him who is the head, even Christ; from whom the whole body, being compacted ana*

---

[1] Ecclus. li. 31. [2] Cant. vi. 8. [3] 1 Cor. i. 10.
[4] Eph. iv. 5. [5] Eph. iv. 4. [6] John xvii. 22.

fitly joined together by that which every joint supplieth, according to the effectual working in the measure of every part, maketh increase of the body unto the edifying of itself in love.[1] According to the grace granted him, each should serve his neighbour; nobody should be despised, nobody should be treated as an outcast, for the Church is like the Ark of Noah, outside of which nobody can be saved.

Then the Church is holy: *know you not that you are the temple of God.*[2] A church when consecrated is washed—so are the faithful cleansed by the blood of Christ: *he hath loved us and washed us from our sins in his own blood.*[3] A church is anointed too—so also the faithful receive a spiritual unction for their sanctification, otherwise they would not be Christians. The Christ means the Anointed One. And his unction is the grace of the Holy Spirit: *now he that confirmeth you in Christ and hath anointed us is God, who also hath sealed us and given us the pledge of the Spirit in our hearts.*[4] Moreover, the Church is holy by the indwelling of the Blessed Trinity: *this is the place of awe, none other but the house of God and gate of heaven.*[5] There, also, is God invoked: *thou, O Lord, art in the midst of us, and we are called by thy name; leave us not.*[6] So then, let us guard against defiling our soul with sin: *for if any man violate the temple of God, him shall God destroy.*[7]

The Church is catholic, that is, universal. First with regard to place: *we have received grace and apostleship for obedience to his faith, in all nations.*[8] Our Lord commanded us, *Go ye into the whole world and preach the gospel to every creature.*[9] The Church has three parts, one on earth, a second in heaven, a third in

---

[1] Eph. iv. 15–16. [2] 1 Cor. iii. 3. [3] Apoc. i. 5.
[4] 2 Cor. i. 21–22. [5] Gen. xxviii. 17. [6] Jer. xiv. 9.
[7] 1 Cor. iii. 17. [8] Rom. i. 5. [9] Mark xvi. 15.

purgatory. The Church is universal with regard to all conditions of human beings; nobody is rejected, whether they be masters or slaves, men or women: *there is neither Jew nor Greek, neither bond nor free, neither male nor female.*[1] It is universal in time, and those are wrong who allow it a limited span of time, for it began with Abel and will last even to the end of the world: *behold, I am with you always, even to the consummation of the world.*[2] And even after, for the Church remains in heaven.

Fourthly, the Church is firm, solid as a house on massive foundations. The principal foundation is Christ himself: *for other foundation no man can lay but that which is laid, which is Christ Jesus.*[3] Secondary foundations are the Apostles and apostolic teaching: hence the Church is called apostolic: *the walls of the city had twelve foundations; and in them the names of the Apostles of the Lamb.*[4] Its strength is signified by Peter, or Rock, who is its crown. A building is strong when it can never be overthrown though it may be shaken. The Church can never be brought down. Indeed it grows under persecution, and those who attack it are destroyed: *whosoever shall fall on this stone shall be broken; but on whomsoever it shall fall, it shall grind him to powder.*[5] Nor can the Church be destroyed by errors: *men corrupted in mind, reprobate concerning the Faith, but they shall proceed no farther, for their folly shall appear to all men.*[6] Nor by the temptations of demons, for the Church will stand, a secure place of refuge: *the name of the Lord is a strong tower.*[7] Though he strives to undermine it, the devil will never succeed: *the gates of hell shall not prevail.*[8] Only the Church

[1] Gal. iii. 28.   [2] Matt. xxviii. 20.
[3] 1 Cor. iii. 11.   [4] Apoc. xxi. 14.   [5] Matt. xxi. 44.
[6] 1 Tim. iii. 8–9.   [7] Prov. xviii. 10.   [8] Matt. xvi. 18.

of Peter, to whose lot fell all Italy when the disciples were sent out to preach, has always stood fast in the Faith. While the Faith has disappeared or has partly decayed in other regions, the Church of Peter still flourishes in faith and free from heresy. This is not to be surprised at, for our Lord said to Peter, *I have prayed for thee that thy faith fail not, and thou, when thou art converted, confirm thy brethren.*[1]

26, 71, 650   Exposition, *Apostles' Creed*

I. TEACHING AUTHORITY

573. When our Saviour sent forth his disciples, he enjoined three duties on them: to teach the faith, to give the sacraments to those imbued with faith, and to lead them on, so steeped, to the observance of divine precepts.

Exposition, *1st Decretal*

574. A man cannot believe unless the truth be proposed to him.

Summa Theologica, 2a–2ae. i. 9

575. The blessed Apostle Peter, to whom our Lord promised that the Church would be built on his confession of faith and that the gates of hell would not prevail against it, in order that the faith of the Church committed to him might persist inviolate, addressed Christ's faithful, *Sanctify the Lord God in your hearts, and be ready always to give an answer to every man that asketh of you a reason of the hope that is in you.*[2] The foundation is faith established in our hearts; it makes us secure against assault and ridicule. It consists in acknowledging the blessed Trinity above all. It glories especially in the cross of our Lord Jesus Christ: *to them*

[1] Luke xxii. 32.   [2] 1 Pet. iii. 15.

that perish foolishness, but to them that are saved the power of God.[1]

78   *de Rationibus Fidei,* 1

576. When you debate with unbelievers, be warned, to begin with, against striving to demonstrate the articles of faith. That would be to minimize their grandeur, for they surpass the minds of angels let alone of men. We believe them because God reveals them. Your intention should be to defend the Faith, not to prove it up to the hilt.

44, 79   *de Rationibus Fidei,* 2

577. Articles of faith in Christian theology are like self-evident principles in philosophy, being so arranged that some are implicit in others. All rational principles can be taken back to the principle of contradiction. Similarly the articles of faith are based on certain primary principles of faith: *he that cometh to God must believe that he is, and that he is a rewarder of them that diligently seek him.*[2] Our faith in God's reality includes everything we believe to be eternally in God, who is our happiness; our faith in his Providence includes all his temporal dispensations for our salvation. From the beginning our faith in the later articles is anticipated; our faith in redemption contains our faith in the Incarnation and Passion of Christ.

Regarding its substance, then, faith does not grow with the passage of time, for whatever has been believed since was contained from the start in the faith of the Ancient Fathers. As regards its explication, however, the number of articles has increased, for we moderns explicitly believe what they believed implicitly. *And God spake unto Moses: I am the God of Abraham, the God*

1 Cor. i. 18.   [2] Heb. xi. 6.

*of Isaac, the God of Jacob; and by my name Jahweh was
I not known to them.*[1] And David says, *I understood more
than the ancients.*[2] And St. Paul, *The mystery of Christ,
which was not known in other ages was not made known
unto the sons of men, as it is now revealed unto his holy
apostles and prophets.*[3]

35, 366 *Summa Theologica,* 2a–2ae. ii. 7

578. Revealed truths, contained in Holy Scripture,
are set forth diffusely, in a variety of styles, and sometimes obscurely, so that for faith to be elicited about its
text disciplined investigation is demanded, and this, all
who need to know cannot manage for themselves, for
most, busied with other concerns, cannot give themselves to study. Hence the need to compile from its
pages a concise summary to be proposed for everybody's
belief. This is the Creed, which is not added to Holy
Scripture, but rather drawn from it.

19, 26, 41 *Summa Theologica,* 2a–2ae. i, 9, *ad* 1

579. A new edition of the Creed is called for when it will
prevent the rise of error. The authority to publish it
goes with the office of pronouncing judicial sentence
on what is of faith, and of deciding what is an authentic
part of the Christian Revelation: the purpose is to keep
our faith steady. To the Supreme Pontiff, who has this
authority, major difficulties are submitted.[4] To Peter,
whom he made Supreme Pontiff, our Lord said, *I have
prayed for thee, Peter, that thy faith fail not, and thou,
when thou art converted, confirm thy brethren.*[5] That one
faith should be held by the whole Church, *that ye all
speak the same thing, and that there be no divisions among
you,*[6] cannot be ensured unless doubts about the faith

[1] Exod. vi. 2, 3.
[2] Ps. cxviii. 100.
[3] Eph. iii. 4–5.
[4] Gratian, *Decretum,* I. xvii. 4.
[5] Luke xxii. 32.
[6] I Cor. i. 10.

be decided by him who presides over the whole Church, and whose decision will be accepted by all. The publication of articles of belief is like the convocation of a General Council or any other commitment affecting the Universal Church: no other power is competent but that of the Pope.

654   *Summa Theologica*, 2a–2ae. i. 10

580. One and the same truth is taught in all the creeds. When errors crop up, more pointed instruction becomes necessary, lest the faith of simple folk slip into heresy. This is the reason why different creeds have been issued: they differ only in this, that occasioned by the instance of heretics, the later ones furnish a fuller explanation of what the previous ones implicitly contained.

98, 105, 369   *Summa Theologica*, 2a–2ae. i. 9 *ad* 2

581. Joy may have a good cause, direct and immediate, and then both cause and effect are to be enjoyed; or it may have an evil cause, indirect and incidental, and then only the effect is to be enjoyed—thus our Redemption occasioned by the betrayal of our Lord by Judas and the Jews. The same distinction works through the Church, which is served both by sound preachers with right intent and by evil preachers with wrong intent, and yet both may bring joy: *What then? notwithstanding, every way, whether in pretence, or in truth, Christ is preached; and I therein do rejoice, yea, and I will rejoice.*[1]

320, 642   Commentary, *Philippians*, i, *lect.* 3

582. Strong faith, even without charity, works wonders. The power of the Holy Ghost operates also

[1] Phil. i. 18.

through wicked men, as when he speaks the truth
through them.

318 Commentary, *1 Corinthians*, xiii, *lect.* 1

583. A heretic who disbelieves one article of faith
lacks the supernatural habit and virtue of faith, either
of dead faith without charity or of living faith with
charity.[1] Here is the reason: the specific character of
a habit depends on its formal motive and object; take
this away, and the nature of the habit is changed. The
formal motive and object of faith is First Truth as
manifested in Holy Scripture and the doctrine of the
Church. A person who does not commit himself to the
doctrine of the Church, as to a divine and unerring rule
proceeding from First Truth as revealed in the Holy
Scriptures, is without the virtue of faith; he assents to
the truths of faith in some other manner. He may be
compared to a man who, agreeing with scientific truths
but not through the proper medium of proof, holds
them by opinion, not by the habit of science.

Clearly a person who accepts the Church as an
infallible guide will believe whatever the Church
teaches. Otherwise he follows his own private judgement, and does not accept the Church's rule when he
picks and chooses for himself. Consequently a heretic
who pertinaciously disbelieves one article is not prepared to follow the teaching of the Church in all
matters. If he is not pertinacious he is not in heresy, but
only in error. A pertinacious heretic, however, is without divine faith in all the other articles of the Creed,
but assents to them from his own opinion.

369, 371, 380 *Summa Theologica*, 2a–2ae. v. 3

---

[1] *Fides informis*—the truly supernatural faith of a Christian
living in sin; *fides formata*—the same virtue quickened by charity
and sanctifying grace.

584. The weightiest authority is the Church's custom. It should be constantly and punctiliously observed. Ecclesiastical writings draw their warrant from the Church's authority. We should take our stand on the Church's traditional teaching, rather than on the pronouncements of Augustine or Jerome or any other doctor.

594   II *Quodlibets*, iv. 7

585. Some godly folk have held that God's omnipotence can unmake the past, in this sense, that what has happened has no longer really happened. The opinion is not heretical; nevertheless, if it involves a contradiction, it is false.

37   *de Aeternitate Mundi*

586. It is unseemly and rather ridiculous for theologians to cite canon lawyers as theological authorities, or to be occupied with points of legal detail.

284   *Contra Retrahentes*, 13

587. I think our embarrassment over some phrases from the Greek Fathers arises from two sources, historical and literary. In the first place, errors which have cropped up have proved occasions for Doctors of the Church to look around more warily. For instance, God's unity of nature was more emphasized after the time of Arius than before. Other heretics as well have marked periods when style has changed. This comes out clearly in the lifetime of one famous doctor, for Augustine began to write more cautiously after the rise of Pelagius; the defences of freewill which he had pushed out against the Manichaeans were seized on by the Pelagians to beset divine grace. That contemporary theologians should take careful and elaborate pains to avoid error is not to be wondered at. When the ancient writers are less exact, then their statements should be fairly explained; on one hand they should not be disparaged and disowned, on the other not drawn out and overstressed.

In the second place, a word may be well chosen in Greek yet not in Latin. East and West profess the same Faith, but their vocabulary is different. The Greeks are orthodox and catholic to call the Father, Son, and Holy Ghost three *hypostases*, but this rings wrong in Latin ears. To us the term suggests three substances. For although *hypostasis* in Greek and *complete substance* in Latin have the same technical meaning, Latin usage applies the term *substance* also to *essence*, which both Easterns and Westerns profess to be single in God. Doubtless there are many similar cases.

A skilled translator's job, therefore, when rendering Catholic theology from one language to another, is to keep the sense while changing the turn of speech in accordance with native idiom. A version where Latin phrases are literally transposed word for word into the vernacular can be awkward and confusing.

98, 369, 507 *Contra Errores Graecorum*, Prologue

2. THE SACRAMENTS

588. We now speak of sacrament in its proper sense— of a sacred thing a sign which sanctifies men.

605 *Summa Theologica*, 3a. lx. 2

589. In this sign three significations can be considered: the cause of our sanctification, namely Christ's Passion, the form of our sanctification, namely grace and the virtues, and the end of our sanctification, namely eternal life. All three are signified: hence a sacrament is a remembrance of the past, a proof of the present, and a promise for the future.

289, 623 *Summa Theologica*, 3a. lx. 3

590. There were sacraments, namely signs of a sacred thing, in the Old Law; for instance the paschal lamb and other legal sacraments. These, however, only signified Christ's grace, and did not cause it. Hence St. Paul speaks of *weak and beggarly elements*,[1] for they neither contained nor conferred grace. The sacraments of the New Law do both. In them Christ's power, says Augustine, secretly works salvation under the covering of things of sense.[2] A sacrament of the New Law is the visible figure of invisible grace, bearing its likeness and serving as its cause. Thus the washing by baptismal water represents the interior cleansing from sin which is caused in virtue of the sacrament of baptism.

The Church's seven sacraments have common and proper features. Common to all is the giving of grace, common to all their being made up of words and things. Christ is their author; he is the Word made flesh, and as his flesh was sanctified and given sanctifying virtue because of the Word united to it, so sacramental things are sanctified and have sanctifying virtue because of the words uttered in them. A word, says Augustine, comes to the elements, and they become a sacrament.[3] Hence these sanctifying words are called the form of the sacraments, and the sanctified elements the matter: for instance, the matter of Baptism is water, the matter of Confirmation is chrism. Every sacrament, too, requires a minister who confers it with the intention of bestowing and doing what the Church bestows and does. If any of these three be defective, that is, if the due form

[1] Gal. iv. 9.　　[2] Isidore, *Etymol.* vi. 19; *PL* LXXXII. 255.
[3] *super Joannem Tract.* LXXX, on xv. 3; *PL* xxxv. 1840.

of words be not used, or the due matter, or if the minister does not intend to bring about the sacrament, then no sacrament is celebrated. Fault in the recipient can be an obstacle to the effect of the sacrament, for instance, if he receives the sacrament for outward show without his heart being prepared: he receives the sacrament, but not its effect, that is, the grace of the Holy Spirit, for *the Holy Spirit of instruction shuns all pretence.*[1] Conversely, there are others who never take a sacrament and yet receive its effect from their devotion and desire.

Other features are peculiar to certain sacraments. Some impress a character, that is, a spiritual and distinctive seal, thus, Baptism, Confirmation, and Holy Order. Such sacraments are never repeated on the same person. Once baptized, you are never baptized again; once confirmed, or ordained, it is the same: the character impressed by these sacraments is indelible. The other sacraments, which leave no character, can be repeated in the same person; not, however, in the same matter. A person can go frequently to Confession and to Holy Communion, he may more than once receive Extreme Unction or make the contract of Matrimony, but the same host, or the same oil for the sick, is not consecrated more than once. Another difference may also be noted, for some are necessary for salvation, for instance, Baptism and Penance, whereas salvation can be reached without the others, so long as they are not held in contempt.

285, 610   *de Articulis Fidei et Sacramentis Ecclesiae*, 2

i. *Sacramental Theory*

591. Sacramental signification is combined from sensible things and words, which are like matter and form

[1] Wisd i. 5.

and make a unity. The words round off and complete the symbolism of the elements—these include outward sensible actions, such as washing or anointing.

Summa Theologica, 3a. lx. 6, *ad* 2

592. He who purposely alters a sacramental formula does not exhibit the intention of doing what the Church does, and therefore would not appear to complete the sacrament. If the words are garbled by mistake or slip of the tongue so as to be deprived of their sense, then the sacrament is not performed. If, however, the sense remains, then the sacrament is valid, for though the words mispronounced may have no meaning when taken alone, usage accommodates them to their due meaning; the sound is changed, but not the sense.

Summa Theologica, 3a. lx. 7, *ad* 3

593. Two rules are to be kept in mind concerning the alteration of sacramental formulas. The first concerns the minister who utters the words: he must have the due sacramental intention. If by adding or omitting words he intends to perform a rite which is not received by the Church, then he does not complete the sacrament, for he does not seem to intend to do what the Church does.

The second concerns the form of words which communicates significance to the sacramental act. Then we must consider whether the alteration changes the due sense of the words. If it does, then the sacrament is invalid.

584   *Summa Theologica*, 3a. lx. 8

594. An act which can have different purposes needs to be directed to a determinate one in order to be effective. Sacramental acts can be performed for different reasons; the washing by water, used in baptism, can also be applied for physical cleanliness, or bodily health,

or play or much else. Therefore it needs to be determined to one end, namely, the sacramental effect, by the intention of the minister. This intention is expressed by the words said in the giving of the sacraments, for example, *I baptize thee in the name of the Father, and of the Son, and of the Holy Ghost.*

The minister acts in the person of the whole Church which he serves. The intention of the Church is expressed in the words he uses, and these suffice for the sacrament unless the contrary outwardly appears, on the part either of the minister or of the recipient.

A minister who is inattentive to what he is doing lacks an actual intention, but he has an habitual intention, which suffices for the sacrament. For example, a priest who intends to do what the Church does when he goes to baptize, but whose thoughts are distracted during the ceremony, duly completes the sacrament in virtue of his first intention. Nevertheless, the ministers of the sacraments should officiate with an actual intention, though this may not be wholly in a man's power, for, despite himself, when he strongly wills to intend something he starts thinking of other matters: *my heart faileth me.*[1]

Summa Theologica, 3a. lxiv. 8, *c. & ad* 2, 3

595. Christ's death is the world-wide cause of salvation. All the same, any universal cause needs to be applied to produce particular effects; consequently determinate remedies need to be applied to men if they are to be brought into the blessings flowing from Christ's death. These remedies, which are the sacraments of the Church, come to us in portions and are bound up with what we can experience.

Several reasons support this conclusion. First, God

[1] Ps. xxxix. 13.

provides for all things according to their condition. To
be led forth from the physical world in order to seize
the spiritual world is our human destiny, and therefore these sacramental reliefs come in sensible guise.
Secondly, instruments are adapted to their principal
cause, and this, as regards human well-being, is the Word
Incarnate. How fitting then that he should come
through to men in bodily fashion, and that divine virtue
should continue to work invisibly in them through
visible appearances. Thirdly, men lapse into sin through
indulging in what their senses offer them. Lest it should
be reckoned that these objects are evil in themselves, or
that sin lies in being attached to them, some have been
hallowed, and their inherent goodness, created by God,
proclaimed. The harm comes when we are inordinately
committed to things of sense, not when we take them
as we should.

Hence we disavow the heretical error of banishing
them from the sacramental life of the Church, an error
which is logical enough on the supposition that physical
things are bad and produced by the author of evil. What
is there awkward about visible and bodily things
ministering to spiritual health? Are they not the instruments of God, who was made flesh for us and
suffered in this world? An instrument's virtue is not its
own, but is imparted by the principal cause which sets
it to work. Hence, the sacraments do not act from the
properties of their natural elements, but because they
have been adopted by Christ to communicate his
strength.

161, 521, 556, 604   IV *Contra Gentes*, 56

596. We are bound to profess that the sacraments of
the New Law in some manner confer grace, and not
merely because they are liturgically instructive: the

Church is not content with the catechism on which the intending convert is grounded, but goes on to give him the sacraments, which cause as well as signify.

Not all theologians are agreed on how the sacraments work. Some contend that no power resides in them, but that when they are received grace is granted by God then specially present; their causality is like that of a *conditio sine qua non*, as, for instance, when by commercial convention the bearer receives so much money on presentation of an equivalent token. So God has covenanted that whoever takes a genuine sacrament will receive grace, not from the outward sign, but from him.

This opinion, which appears to have been held by the Master of the Sentences,[1] does not sufficiently bring out the greater dignity of the Christian sacraments when compared with the sacraments of the Old Law. If you scrutinize the matter you will find that a condition is not really a cause and amounts to no more than a sign; a receipt is the sign that something has been received, an abbot's crozier that jurisdiction has been conferred.

We should go farther and affirm that the sacraments of the New Law really contribute to the reception of grace. Two kinds of cause produce an effect, a principal cause and an instrumental cause. A principal cause acts from itself by its own inherent quality, innate or acquired, natural or artificial, as the case may be: thus sun lights the air, and fire heats water. An instrumental cause, on the other hand, acts not precisely by its own quality, but in virtue of the influence of the principal cause. An instrument acts because it is acted on; a motion received from outside plays the part equivalent to that of the inherent active power in the principal cause. The carpenter selects a saw to make a chest because its

---

[1] Peter Lombard (iv. 1).

proper action is to cut, but the effect, namely to cut with art, goes beyond what the tool can do; it is achieved by the craftsman who wields it. There are two operations in play, one from the instrument, the other from an imparted motion exceeding its own proper form. The conclusion is that neither the sacraments nor any other creature can be the principal causes of grace, which is produced solely by divine power, but that they are instrumental causes.

Damascene says that the Godhead communicated a quality of divine virtue to Christ's human nature, which was its organ.[1] Christ touched lepers, and they were cleansed; his human action was really instrumental in the cure. Likewise his human nature entered into the spiritual effects of divine power. He shed his blood, and we are purified: *he washed us from our sins in his own blood*;[2] and again, *being justified freely . . . through faith in his blood*.[3] His manhood, therefore, is the instrumental cause of our righteousness. It was composed of spirit and matter; spiritually he comes to us through faith, and corporeally through the sacraments, that we may make his holiness our own. The noblest sacrament, consequently, is that wherein his body is really present. The Eucharist crowns all the other sacraments; and though all are instruments of grace, and his life and death work through them all, it is there that sacramental causality reaches its height.

521   Disputations, xxvii *de Veritate*, 4

597. God does not adopt sacraments or secondary intermediate causes because his activity depends on them, but because they suit the effects he brings about. It is not his need, but our benefit, that is consulted; divine

---

[1] *de Fide Orthodoxa*, iii. 15; *PG* xciv. 1049.
[2] Apoc. i. 5.   [3] Rom. iii. 24–2

blessings are offered us through human modes of activity, namely, through objects of sense.

438, 607   Disputations, xxvii *de Veritate*, 4, *ad* 16

ii. *Sacramental Grace and Character*

598. Grace should not be reputed to be in the sacraments as though they were receptacles or vessels.

Summa Theologica, 3a. lxii. 3, *ad* 1

599. Grace is in the sacraments like an effect in a cause, not like an accident in a substance. Effect can be in cause in two ways. First, the cause may be responsible for the effect; human acts are thus said to be in us. No effect is thus present in its instrumental cause, which is productive only when it itself is set in motion from outside. So when the sacraments are classed as instruments we should not entertain the notion that grace resides in them.

But, secondly, effect may be present in cause through likeness. Here four types of presence can be considered. First, when the specific nature of the cause is really repeated in the effect. Second, when the nature of the cause is really repeated but with a difference of kind or degree.[1] Third, when the likeness of the effect pre-exists in the cause, not physically, but ideally, as when works of art are conceived in the artist's mind—the form of a house is then in the mind as an intelligible

---

[1] The first is called a 'univocal cause', as when like begets like according to the same species. The second is called an 'analogical cause', and sometimes an 'equivocal cause', as when the cause is of a nature higher than the effect. *Bos generat bovem et sol*: to Aristotelean Scholasticism the saying meant that the bull is the univocal cause of the calf, but that the generation is effected within the universal causation of the sun. *Being* is an analogical term, not a univocal term. Consequently, a cause of being is an analogical cause, as is every full metaphysical cause.

plan, not on the ground. Fourth, when the likeness of the effect is not really in the cause's nature nor settled there as an idea, but is somehow related to its causal influence. Only so are the likenesses of effects in their instrumental causes; for an effective meaning passes from the principal cause through an instrumental cause. Only by this type of presence is grace in the sacraments; as such they are but outward signs, and of themselves cannot directly and immediately reach to sanctifying grace.

117   Disputations, xxvi *de Veritate*, 7

600. If sacramental grace added nothing to the grace of the virtues and the Gifts of the Holy Ghost, there would have been no point in instituting the sacraments for the benefit of those endowed with these virtues and Gifts. Yet there is no redundance in the works of God. Therefore it seems that sacramental grace is additional to the grace of the virtues and the Gifts.

A comparison will illustrate the position. Sanctifying grace itself perfects the soul's substance, which thereby partakes of, and is likened to, the divine being. But from the soul's substance faculties flow. Likewise from sanctifying grace qualities of activity flow. These are called the virtues and Gifts; they are in the soul's faculties, and equip them for their activities. Now the sacraments aim at certain effects necessary for the Christian life; for example, the purpose of Baptism is a spiritual rebirth, wherein a person dies to sin and becomes a member of Christ. This is a special effect, outside the run of normal unassisted activities. Similar purposes are proposed by the other sacraments. The virtues and Gifts add to sanctifying grace a special bent towards the proper activities of our faculties, and similarly, sacramental graces add to sanctifying grace, and to the virtues and Gifts, a special divine help which assists us to reach the purpose of the sacraments.

315, 414, 454   *Summa Theologica*, 3a. lxii, 2

601. A character is a kind of seal, which marks a thing as being set apart for some particular purpose; thus a coin is marked for use in the exchange of goods, and soldiers wear a badge to show they are deputed to some special military office. The faithful are deputed to a twofold end. First and principally to the enjoyment of glory; for this purpose are they sealed with grace. *Mark thou upon the foreheads of the men that sigh and mourn.*[1] And again, *hurt not the earth, nor the sea, nor the trees, till we sign the servants of our God on their foreheads.*[2] But secondly, each of the faithful is commissioned to receive, or to bestow on others, activities appropriate to God's worship. This, properly speaking, is where sacramental character plays its role. All Christian ritual derives from Christ's priesthood. Consequently the sacramental character manifests Christ's character, and configures the faithful to his priesthood.

632   *Summa Theologica*, 3a. lxiii. 3

602. Grace is not necessarily a permanent possession; it is a heightened quality of soul, but it responds to the condition of its subject, and the soul is variable because of its freewill. Sacramental character, however, is an instrumental power, and takes its steadiness from its principal cause. It is indelible, from the indefectibility of Christ's priesthood, not of the soul itself.

311, 628   *Summa Theologica*, 3a. lxiii. 5, *ad* 1

603. We share in Christ's Passion through all the sacraments, for through them all we take its effects to ourselves and are sanctified, being cleansed from sin by

[1] Ezek. ix. 4.   [2] Apoc. vii. 3.

grace. Not all the sacraments, however, appoint us to a post, either for doing or receiving, in the system of worship centred on Christ's priesthood. Penance restores a sinner to his pristine condition, but has no special hierarchical effect; the Eucharist, too, conducts us to no further sacramental duty or right, rather is it the fulfilment of all the sacraments. Three sacraments confer a character, Baptism, Confirmation, and Holy Order; these are the sacraments which consecrate human beings and liturgically set them apart in the economy of divine worship.

569 *Summa Theologica*, 3a. lxiii. 6, *c. & ad* 1, 2

iii. *Seven Sacraments*

604. The courses of physical and spiritual life run parallel, and the sacramental elements correspond to the provisions of bodily needs. These fall into two groups, affecting respectively the life-receivers and the life-givers.

The first group covers three essential phases in human development. A man must be born to begin with, afterwards he must reach his proper stature, and in order to be sustained and grow he must eat: these three correspond to the three vegetative functions of reproduction, growth, and nourishment. They are matched in the life of the spirit: Baptism is a spiritual birth, Confirmation a setting up in full strength, the Eucharist a special food. Then there is the case of sickness, an incidental phase. For our healing Penance cures our soul only, but the effects of Extreme Unction may well spread from the soul to the body.

Of the people who give and govern life some are responsible for its natural origin, namely parents, others for its civilized and peaceful continuance, namely kings and rulers. Matrimony is for a man and a woman to beget children and bring them up in God's service; they bear them physically and rear them spiritually. Holy Orders are for those who kindle and keep the life of the spirit through their ghostly ministrations.

590   iv *Contra Gentes*, 58

1. *Baptism*

605. Note three features in the sacrament of baptism: the mere sacrament, or outward sign, namely, the water which flows away; next, and this is part sign and part signified, namely, the character which remains; finally, the inner significance, namely, sanctifying grace, and this sometimes stays and sometimes goes away.

330   *IV Sentences*, iii. 1. iv, *ad* 1

606. In Baptism Christ's Passion works a regeneration; a person dies entirely to the old life and takes on the new. Therefore Baptism washes away the whole guilt of punishment belonging to the past. Although the virtue of Christ's Passion works a healing in the other sacraments, as in Penance, this healing does not demand that all the after-effects of infirmity should be suddenly cleared up.

267, 549   Commentary, *Romans*, xi, *lect.* 4

607. The efficaciousness of baptism by water flows from the Passion of Christ, to whom the baptized person is configured, and, further back, as from a first cause, from the Holy Spirit. An effect depends on its first cause. Observe, however, that the first cause surpasses all secondary causes, and is not committed to producing the effect always through the same means. Consequently, apart from baptism by water, a person may obtain the grace of Baptism from Christ's Passion because he is made like to Christ in his sufferings: *these are they who have come out of great tribulation, and have washed their robes, and made them white in the blood of the Lamb.*[1]

For a similar reason a person who is baptized neither by water nor by blood may obtain the grace of Baptism through the power of the Holy Spirit, because the Spirit moves his heart to believe God and love him and to be contrite for his sins. This is called the baptism of penitence.[2] *When the Lord shall have washed away the filth of the daughters of Sion, and shall have purged the blood of Jerusalem from the midst thereof by the spirit of judgment, and by the spirit of burning.*[3]

Blood and desire, both are called baptisms, for they supply the place of Baptism and produce its effect, though neither are sacraments, since they are not official signs.[4] Augustine recalls how the blessed Cyprian took not lightly the words addressed to the unbaptized thief, *To day thou wilt be with me in Paradise,*[5] for his sufferings took the place of Baptism. Augustine's own considered conclusion is that faith and the heart's conversion can supply in those straits when succour from the rites of Baptism is out of the question.[6]

187, 385, 629   *Summa Theologica*, 3a. lxvi. 11, *c. & ad* 2

2. Confirmation

608. The sacraments of the New Law are instituted to bring about special effects of grace. Accordingly, where a special occasion occurs there a special sacra-

---

[1] Apoc. vii. 14.
[2] More commonly, the baptism of desire, or *baptismus flaminis*.
[3] Isa. iv. 4.
[4] Nor do they impress the sacramental character.
[5] Luke xxiii. 43.
[6] *de Baptismo contra Donatistas*, iv. 22; *PL* XLIII. 173.

ment is provided. Things of sense bear the likeness of things of mind, and turning points in the life of the body have their equivalents in the life of the spirit. Coming of age ends a definite period; after that a man is capable of acting for himself: *when I was a child, I spoke as a child, I understood as a child, I thought as a child; but when I became a man, I put away childish things.*[1] By the process of being born we receive bodily life; by the process of growing up we become adult. So is it in the life of the spirit; born by baptism, we reach our full stature by confirmation.

Summa Theologica, 3a. lxii. 1

609. Full spiritual strength consists in the ability to confess the Christian Faith in any company, without shyness, embarrassment or dismay: fortitude casts out cowardice. The sacrament which gives strength to those who are reborn by Baptism is for those who would fight for Christ. Soldiers wear their leader's badge, and those who are confirmed are signed with the cross of Christ: this is the sign under which they go out to battle and conquer. They receive it on their foreheads, to show they will confront temptation and unashamedly maintain their cause. They are sealed with a blend of oil and balsam, called chrism—oil, to symbolize the power of the Holy Ghost, by whose unction Christ is called the Anointed, and we are called Christians, also because then we campaign under Christ; balsam, to symbolize the good odour of those who profess Christ while mixing in the world. We are enrolled by bishops, who are like the leaders in Christ's army: the imposition of hands reminds us that virtue and strength come from Christ.

443   iv *Contra Gentes*, 60

[1] 1 Cor. xiii. 11.

610. There are various views regarding the institution of the sacrament of Confirmation. Some think it was instituted neither by Christ nor by the apostles, but by a Council of the Church at some later period.[1] Others that it was instituted by the apostles.[2] These opinions cannot be sustained, for the founding of a new sacrament is reserved to that excellence of power which is Christ's alone. Let us say that Christ instituted Confirmation, but by promising rather than by presenting it.

Summa Theologica, 3a. lxxii. 1, *ad* 1

3. *Holy Eucharist*

611. Here, Lord Jesus, art thou both shepherd and green pasture.

Maundy Thursday Sermon[3]

612.

Godhead here in hiding, whom I do adore
Masked by these bare shadows, shape and nothing more,
See, Lord, at thy service low lies here a heart
Lost, all lost in wonder at the God thou art.

Seeing, touching, tasting are in thee deceived;
How says trusty hearing? That shall be believed;
What God's Son hath told me, take for truth I do;
Truth himself speaks truly, or there's nothing true.

On the cross thy Godhead made no sign to men;
Here thy very manhood steals from human ken;
Both are my confession, both are my belief,
And I pray the prayer of the dying thief.

---

[1] Alexander of Hales put it down to the Council of Meaux, 845.

[2] So Peter of Tarentaise, St. Thomas's colleague at Paris, afterwards Master General of the Dominicans, and afterwards Pope Innocent V.

[3] Preached before Urban IV.

I am not like Thomas, wounds I cannot see,
But can plainly call thee Lord and God as he;
This faith each day deeper be my holding of,
Daily make me harder hope and dearer love.

O thou our reminder of Christ crucified,
Living Bread, the life of us for whom he died,
Lend thus life to me then; feed and feast my mind,
There be thou the sweetness man was meant to find.

Jesu, whom I look at shrouded here below,
I beseech thee send me what I long for so,
Some day to gaze on thee face to face in light
And be blest for ever with thy glory's sight.

Hymn, *Adoro te devote*[1]

613. Among the immeasurable benefits God's goodness has bestowed on Christian people is a priceless
dignity: *for what nation is there so great, who hath gods
nigh unto them, as the Lord our God is unto us?*[2] The
only-begotten Son of God, intending to make us *partakers of the divine nature,*[3] took our nature on himself,
becoming man that he might make men gods. Everything of ours he adopted he turned to our salvation. His
body he offered to God the Father on the altar of the
cross as a sacrifice that we might be reconciled; his blood
he shed both as a price to redeem us from wretched
bondage and as a cleansing from all sin.

He has left his faithful his very body for food and his
very blood for drink, nourishment for them under the
appearance of bread and wine, and an abiding memorial
of his noble engagement. O how precious then, how
marvellous, how health-giving, how well-appointed his
banquet! Nothing more precious, for in the Lord's
Supper the food put before us is not the flesh of bulls

[1] Translation by Gerard Manley Hopkins, 1844–89.
[2] Deut. iv. 7.   [3] 2 Pet. i. 4.

and goats, as in olden times, but Christ himself, our
very God. Nothing more marvellous, for there it comes
to pass that the substance of bread and wine is changed
into the body and blood of Christ. He is there, perfect
God and perfect man, under the show of a morsel of bread
and a sup of wine. He is eaten by his faithful, but not
mangled. Nay, when this Sacrament is broken, in each
piece he remains entire. The appearance of bread and
wine remain, but the Thing is not bread or wine. Here
is faith's opportunity, faith which takes what is unseen
or disguised, and keeps the senses from misjudging
about the wonted appearances.

Nothing more health-giving, for in this Sacrament
sins are purged away, strength renewed, and the mind
fortified with generous spiritual gifts. Offered in the
Church for the living and the dead, it is meant for all,
and all gain its benefits.[1] Nothing is better-appointed,
for the sweetness of this sacrament none can tell. There
comfort is drawn from the well-head of the spirit; there
is found the memorial of Christ's exceeding love for us
in his sufferings. That he might bring his boundless
love home to the hearts of his faithful did he found this
sacrament, after he had celebrated the Passover with
his disciples, when the Last Supper was ending: *Jesus
knowing that his hour was come that he should depart out
of this world, unto the Father, having loved his own
which were in the world, he loved them to the end.*[2] This
sacrament is the everlasting *showing forth of his death
until he come again;*[3] the embodied fulfilment of all the
ancient types and figures; the mighty joy of them that
sorrow until he shall come again: *their heart shall rejoice, and their joy no man shall take from them.*[4]

399, 560   Breviary Lessons, *Corpus Christi*

[1] Here ends the Nocturn.   [2] John xiii. 1.
[3] 1 Cor. xi. 26.   [4] John xvi. 22.

614. *Except a corn of wheat fall into the ground and die, it abideth alone.*[1] Corn is used for bread and for seed. If it is ground into flour it never sprouts or bears fruit. Our Lord, then, is speaking of seed, and when he says, *unless it die,* he means that it should be transformed, not that it should lose its fertility: *that which thou sowest is not quickened, except it die.*[2]

As God's words are like seed in man's soul, borne by word of mouth to produce the fruit of good works— *the seed is the word of God*[3]—so the Word born in flesh is the seed of the world, compared to the mustard seed,[4] and harvested in a rich crop. Christ is compared to the corn also because he came to nourish and sustain man's mind: *bread which strengtheneth man's heart.*[5] *The bread which I shall give is my flesh, which I will give for the life of the world.*[6]

561   Commentary, *St. John,* xii, *lect.* 4

615. Christ's true body, born from the Virgin Mary, is contained in the sacrament of the altar. To profess the contrary is heresy, because it detracts from the truth of Scripture, which records our Lord's own words, *This is my body.*[7] Persuading arguments may be found for the doctrine. One is that Christ would not be so intimately united to us were we to share only in his power: how much better that he should give us his very self, not merely his effects, for the perfect joining of head and members. There are other advantages too: what a proof of friendship, that he should feed us himself; what a lift to hope, that we should be offered such familiar intercourse; what a test for faith, which merits by believing beyond reason and against sense. There are many

---

[1] John xii. 24.   [2] 1 Cor. xv. 36.
[3] Luke viii. 11.   [4] Matt. xiii. 31.   [5] Ps. ciii. 15.
[6] John vi. 51.   [7] Matt. xxvi. 26.

others as well, which cannot be exhaustively dealt with now.

28, 567   *IV Sentences*, x. 1

616. That Christ's true body and blood are present in this sacrament can be perceived neither by sense nor by reason, but by faith alone, which rests on God's authority. On the text, *This is my body which is given for you,*[1] Cyril comments that we must not doubt that this is true, but must take our Saviour's words on faith; he is truth, and does not lie.[2]

The doctrine first of all brings out the dignity of the New Law. The sacrifices of the Old Law figuratively contained the true sacrifice of Christ's Passion: *the law having the shadow of the good things to come, not the very image of the things.*[3] Rightly the New Law should surpass the Old, and offer Christ, not only in sign and figure, but in very truth. Therefore this sacrament, in which Christ is really present, is the culmination of all the other sacraments in which his power is shared.

Secondly, the mystery matches Christ's charity, which caused him to assume true human nature in order to save us. Aristotle notes that it is in the name of friendship that friends should live together.[4] Christ promised to reward his friends with his bodily presence: *wheresoever the body is, there will the eagles be gathered together.*[5] Even during our pilgrimage he does not absent himself, but through his veritable body and blood joins us to himself: *he that eateth my flesh, and drinketh my blood abideth in me, and I in him.*[6] By such familiar intercourse is this sacrament the greatest pledge of charity and encouragement of hope.

[1] Luke xxii. 19.
[2] *Explanatio in Lucae Evangelium*, xxii. 19; *PG* LXXII. 911.
[3] Heb. x. 1.   [4] *Ethics*, ix. 12, 1171^{b}32.
[5] Matt. xxiv. 28.   [6] John vi. 57.

Thirdly, the mystery invites an act of complete faith, accepting both the divinity and humanity of Christ: *you believe in God, believe also in me*.[1] Faith is of things unseen; Christ's Godhead was hid, and in this sacrament so also is his manhood.

286, 399, 555, 557   *Summa Theologica*, 3a. lxxv. 1

617. Christ's true body, present in this sacrament, does not come there by local change, for it is not confined there as though in a place. We must conclude, then, that the presence starts from the conversion of bread and wine. This conversion, unlike natural changes, is wholly supernatural, effected by God's power alone. Wherefore Ambrose says that it is clear that the Virgin mothered Christ miraculously, and what we consecrate is the body born from the Virgin: why then seek natural laws ruling Christ's body?[2] And Chrysostom, when commenting on the text, *The words that I have spoken to you are spirit and life*,[3] remarks that they are indeed spiritual, having nothing carnal about them, or developed by nature, for they are lifted above earthly necessity and the laws there in force.[4]

Every efficient cause acts because it is active and actual. A created cause is limited in its activity, since it is of a determinate kind; that is why its action bears on a determinate actuality. The determinate existence of a thing is defined by its form. Therefore no physical cause, or created cause, can act except by changing forms. For this reason the deepest changes, according to the laws of nature, are transformations. But God is infinite actuality, and therefore his activity covers the whole of reality: he is not restricted to the production

---

[1] John xiv. 2.
[2] *de Mysteriis*, 9; *PL* xvi. 424.   [3] John vi. 64.
[4] *Commentarius in Joannem*, Hom. xlvii; *PG* lix. 265.

of substantial changes, when diverse forms succeed one another in the same material subject; he can change a whole reality, in such a way that the whole substance of this is changed into the whole substance of that.

Such is the activity of divine power in this sacrament. The whole substance of bread is converted into the whole substance of Christ's body, the whole substance of wine into the whole substance of his blood. This is not a transmutation or transformation; it is not catalogued under the ordinary physical processes, but is given the special name of transubstantiation.[1]

136, 141   *Summa Theologica*, 3a. lxxv. 4

618. Lanfranc says that through the seen species of bread and wine we honour unseen things, namely, flesh and blood.[2] It is evident to the senses that all the accidents of bread and wine remain after consecration. Such is the reasonable course of divine Providence, for it is abominable to eat human flesh and drink human blood. That is why Christ's body and blood are offered to us under the species of what we are accustomed to take, namely, bread and wine.

11   *Summa Theologica*, 3a. lxxv. 5

619. *Hic est calix sanguinis mei* is a figurative expression, which can be understood either by metonymy or by metaphor. Metonymy signifies the container for

---

[1] Change comes under the general scholastic heading of *motus*, movement. Change may be either of accident or of substance. Of accident, thus the successive changes of a thing in space and time, the alteration of its qualities, the growth or shrinkage of its quantity. Of substance the normal example is substantial transformation resulting from substantial generation and corruption. Creation (and annihilation) are not changes in the strict sense, because of the lack of two real terms, either *before* or *after*.

[2] *de Corpore et Sanguine Domini*, 13; PL CL. 423.

the contained, and the sense, which is then, *This is my blood contained in the chalice*, is justifiable, for Christ's blood is sacramentally consecrated as drink for the faithful, an idea better conveyed by the term *cup* than *blood*. By metaphor Christ's Passion is signified, as when he himself said, *Father, if it be possible, let this chalice pass from me.*[1] The sense of the consecration formula is then, *This is the chalice of my Passion.*

28, 33   *Summa Theologica*, 3a. lxxviii. 3, *ad* 1

620. Does an unbeliever profess that the changing of bread and wine into the body and blood of the Lord is impossible? Then let him consider God's omnipotence. Admit that Nature can transform one thing into another, then with greater reason should you admit that God's almighty power, which brings into existence the whole substance of things, can work, not as Nature does, by changing forms in the same matter, but by changing one whole thing into another whole thing.

If he objects that such a change flies in the face of the appearances, since no change is observable, let him consider how divine things are proposed to us under visible coverings. Christ is taken under the species of bread and wine as spiritual refreshment, and not as common food and drink, in a horrible and cannibal manner. Nor should we say that these appearances exist only in the imagination, as though by some illusion of magical art; fiction of any sort does not go with sacramental truth. God is the creator of substance and accident; he can preserve accidents though their proper subject has been changed into something else, for his omnipotence can both produce and keep in being the effects of secondary causes without those causes.

187   *de Rationibus Fidei*, 8

[1] Matt. xxvi. 39.

621. Every localized body is in place, after the manner of a thing with dimensions, commensurate by its quantity to the place it occupies. Christ's body is not present in place in the sacrament of the Eucharist in this manner. It is present in the manner of substance involved in dimensions. The substance of Christ's body succeeds to the substance of bread, and as the bread's substance was not localized under its dimensions directly as a substance, but through its quantity, no more is Christ's body. Note this difference, however, between the substance of bread and the substance of Christ's body; the bread was the subject of those dimensions, but the body of Christ is not. The bread was there because of its dimensions; localized, as in the case of any other physical body, through its own quantity. The substance of Christ's body, however, is related to a place through the dimensions of something else, namely of something that was bread. His own proper dimensions are related to his sacramental place only through his substance: this is above the nature of a localized body. In no sense is the body of Christ pinned down to a spot in this sacrament.

Summa Theologica, 3a. lxxvi. 5

622. Is Christ's body localized in this sacrament? He is said to be on the altar, or in the church; all the same, properly speaking, his body is not really localized in this sacrament, for he is not there through his own proper dimensions, and his relation to the sacrament is not that of placed to place.

Does his body move when the host is lifted up? The motion is certainly not like that of other natural bodies, which are shifted either directly through their own proper dimensions or indirectly through the vehicles which transport them from place to place. The relation of Christ's body to the sacramental dimensions is not that of a body to its own proper dimensions. Only to the extent to which Christ's body can be said to be in a place because of the sacramental quantity can movement in place be attributed to it.

Declaratio xxxvi *Quaestionum*, 33, 34[1]

623. In a sacrament we may consider the sacrament itself, that is, the sign, and the reality there. The reality in the Eucharist is the unity of Christ's mystical body, outside of which there is no salvation. There is no access to heaven save through the Church, as there was no escape from the flood save in Noah's Ark. Yet the reality of a sacrament may be possessed before the sacrament itself is received, by virtue of desire. So may a man reach salvation, as in the case of Baptism.

607 *Summa Theologica*, 3a. lxxiii. 3

624. Two qualities are required in the recipient, love desiring to be conjoined to Christ, fear reverencing the sacrament. The first bids us approach, the second holds us back. If anybody knows from experience that daily Communion increases fervour without lessening reverence, then let him go every day. But if anybody finds that reverence is lessened and devotion not much increased, then let him sometimes abstain, so as to draw nigh afterwards with better dispositions.

Each person should be left to his own judgement. This is Augustine's advice,[2] who quotes the examples of Zacchaeus, who made haste and came down from the tree and received Christ with joy,[3] and of the centurion, who confessed, *Lord, I am not worthy that thou shouldst*

---

[1] To a Venetian lecturer.
[2] *ad Inquisitiones Januarii*, 3; PL xxxiii. 201.
[3] Luke xix. 6.

enter under my roof.[1] Both honoured our Saviour, though in different ways, and both found mercy.

IV Sentences, XII. iii. 1. *iv*

625. *We have therefore a great high priest that hath passed into the heavens, Jesus, the Son of God.*[2] A priest's office is to be a mediator between God and the people, forasmuch as he bestows divine blessings on the people and offers up their prayers to God, and in some manner renders satisfaction to God for their sins. *Every high priest taken from among men is ordained for men in the things that appertain to God, that he may offer up gifts and sacrifices for sins.*[3] Appropriately, then, is Christ a priest: *for through him gifts are bestowed on men, by whom he hath given us exceeding great and precious promises, that by these you may be made partakers of the divine nature.*[4] Furthermore, he reconciles the human race to God, for in him it *hath well pleased the Father that all fullness should dwell, and through him to reconcile all things unto himself.*[5]

553, 566   *Summa Theologica,* 3a. xxii. 1

626. For two reasons the celebration of the Eucharist is called the immolation of Christ. First, because, as Augustine observes, the usage is to call images by the names of the things they represent; when we look at a fresco we say, there is Cicero, or, there is Sallust.[6] The celebration of this sacrament, the holy mass, is an image representing Christ's Passion. That was the real immolation. Therefore Ambrose says, The host was offered once in Christ, powerful for everlasting salvation. What

---

[1] Matt. viii. 8.
[2] Heb. iv. 14.   [3] Heb. v. 1.
[4] 2 Pet. i. 4.   [5] Col. i. 19.
[6] *de Diversis Quaestionibus ad Simplicianum,* ii. 3; *PL* XL. 143.

then about us? Do we not offer it every day, in record of his death?[1]

Secondly we consider the effect of the Passion. Through this sacrament we are made partakers of the fruit of our Lord's Passion. Wherefore the Missal says, As often as the memory of this victim is kept the work of our redemption is renewed.[2]

The first reason applies outside the Eucharist, for Christ may well be said to have been so immolated even in the figures of the Old Testament: *the book of life of the Lamb, which was slain from the beginning of the world.*[3] The second reason is peculiar to this sacrament; there only in its celebration is Christ immolated.

There is one Christ, not many offered by Christ and by us. For Christ was offered once, and his sacrifice was the original of ours. There is one body, not many, and so, wherever he is offered, the sacrifice is one and the same with his.

551, 560   *Summa Theologica*, 3a. lxxxiii. 1, *c. & ad* 1

4. *Penance*

627. Certainly we receive grace from Baptism, Confirmation, and the Eucharist; yet we do not thereupon become impeccable. The free gifts of grace are received as habitual dispositions of the soul; but we do not invariably act according to them, any more than we do from other habits. Grammarians can express themselves correctly, or they can, if they choose, commit solecisms. It is the same with the moral virtues: just men may act against justice. The use of good habits is governed by freedom, and the will is faced with alternatives.

[1] Gratian, *Decretum*, III. ii. 58.
[2] Secret Prayer; 9th Sunday after Pentecost; 7th Sunday after the Octave of Trinity, Dominican rite.
[3] Apoc. xiii. 8.

We who have received grace may still sin by acting against it.

Impeccability supposes that the will is fixed in good, and this in its turn supposes that the will has found its last end and is at rest there, without possibility of distraction. Until we have arrived there sin is always possible, and in the meantime, while we are able to receive sacramental grace, we are not impeccable. Remember that the purpose of the sacraments is to help us on our way to our last end.

Moreover, every sin happens because of some lack of knowledge: as Aristotle says, every bad man is an ignorant man.[1] *Do they not err who devise mischief?*[2] Our will is secure against sin only when our mind is secure against ignorance and error: sacramental grace does not guarantee this immunity.

Again, our varying moods exercise a great influence on the phases of wickedness and virtue. This instability, which is not completely checked by sacramental grace, remains ours so long as soul is joined to a changeable body.

Finally, to admonish people not to sin when sin they cannot would be quite uncalled for. Yet evangelical and apostolic teaching so admonishes the faithful who have already received the grace of the Spirit through the sacraments. *Looking diligently lest any man fail of the grace of God; lest any root of bitterness springing up trouble you.*[3] *Grieve not the holy Spirit of God, whereby you are sealed unto the day of redemption.*[4] *Let him that thinketh he standeth take heed lest he fall.*[5] St. Paul confessed of himself, *I keep my body, and bring it into subjection, lest that by any means, when I have preached to others, I myself should become a castaway.*[6]

---

[1] *Ethics*, iii. 2, 1110^{b}27.   [2] Prov. xiv. 22.
[3] Heb. xii. 15.   [4] Eph. iv. 30.
[5] 1 Cor. x. 12.   [6] 1 Cor. ix. 27.

Accordingly, we deny the error of heretics who have held that once a man has received the grace of the Spirit he can sin no more, and that a man who does sin has in fact never received the grace of the Spirit.

233, 310, 414, 647   IV *Contra Gentes*, 70

628. Furthermore, a man who falls into sin after receiving sacramental grace can be again restored to grace. There is no doubt about it. This much must be allowed to human mutability, that if we can go from grace to sin, so also can we go back to virtue. Good is more powerful than evil; if we can stray away, much more can we be recalled. While we live we can never be so stuck in evil that divine grace cannot get us out.

Sacramental grace frees us from the sins we committed beforehand. *Know ye not that the unrighteous shall not inherit the kingdom of God. Be not deceived: neither fornicators, nor idolators nor adulterers, nor effeminate, nor abusers of themselves with mankind, nor thieves, nor covetous, nor drunkards, nor revilers, nor extortioners, shall inherit the kingdom of God. And such were some of you: but ye are washed, but ye are sanctified, but ye are justified in the name of the Lord Jesus, and by the Spirit of our God.*[1] Now the grace granted in the sacraments does not lessen nature, but rather increases it. Part of the goodness of human nature is that it is always capable of being lifted up from sin to righteousness; this goodness remains, even despite a fall from grace previously held.

If those who sin after Baptism could never return to grace, they would lose all hope of salvation. Despair is the path to unrestrained sin: *who despairing have given themselves over to lasciviousness, to work all uncleanness with greediness.*[2] There is nothing more dangerous than

[1] 1 Cor. vi. 9–11.   [2] Eph. iv. 19.

teaching which would cast men into the pit of despair. If a man could not return to righteousness if he fell into sin after receiving the sacraments, what a risky business it would be ever to receive them. Assuredly, the teaching is unhelpful. So we deny it.

Our refusal to rule out a restoration to grace is confirmed by the authority of Holy Scripture. *My little children, these things I write unto you, that you sin not. And if any man sin, we have an advocate with the Father, Jesus Christ the righteous, and he is the propitiation for our sins.*[1] St. Paul wrote of the sinful Corinthian, *You should pardon and comfort him, lest perhaps he be swallowed up with overmuch sorrow.*[2] Later he wrote, *I rejoice, not that you were made sorrowful, but that you were made sorrowful unto penance.*[3] The prophet cries, *Thou hast played the harlot with many lovers, yet return again to me, saith the Lord.*[4] And again, *Turn thou us unto thee, O Lord, and we shall be turned; renew our days as of old.*[5]

249, 267, 305, 494   iv *Contra Gentes*, 71.

629. Baptism itself obviously provides no remedy if somebody falls into sin after Baptism. Yet lest he be sent away as a hopeless case, God's generous mercy and Christ's strong power have established another sacrament. As those who are delivered into natural life may be cured of a disease which saps their constitution, not by being born again, but by restoring the balance of health, so after Baptism we are not healed by Baptism, which is a spiritual rebirth and not repeated, but the sacrament of Penance, a sacramental cure which purges us from sin.

Observe that physical recovery is sometimes wholly

[1] 1 John ii. 1–2.   [2] 2 Cor. ii. 7.
[3] 2 Cor. vii. 9.   [4] Jer. ii. 1.   [5] Lam. v. 21.

from within, as when a man pulls round on his own, and sometimes partly from within and partly from without, as when medicine assists nature. Never is it wholly from without, for some vital principles must remain on which the treatment can work. Spiritual healing, however, cannot come about wholly from within, for we cannot be freed from sin by our own efforts without the help of grace. Nor, on the other hand, is it exclusively from outside, for the soul is not restored to vigour unless its own voluntary motions are set to rights. Consequently, spiritual soundness is produced both from within a man and from without, through the sacrament of Penance.

Let us continue the analysis. A complete physical cure requires the repair of all the inroads of disease. Similarly, a spiritual cure is not complete until the sufferer has been extricated from the wreckage of sin. The damaging effects are three. The first is a mind out of the true, a mind turned away from God's immortal goodness to vanity. The second is the debt of punishment incurred. The third is the weakening of moral energy, for he has become more prone to evil, and tardier about doing good. All three are covered by the sacrament of Penance.

The first element of Penance is a redirection of mind, which, sorrowing for sin and proposing amendment, must turn again to God and away from sin: all this belongs to *contrition*. Without grace and charity this conversion is impossible. By contrition the offence against God is blotted out and the debt of eternal punishment cancelled, for such separation from God is incompatible with charity. This contrition springs from within, that is from freewill helped by divine grace.

The merits of Christ, who suffered for the entire human race, expiate for all sins. To be freed from sin, therefore, a man must cleave, not only to God, but also to our mediator, Jesus Christ, through whom sins are pardoned. Spiritual health lies in the conversion of mind and heart to God, which health cannot be obtained except from the physician of our souls, Jesus Christ, who saves his people from their wickedness, whose merit is ample to take all sins utterly away: he it is *who taketh away the sin of the world.*[1]

Not everybody, however, reaches the full effect of forgiveness, but each in proportion to his union with Christ, who suffered for our sins. Our union with Christ in Baptism is not of our own doing; it is not accomplished by our own inner activity, for nothing begets itself: it is the work of Christ, *who regenerates us unto a lively hope.*[2] The baptismal regeneration of sins is wrought by Christ's power; he joins us perfectly and completely to himself, so that not only is all impurity of sin washed away, but also all debt of punishment with it. In the spiritual healing of Penance, however, we are joined to Christ as the result of our own activity charged with divine grace. For this reason the debt of punishment is not always completely or equally remitted. It may happen that the turning to God and the detestation of sin is so intense that a complete remission of sin is the result, as regards penalty as well as fault. But this does not always happen; contrition may take away fault and guilt and the debt of eternal punishment, but leave the obligation of undergoing temporal punishment in accordance with divine justice.

A sentence of punishment for crime is a judicial act, and so the penitent, committing himself to Christ to be healed, is prepared to make the retribution pronounced by Christ through his ministers. No one can judge about faults of which he is not cognisant. *Confession,* therefore,

[1] John i. 29.   [2] 1 Pet. i. 3.

enters as the second element of this sacrament, that fault may be made manifest to Christ's ministers. The minister to whom confession is made is the delegate of Christ, who is the judge of the living and the dead.

Judicial power has two parts, the authority to pass a verdict, and the authority to pronounce sentence. These are called the two keys of the Church, namely, the power of discerning and the power of binding and loosing. They were committed by our Lord to Peter: *I will give unto thee the keys of the kingdom of heaven.*[1] Do not misunderstand, this power was not restricted to him personally, but was meant to spread out from him to others, otherwise the welfare of the faithful would not be sufficiently provided for. It is Christ who opens for us the gates of heaven; he who gives effect to these keys. Therefore, as salvation requires Baptism, received either sacramentally or by desire (when necessity, not contempt, forbids the sacrament), so also the salvation of those who sin after Baptism requires that they submit themselves to the power of the keys, either by actually going to Confession, or by intending to do so in due season. We are saved only through Jesus Christ: *there is no other name under heaven given to men among men whereby we must be saved.*[2]

Finally, let us draw another comparison and consider that as Baptism may be effective in forgiving sins before it is sacramentally received, namely by desire, though its sacramental effect is fuller as regards both the forgiveness of sins and the obtaining of grace—sometimes, indeed, sins are then forgiven and grace conferred for the first time—so the keys of the Church may have an effect on somebody before he actually submits to them, given the proper intention, though a fuller grace of forgiveness comes when he actually goes to Confession;

[1] Matt. xvi. 19.   [2] Acts iv. 12.

indeed it may happen that it is conferred during the absolution itself.

If, therefore, an ampler effect of gracious pardon is then granted to him who is already forgiven, it follows that the Church's minister, who absolves in virtue of the keys, must release the penitent from some of the debt of temporal punishment to which he was bound when he was contrite but unabsolved. He enjoins the penitent to pay what remains; the fulfilling of this obligation is called *satisfaction*. This is the third element of Penance, and this, when complete, clears away all the burden of sin. Eventually a person's human weakness is cured. He then keeps away from all evil and grows familiar with good; he bends his spirit to God by prayer, he masters his flesh by fasts, he joins himself to his brothers and sisters, from whom guilt had separated him, by giving generously of his goods.

The minister of the Church exercises judgement when the keys are applied. This power of judgement is reserved to the authority in charge. Not any priest can absolve from sin, as some have mistakenly thought, but only that priest who has duly received jurisdiction.

223, 247, 256, 640   IV *Contra Gentes*, 72

630. Having read the pamphlet you showed me, I discovered the extremely rash statement that a priest in giving absolution should not use the Form, *I absolve you*. This is I judge presumptuous, because it goes against the Gospel. Our Lord said to Peter, *Whatever thou shalt bind on earth shall be bound in heaven*.[1] He was speaking of the power of the keys. Afterwards he went on to declare, *And whatsoever thou shalt loose on earth shall be loosed in heaven*. Clearly he who absolves has the power of the keys, and to say that he should not

[1] Matt. xvi. 19.

say, *I absolve you*, to a person whom our Lord absolves is presumptuous, not to say erroneous. Our Lord's very words establish the form. For as he said, *Go ye therefore and teach all nations, baptizing them*, &c.,[1] and as the proper form of Baptism is for the minister, to whom our Lord attributes the act, to say, *I baptize you*, so also should the minister to whom our Lord has granted the power say, *I absolve you*.

647   *de Forma Absolutionis Sacramentalis*[2]

631. The Church's ministers do not remit sin of their own authority and principal efficient causes. Only God can do that: *I am he that blots out thy iniquities for my own sake*.[3] They should not be called givers of grace, for this implies authority, but rather ministers of the granting of Christ's grace.

596   *I Sentences*, xiv. iii, *ad* 3

5. *Holy Orders*

632. The sacrament of Holy Orders relates to the performance of a function in divine worship; it conveys the power to discharge certain sacred acts. Though interior perfection is called for, a man is not committed to the life of canonical perfection, except in so far as the reception of Holy Orders in the Western Church carries with it a vow of continence, which is one of the instruments of perfection.

490   *Summa Theologica*, 2a–2ae. cxxxiv. 6

633. Such is its dignity that the sacrament of the Eucharist is not consecrated save in the person of Christ. Whoever acts for another must have power con-

---

[1] Matt. xxviii. 19.
[2] To the Dominican Master General.
[3] Isa. xliii. 25.

ferred by the other. By Baptism Christ grants the power of receiving this sacrament, by Holy Orders the power of consecrating it, for ordination places a man in the ranks of those to whom Christ said, *Do this for a commemoration of me.*[1]

615 *Summa Theologica,* 3a. lxxxii. 1

634. Once upon a time there was no difference of style between bishops and priests. Bishops were those who superintended, as Augustine notes,[2] while priests, or presbyters in Greek, meant elders. St. Paul, for instance, calls both priests: *let the priests that rule well be counted worthy of double honour.*[3] He addresses the priests of Ephesus as bishops: *take heed therefore unto yourselves, and to all the flock, over which the Holy Ghost has made you bishops to rule the Church of God.*[4] Nevertheless a real distinction of rank existed between them. The Gloss, commenting on the text, *After these things the Lord appointed also other seventy-two,*[5] says that the form of bishops was found in the Apostles, the form of priests of the second rank in the disciples. The difference was afterwards expressed in name and style, and the denial of the difference is reckoned a heretical tenet by Augustine.[6]

580 *Summa Theologica,* 2a–2ae. clxxxiv, 6, *ad* 1

6. *Matrimony*

635. The Mother of God was both a maid and espoused. Virginity and wedlock are honoured in her person. She is a challenge to heretics who disparage either one or the other.

538 *Summa Theologica,* 3a. xxix. 1

[1] Luke xxii. 19.
[2] *de Civitate Dei,* xix. 19; *PL* xli. 647.
[3] 1 Tim. v. 17.   [4] Acts xx. 28.
[5] Luke x. 1.   [6] *de Haeresibus,* 53; *PL* xlii. 40.

636. Married friendship is useful, delightful, and honourable. It serves to provide for domestic life. It brings the delight of sex, and the physical pleasure animals have. And if husband and wife are fair to one another, their friendship is expressed in virtue proper to them both, rendering it mutually agreeable.

399   Commentary, *VIII Ethics*, lect. 12

637. *Two shall be in one flesh.*[1] For one woman to have many husbands is unlawful, for then a child would not know his father. On this count alone it might be all very well for one man to have many wives, but it would disregard the liberal friendship which should flourish between husband and wife. Friendship spells equality. Experience shows that women are treated like servants when polygamy is the rule.

269   III *Contra Gentes*, 124

638. A genuine marriage is complete. Complete is perfect. The primary perfection of anything dwells in its form, which determines the specific nature; the secondary perfection in activity, whereby somehow it reaches to its purpose or end. The form of matrimony consists in an inseparable union of minds; a couple are pledged to one another in faithful friendship. The end is the begetting and upbringing of children, through marriage intercourse and shared duties in which each helps the other to rear children.

The Virgin Mother of God and Joseph were completely married as regards the form; both consented to the marriage bond, though not expressly to marriage intercourse—unless under the condition that it pleased God. Mary was called Joseph's wife by the angel: *fear not to take unto thee Mary thy wife.*[2] Augustine com-

---

[1] Gen. ii. 24.   [2] Matt. i. 20.

B 4007   C C

ments that she is called wife because of the first promise of the espousals, she whom Joseph had never lain with, or ever was to.[1] As regards the generative act, the marriage was not consummated, but the second perfection was assured in the upbringing of the child. Wherefore Augustine remarks that every good of marriage was there present—sacrament, faithfulness, and child.[2]

488 *Summa Theologica*, 3a. xix. 2

639. The efficient cause of Matrimony is the mutual consent of the partners expressed in words about their undertaking here and now. Marriage has three blessings. The first is children, to be received and raised for God's service. The second is the loyal faith whereby each serves the other. The third is the sacrament, which signifies the inseparable union of Christ with his Church.

29 *de Articulis Fidei et Sacramentis Ecclesiae*, 2

7. *Extreme Unction*

640. Because body is instrument of soul, and an instrument should serve and suit the principal cause, it follows that body should be aptly disposed to soul. From sickness of soul, which is sin, body also sometimes contracts sickness; such is the provision of divine justice. It is true that bodily sickness can be for spiritual health, when endured humbly, patiently, and as satisfaction for sin; it can also hinder spiritual health, by stopping the play of the virtues.

Rightly, therefore, spiritual medicine should be applied to counteract the spread of sin into the body, and, when this is expedient for salvation, to cure bodily

---

[1] *de Nuptiis et Concupiscentiis*, i. 11; *PL* xliv. 420.
[2] Ibid. ii. 12; *PL* xliv. 421.

infirmity as well. To this end the sacrament of Extreme Unction is designed. *Is any sick among you? Let him call in the priests of the Church, and let them pray over him, anointing him with oil in the name of the Lord. And the prayer of faith shall save the sick man.*[1]

Non-recovery of physical health should not be held against the virtue of this sacrament, for sometimes, even when the sick are worthily disposed, their bodily cure is not expedient for their spiritual salvation. Nor is Extreme Unction then received in vain, for it offers remedies against certain consequences of sin, namely, a proneness to evil and a lethargy about good, and all the more so because these psychological ills are nearer to sin than is physical infirmity. Certainly these after-effects of sin may be cured by penitence; yet when somebody, either from negligence or because of the press of other business, or even because time is so short, may not altogether have rid himself of them, this sacrament comes as a salutary help; it may finish the treatment, and free the sufferer from the debt of temporal punishment, so that his soul is not kept away from glory on its departure from the body.

Past sins may escape notice, or not be held in memory, and so each cannot be purged by penitence. There are also the daily sins, which we do not avoid in the ordinary run of life, from which also we should be cleansed if our soul is to be fit for heaven. This sacrament is then the last, and, as it were, the finishing touch to our spiritual cure and our preparation for heaven.

178, 267, 627   IV *Contra Gentes*, 73

641. The matter of Extreme Unction is olive oil blessed by a bishop. It should not be given except to

[1] James v. 14.

the sick in the danger of death: they should be anointed on the organs of the five senses; on eyes for seeing, on ears for hearing, on nostrils for smelling, on the mouth for speaking and tasting, on the hands for touching, on the feet for walking. Some also anoint the loins, where lust has been lively. The form of the sacrament is this: By this anointing and his fondest mercy may the Lord be gentle with you whatever your failure through sight, and so forth. Its minister is a priest; its effect a healing of mind and body.

664 *de Articulis Fidei et Sacramentis Ecclesiae*, 2

3. DISCIPLINE

642. Religion, a part of the moral virtue of justice, offers due worship to God. One of its elements is the service offered, which is like the subject-matter and object of religion; another is its relation to the person to whom it is offered, who is God. The acts by which God is served do not reach through to God himself, as faith does, where God is both object and end; we believe God because of God. He is offered due worship in that the acts, offerings, sacrifices, and so forth, which serve him are performed out of reverence for him. God himself is certainly the end or purpose, but not the subject-matter or object of the virtue of religion. It is not a theological virtue, of which the object is the ultimate end, but a moral virtue, occupied with means to that end.

349, 438 *Summa Theologica*, 2a–2ae. lxxxi. 5

643. As the office of temporal princes is to enact legal precepts which are arbitrary applications of the Natural Law to temporal business affecting the commonwealth so also the office of ecclesiastical prelates is to command by statute matters which affect the common welfare of the faithful, that is, their spiritual welfare.

279   *Summa Theologica*, 2a–2ae. cxlvii. 3

644. Three stages have to be passed in order to reach perfect friendship with God. External goods have to be renounced. Carnal thoughts have to be left behind. Life has to be given up, either by suffering death for Christ or by denying one's own will. Whosoever binds his whole life by vow to these works of perfection assumes the status of perfection. Such is the religious life.

Again, perfect brotherly love includes three qualities: that enemies are loved and served; that one's life is given to one's neighbours, either by risking death for them, or by living it completely at their service; and that it is spent on their spiritual welfare. Clearly bishops are held to all three.

To the Church has been committed care for all men, among whom many will be found to hate, revile, and persecute. But enemies and assailants should be repaid with love and kindness. Such was the example of the Apostles, and bishops are their successors, who must dwell in the midst of their persecutors. Such was our Lord's command: *Behold, I send you forth as sheep in the midst of wolves; be ye therefore wise as serpents, and harmless as doves.*[1] In expounding the text, *Whosoever shall smite thee on thy right cheek, turn to him the other also,*[2] Augustine says that mercy is best shown by those who realize how much must be endured from those well loved, from babies and foolish ones, from whom and for whom they are prepared to suffer more, for the sake of salvation.[3] The Master and Doctor of our souls taught his disciples that they would have to bear with

---

[1] Matt. x. 16.   [2] Matt. v. 39.
[3] *Lib. de Sermone Domini in Monte*, i. 18; *PL* xxxiv. 1258.

equanimity the imbecilities of those whose welfare they would foster, for all wickedness comes from foolishness. St. Paul says, *being reviled, we bless; being persecuted, we suffer it; being defamed, we entreat.*[1]

Bishops are also bound to lay down their lives for the salvation of their subjects. Our Lord says, *I am the good shepherd; the good shepherd giveth his life for his sheep.*[2] Gregory explains how the wolf comes down on the flock whenever scoundrels and robbers oppress the little ones of Christ.[3] The hireling, who seems a shepherd but is not, abandons his flock and flees, fearing death and not daring to resist injustice. Hence it is an obligation of a bishop's pastoral office that mortal danger is no reason for deserting the flock committed to his care, for he is bound, in virtue of his office, to lay down his life for his brethren.

Similarly, he is bound to dispense spiritual blessings, for he represents *the man Jesus Christ, the one mediator between God and men,*[4] who was prefigured by Moses when God spoke to his people, *I stood between you and the Lord at that time.*[5] He impersonates the people when he offers prayers and petitions to God: *for every high priest taken from among men is ordained for men in things pertaining to God, that he may offer both gifts and sacrifices for sins.*[6] On the other hand, he acts in God's person when he turns towards the people, by our Lord's power ministering to them doctrine, example, and sacraments: *for what I have pardoned, if I have pardoned anything, for your sakes have I done it in the person of Christ.*[7]

To this perfection a bishop obliges himself at his

---

[1] 1 Cor. iv. 12–13. [2] John x. 11.
[3] *Homil. in Evangel,* xiv; *PL* LXXVI. 112.
[4] 1 Tim. ii. 5. [5] Deut. v. 5.
[6] Heb. v. 1. [7] 2 Cor. ii. 10.

consecration, a religious also at his profession. *Fight the good fight of faith; lay hold on eternal life where-unto thou art called, and hast professed a good profession before many witnesses.*[1] Human contracts are invested by human law with some ceremony that they may be the more binding, so also the pontifical state is assumed and religious profession celebrated with solemnity and benediction.

486, 491   *de Perfectione Vitae Spiritualis,* 16

645. *How shall they preach, except they be sent?*[2] Nobody, however learned or holy, should preach unless commissioned by God and ecclesiastical authority. A cause can act only on its proper material. Preaching, exhorting, teaching, which are the public concern and care of the Church, are committed to the bishops, who only can exercise this official authority. Everybody is bound to do what good lies in his power—this is not every sort of good. The Lord *gave every one commandment concerning his neighbour,*[3] that is, to give them private and familiar advice.

488, 572, 581   XII *Quodlibets,* xviii, 27

646. By common consent human will can institute juridical rights so long as they are not contrary to natural justice. These matters make up the field of positive law.

433   *Summa Theologica,* 2a–2ae. lvii. 2, *ad* 2

647. Some theologians are of the opinion that any priest may absolve anybody from any sin, and though he may act unlawfully, nevertheless the penitent is absolved. Their reason is that priestly ordination simultaneously confers the power of consecrating the body of Christ and the power of the keys, that is, of

[1] 1 Tim. vi. 12.   [2] Rom. x. 15.   [3] Ecclus. xvii. 12.

locking and unlocking. The teaching is erroneous, for
nobody on his own authority can absolve persons who
are not in some way his subjects. An act requires its
proper matter on which to work; sacramental absolution
is essentially a judicial act, which is effective only with
subjects and subordinates. He who has no subjects
cannot absolve. Jurisdiction settles what is the determinate material on which a priest can act. It is quite
otherwise with the sacrament of the Eucharist, which
already has determinate matter. In the case of a priest
to whom no charge is committed, the keys are chained;
as the jurists say, he has the *clavis ligata*.

Others teach that by the power of a higher authority
nobody can absolve a subject of a lower authority
without the consent of that authority; for instance, the
bishop cannot override the parish priest by giving
absolution to a parishioner. This also is erroneous.
Absolution requires these two, sacerdotal power and
jurisdiction. A bishop has immediate jurisdiction over
everybody in his diocese, and can hear their confessions.
So can any priest when duly commissioned by him,
and with stronger reason when commissioned by the
Pope.

629   XII *Quodlibets*, xix. 30.

648. The faith of Christ is the origin and cause of
justice: *the righteousness of God is by faith of Jesus
Christ.*[1] Faith does not detract from the order of justice,
but rather establishes it more firmly. The order of justice requires that subordinates should be obedient to
their superiors; otherwise civilization could not be kept
going. Therefore, the faithful are not excused from the
obligation of obedience to their rulers.

436, 656   *Summa Theologica*, 2a–2ae. civ. 6

[1] Rom. iii. 22.

649. *Servants, be subject to your masters.*[1] *Whosoever resisteth the power, resisteth the ordinance of God.*[2] Obedience observes what is due and right in carrying out a command. This right is based on an order of things scaling down from God. Authority has the power to constrain spiritually as well as temporally, and to bind the conscience. Hence a Christian is bound to obey the authorities when their power is from God, but not otherwise.

Authority can fail to derive from God for two reasons; the first affects its acquisition, the second its exercise.

With regard to the first, the defective personal character of the man who comes into power and the defective means employed on his behalf are two separate questions. Merely personal unworthiness as such does not invalidate the possession of legitimate power, since the inner form of authority is from God, which is the cause of the duty of obedience, and the reason why subjects are to obey unworthy superiors. But the usurpation of authority, through simony, violence, or some other illicit means, is another matter. This prevents the setting up of any right to rule; he who snatches power by force is not truly lord and master. And so a subject with the ability to do so may repudiate the usurper's claims, unless it so happens that his power is subsequently legitimized, either by the consent of subjects or the intervention of a higher authority.

With regard to the abuse of power, or defective exercise, two situations can be considered, of immorality and of illegality. When what is officially commanded is contrary to the very purpose for which authority is ordained, for example, if sin is commanded, which is against the virtue to which authority is supposed to

[1] 1 Pet. ii. 18.　　　　[2] Rom. xiii. 2.

contribute, then the subject is not only not bound to obey, he is also bound not to obey, in imitation of the holy martyrs who suffered death rather than carry out the impious commands of tyrants. But when authority commands what goes outside the bounds of its competence, when, for example, a lord exacts tribute to which a subject is not obliged, and in other such cases, then the subject is not bound to obey, nor is he bound not to obey.

436 *II Sentences*, XLIV. ii. 2

650. The diversity of states and offices in the Church serves, first, the integrity of the Church, second, the carrying out of the Church's action, third, the dignity and beauty of the Church.

First, essential perfection, which is single and simple in God, is broken up and manifold in creatures. The plenteousness of grace, all collected together in Christ, who is the Head, descends in different kinds and degrees to his members, so that the body of the Church may be made perfect: *and he gave some, apostles; and others, prophets; and some, evangelists; and some, pastors and teachers, for the perfecting of the saints, for the work of the ministry, for the edifying of the body of Christ.*[1]

Second, different men should be appointed to different jobs, so that the Church's work may be carried out in a more orderly and expeditious fashion. *As we have many members in one body, and all members have not the same office; so we, being many, are one body in Christ.*[2]

Third, splendour and richness should be set out and arrayed. *When the Queen of Sheba had seen all Solomon's wisdom, and the house that he had built, and the sitting of his servants and the attendance of his ministers, there was no more spirit in her.*[3] And again, *in a great house*

[1] Eph. iv. 11.   [2] Rom. xii. 4–5.   [3] 3 Kings x. 4–5.

there are not only vessels of gold and of silver, but also of wood and of clay.[1]

321, 562   *Summa Theologica,* 2a–2ae. clxxxiii. 2

651. Layfolk are united spiritually to Christ through faith and charity, but not by active sacramental power. Theirs is a spiritual priesthood, to offer spiritual sacrifices: *the sacrifice God loves is a contrite spirit.*[2] *Present your bodies a living sacrifice, holy, acceptable unto God, which is your reasonable service.*[3] *You are a holy priesthood, to offer up spiritual sacrifices, acceptable to God by Jesus Christ.*[4]

632   *Summa Theologica,* 3a. lxxxii. 1, *ad* 2

652. Human legislation may be either just or unjust. If just, then the laws laid down by human authority draw from the eternal law their power of obliging in conscience: *by me kings reign, and lawgivers decree just things.*[5]

Laws are called just on the three counts of end, author, and form. By their end, when ordained to the common welfare; by their author, when the legislator does not go outside the bounds of his authority; by their form, when the burdens imposed on subjects are fairly distributed and promote the common good.

Legislation is illegal when it conflicts with human goodness according to the three norms given above, and is immoral when it conflicts with divine goodness and the eternal law. The illegality of the decrees may come from their end, when burdensome regulations are imposed to indulge the ruler's greed or vanity, not to promote the common welfare; from their author, when the legislator exceeds the power vested in him; and from their form, when although the intention may

---

[1] 2 Tim. ii. 20.   [2] Ps. l. 19.   [3] Rom. xii. 1.
[4] 1 Pet. ii. 5.   [5] Prov. viii. 15.

be to serve the common good their effect is to load people inequitably. Ordinances of this sort offer violence rather than reasonable direction; Augustine says that what is not just is not seemingly a law.[1] They do not bind in conscience, except on occasion, when it may be necessary to avoid public disorder or scandal; then a man ought to cede his rights: *whosoever will force thee one mile, go with him the other two; and if a man take away thy coat, let go thy cloak also unto him.*[2]

Secondly, ordinances are immoral when they are contrary to divine goodness; for example, tyrannical legislation which enforces idolatory or anything else against the divine law. Under no circumstances are such laws to be obeyed: *we must obey God rather than man.*[3]

215, 288, 320   *Summa Theologica*, 1a–2ae. xcvi. 4

653. Is the contemporary Church identical with the Church of Apostolic times? It seems not, because first, how different now the sumptuary customs when prelates go clad in silver and gold, and second, how unlike Christ and the Apostles the Church which now owns estates. On the other hand, let us remember, *Lo, I am with you always, even to the end of the world,*[4] a promise not confined to the Apostles, who are now dead, while the world still goes on.

I answer by saying that the present Church is identical with the early Church. The sacraments are the same, the authority the same, the profession of faith the same. *Is Christ divided?*[5]

With regard to the first difficulty, the passage in St. Matthew's Gospel where our Lord commands his

---

[1] *de Libero Arbitrio*, i. 5; *PL* xxxii. 1227.
[2] Matt. v. 40–41.   [3] Acts v. 29.
[4] Matt. xxviii. 20.   [5] 1 Cor. i. 13.

disciples to travel very light[1] has been expounded by
the Fathers in three ways. First, according to its mystical
sense: *carry not gold*, that is, do not sell your spiritual
ministrations for money; *nor two coats*, that is, be not
double minded. Then there is the literal sense: advice
is not of precept, but of counsel; he who does not follow
it does not sin, he who follows it does better. The moral
is this, when you go out to preach do not worry about
the expenses. The people owe you your keep: *the
labourer is worthy of his hire*;[2] there is no need to carry
money, for those to whom you preach will meet the
costs. After all, St. Paul did not observe this rule, but
earned his living as a tentmaker. A third patristic explanation is that it was indeed a command, but restricted
to the circumstances of the disciples' first preaching
commission. Our Lord sent them twice, before his
Passion to the Jews, when he said, *Walk not in the ways
of the Gentiles*,[3] and then after his Resurrection to the
Gentiles, when he said, *Teach all peoples*.[4] It was the
custom of the Jews to support their rabbis, and consequently the disciples could earn money without giving
offence. But the Gentiles had no such custom: it would
have upset them and made them think the Apostles
were preaching as an excuse for begging. Hence St.
Paul did not keep this rule, and our Lord said before the
second preaching commission, *He who has a bag let
him take also a staff*.[5]

In answering the second difficulty, we may distinguish between different periods in the Church. At
the beginning, governors were hostile to Christianity,
and, far from supporting the faithful, they killed them.
But now times have changed; rulers are schooled in the
service and fear of Christ, and are sometimes vassals of

---

[1] Matt. x. 9–10.   [2] Matt. x. 10.   [3] Matt. x. 5.
[4] Matt. xxviii. 19.   [5] Luke xxii. 36.

the Church. Conditions are different, but the Church is the same.

488, 571   XII *Quodlibets*, xiii. 19, *c. & ad* 1, 2

654. The Pope possesses such plenitude of power within the Church that he can dispense from purely ecclesiastical regulations, which are ordinances which belong to positive law, that is, human law. But he can give no dispensation from the precepts of the divine law and the Natural Law; their force comes from divine decree. The divine law of which we speak is found in the Mosaic moral law and the Gospel Law. There is this difference between them: whereas the Old Law determined many points of ceremonial observance and juridical procedure regulating the fair dealing of men with one another, the New Law, which is the law of freedom, descended to less detail. It contents itself with the moral precepts of the Natural Law, for the articles of faith are explicit, and the sacraments are efficacious. Further arrangements for regulating human affairs and divine worship were freely left by Christ, the giver of the New Law, to be settled by the bishops of the Church and the princes of Christian peoples. Accordingly they belong to human law, where the Pope has dispensing power. In matters of the Natural Law, the articles of faith, and the sacraments, he cannot dispense, and any claim to such power is not authentic, but a pretence.

274, 283, 579   IV *Quodlibets*, viii. 13

655. Unbelievers who have never accepted the Faith should be subjected to no compulsion at all, for belief is an act of freewill. Given the power, however, the faithful may use force to prevent unbelievers from impeding the Faith by blasphemy, or evil persuasion, or open persecution.

375   *Summa Theologica*, 2a–2ae. x. 8

656. Unbelief in itself is not incompatible with the rights to own and to rule, which derive from the *jus gentium*,[1] or human law common to many nations. The distinction between believers and unbelievers is a matter of divine law, which does not abrogate human law.

He who sins through disbelief may be deprived, by judicial sentence, of his right to rule—as also, sometimes, for other faults. But to punish unbelief in those who have never embraced the Faith is not within the Church's power. *What have I to do to judge them that are without?*[2]

276, 292, 386   *Summa Theologica*, 2a–2ae. xii. 2

657. Spiritual power and secular power both derive from divine power. Consequently the secular power is subject to the spiritual power only to the extent that it is so subordinated by God, namely, in matters relating to the soul's salvation, where the spiritual power is to be obeyed before the secular. In matters of political welfare, however, the temporal power should be obeyed before the spiritual: *render to Caesar the things that are Caesar's.*[3] That is the rule, unless historically it happens that secular power is joined to spiritual power, as in the Pope, who occupies the peak of both powers,[4]

[1] *Jus Gentium*: a mixture of tribal law and local Roman Law, later given the dignity of representing what all nations agreed to be right. St. Thomas places it midway between the Natural Law and positive human law: its precepts are derivative conclusions of the principles of Natural Law, but are too universal to be treated as the *ad hoc* regulations of Civil Law.

[2] 1 Cor. v. 12.   [3] Matt. xxii. 21.

[4] Despite the peroration, which might be misleadingly taken to mean that St. Thomas shared the political views of the thirteenth-century canonists, the reference is probably to the Pope's power in his own dominions.

according to the dispensation of Christ, who is both priest and king; a priest for ever according to the order of Melchisedek, and the King of kings and Lord of lords, whose power shall not fail, nor dominion pass away, for ever and ever. Amen.

436 *IV Sentences*, xliv. iii. 4

XI

The Last Things[1]

658. *The word I have spoken, the same shall judge him in the last day.*[2] Things in a process of change are not fit subjects for judgement before they have come to a stop; no action can be fully assessed before it is finished and its results are evident. What may seem to be profitable at first may turn out to be damaging. Judgement cannot be pronounced on a man until he has run his course; until then he can switch from good to evil or from evil to good in many ways, from bad to worse or from good to better. *It is appointed unto men once to die, and after this the Judgment.*[3]

All the same, reflect that although a man's personal career ends with death, his life still goes on in a sense, and is affected by what happens afterwards. He lives on in men's memories, and his reputation, for good or ill, may not correspond to his real character. He lives on also in his children, who, so to speak, are part of their parents: *his father is dead, and he is as if he were not dead, for he has left one behind him that is like himself*[4]—though good parents may have wicked children, and wicked parents good children. Furthermore, he survives in the results of his actions: infidelity continues to breed

---

[1] There is a matter-of-fact air about St. Thomas's eschatology. The future state of mankind seems to develop easily from the conditions of the present. Human beings will be held accountable for what they have done, and be punished or rewarded in their souls and bodies. True human bodies will rise again, not ghostly semblances. Some hints of what heaven will be like appear from human cravings which exist unfulfilled on earth.

[2] John xii. 48.   [3] Heb. ix. 27.   [4] Ecclus. xxx. 4.

until the end of time from the deceits of Arius and other
seducers, and Christianity continues to grow from the
teaching of the Apostles. Then again, he continues in
his body, sometimes given honourable burial, sometimes
left unburied, but always eventually crumbling into
dust. Finally, he lasts in the projects on which he had
set his heart, which sometimes come to quick failure
and sometimes endure longer.

All these affairs are submitted to Divine Judgement,
but a full and public verdict cannot be pronounced and
sentence passed while time rolls on its course. How
right and proper, then, a final judgement on the last
day, when everything whatsoever about a man will be
manifestly displayed.

183, 393 · *Summa Theologica*, 3a. lix. 5

659. Christ's human deeds and sufferings free us from
physical and moral evil, and bear us along to spiritual
and eternal blessings. The person who has gained riches
is the person who should distribute them. The bestowal
calls for judgement, that each may receive according to
his deserts. Fittingly, therefore, is Christ in his human
nature made judge over the men he has delivered: *the
Father has given him judgment also, because he is the Son
of man.*[1]

There are other reasons too. Those to be judged
should confront their judge. God's is the supreme
authority, but to gaze on the Divinity is the reward, of
which some have rendered themselves unworthy, while
others will be granted it after judgement. It is appropriate, then, that all, good and bad, should see Christ
in the human nature he assumed.

Again, events turn full circle when Christ, who
suffered under Pontius Pilate and allowed himself to

[1] John v. 27.

be unjustly condemned, is lifted up to judge the living and the dead in acknowledgement of the extreme humiliation he underwent: *thou hast fulfilled the judgment of the wicked; justice and judgment take hold on thee.*[1] Judicial prerogatives are displayed, not in modesty which makes for merit, but in glory which gives the reward. *Then shall they see the Son of Man coming in a cloud with power and great glory.*[2]

The sight will fill the elect who love him with joy: *thine eyes shall see the king in his beauty.*[3] The wicked, however, will be filled with shame and lamentation: *now must they heed, those envious ones, and to their own confusion; fire shall consume thy enemies, O Lord.*[4] Majestic will he come to the Great Assize, yet showing the marks of his blessed Passion, not flaws, but fair trophies, which the blessed will behold with gratitude at their deliverance, but sinners with shame because of their past scorn. *Behold, he cometh; and every eye shall see him, and they also who wounded him; and all the tribes of the earth shall wail because of him.*[5]

302, 477, 522   *Compendium Theologiae*, 141

660. Perfect activity of a conscious being is invariably pleasurable activity. Pleasure is not restricted to touch and taste, but can be present in every sense, and above all in the mind's contemplation. Of all activities those are most pleasurable which are most perfect. The most perfect activity is of sense and mind well adapted to the best objects which come before them.

75   Commentary, *X Ethics, lect.* 6

661. Happiness consists in acting, not in a state of preparedness.[6] Enjoyment belongs to the best human

---

[1] Job xxxvi. 17.
[2] Luke xxi. 27.
[3] Isa. xxxiii. 17.
[4] Isa. xxvi. 11.
[5] Apoc. i. 7.
[6] *Ethics*, x. 4, 1175^{a}5.

activity, since it is the final part of human happiness. Man's best activity is the activity of his highest power, namely his mind, on the noblest object, who is God. Therefore the whole substance of our beatitude centres on the vision of the Divinity itself: *now this is eternal life, that they may know thee, the only true God.*[1]

This vision, unmediated by any representation, is directly of the thing itself, which enters the mind. Here is possession displacing hope's desire, even as vision displaces faith's belief, a possession which follows vision even as hope may sometimes follow faith. What is seen is received, and the union is one of mutual entering in by love: *he that abideth in charity abideth in God, and God in him.*[2] Then is our happiness complete, for the highest delight rises from our being united with what fits us best. Note that enjoyment, which is an act of will through charity (always supposing the other abilities and virtues) denotes the complement of happiness, not the decisive point.[3]

7, 46, 77, 150   *I Sentences*, 1. i. 1

662. Through Christ we are delivered from the evils inherited through the sin of our first parents. Not only guilt descends on us, but also death, which is its penalty: *by one man sin entered into this world, and by sin death.*[4] From both, then, we have to be delivered by Christ: *for if by the offence of one many died, much more the grace of God and the gift, by the grace of one man, Jesus Christ, hath abounded unto many.*[5] Christ enacted both our deliverances in himself. He willed to die in order to free us from sin: *as it is appointed unto men once to die,*

---

[1] John xvii. 5.   [2] 1 John. iv. 16.

[3] An example of St. Thomas's intellectualism. The Dominicans differed from the Franciscans in stressing that happiness is an act of mind.

[4] Rom. v. 12.   [5] Rom. v. 15.

so also Christ was offered once to exhaust the sins of many.[1]
He willed to rise again in order to deliver us from death:
*now Christ is risen from the dead, the first fruits of them
that sleep; for by a man came death, and by a man the
resurrection of the dead.*[2]

With regard to the forgiveness of sin, we lay hold
of the effects of Christ's death in the sacraments; as
regards our liberation from death, we come to the
effects of his resurrection at the end of the world, when
by his power all will rise again: *if Christ be preached,
that he arose again from the dead, how do some among you
say that there is no resurrection of the dead? If there be no
resurrection of the dead, then Christ is not risen again.
And if Christ be not risen again, then is our preaching
vain; and your faith is also vain.*[3]

Some have misunderstood this teaching; they have
not believed in the resurrection of the body, and have
strained to twist the words of Holy Scripture to mean
a spiritual resurrection, a resurrection from sin through
grace. They have St. Paul against them; *Shun profane
and vain babblings,* he says, *for they grow much towards
ungodliness, and their speech spreadeth like a canker; of
whom are Hymeneus and Philetus, who have erred from
the truth, saying that the resurrection is past already:*[4] these
men were, of course, referring to a spiritual resurrection.
That St. Paul believed in a bodily resurrection is clear:
*it is sown a natural body, it shall rise a spiritual body;
for this corruptible must put on incorruption, and this
mortal must put on immortality.*[5] *This corruptible* and
this mortal is our present body, and this is the thing
which rises again. To deny this, and to affirm a purely
spiritual resurrection is against the Christian Faith.

---

[1] Heb. ix. 27.
[2] 1 Cor. xv. 20–21.
[3] 1 Cor. xii. 12–14.
[4] 2 Tim. ii. 16.
[5] 1 Cor. xv. 44, 53.

Our Lord promised both resurrections, spiritual and bodily. *Amen, amen, I say unto you, that the hour cometh, and now is, when the dead shall hear the voice of the Son of God; and they that hear shall live.*[1] The text seems to indicate the spiritual resurrection, already coming about when men were joining themselves to Christ through faith. Then our Lord went on to say, *The hour cometh, wherein all that are in the graves shall hear the voice of the Son of God.*[2] And this indicates the bodily resurrection, for bodies, not souls, are in graves.

The resurrection of the body was expressly foretold in the Old Testament: *I know that my Redeemer liveth, and in the last day I shall rise out of the earth; and I shall be clothed again with my skin; and in my flesh I shall see my God.*[3]

It is supported also by sound reasons. For the human soul is immortal, and continues after its separation from the body. Yet union with body is essential to it, for by its very nature soul is form of body. Without body it is in an unnatural condition; and what is unnatural cannot go on for ever. Therefore the soul, which is perpetual, is not for ever apart from the body, but will be reunited with it. The soul's immortality, therefore, seems to demand the eventual resurrection of the body.

Next, within man is a natural drive towards happiness, which is his ultimate completion. If an element is lacking then perfect happiness has not been attained, and his instinctive appetites are not completely at rest; for everything made to be perfect desires to be perfect. A disembodied soul is to that extent incomplete; it is a part out of its whole. We cannot reach final perfection so long as our soul is not quickening our body, and since in this life perfect happiness is impossible, human completion requires the resurrection of the body.

[1] John v. 25.   [2] John v. 28.   [3] Job xix. 25–26.

Moreover, divine Providence sees that men get their deserts, penalties for wrongdoers, rewards for those who have done well. Now the persons who do ill or well in this life are human beings of flesh and blood. Punishment and reward, then, are due to them both in their bodily and in their spiritual life. The reward is not possible in this life, where sins frequently go unpunished. *Why then*, asks Job, *do the wicked live, why are they advanced, and strengthened with riches?*[1] It is right, then, to postulate a reunion of souls with bodies, in order that human beings may be fitly punished and rewarded.

178, 517, 567   III *Contra Gentes*, 79

663. Our wills cannot be quite at peace until our natural appetites are altogether satisfied. Realities congenitally united always want, as it were, to be together: within everything there is an impulse towards natural integrity. Since the human soul is essentially an embodied thing, a natural desire rises within the soul for union with the body; its will cannot be utterly stilled until it be reunited with the body, in other words, until man rises from the dead.

A crowning achievement supposes a firm foundation. The culmination, when a thing attains its last end, supposes that it is basically complete in its nature. To be ultimately fulfilled the soul must be complete. Therefore, it must be combined with the body, for of its very nature it is man's substantial form, a part of him, and incomplete when existing outside its proper whole. Therefore, man's ultimate perfection demands the reunion of soul and body.

What is adventitious and unnatural is not perpetual. Soul is bereft of body by outside forces acting against

[1] Job xxi. 7.

its nature. Since it is immortal, we infer that soul will be again joined to body.

664. The human beings that rise again are the identical human beings who lived before, though their vital processes are performed in a different way. Now their life is mortal; then it will be immortal. The generative impulse in living nature intends a kind of immortality, but in restoring human nature God's intention is stronger. The resurrection is not designed to perpetuate the human species—this could be served by continuous interminable generation. Its purpose is to perpetuate the individual.

Even were men to die again after the resurrection they would still not remain for ever without their bodies, which again would rise, and again die, and so on indefinitely. This never-ending cycle of life and death would lead nowhere. On purely reasonable premisses the more probable conclusion is that the first resurrection is final.

When we say that men are immortal after the resurrection, and deny that they are no longer mortal, we read no specific or numerical change into them. They are still of the same kind and are still the same individuals as before. The term *mortal* attributes no specific difference to a subject; it designates a liability to undergo change, and, though it is used as a kind of differentiating predicate, it means no more than that man's body is composed of warring principles, which can, under certain circumstances, make it break up. But when we say that the body is no longer mortal in fact we do not alter its material. Men do not assume a heavenly or ghostly kind of body. Their bodies remain truly human, though they are invested with an immortality coming from a divine strength which enables the soul so to dominate the body that corruption cannot enter. Any reality remains in being so long as it is possessed by form.

180, 206, 340 *Compendium Theologiae*, 155

665. Let us investigate the properties of the risen body. Our starting-point is this, that soul is the substantial form of body and its active moving principle. It gives the body its human substantial reality, and, not only that, it is the principle of the proper characteristics that follow from its union with the body. The stronger the form the deeper its impression on its material, the firmer its grip, and the abler it is to resist encroachment from without; the greater the light and warmth so much the more are the dark and cold kept out. The blessed soul is joined with God and is at the height of its excellence and vigour, and so it confers on the body, divinely restored to it, substantial being at its best. Entirely possessed by soul, the body will then be fine and spirited. Then also will it be endowed with the noble lightsomeness of beauty; it will be invulnerable, and no outside forces can damage it; it will be lissom and agile, entirely responsive to the soul, like an instrument in the hands of a skilled player. These are then the four conditions of the glorified body: fineness, radiance, impassibility, and agility. *It is sown in corruption, it is raised in incorruption*—beyond hurt; *sown in dishonour, raised in glory*—beautiful; *sown in weakness, raised in strength*—quick and nimble; *sown a natural body, raised a spiritual body*—delicate and supple.[1]

178 *Compendium Theologiae*, 168

666. At his transfiguration Christ showed his disciples the splendour of his beauty, to which he will shape and

[1] 1 Cor. xv. 42–44.

colour those who are his: *he will reform the body of our lowness configured to the body of his glory.*[1] At other times also he anticipated his resurrection, and showed some of the endowments of a glorified body; of light-footedness, when he walked on the waves; of delicacy, when he broke not open the Virgin's womb; of invulnerability, when he escaped unhurt from the Jews who wished to stone him or cast him to the ground.

521, 526   *Summa Theologica*, 3a. xlv. 1, *ad* 3

667. When by divine grace a man is admitted into the blessed company and shares in divine happiness, he becomes a citizen of the Heavenly Jerusalem.

403   Disputations, *de Caritate*, 2

668. There will be *a new heaven and a new earth,*[2] and there, in the *city that lieth foursquare,*[3] angels can be compared with men, *according to the measure of a man, that is, of the angel.*[4] With respect to God's love, and to grace and glory, some angels will be mightier than human beings, and some human beings will be enthroned above the angels. Nevertheless, the condition of angelic nature is superior to that of human nature. God did not assume human nature because he loved it more, but because it needed him more: a good master may lavish more care on a sick servant than on a healthy son.

310   *Summa Theologica*, 1a. xx. 4, *ad* 2

669. Whatsoever can make us joyful, there it is in heaven, and superabundantly. *For then shalt thou have thy delight in the Almighty.*[5] *In thy presence is fullness of joy; at thy right hand there are pleasures for evermore.*[6] Is honour desired? There it is: *thou hast made us unto*

---

[1] Phil. iii. 21.   [2] Apoc. xxi. 1.   [3] Ibid. 16.
[4] Ibid. 17.   [5] Job xxii. 26.   [6] Ps. xv. 11.

our God priests and kings.[1] Is knowledge desired? There
also is the secret, the most perfect reason of every truth
and everything we want to see: *all blessings come with
wisdom.*[2] *The desire of the righteous shall be granted.*[3]
Complete security will be enjoyed; it will not be as
now, when the more we love the more we need and
the more we have cause to fear. *My people shall dwell in
the beauty of peace.*[4] *They shall dwell safely, and shall
be quiet from fear of evil.*[5] There also the blessings of
companionship, and most pleasant they will be, when
one loves another as himself, and both rejoice together,
and the gaiety of one is the happiness of all: *all the
world rejoicing finds its dwelling place in thee.*[6]

175, 397   Exposition, *Apostles' Creed*

670. Happiness which is final and God's own we call
eternal life—the term *life* here has the same meaning as
when we speak of life being the activity of the quickening soul. There are as many degrees of life as there are
functions of soul. The highest is the vital activity of
mind. Object gives meaning to activity, and therefore
the vision of the Divinity is called eternal life: *this is
eternal life, that they may know thee, the only true God.*[7]
In our present life we stretch out, as though to a person
far away: *while we are in the body, we are absent from
the Lord, for we walk by faith and not by sight.*[8] But
when we shall see him really present to us then our
inmost self will be embraced; we shall be like a lover
who has long searched and at last the beloved is found:
I held him, and would not let him go.[9]

64, 205, 209   *Compendium Theologiae*, 155

---

[1] Apoc. v. 10.   [2] Wisd. vii. 11.   [3] Prov. x. 24.
[4] Isa. xxxii. 18.   [5] Prov. i. 33.   [6] Ps. lxxxvi. 7.
[7] John xvii. 3.   [8] 2 Cor. v. 6.   [9] Cant. iii. 4.

Index